BIOGRAPHICAL TRUTH

BIOGRAPHICAL TRUTH

The Representation of Historical Persons in Tudor-Stuart Writing

JUDITH H. ANDERSON

Yale University Press
New Haven and London

Published with the assistance of the Elizabethan Club of Yale University from the foundation established in memory of Oliver Baty Cunningham of the Class of 1917, Yale College.

Designed by Nancy Ovedovitz and set in VIP Janson type by Northeast Typographic Services, Inc., Meriden, Connecticut. Printed in the United States of America by Edwards Brothers Inc., Ann Arbor, Michigan.

Library of Congress Cataloging in Publication Data

Anderson, Judith H.
Biographical truth.
Includes index.
1. English literature—Early modern, 1500–1700—History and criticism. 2. Biography (as a literary form). I. Title.
PR428.B55A52 1984 820'.9'351 83-14520
ISBN 0-300-03085-1

1 3 5 7 9 10 8 6 4 2

For Bea, Nita, and Marie, who together have inspired so many of my fictions

CONTENTS

ACKNOWLEDGMENTS

The writing of this book has been for me an adventure, an education, and a pleasure. During it, I have been assisted by a grant from The Huntington Library, by a summer stipend and a senior research fellowship from the National Endowment for the Humanities, and by supplemental support from Indiana University; I am grateful to each of these institutions. For their encouragement at various times, I particularly wish to thank Louis Martz, Kenneth Gros Louis, Foster Provost, Rudolf Gottfried, Harry Berger, Richard Lanham, A. C. Hamilton, and Carol Sicherman. For many kindnesses, I am likewise indebted to the staff, Fellows, and fellow-travelers of The Huntington Library.

I also wish to express my gratitude to my colleagues Philip Daghlian and Georges Edelen, both of whom read the book in manuscript, saved me from error, and endeavored in vain to dissuade me from using the word *licentious* licentiously. Andrew Weiner's generous reading of the manuscript influenced—unknown to him—its present ending. L. C. Rudolph of the Lilly Library was most helpful when consulted on genealogy. Talbot Donaldson, my husband, has been throughout the writing of this book reliably *there*, throughout seeming disasters, recurrent demands, more than a few readings, and many wonderful times.

Finally, I am grateful to Ellen Graham, editor in the Yale University Press, for her unfailing tact and good judgment, and to Alexander Metro, my copy editor, for his patient assistance.

Bloomington
December 1982

GENERAL INTRODUCTION

This study examines the ways historical persons were seen, understood, and depicted by writers of biography, drama, and history in Tudor-Stuart England. During this period the perceived relation of the mind and especially of the imagination to the material and factual world was changing, and with it, the conception of truth and its relation to fiction. Although these changes bring the relations of imagination and fact, fiction and factual truth, nearer to those of our own time, such relationships remain both closer and freer for the earlier period than they are for us. Biographical truth, my subject, catches these changing relationships in a particularly human and immediate expression.

While my study of biographical truth draws on portraiture, the chronicles, and other contemporary evidence of various sorts, the texts I have chosen to treat in detail are peripherally or essentially literary: Bede's *Life of Saint Cuthbert* (used as an example of earlier conventions), Cavendish's *Life of Cardinal Wolsey*, Roper's *Life of Sir Thomas More* (along with Harpsfield's *More*), Walton's *Life of Dr. John Donne*, More's *History of King Richard III*, Shakespeare's *Richard III* and *Henry VIII*, and Bacon's *History of King Henry VII* (along with Herbert of Cherbury's *Henry VIII*). I should note two other principles for selecting these texts: (1) since early biography is a radically mixed form, a cross between history and literary art, instead of studying it in an isolation that is to my mind distorting, I have grouped it with forms closely allied to it in an effort to expose and to explore their connections; (2) considering the relatively unfamiliar nature of many early biographical and historical works and my need to establish a factual basis for discussion of each work (i.e., one cannot determine what a Tudor-Stuart writer does to fact unless one first establishes what facts he is using), I have chosen texts that create an increasingly familiar historical context. My argument addresses some broad issues in Renaissance studies whose implications extend to other periods and disciplines, and I hope in this way to make it more easily accessible to a wider audience.

Biographical fiction is as much the concern of my study as biographical truth. Although the phrase *biographical fiction* would have puzzled most of the writers whose works I examine, these same writers repeatedly used the word and notion of *truth* when referring to their biographical works, in which, from a modern point of view, fiction is unquestionably present. To our eyes, biographical truth thus embraces biographical fiction in Tudor-Stuart England. But how far writers of the period recognized this fact would be debated by many scholars. That is, the phenomenon of biographical fiction is common in the period—indeed, is virtually a way of *Life*, of living and of writing—yet consciousness of it in the period itself as anything beyond simple truth has so far proved less clear. To show that such consciousness is increasingly and undeniably present is to a considerable extent the object of this study. As applied to the Tudor-Stuart period, then, *biographical truth* is a phrase designed to raise questions about biography and truth as historical conceptions, and it specifically includes the possibility of fiction, the deliberate and creative shaping of fact.

Biographical truth sharpens the focus on the larger question of relationship between fiction and fact in the Tudor-Stuart period. Biography—or life-writing, as with greater historical accuracy we should call it—itself occupies a middle ground between history and art, chronicle and drama, objective truth and creative invention—Holinshed and Shakespeare, so to speak. Biographical truth, while most explicitly and exclusively a concern in life-writing, is therefore not a conception limited to a single genre or form. It exists not only in biography but also in other forms, and I have traced its alterations and similarities in passing from one type of form to another, as well as its defining form in biography. In fact, not to trace them would have been almost an impossibility, because the forms themselves are so mixed, their subjects and methods overlapping: biographies draw on chronicles, chronicle-histories include huge excerpts from the *Lives*, and poetic versions of similar materials variously derive from and contribute to these other less fictional forms.

Thus this book is not a history of Renaissance biography, an undertaking which would have duplicated Stauffer's monumentally inclusive and summary work.[1] I am concerned with a certain artistic awareness, with a conception of truth, and specifically with their bearing on the presence and understanding of fiction in biographical-historical literature of the English Renaissance. I have selected fairly complex, important examples of life-writing and related forms in the period because they speak most profitably to these concerns. Such examples are superior to the run-of-the-mill and tend to explain more about a conception of biographical truth in lesser works than would be the reverse. Including and developing more possibilities, they are more fully representative.

A special word might be added about the exclusion of John Foxe's *Acts and*

Monuments from my primary texts and the presence of works by the Venerable Bede and, as biographers go, the nearly as venerable Izaak Walton. In terms of my discussion Foxe's book has analogies both with Bede's and with those of the chronicle-historians. On the one hand, its lives are focused on a single issue and a limited sequence of temporal events, and for these reasons they are formulaic and repetitive despite their variety of objective details: Foxe's book is not about men but about martyrs; if it is anyone's biography, it is the Spirit's. On the other hand, the scope of Foxe's book, the absence of a primarily individual focus and the presence of realistic fact and detail, indicates its closeness to history and chronicle. Foxe's book itself is thus of mixed form, and although it cannot be equated in every respect with the works I treat, they represent major elements in it.

I have chosen to treat a traditional, relatively early saint's *Life*, namely Bede's *Cuthbert*, in order to establish characteristics of the hagiographic tradition clearly and economically as background for later biographies. Bede's *Cuthbert* is especially appropriate to this purpose because of its native English setting and historicity for Bede and because Bede himself—like More and Bacon—was an historian. I have included Walton's *Life of Donne* largely because it sums up so much of what preceded it, including the hagiographic tradition. To label Walton's *Donne*, last revised in 1675, a Stuart work in the usual pre-Commonwealth sense might be stretching the case, but Walton's first version of the *Donne* was published in 1640. Thus it was technically pre-Commonwealth in addition to being pre-Commonwealth in spirit. Like Milton, Walton (1593–1683) belongs more than half to the Renaissance but belongs to the coming age also. He gathers up earlier strands and alters them profoundly.

Three important studies, all published in the past decade, have enough bearing on the present undertaking to merit discussion here. They are William Nelson's *Fact or Fiction: The Dilemma of the Renaissance Storyteller*, Hayden White's *Tropics of Discourse: Essays in Cultural Criticism*, and Stephen Greenblatt's *Renaissance Self-Fashioning: From More to Shakespeare.*[2] My purpose in discussing them is to suggest representative, if not always compatible, contexts for my own concerns and thus to distinguish these concerns more clearly.

The relevant portion of Nelson's study exists in two versions that differ slightly but significantly, and so I shall refer briefly to both of them. In the earlier version, Nelson's "purpose is to describe the way in which fiction comes to be recognized, defined, and distinguished from history in the Renaissance."[3] In *Fact or Fiction*, the later version, he seeks "to trace the history" of the "defensive attitude" toward fiction found in such an apologist as Sir Philip Sidney, "to examine the reasons for it, and to consider its consequences for . . . fictitious narrative" in the sixteenth and seventeenth centuries.[4] Whereas Nelson's earlier emphasis is on the distinction between fiction and history, mine is on their convergence; whereas his later emphasis is on a defensive attitude toward fiction, mine is on the tendency present in life-writing to trust to it, even at times too much.

These differences result from the kinds of texts we set out to examine, from our approaches to them, and from the range of meanings we assign to words like *truth* and *fiction*. Nelson's primary interest is *fictitious* narrative, while mine is literature specifically objective and factual in reference or in derivation. Nelson characteristically approaches his narratives through explicit statements by Renaissance (or earlier) critics and apparently views these statements as the reliable boundaries of interpretation. For the purposes of his study, however, he defines *fiction* narrowly as "invented narratives of verisimilar actions in contemporary and familiar settings, the usual stuff of the novel from *Pamela* onward."[5] As he observes, this is neither Sidney's usage in *A Defence of Poetry* nor that of the Renaissance generally. By *truth*, he means "the correspondence of a tale with things that have happened, the kind of correspondence that should obtain between the testimony of a witness in a courtroom and the events he describes."[6] This is what Virginia Woolf distinguishes from "truth of fiction" as "truth of fact," what Northrop Frye distinguishes from "the constructive elements in thought" as "its descriptive elements," and what Hayden White distinguishes from "the truth of [internal] coherence" as "the truth of [external] correspondence."[7]

Suffice it to say that my own study, like the works it examines, is concerned with both kinds—otherwise aspects—of truth. Some paragraphs earlier I glossed *fiction* as "the deliberate and creative shaping of fact." To define it more fully, I should substitute for *fact*, the phrasing "some reality, whether ideal or actual, outside itself" and should promptly add that for the purpose of the present study the reality shaped is more precisely actual and still more simply factual.[8] For clarity's sake I shall stick with my earlier gloss, the historical warrant for which lies in the following chapters. In turning next to Hayden White's metahistorical essays, however, I should reemphasize that the phenomenon of fiction in biographical-historical writings, not the word, is what really concerns me. The word, as noted before, refers in this book to what most Tudor-Stuart authors were inclined to call, and to regard as, truth.

Extending the views of R. G. Collingwood and Northrop Frye on the relation of the imagination to historiography, White argues repeatedly for a similarity between the activity of the creative writer and that of the historian: "Novelists might be dealing only with imaginary events whereas historians are dealing with real ones, but the process of fusing events, whether imaginary or real, into a comprehensible totality . . . is a poetic process."[9] Sir Philip Sidney, though scoffing at the claims of historians, had something of the same insight when he remarked, "Many times . . . [the historian] must tell events whereof he can yield no cause; or, if he do, it must be poetically," that is, "fictionally," according to Sidney's usage in the *Defence*.[10] For White, as for Sidney's scoffing insight, there is poetry "in every historical account of the world," and it matters little "whether the world is conceived to be real or only imagined; the manner of making sense of it is the same." The identification of truth—all real truth—with fact and the consequent opposition of fiction to fact and to history are an early-nineteenth-century development, according to White, although his remarks about the eighteenth century imply that its roots might lie there.[11]

Provocative and pertinent as White's thought surely is, it cannot be applied full strength to Tudor-Stuart texts. It assumes a fidelity to evidence and a sense of factual accuracy that are just beginning to be important in the Renaissance. It also tends to assume a stable meaning for *truth* and *fiction* and for their relationship in periods prior to the nineteenth century. One contribution I hope the present study might offer is a more accurate, detailed background for modern views like White's. Nothing, however, is further from my intention or ability than to deal with the philosophical question of what history as such *is*, except in the basic or ad-hoc terms necessary to my discussion of particular texts. In such terms, history might be said to deal with persons and events that actually existed or happened, were localized in time and space (as Collingwood puts it), and were in principle (as White puts it) observable.[12] Beyond this basic and partial definition, my concern with history is what certain representative authors in a particular time and place, namely Tudor-Stuart England, took the biography present in historical forms of writing to be.

The third point of reference invoked for this study is Greenblatt's *Self-Fashioning*, with which it shares some general ground. As Greenblatt himself writes, self-fashioning "crosses the boundaries between the creation of literary characters, the shaping of one's own identity, the experience of being molded by forces outside one's control, the attempt to fashion other selves." Like the fashioning of one's self and of another's self in actuality or in literature, life-lived and *Life*-written often resist distinction in biography. This phenomenon is not exclusive to the Renaissance, although it might very well have special—and presently debatable—meaning there. Its major meaning for me is an increasing artistic awareness, a reflectivity on itself, whereas for Greenblatt its meaning seems primarily to involve "the relations of power." In its simplest form, he explains, "the *power to impose* a shape upon oneself is an aspect of the more general *power to control* identity—that of others at least as often as one's own." Fashioning, so described, begins to sound like the Iron Maiden, and its pertinence to such *Lives* as Walton's or Cavendish's sounds pretty farfetched.[13]

With the possible exception of Shakespeare's *Richard III*, imposition of the theories of selfhood and power in *Self-Fashioning* on the works I examine would identify their concern for truth with a drive for power, and their artistic awareness with self-deception: it would thereby deny the integrity of *their* fiction. While such reductions might pertain in certain cases, they are not historically, or ideologically, or humanly necessary. In Shakespeare's *Richard,* as I shall argue, the fiction in human wholeness is a crucial concern, but considerable ingenuity would be required to fit even this play to Greenblatt's ten conditions governing the examples of Tudor self-fashioning he analyzes.[14] Still, such a fit could at least be fashioned in the monstrous Richard's case, but it would reveal an empty, unfulfilled identity whose relation to other cultural phenomena is oblique rather than normative. Distortion like Richard's can be wonderfully revealing, and yet it remains distorted, not simply heightened.

Although less obviously relevant to my present undertaking, Greenblatt's fine earlier book on Ralegh and Joseph Anthony Mazzeo's still earlier essay, "Castiglione's *Courtier:* The Self as a Work of Art," once served as catalysts to it, and as such they testify more accurately to lines of relationship than does *Self-Fashioning*.[15] These lines are evident in Greenblatt's description of "key moments in Ralegh's career" when "the boundaries between life and art completely break down" and "the conventional distinction between reality and the imagination must give way to a sense of their interplay." In my present work, however, the interplay of art and life is not seen so irrevocably in a context of crises and breakdown but rather more in contexts of reflection, invention, and even conviction. Insofar as I use the word *fashioning* in subsequent pages, it implies a complementary (and complimentary) relation to such earlier studies as Greenblatt's and Mazzeo's without implying any theoretical framework not otherwise stated. Beyond these facts, the verb *to fashion,* common in the Renaissance, means simply "to make," "to shape," or "to form."[16]

A definition of biography remains to be offered but is surprisingly hard to give. Any definition that includes early biography is bound to be irreducibly ambiguous, and any one that does not is misleading. "The history of a particular human life" is a definition essentially derived from Dryden and one to which Bacon would have assented, even while he distinguished *Lives* from other types of histories like chronicles.[17] This definition is desirable for its openness and accurate reflection of the practice of earlier life-writers. Its openness includes changing conceptions of the nature and purpose of history (e.g., essentially moral or not) and changing convictions regarding what a human life means or, in this sense, really is. Such views differ radically, for example, in the instances of a Bede and a Bacon.

While Dryden's definition acknowledges the relationship of history and biography and their actual combination in Renaissance practice, however, it blurs the distinction between them. The same distinction perhaps overexercises the modern scholar's indignation. Collingwood, for example, labels biography at its best pure "poetry" and at its worst "an obtrusive egotism," and he disclaims any relation whatsoever between it and history. Persuaded of the urgency of dissociating history from scientific models and therefore of separating its subject matter from the purview of science, Collingwood achieves his disclaimer by defining human life reductively as the life span of a "human organism"; he thus replaces biography with biology.[18] Stauffer, to take a second example, repeatedly decries the "confusion" of history and biography, "Life and Reign," that he finds in so many biographies before 1700. Yet in criticizing the absence of distinction, he places a disproportionate and somewhat anachronistic emphasis on factual details and intimate dimensions of personality in biographical writing. Historically, insofar as early periods distinguished the two types of writing, there is more frequent evidence for distinction in terms of the larger design of the work, such as scope, focus, and perspective.[19]

A better definition than Dryden's, in my view, is John A. Garraty's: "biography is the reconstruction of a human life."[20] Replacing the troublesome word *history*, the word *reconstruction* carries a promising resonance of its own, reminding one of the "constructive elements" of artistic thought, as Frye calls them, and of "the constructive imagination," as Collingwood describes an essential means by which the historian imagines or constructs a picture of the past.[21] At the same time, the word *reconstruction* at least suggests the more descriptive, factual, or preexistent content and elements of form in a written *Life*. Again, what *life* means in Garraty's definition and therefore what the aims and methods of the written *Life* will be, remain, pending further description, still open.

Approximately the first third of my study treats early biography directly, examining Bede's through Walton's *Lives* in detail. It identifies the kinds of truth and the nature of the awareness present in each work. Moving from Bede's confidence in his own objectivity to Walton's nervously self-conscious subjectivity, it shows the emergence, then the development, of an awareness of fiction in biography, an awareness of forming and even contriving the human image.

This section is followed by discussion of More's *History of Richard*, which has variously been claimed as history, as biography, and essentially as drama; and by discussion of Shakespeare's two plays: *Richard III*, written early in his career and largely based, via the chronicles, on More's *History;* and *Henry VIII* (whether Shakespeare's in whole or in part), written late and drawing, via the chronicles, on Cavendish's *Life of Wolsey*. Much of More's studied fiction in the *Richard* belongs to the tradition of literary portraiture or Renaissance life-writing, and the two plays exhibit a self-conscious concern with the historical and biographical traditions—as traditions of interpretation—that Shakespeare finds interlocked in the chronicles. I should note in passing that research for this section has led to a revised view of Shakespeare's use of Stow and, via Stow, of Cavendish.

The final third of the study deals with Bacon's theory and practice of civil history-writing, of which Bacon considers life-writing a major form. Here the tradition of life-writing has led me to modify the customary interpretation of Bacon's theory and to reduce the distance between it and his practice in *Henry VII*. I have aligned his theory with a number of his views on science, language, and philosophy, in this way relating the topic of biographical truth to the general intellectual developments of the seventeenth century. The kind of truth and the nature of the awareness demonstrably present in *Henry VII*, however, remain my chief concerns. I can hardly do better at this point than to anticipate my later discussion: in Bacon's own word for the historian—a word poised equivocably among rhetorical, imaginative, and scientific meanings—he is an *Inventor* of truth as it inheres in human "individuals . . . circumscribed by place and time." The truth he invents in *Henry VII* is radically different from that of life-writers like Bede or Walton, but not in every respect different are his methods and the commitment to fiction underlying them.

PART I

ONE
BIOGRAPHICAL TRUTH

Bede's *Life of Saint Cuthbert*, Cavendish's *Life and Death of Cardinal Wolsey*, Roper's *Life of Sir Thomas More*, and Walton's *Life of Dr. John Donne* were written by men whose lives overlapped those of their subjects in years, location, and experience. The monk Bede may never actually have met the monk Cuthbert, but while Cuthbert was still living and after his death, Bede lived about fifty miles from Lindisfarne, where Cuthbert was notable as a holy recluse and briefly as a bishop. George Cavendish served Wolsey as his gentleman-usher, or personal attendant, for nearly a decade. William Roper, More's son-in-law, lived in More's household for "sixteen years and more." Izaak Walton was Donne's parishioner and knew him in some degree while Donne was Dean of St. Paul's.[1] Although the extent to which these authors' lives touched those of their subjects varies, being greatest in the cases of Cavendish and Roper and least in the case of Bede, each is culturally, geographically, and temporally close enough to his subject to minimize the quaint misconceptions and fictional license that mere distance invites.

Each of the four biographies presents itself as truth and, it is soon clear, as a different kind of truth. Together, they make us wonder what truth there is in the biography of earlier periods, and what, in truth, early biography itself might be. Of the four, Bede, an historian as well as a biographer, lays the most explicit claim to impartial and objective truth: "I have presumed to write nothing about so great a man without the most rigorous investigation of events [in his life], nor finally to offer what I had written for widespread use without the painstaking examination of trustworthy witnesses . . . I have taken care to commit to parchment a plain, dependable account of the truth, as I have ascertained it, in simple language from which, in the interest of clarity, all the obscurities of supersubtlety have been removed."[2] But a modern reader is likely to be startled by Bede's adding, "When you [monks at Lindisfarne] talked together with us, you brought forward many other facts about the life and virtues of this blessed man no less important than the ones we have written down and certainly worthy of record, were it not well known to be unseemly and improper to insert new material or to add to a work carefully thought out and completed."[3] According to Bede, the pattern has been perceived and woven, and its truth should not be disturbed. The *vita* has been written and has now, it appears, a life of its own.

Like a good historian, Bede sees to it that certain additional facts about Cuthbert, namely, subsequent miracles at his tomb, are recorded in *The Ecclesiastical History of the English People:* "Some of these [miracles] we have formerly recorded in the book about his life, but in this present history, we have considered it fitting to add some that recently have come to our attention."[4] We might suppose that for Bede history is more flexible and open, less whole, less finished, even less nearly perfect as yet than a life. History, like the chronicles that record and most nearly approximate it, continues in a way that the individual human life clearly cannot: death is a finisher, an end and, ideally, a completion. A *Life* "carefully thought out and complete" requires more shaping and a clearer, simpler pattern than a history. Perhaps a *Life* is more of a whole because it is more of a fiction, although I should add that the notion of self-conscious or even explicit fiction is foreign to Bede's avowed intentions. The shaping and the pattern are for him the discovery and expression of truth.

Discussing Bede's *Life of Cuthbert,* Stauffer observes that "Bede did not distinguish in his mind between history and biography."[5] According to Stauffer, Bede's treatment of Cuthbert in the *History* is merely a condensation of his *Life of Cuthbert* in order "to fit the perspective" of history. The *Life* is therefore not a different kind of work, using different kinds of materials, such as table talk and intimate anecdotes; essentially, Stauffer determines, the two treatments are the same.

Yet it is precisely the "perspective" of the historian that essentially distinguishes the treatment of Cuthbert in the *History* from that in the *Life*.[6] In the *History,* Bede omits nearly all the miracles recorded in the *Life,* retaining only a few exemplary ones and adding two miracles at Cuthbert's tomb that subsequently came to his knowledge. Except in the interest of a fuller record and of the extension of Cuthbert's miraculous presence further into contemporary history, there is little to choose between the miracles that Bede adds to the *History* and those from the *Life* that he leaves out. In the *History,* however, Bede fits the chronological outline of Cuthbert's life to his own larger vision of God's work in the national life of England and implicitly in the world as a whole.[7] The effect of his condensation of the *Life* is to heighten our sense of Cuthbert as a public force and figure and, in comparison to the *Life,* to diminish our sense of him as a unique and private holy man, indeed, a hermit. The difference between Bede's treatment of Cuthbert in the *Life* and in the *History* finally has less to do with the materials Bede uses than it does with the distinction between Bede's historical and biographical perspectives, that is, less to do with kinds of facts than with the context in which Bede places them and the angle from which he views them.[8]

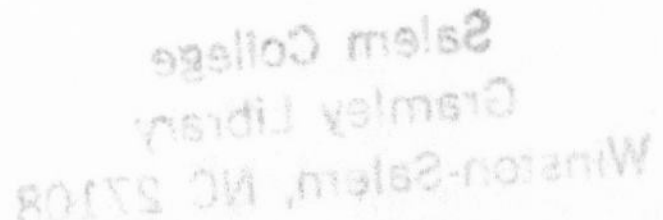

More information about Cuthbert's behavior and manners with intimates might have enriched Bede's *Life*, but I should argue that such material is not essential to the biographical perspective. In regard to the biography of the past, "realistic," or factual, psychological, intimate, standards of excellence are about as suitable as the standards of nineteenth-century novels are to the assessment of allegorical narrative or as the standards of documentary realism are to the assessment of medieval romance. Stauffer's evaluative phrase, a "biographer in the modern spirit," means quite simply a modern man: for him, "real" biography offers us a person who begins to look like us or, rather, like the way we picture ourselves.

When the history of biography is rewritten—if it ever can be, given the diversity of this human form—it ought not to be so simply equated with the history of *modern* personality and characterization. The history of biography—not life, but life-writing—is the literary history of the ways actual individual human beings have been seen, understood, and fashioned by another. Its essential truth is a matter of perception, insight, and judgment—never reducible to fact and at times, like life itself, irreconcilable with certain kinds of fact: witness *Cuthbert*. To a greater or lesser extent, biography is inseparable from fiction.

The three Tudor-Stuart biographies to which we turn *(Wolsey*, *More*, *Donne)* suffice to chart the distant beginnings of an awareness of the fictive element in biography. Put another way, they suggest how the cultural acknowledgment of such an element developed. As I did with Bede, I shall examine first the avowed intention of each author, which he states in a prologue or an opening paragraph, and turn later to the bodies of the works themselves.

Unlike Bede's *Life* of the holy Cuthbert, Cavendish's *Life* of the worldly Cardinal Wolsey exhibits from its opening sentence an indignant awareness of controversy, falsehood, and deception—of the "innvmerable lyes . . . (which prima facie) sheweth forth a vysage of trwthe."[9] At least eleven times in his brief Prologue, Cavendish uses forms of the words "truth" and "untruth." Since Wolsey's death Cavendish writes, "I haue hard dyuers sondry surmysis and Imagyned tales made of his procedynges and doynges whiche I my selfe haue perfightly knowen/ to be most vntrewe" (4). Explaining the futility and danger of answering such tales sooner "accordyng to the trouthe," Cavendish commits "the treuthe to hyme that knowyth all trouthe" and then adds, "in my Iugement I neuer sawe thys realme/ in better order quyotnes and obedyence/ than it was in the tyme of his auctoryte and Rule/ ne Iustice better mynestred with indifferencye/ As I could euydently prove/ If I shold not be accused of to myche affeccion *or elles that I setforthe more than trouthe/* I wyll therfore here desist to speke any more in his commendacion/ And proced fyrst to his orygynall begynnyng" (4: my emphasis). It is appropriate here, where Cavendish explicitly identifies his proceeding as the telling of truth, that he should at once distinguish truth from his personal judgment and suggest by including that judgment some awareness of the relevance or inevitability of his own presence in the work. Perhaps it is not too fanciful to suggest that the phrases Cavendish uses earlier to describe falsehood, "prima facie" and "vysage of trwthe," in combination stretch elusively toward the image of a human face [*facie*, visage]. In this case, biographical falsehood, like biographical truth, has a peculiarly human countenance; it, too, is inseparable in biography from a human life and a human judgment.

Roper's claim to truth in *The Life of More* is less explicit than Bede's and Cavendish's, but it is unmistakably present and persuasive: "I, William Roper, thoughe most vnworthy, his sonne in lawe by mariage of his eldest daughter, knowing [at this daye] no one man [livinge] that of him *and* of his doings vnderstood so much as my self, for that I was contynually resident in his house by the space of xvj yeares and more, thought it therefore my p*ar*te to sett forth such matters towching his life as I could at this present call to remembraunce."[10] The reliability of Roper's testimony is implicit in its measured rhetoric and in its careful statement of his identity, circumstances, and qualifications, all calling to mind a legal document. From Roper's first word, the formal clauses that precede the declaration of Roper's identity reinforce this impression: "FORASMUCHE as S*ir* Thomas Moore, knighte, sometyme lorde Chauncelor of England, a man of singular vertue *and* of a cleere vnspotted consciens, as witnessethe Erasmus. . . ." In the hands of the lawyer Roper, the opening of *The Life* has the authoritative ring of a deposition or a final testament. For all the impression of forthright honesty, however, the technique here is essentially figurative; it is that of allusion.

Looking again at the opening, we see that Roper lays explicit, special claim to an understanding of More and his doings. Roper's choice of the word "understood" is itself telling. This word includes factual knowledge but also assessment and sympathy. Roper's claim is slightly less objective but humanly truer than disembodied truth, and the biographer's presence, indeed his role in *The Life*, is acknowledged more fully in it.

At this point I shall raise, though not entirely answer, another question: to what extent are Roper's choices—his deliberate words and phrases—conscious literary strategies? For example, is the apparent allusion to a legal document the deliberate use of a figurative technique? Like Cavendish, Roper is aware of his interpretative presence in *The Life of More* and of his role as an actual actor in it. At the beginning of his biography, Roper is considerably more aware of both than is Cavendish at the beginning of his. Yet Roper's choices, while "right" and "artful," seem also in part instinctive and merely fortunate. They seem "natural." Although deliberate, they are not explicitly or openly self-conscious when *The Life* begins. Here, for instance, Roper's biographical art is a far cry from the sometimes precious self-consciousness of Nicholas Harpsfield's biography of More, the lengthier successor to Roper's *Life*, which it incorporated.

A brief sampling of references to the biographer's art in Harpsfield's "Epistle Dedicatorie" sets Roper's more understated approach to biography in clearer perspective. To Harpsfield, the biographer presents a "liuely Image" of an actual human person that compares favorably with the "deade image" a sculptor (even Lysippus) or a painter (even Apelles) might make: so "ought the liuely Image of [*More,*] this woorthy man (whom not his deade image, being neuer so artifically and exquisitely sett forth, but his notable doinges and sayinges doo to vs most exactly represent) to be by some singuler artificer and workeman sett forth to the world, and . . . by some other more then my selfe."[11] Harpsfield sees the biographer first as an artificer who works a living, moving image out of a person's words and acts. The biographer is clearly an artist. Shortly thereafter, in a self-conscious assemblage of unlikely images, the biographer becomes a farmer or breeder, a gardener or flower-arranger, a fashioner of decorated wreaths—in each case, a shaper of natural materials. Addressing Roper in the dedicatory epistle, Harpsfield describes the biography he is sending to him: "ye shall receaue, I will not say a pigg of your owne sowe (it were too homely and swinish a terme) but rather a comely and goodly garlande, a pleasaunt, sweete nosegaye of most sweete and odoriferous flowers, picked and gathered euen out of your owne garden; ye shall receaue a garlande decked and adorned with pretious pearles and stones" (6). Biography is—mirabile dictu—the bristling offspring of Roper's materials and Harpsfield's brain.

Of the four biographies central to this section—Bede's, Cavendish's, Roper's, Walton's—Walton's *Life of Donne* is from the start the most obviously self-conscious about biographical art (or artlessness) and about the problematical nature of biographical truth. I should add a caveat, however. Walton's awareness is not "modern," if by "modern" we mean that of the twentieth century, but it still extends significantly beyond that of the others. At the same time, the example of Harpsfield, whose biography of More is, like Roper's, a product of the middle sixteenth century, can serve to remind us that self-conscious biography did not suddenly spring full-blown in the mid-seventeenth century. Indeed, although there are wide, even vast differences between the biographies of Bede and Walton, Bede's desire to avoid altering the pattern of the *Life of Cuthbert* is not entirely unlike what David Novarr's discussions of Walton's revisions have shown us about Walton's belief in and commitment to the pattern he has once established in *The Life of Donne*.[12]

Walton's introduction does not promise us, as does Bede's, "a plain, dependable account of the truth, as I have ascertained it, in simple language," but it promises us "*the best plain Picture*" of Donne's life that he can draw or, as he puts it, that "*my artless Pensil, guided by the hand of truth, could present to* [the world]."[13] Verbally, at least, "simple language" and a "*plain Picture*" sound a similar note, but artlessness sounds a new one. Examined more closely, Walton's image of artlessness is curiously artful. Whereas Bede transcribed the materials of simple truth, Walton's artless pencil is *guided* by truth. Walton's claim to veracity and his confidence of it are more guarded. His claim is also more artificial than are the direct statements of Bede's Prologue, being a classic example of the familiar modesty topos. Further, it contrasts sharply with Bede's avowed effort to avoid obscurity or ambiguity. After all, whose "hand" is guiding the artless pencil? God's? Walton's? and if plain truth's, what is plain truth doing with a hand in the first place? Figurative language, as Hobbes, Walton's contemporary, informed us, is not the surest means to plain and simple truth. Reflecting on Walton's supposed artlessness, we might recall that Roper is, in his own word, "unworthy" of his biographical task when he begins *The Life of More*, but Roper's concern is for himself, for his mental and moral unworthiness, rather than for the unworthiness of his art.

Toward the end of his introduction to *The Life of Donne*, Walton again in effect couples artlessness with plainness and both of them with truth. He assures us that "*the beholder . . . shall here see the Authors Picture in a natural dress, which ought to beget faith in what is spoken: for, he that wants skill to deceive, may safely be trusted.*" A natural dress is a plain one, and since we ought to credit what is spoken and might safely trust its speaker, what we are attending to is truth. This time it is clearer that we cannot take Walton's words (whatever he meant by them) to mean "objective truth." His words here invite our assent, our involvement, and even our sympathy. Indeed, the author's voice—another figurative and relatively subjective dimension—is to be our major guarantor, or speaker, of truth.

Throughout *The Life of Donne* Walton not only uses figurative language but variously echoes and quotes phrases, stanzas, and whole poems written by Donne himself. In this way he deliberately employs Donne's own fictions, his poems, to depict Donne's life and more especially to lend the reality of emotional involvement to the biography. His doing so is surprising in view of the nervousness about poetic utterance which Walton evinces in the biography, for example, when he insists that testimony to the persuasive power of Donne's preaching "is a known truth, though it be in Verse" (49), which he then cites; or when he digresses for well over a hundred words, including references to Prudentius, King David, and Hezekiah, in order to defend Donne's composition of a poem while on his deathbed (66–67). Walton distrusts the imagination even as he recognizes its truth and makes use of it. In actual fact he appears only able to convey his "true" picture, the biography, by invoking imagination again and again.

The verses of Charles Cotton affixed to *The Life of Donne* in 1675 conveniently illuminate Walton's position:

And, though to Verse, great reverence is due;
Yet, what most Poets write, proves so untrue,
It renders truth in Verse, suspected too.

The memories of virtuous men deserve something "*more sacred*" and "*intire*," Cotton adds, and he continues, "*This, History can give.*" Such history—"*truths so candid*" and "*stile so pure*"—he salutes Walton for presenting in his *Donne*. Verse themselves, Cotton's sentiments display the suspicion of versified truths that we find in Bacon and to an extent even in the poet Ben Jonson. In Walton's work as well, there is a touch both of plain honesty and of artistic self-consciousness when he uses figurative or poetic utterances and yet warns us about them. This is the kind of human logic, or illogic, that we find everywhere in the age and find elsewhere in Walton, for example, when he calls our attention to his own postures or digressions. We may or may not like Walton's biographical art, but it proves to be self-conscious.

Walton's addresses to the reader sound as if they came straight out of an eighteenth- or nineteenth-century novel, out of a work of outright fiction, like Fielding's, Sterne's, or Thackeray's: "*Reader, This sickness continued long, not only weakning but wearyng him so much, that my desire is, he may now take some rest*" (60). Several pages later Walton notes, "*But I return from my long Digression,*" and then proceeds, "We left the Author sick in *Essex,* where he was forced to spend much of that Winter" (73). What I might term the "dear-reader form of address" is not, of course, peculiar to Walton's biographies. What strikes us about Walton's use of this form, whether explicitly or implicitly, are frequency and dramatic directness. The dear-reader form occurs in Harpsfield's *More,* for example, but there it is used more formally and far less noticeably. For Harpsfield the reader is not imagined so fully; his audience is less real.

Two examples from Harpsfield will clarify this distinction. The first is an apology, very much pro forma: "In the meane season, good Reader, if thou thinke I passe and exceede iust measure, and wouldest I should shewe by and by what motions I haue that leade me to this censure, I praye thee spare me a litle while, and geue the more vigilant and attentiue eare to the due and deepe consideration of that I shall truely and faythfully sett forth touching this man" (11–12). Harpsfield's rhetoric, especially his insistently paired terms (pass/exceed, would/should, by/by, vigilant/attentive, due/deep, truly/faithfully), militates here against intimacy. It can also distract us from the directness of an address, as in the following passage concerning Margaret, More's eldest daughter: "And to say the truth, she was our Sappho, our Aspasia, our Hypathia, our Dam[o], our Cornelia. But what speake I of these, though learned, yet Infidels? Nay, rather, she was our christian Fabiola, our Marcella, our Paula, our Eustochium. We will nowe, gentle Reader, geue thee a little taste of her learning and of her readie, pregnant witt. St Ciprians workes had beene in those dayes manye times printed . . ." (80–81). The juncture of gentle reader with what we might call clerical high style is too perfunctory and abrupt to ensure participation.

Even when Walton does not address his readers directly, he seems to engage them directly: "And now, having brought him through the many labyrinths and perplexities of a various life: even to the gates of death and the grave; my desire is, he may rest till I have told my Reader, that I have seen many Pictures of him . . . And, I now mention this, because . . ." (79). Walton's engaging the reader derives from his own dramatized engagement with his biographical materials. In the lines just cited, Walton's involvement pushes into the text itself, giving us more of a sense of his presence than of Donne's; very soon after, Walton not merely imagines the reader's responses but actually dramatizes them in the text: "And, the view of . . . [two pictures] might give my Reader occasion, to ask himself with some amazement, *Lord! How much may I also, that am now in health be chang'd, before I am chang'd?*" (80).

Walton's dramatic sensitivity is highly developed, but his impulse to dramatize is that of the novel rather than of the stage. His own relation to the reader and to his characters, his authorial role, is as important as relations among the characters themselves. We might relevantly think again of Walton's introduction to *The Life of Donne*, with its invitation to the reader's faith and trust, to a response in large part subjective.

I began this discussion of Walton's biographical consciousness, the approach to biographical truth that he avows, by comparing it to the simpler, more straightforward, and more confidently objective avowals of Bede in the Prologue to *Cuthbert*. As we have seen, Walton's biographical consciousness—his biographical awareness, as apart from the actual facts and events of the life he records—is more fictional, in the Renaissance sense of the word, more artificial. Such distinctions in attitude and approach will prove radically to affect biographical truth itself, the texture, structure, techniques, purpose, content—the sum reality—of the four biographies central to this section.

The ends of Walton's *Donne* and Bede's *Cuthbert* demonstrate this effect quite clearly. Cuthbert's death occurs in Bede's thirty-ninth chapter; the following seven chapters are devoted to the miracles that attested to his sanctity posthumously: a prophecy fulfilled, miraculous cures, the preservation of Cuthbert's body intact. The miracles at or near the tomb receive special emphasis, as is customary at the end of a saint's *Life*. Walton's *Donne* has some generally recognized analogies with a saint's *Life*, however much it might also differ from one, and they include the recounting of significant events at Donne's tomb, namely, the mysterious strewing of Donne's grave with splendid flowers "morning and evening for many days" by some "who were never yet known," and some other unknown admirer's writing an epitaph with a coal over the grave: "Donne's *Body only, lyes below*." But it is Walton's presentation of a third "Honor done to his reverend Ashes" that truly reveals the extent and nature of the relation between *The Life of Donne* and a saint's *Life*, such as Bede's. Walton describes Donne's monument as being "as lively a representation" of him "as Marble can express; a Statue indeed so like Dr. *Donne*, that . . . *it seems to breath faintly; and, Posterity shall look upon it as a kind of artificial Miracle*" (83). An artificial miracle is both man-made and made by art. I strongly suspect that Walton knew the extent to which his *Life* of holy Dr. Donne is an artificial saint's *Life*—not an untruth certainly, but a fiction.

TWO
BEDE:
Conventions of Portrayal

From first to final chapter, Bede presents Cuthbert's *Life* in the terms traditional to Christian sanctity and in the pattern traditional to a saint's *Life*. At the beginning of the *Life*, a little child suddenly appears to warn Cuthbert, himself a fun-loving boy of eight years, that he should devote his life to virtue.[1] Prophetically, the child addresses Cuthbert as "most holy bishop and priest."[2] Cuthbert is thus called or marked from youth to be a man of God, and from the time he hearkens to the call he experiences and summons miraculous powers. The body of the *Life* concerns his human and superhuman labors in Christ's service as monk, preacher, hermit, and bishop and, as his death draws near, records his increasingly clear premonitions of it, his farewell speech to his followers, and then his death and the subsequent miracles at his tomb. In outline these events conform to the basic structure of hagiographic biography as Bede inherits it.

The miraculous details of Bede's biography similarly belong to tradition, and Bede is at some pains to point out this fact. For example, he introduces the story of the prophetic child's warning with the observation that until this time young Cuthbert cared only for play and games: "so that it could be said of him as of the blessed Samuel: 'As yet Cuthbert did not know the Lord, neither was the word of the Lord revealed unto him.' " Within a few lines comes another biblical reference, this time a third-person adaptation of Paul's words in I Corinthians 13:11: "For when he was a child he understood as a child, he thought as a child; but after he became a man he put away childish things completely."[3] Such references to a tradition of holy men are frequent, explicit, and conspicuous. Often they frame or climactically point an incident. They impart a quality of single-mindedness to the narrative that is distinctive.

Bede refers Cuthbert's deeds to those of latter day saints, as well as to the Bible. In one chapter he carefully explains that Cuthbert has imitated the miracles of two of the fathers, Benedict and Marcellinus, first by dispelling diabolically induced phantom flames and second by checking real ones; and a few chapters later he notes that Cuthbert has imitated two more: "namely, in having brought water from the rock, a deed of the blessed father Benedict, who is reported to have wrought an almost identical miracle in the same way, excepting only that he brought it forth more abundantly because there were more who were suffering from lack of water. Further, in having ordered the birds from the grain he was following the example of the most reverend and holy father Anthony, who with one speech restrained the wild asses from harming the little garden that he had planted himself."[4] As the *Life* proceeds and such references mount, we realize it is not saying that Cuthbert is like these saints but that he *is* one of them. They live again, not just figuratively in his spirit, but literally and exactly in his very acts. The literal directness of imitation is striking and strange and displaces our customary sense of relationships. This phenomenon is difficult to describe, but it is as though we were dealing with identical twins rather than with father and son or with close cousins—with identity rather than with resemblance, with one rather than several dimensions of historical time and space.[5]

Appropriately near the end of the *Life*, Bede attributes a miracle to Cuthbert that refers more directly and specifically to one of Christ's. Cuthbert requests water, which is drawn fresh from a well, blesses it, drinks a little, and returns the cup to the priest who brought it. Having received permission to drink from the same cup, the priest does so, "and it seemed to him as if the water had taken on the taste of wine, and wishing to have as witness of such a miracle a brother who was standing near by, he handed him the cup. And when he too drank, he also tasted wine on his palate instead of water."[6] Tactfully Bede does not tell us Cuthbert knew that his tasting the water had transformed it or whether he was more generally aware of such Christ-like powers.

Elsewhere, however, Bede shows us that Cuthbert consciously imitated the works and words of earlier godly men, a biographical fact which focuses other questions about the source of fiction and the nature of truth in this *Life*. The relevant passage informs us that occasionally when Cuthbert was particularly pressed to find a model of godly "living for those still alive" he would refer to his own life: "Sometimes he indeed did this openly, but sometimes he took pains to do it in a veiled manner, as if in another's person. Nevertheless those who heard understood that he was speaking of himself after the example of the teacher of the Gentiles, who now recounts his virtues openly and now speaks under the guise of another person, saying: 'I know a man in Christ who fourteen years ago was caught up even to the third heaven.' "[7] This passage suggests a number of superimposed images: reading it, we might imagine Bede—or rather, Bede's *Life*—pointing to Cuthbert pointing to his own life pointing to St. Paul's. There are multiple layers in the *Life* but little sense of a receding plane.

It is commonplace to observe that a holy man like Cuthbert imitated the lives of Christ and the saints, but we tend to forget the reality and the implications of such imitation when we talk about biography. We expect to find typology in literature (obviously including the Bible) but not in real life. It is entirely credible that as a result of deliberate imitation and eventually of total immersion in the lives of Christ and the saints, Cuthbert's behavior—words and gestures that now came effortlessly and almost instinctively to him—would suggest to others already aware of these lives the reembodiment of them in him. If our own culture believes, as it purports to do, that behavior, including language, shapes perception, it should be conceivable to us that (the reality of miraculous powers aside) Cuthbert became what he thought he was during those years of concentration and isolation and this was his truth, as well as his biographer's.[8] I need hardly add that this truth looks to modern eyes very much like fiction.

The reader might already have noticed that the essential ambiguity of the words "life" and "*Life*," the one lived and the other written, makes the relation between truth and fiction in Bede's biography more problematic than it seems at first glance. We cannot always separate life-lived and life-written because, as we have them in the biography, they are not in fact wholly separate. Bede's *Life* is also Cuthbert's. To vary my earlier statement, a life, as well as a *Life*, is perhaps more whole when it is more of a fiction.

We can distinguish certain patterns in the *Life of Cuthbert* as Bede's, for example, the contrast established between the comparisons of Cuthbert's experiences to biblical ones—especially but not exclusively to those of Old Testament figures—early in the *Life* and the later comparisons of Cuthbert's miracles to those of the New Testament and the monastic saints.[9] The early comparisons tend to be editorial and external to Cuthbert's present understanding of them; the later comparisons are fully dramatized in the text, their significance available to Cuthbert himself. Cuthbert helps to shape the later events to a greater extent. His hand, so to speak, becomes relatively harder to distinguish in these events from Bede's.

Bede's biography of Cuthbert is imaginatively and conceptually true—true not in opposition to factual, natural truth but often quite simply apart from it. Firmness, discipline, trial, even suffering are present in the *Life of Cuthbert*, but there is no real defensiveness, no anxious denial of hostile realities. The work is in this sense serene and, once again, single-minded. In the second chapter of the *Life*, Bede relates how young Cuthbert's infected knee was cured by the advice of a mysterious horseman, who, Cuthbert soon realized, was really an angel "sent by One who once deigned to send the Archangel Raphael to cure Tobias' eyes." Then Bede offers the historical evidence for this event: "if it seems incredible to anyone that an angel appeared on horseback, let him read the history of the Maccabees where angels on horseback are said to have come to the defense both of Judas Maccabeus and the Temple itself."[10] Here the Bible is not verified by life, but life by the

Bible. Bede refers to the Bible not for analogy but for proof. He is aware of the claims of experience ("if it seems incredible to anyone") but he is not at all pressured by them. A truth different from that of normal experience, rather than in flat opposition to it, simply takes precedence.

As quotations from the *Life* have already suggested, Bede is everywhere in this work, glossing, comparing, explaining. Repeatedly he enters the biography to identify the witnesses who reported Cuthbert's miracles, usually noting their names and stations in life: "as Herefrith, a priest of the saint's own community and at one time the abbot of the monastery of Lindisfarne, testifies Cuthbert himself was accustomed to recount"; one of the brothers who tasted the water-turned-wine "related the story to me himself, for he later stayed for a considerable time in our monastery at the mouth of the River Wear"; "These things a devout priest of our monastery at Wearmouth named Ingwald told me he had heard from Cuthbert himself, then a bishop"; King Ecgfrith's servant Baldhelm "is still alive and holding by appointment the office of priest in the church of Lindisfarne . . . and he is the one who made known to me this very miracle that I am repeating"; "Let me describe his death in the words of that man whose report declared it, namely Herefrith."[11]

Bede does not hesitate to refer to himself occasionally in other ways, for instance, when reporting the response of Bishop Eadberht to a miracle at Cuthbert's tomb: "And as he wondered, he added the following words, which I once put into verses."[12] Another time we hear Bede's voice in a manner that suggests more about the nature of his own involvement in this work. He refers once again to Cuthbert's miraculous quelling of real flames: "But I and those like me, conscious of our weakness and ineffectuality, are indeed certain that we dare take no such measures against material fire but uncertain whether we can escape unharmed from that inextinguishable fire of future punishment." Upon further reflection he adds that a gracious Savior will enable them "even now to extinguish the fires of vices, unworthy though we be, and to escape the flames of punishments in the next world."[13] Bede points the moral of this miracle, expanding its significance figuratively, and he thus brings it home. In fact the *Life* becomes in Bede's hands a sermon for others and a sustained meditation for Bede himself.[14]

We perceive the exemplary purpose of this *Life* clearly at moments when Bede addresses us inclusively: "Whence it is beneficial to remember that this is the transforming power of the Most High, whose miracles, memorable from the beginning, cease not to shine in the world."[15] For all his efforts to review the testimony of witnesses to Cuthbert's miracles, Bede actually relied heavily on an earlier *Life* of the saint written by an anonymous monk of Lindisfarne, which is the evident source for about three-quarters of the miracles he records.[16] It therefore seems likely that Bede embellished and artistically improved the earlier *Life* as an act of reverence and devotion.

Despite the steadiness of Bede's presence in the *Life*, he is not really so noticeable as, say, Walton is in *The Life of Donne*. The impersonal constructions of Latin reinforce the impression of his personal restraint, but they do not account for it. Bede maintains a degree of narrative distance from the events he describes, not putting himself in Cuthbert's presence or trying to penetrate the workings of his mind. Bede's personal references—his presence in the *Life*, as apart from his authorship of it—do not call attention repeatedly to themselves. His own presence in the work is incidental to its truth. He is not insistently, nervously self-conscious, as Walton memorably can be.

Earlier I remarked that the *Life of Cuthbert* suggests a single dimension of historical time and space. My own efforts to discuss the *Life* have repeatedly led back to this suggestion. Instead of the phrases that ordinarily occur in description of a narrative or historical sequence—having done this, he did that; after this, then that; because this was so, that happened next—any discussion of *Cuthbert* leads to a search for variations on the phrase "at one point" (e.g., elsewhere, in one chapter, early in the *Life*, later in the *Life*, at another point).

The openings of many of Bede's chapters are, we might say, cases in point: "Now on a certain day, while he was going round his diocese . . ."; "Let me also relate a certain miracle wrought by the blessed Cuthbert after the example of the previously mentioned father Benedict"; "Many who were present have testified to a miracle of healing, not unlike this last one . . . For while, according to his custom, he was passing through all the people teaching, he came into a certain village"; "Nor do we think we ought to pass over in silence a miracle which, we have learned . . ."; "Not long after this time the same servant of the Lord, Cuthbert, came by invitation to the same city of Lugubalia [Carlisle]"; "Now on a certain day when he was to preach to the people according to his custom, he left the monastery . . ."; "Now at a certain time while the most holy shepherd of the Lord's flock was traveling around checking his sheepfolds. . . ."[17]

There are several exceptions to this arbitrary setting of the narrative, but even they are characteristically general—"after he completed many years in the same monastery, he finally entered with joy into the recesses of a solitude he had long desired, sought, and striven after"—or else they are incidental to Cuthbert's life: "When King Ecgfrith, in a rashly daring move, led his army against the Picts and was devastating their kingdoms with cruel and savage force, Cuthbert, the man of God, knowing the time at hand about which he had prophesied the year before to the King's sister, foretelling that the King would not live longer than one year, came therefore to the town of Carlisle."[18] The dominant impression we receive from the *Life* has little to do with scenery or historical background or, indeed, with the temporal rhythm of a life as we know it. So many important signs and miracles in the *Life* happen "suddenly," without any rational cause or sequential context.[19]

Pattern abounds in the *Life of Cuthbert*, but there is something aggregative and arbitrary about its parts, especially about the order of them. The general pattern of this saint's *Life*, blessed childhood through posthumous miracles, is firmly conceived, and individual chapters exist primarily to illustrate it, but they do not relate causally or sequentially to one another. Incidents reflect the development of the encompassing saintly pattern, instead of generating it. They are so many juxtaposed still shots rather than a moving picture. Although there is deepening commitment in the *Life of Cuthbert*, there is no change in it once the saint commits himself to a monastery in the fourth chapter of a work forty-six chapters long: to cite phrases characteristic of Cuthbert's progress—or stasis—once more, "after he completed many years in the same monastery, he finally entered . . . into the recesses of a solitude he had long . . . sought." In the phrase "long sought," the "many years" of Cuthbert's past become simultaneous with the solitary "recesses" of his present state. The general pattern is preordained and established; it is manifestly imposed on experience.

Although Bede's *Life of Cuthbert* is conventional in structure and generally vague in historical setting, the details of its separate vignettes can be realistic or simply human: "the bitter insults" that Cuthbert met at chapter meetings when he first came to Lindisfarne, or the five onions, one "less than half gnawed away," which sustained him during an illness just before his death; the peasants who jeer at the monks for doing away with the old ways of pagan worship, or Cuthbert's "boots of skin," left on his feet for months on end because he was too engrossed in prayer to think to remove them.[20] There is nothing miraculous about Cuthbert's trips into the countryside: "He used especially to travel through those parts and to preach in the villages placed far away in the steep and rugged hills where others dreaded to visit and poverty and rudeness alike prevented approach. Yet he gave himself up gladly to this pious work and taught the villagers so assiduously that, leaving the monastery, he often did not return home for an entire week . . . and sometimes not even for a full month; remaining instead in the hills, he called the rough villagers at once by preaching and by virtuous example to heavenly concerns."[21] Little imaginative effort is needed to sense the human reality in these glimpses of primitive Christianity.

Like them, the characterization of the redoubtable Abbess Aelfflaed—holy virgin, "mother of the handmaids of Christ," and hardly less important, sister of King Ecgfrith—is better, warmer, and more real than a fiction without relation to human lives would ever be.[22] The Abbess holds Cuthbert in special regard, consulting him, wheedling prophecies out of him, and not easily taking an unprophetic no for an answer. She has in her the blood, if only a few drops, of those meddlesome, intriguing, immensely helpful royal sisters and religious ladies of romance and history. In short, it is not the absence of human detail or realistic potential but the presence of conceptual pattern and devotional purpose that truly distinguishes Bede's biographical work. The *Life of Cuthbert* does not negate one kind of awareness or one kind of truth, but it affirms another kind overwhelmingly.

THREE
CAVENDISH
Patterns without Meaning

Cavendish's *Life and Death of Cardinal Wolsey* is imbued with moral pattern and purpose, but both, considered as sequels to the defining qualities of Bede's *Cuthbert*, seem ironic by contrast. The first word of *The Life of Wolsey* subsequent to the Prologue is *truth*, which, for all its momentous ring as an opener, turns out to be the pedestrian truth of known fact: "**Trewthe it ys/** Cardynall wolsey somtyme Archebisshope/ of york/ was an honest poore mans Sonne borne in Ipsewiche with in the Countie of Suffolk." By the end of *The Life*, however, truth is less simple and considerably less seamless. There King Henry VIII promises to make Cavendish his gentleman-usher as a reward for his "trewthe and honestie." A few lines later, on his way to give the oath required of an usher, Cavendish encounters Master Kingston, Constable of the Tower, who delivers to him an immediate summons from the King's Council and accompanies it with a warning of his own: "And if you tell theme the treuthe . . . what he [the dying Wolsey] sayd you shold vndo your self" (184–85). Within moments, the truth which preserves becomes a denial of plain fact and former loyalty, an acknowledgment that truth is defined by existing power. Cavendish makes (or at least mouths) this acknowledgment but promptly rejects it in his own life by abandoning the Court that has exacted it from him.

Dramatically, without editorial comment and with impressive artistic control, Cavendish gives us in this incident one of the most effective, revealing, and bitterly ironic glimpses of Henry and his Court available in descriptions of the period. It is a picture at some remove from the simple truth of Cavendish's opening sentence. We shall return to this incident later, but for the present it serves to suggest the extent to which *The Life of Wolsey* is characterized by ambiguity and irony, developing understanding, mixed motives, changing roles, and even some inconsistency of attitude, perhaps the unavoidable result of Cavendish's effort to present a complex and self-contradictory life "accordyng to the trouthe."

The briefest outline of *The Life of Wolsey* makes moral and structural patterning evident. *The Life* begins with an account of young Wolsey's precocity in learning and proceeds to his rapid promotion; it ends with his premonitions of death, his deathbed speech to those attending him, and the aftermath of his death. *The Life* divides neatly into two halves, the first presenting Wolsey's rise and triumphs, the second presenting his fall from favor and his death. In the middle of the work, like a pivot between Wolsey's triumphs and tribulations, come the formal divorce proceedings against Queen Catherine, and in them we find the thematic center of *The Life*, the question of conscience.

Pattern extends to smaller details, to the recurrence of key words, such as "will," "favor," "estimation," "pleasure," and the pointed contrasting of images and events from the first and second halves of *The Life:* for example, the contrast between the Cardinal's needs in glory and in disgrace, first the valance of "ffynne Scarlett clothe enbrodered ouer and ouer with clothe of gold" and much later the "Red bokerham bagg" holding only three "shyrtes of heare" (45, 162); or the "golden world" of young Henry VIII, the "hevynly paradice" of a banquet at the Cardinal's palace, and the "fooles paradice" offered old Wolsey when under arrest (11, 70, 173). Especially interesting are the contrasts between Wolsey's early journeys to the Continent and the journeys he makes late in *The Life,* north to York and then south again, en route to the Tower. In the first journey reported, Wolsey's pacing and staging of events, his seeming control of time and space, are incredible even to King Henry VII; remembering them, we are likely to find a sign ominous for Wolsey's future in the very haste of his later return from the great embassy to France. This haste balances so ill the earlier orchestration of his movements that it also serves to suggest their lack of substance. Then, on the final journey of his life, Wolsey rides as a prisoner, escorted by members of the King's Guard who were once Wolsey's own servants, the living symbol of one who has lost control of his movements.

Examples of patterning in Cavendish's work seem almost inexhaustible and numerous additional ones could be cited. Despite this fact *The Life* does not impress us with a sense of order so rational or even so meaningful as we might expect. What pattern in *The Life of Wolsey* signifies or that it ultimately signifies is not so clear as it was, for instance, in Bede's *Life of Cuthbert*. Cavendish himself is not always sure of its meaning, now seeing in it the arbitrary malice of the Goddess Fortuna, and now the design of God.[1]

Cavendish tells us that Wolsey, while still a long way from the top, lacked nothing to please his fancy or to enrich his coffers:

> ffortune smyled so vppon hyme/ but to what end she brought hyme/ ye shall here after/ Therfore lett all men to whome ffortune extendythe hir grace not to trust to myche to hir fikkyll fauor and plesaunt promysis vnder Colour wherof she Cariethe venemous galle/ ffor whan she seyth hir seruaunt in most highest Auctorytie And that

he assuryth hyme self most assuredly in hir fauour/ than tournythe she hir visage And plesaunt countenaunce vnto a frownyng chere And utterly forsakyth hyme/ suche assuraunce is in hir inconstaunt fauour and Sewgerd promyse. [13]

The passage continues in exactly this vein. Although the Boethian view that Fortune is subservient to Divine Providence is available to Cavendish, this passage is a far cry from it. Cavendish's gloomy fatalism here is at odds with another view that appears somewhat later:

But ye/ may se whan ffortune begynnythe to lower howe she can compasse a matter to worke displeasure by a farre fetche/ **ffor nowe** marke good reder the grudge howe it began that in processe burst owt to the vtter ondoyng of the Cardynall/ **O lord** what a god art thou that workest thy secrettes so wondersly whiche be not perceyved vntill they be brought to passe and ffynysshed. [34]

There is a note of genuine discovery in this passage, discovery so immediate that its steps are not even fully expressed. The passage jumps from the irrational malice of Fortune, by now familiar enough to the reader to trigger expectations of another fatalistic lament; to Anne Boleyn's grudge, a cause both human and understandable; to apparent illumination ("**O lord** . . .") and to a conviction of purpose and design. Its final clause—"whiche be not perceyved vntill . . . brought to passe and ffynysshed"—seems to comment not only on human perception of God's ways but also on the process of discovery, of inspired insight, which the passage itself *expresses* rather than explains. This commentary indicates that understanding in *The Life of Wolsey*, as in life itself, is progressive, though not necessarily consistent or entirely rational. Cavendish himself warms to his new insight as he continues the same passage without pausing: "marke thys history folowyng/ good reder/ And note euery circumstaunce/ And thou shall espie at thyn eye the wonderfull workes of god agaynst suche persons as forgettithe god and his great benefites." As in this instance, there is a definite progress in Cavendish's interpretation of Wolsey in *The Life* and, to all appearances, in his understanding of Wolsey as well.

There is also progress in the nature and meaning of patterns in *The Life of Wolsey*. The first half of *The Life* has a foreground of banquets, processions, embassies, crowded rooms sparkling with candles and cloth of gold, splashes of black velvet against crimson, scenes of ceremony, sport, and disguise. With Wolsey's fall from power in the second half, this foreground recedes, and personal conversations and disclosures come to the fore; individual characters stand out more sharply; and a single word, act, or gesture carries more weight. Here we see more of Wolsey himself and also of Cavendish. Wolsey's gentleman-usher becomes more important to him when he is relatively isolated and in disfavor and so plays a more central part in Wolsey's *Life*. Here Cavendish's portrayal of Wolsey becomes increasingly dramatic and ambiguous, irreducible to moralization. *The Life* thus becomes more of a human story than a record of brilliant images and stately events. Now the human motives underlying events are either commented on directly or, more often, presented without explicit comment but in a way so designed, so inviting to analysis, that we are compelled to attempt it.

Early in *The Life*, descriptions often occur in seriatim fashion—"**Now wyll I declare** vnto you his order in goyng to westmynster hall dayly in the tearme season" (22)—and our dominant impression is likely to consist of pageantry and processions:

> And after masse he . . . wold issue owt in to theme apparelled all in red in the habytt of a Cardynall whiche was other of fynne skarlett or elles of crymmosyn Satten/ Taffeta Dammaske/ or Caffa . . . and vppon hys hed a round pyllion with a nekke of blake velvett . . . he had also a tippet of fynne Sables a bought his nekke/ holdyng in his hand a very fayer Orrynge . . . agaynst the pestylente Ayers . . . There was also borne byfore hyme first the great Seale of Englond/ And than his Cardynalles hatt by a noble man or some worthy Gentilman right Solemply barehedyd . . . thus passyng forthe with ij great Crossis of Syluer borne byfore hyme with also ij great pillers of syluer/ And his seriaunt at Armez with a great mase of syluer gylt . . . thus passed he down frome his chambers thoroughe the hall/ And whan he came to the hall doore ther was attendaunt for hyme his mewle trapped all to gether in Crymmosyn velvett and gylt Stirroppes/ whan he was mounted/ with his crosse berers/ and Piller berers also/ vppon great horsis trapped with red skarlett Than marched he forward with his trayn and furnyture . . . hauyng abought hyme iiij^{or} footmen with gylt pollaxes in ther handes/ And thus he went vntill he came to westminster hall doore. [23–24]

Especially as we look back from the second half of *The Life*, we realize the extent to which processions are an ordering device in its first half; we realize as well that they are more than shows superficially filling the earlier half of Cavendish's work, as indeed the triumphant years of Wolsey's life. To a great extent, they are the substance of both. There is a massive, physical reality about these processions but also a curious unreality. They emphasize the external, the visual, and above all the formal side of life exclusively, with the result that their very tangible reality seems fantastic. They are so detailed and so real in one respect that they leave us groping for another, for some kind of real meaning or some kind of inwardness. It is hardly irrelevant to this impression that Cavendish wrote his biography of Wolsey between 1554 and 1558, the bulk of it more than a quarter of a century after Wolsey's death: in retrospect, once Wolsey's power collapses, his processions are patterns with meaning that is uncertain or perhaps is not real at all.[2]

Later in *The Life*, scenes set in a window are especially notable. Twice between the divorce trial and the King's recalling the Great Seal from the Cardinal's possession, Henry leads Wolsey into a great window for secret conversation, as Cavendish, out of earshot, watches them. On another occasion, Cavendish finds Thomas Cromwell in a great window, weeping, praying, and, more convincing, making plans for his future. Wolsey goes "strayt in to the great wyndowe" before emotionally addressing the servants who, without reward, remain faithful to him in his disgrace (107). Later, Cavendish reports, Wolsey talks secretly and at length in a great window with two messengers from the King and then affixes his seal to the petition they carry. In another related image, the Earl of Northumberland, standing at "a wyndowe/ by the chymney" in Wolsey's bedchamber, arrests Wolsey of high treason (155). The Earl of Shrewsbury, who holds Wolsey in custody, speaks daily with the Cardinal, "commonyng vppon a benche in a great wyndowe," and they sit "vppon a benche in a great wyndowe" when the Earl tells Wolsey that Master Kingston has come to take the Cardinal to the Tower (164, 171). At the very end of *The Life*, Cavendish himself stands with Kingston, Ratcliff, and the Duke of Norfolk in a window when he suddenly makes known his decision to abandon Henry's hypocritical court and to return to the country. All these scenes set into a great window or before a recessed window occur in the second half of *The Life*, and as they accumulate there, they testify to a growing sense of recesses and depths, a growing innerness.

Whereas processions are staged by Wolsey and are, so to speak, his pattern, the pattern of window scenes is Cavendish's, imposed by his process of association and not by Wolsey's design. In two of these scenes, Wolsey is not even present; Cavendish is an observer or an actor in them all. The processional patterns are presented objectively, from outside, to Cavendish's memory; the window scenes have the character of a subjective pattern, of images memorable only because associated by the mind that finds them striking. Cavendish's descriptions of Wolsey's ceremonial arrangements in the first half of *The Life* have something of a recitation about them. They are memorized arrangements; the window scenes are an arrangement creatively discovered by Cavendish in Wolsey's *Life*, although presumably also true to the actual events of the Cardinal's life.

In Wolsey's actual ceremonial arrangements, the patterns he imposed on historical movement, the life Cavendish records seems itself to become an unreal surface. But in the more subjective and personal patterns that Cavendish perceives, historical fact, selected and arranged creatively, takes on the meaningful coherence and depth of fiction. In them we are actually able to see life becoming a fiction that has real significance, indeed, I should say, a fiction in which there is persuasively real human truth.

It is no coincidence that the last scene set in a window centers on Cavendish himself. At the end of Wolsey's life, Cavendish is the main character, and the *Life* he depicts is his own. The relation between the lives of Wolsey and Cavendish—lives-lived and *Life*-written, historical facts and fictional coherence—could hardly be more fully realized. Cavendish's presence as a character in an historical role and as a perceiving consciousness is increasingly evident and effective in *The Life of Wolsey*. For Cavendish *The Life* becomes progressively an exploration of Wolsey's meaning and of his own comprehension of it. The two evolve inseparably. It is noteworthy in this regard that Cavendish spends roughly half *The Life* on Wolsey's first fifty-odd years and half on his last year of life. The last year is treated in much more depth, and questions about the nature of Wolsey's awareness and control become focal in it.

Wolsey's fall from power in the second half of *The Life* induces a rise in awareness, a qualified and somewhat ironic alteration of his perception and values. His moving, if perhaps also too tearful, address to his loyal servants is part of this alteration, as is his decision, while lodging in the Charterhouse of Richmond just before his final journey to York, to don a hair shirt: "And at after nones he wold sytt in contemplacion with oon or other of the most auncyent ffathers of that howsse in his sell/ who among theme and by ther councell perswadyd [him] frome the vaynglory of thys world/ And gave hyme dyuers shirtes of heare the whiche he often ware after ward (wherof I ame certyn)" (130). Surprising as Wolsey's new-found asceticism might be, it leads us to recall seeming inconsistencies in his behavior noted by Cavendish early in *The Life:* "he hard most comenly euery day ij massis in his privye closett/ And there than seyd his dayly seruyce with his chapleyn (And as I hard his chapelyn say beyng a man of credence/ and of excellent learnyng) that the Cardynall what bysynes or waytie matters so euer he had in the day he neuer went to his bed with any part of his devyn seruyce onsayd/ yea not so myche as oon Collect" (22–23). There are, of course, many possible reasons for Wolsey's donning a hair shirt—superstition, hypocrisy, and fear among them—and the same range of interpretative choices applies to his earlier devotional exercises. The passage just cited settles nothing about Wolsey's motives, but it renders Wolsey's hair shirt a development that is less startling, less abrupt, less out of character.

The hair shirt admittedly remains almost too good and too conventional to be true. But a more interesting, complex, and ultimately more credible expression of alteration in Wolsey is the recurrent and pervasive recall in his words and actions of a holy tradition of churchmen and martyrs, most often of Christ Himself. Virtually from the moment when Wolsey's fall becomes irreversible and he conveys the Great Seal to the King, his statements begin to echo the Bible, lending a strange life indeed to its sacred myths. Referring to the King, who has just claimed the Cardinal's worldly possessions, Wolsey declares, "I wold all the world knewe and so I confesse to haue no thyng other riches, honour, or dignyty that hathe not growen of hyme and by hyme therfore it is my very dewtie to surrender the same to hyme agayn as his very owen . . . or elles I ware an onkynd seruaunt" (100). The echoes are conflated but persistent, very much the way echoes of well-known passages occur in actual life. They hold memories of I Chronicles 29:12: "And rychesse and honour come of the and thou raygnest ouer all, and in thyne hande is power and strength, and in thyne hande it is to make great, and to gyue strength vnto all."[3] More generally they recall the situation of the parable of the talents and perhaps evoke distant contrasts with other unjust servants in the parables (Matt. 25:14–27, 18:23–30; Luke 16:1–8). Whether Wolsey's words arise from conviction or convenience, they serve to remind the King that the Cardinal's amassing of vast riches and power has been a good investment, since it really belongs to the throne, and that the Cardinal has been a good and faithful servant rather than an unprofitable or unjust one.

Wolsey's submission to Henry is swift, easy, pious, and complete. Although we question the motives behind his biblically resonant statements, they are undeniably effective and almost disarming, as—the word "almost" excepted—he doubtless intends them to be. Wolsey's earlier career, as Cavendish depicts it, gives us reason to suspect that the Cardinal's initial motives in submitting are political, self-serving or at least self-preserving. We are not surprised when Wolsey later tells Cavendish that he surrendered to Henry without any recourse to justice in an effort to move the King's conscience without losing his favor, for "his ffauor oons lost . . . is but oonly deathe" (137). Yet our reservations about Wolsey's motives, especially those arising after the fact, do not cancel the surprising effect of his submissive statements and fail adequately to account for their scriptural resonance.

Other passages and considerations challenge the assumption that Wolsey's submission is merely political. Throughout Cavendish's *Life*, the Cardinal confuses the values of heaven and earth and more subtly and alarmingly confuses the King with God. Cavendish's biography leads us to believe that such confusion is genuine, or rather, not fully conscious. Cavendish offers little, if any, direct comment on Wolsey's confusion but instead leaves us to the ambiguities of motive and meaning that Wolsey's own words and actions, as presented by Cavendish, increasingly press upon us.

Shortly after his initial submission to Henry, Wolsey reproaches himself for this very confusion, in his own words, for being "allwayes contentyd and glade to accomplysshe . . . [the King's] desier and commaundement (byfore God) whome I owght most rathest to haue obeyed/ the whiche necligence nowe greatly repentithe me" (114). Wolsey's understanding of this failure is fitful and elusive. He is neither entirely blind to it nor quite able to overcome it and to face the worldly consequences. The passage just quoted, for example, occurs near the end of another speech of submission, albeit a less wholehearted one than before: "And allthoughe I myght Iustly stand in the tryall with . . . [the King] ther in/ yet I ame content to submyt my self to his clementsye . . . I ame Intierly his obedyencer/ and do entend (god wyllyng) to obey and fulfyll all his pryncely pleasure in euery thyng . . . whose wyll and pleasure I neuer yet disobeyed" (113–14). Wolsey's self-reproach breaks illogically into his submission at just this point, as if the Cardinal had overheard himself and were beginning to have second thoughts about the alignment of God's will with Henry's will and pleasure.

Near the end of his life, Wolsey declares in another biblical reminiscence, this time of the Psalms, that the King "is my stafe that supportethe me"

(165);[4] and even on his deathbed, ambiguity plagues the Cardinal's awareness: "But if," he laments, "I had serued god as dyligently as I haue don the kyng he wold not haue gevyn me ouer in my gray heares" (178–79). God or the King would not have given him over? The ambiguously placed pronoun "he" mocks Wolsey's final realization with a wavering referent.[5] Wolsey's earlier expressions of submission to Henry, couched in terms of submission to God, may be almost instinctual for him—a habit of mind that is less a politic compliment than a real confusion, an ingrained and inadvertent self-betrayal.

The Cardinal's words show us repeatedly that the Bible was in a complex, baffling, human way part of his consciousness. Remembering Wolsey's career, we are hardly surprised that it should be so: his amazing learning in youth and his training as a priest, his position as fellow and teacher at Oxford, his daily exposure to biblical readings in the Mass and in his Office. The biblical phrases Wolsey utters in his fall come naturally to him, yet they invite our seeing first a cunning, then an ironically habitual, employment of words whose full implications Wolsey himself does not hear. Simultaneously they invite our recognition of a new awareness, one that Wolsey is increasingly, if at last imperfectly, to grasp. Wolsey's speeches thus express the ambiguity of his own awareness and do so dramatically.

Wolsey's actions—witness the hair shirt—assert meaning more flagrantly. The series of events which distinguishes Wolsey's journey to York and essentially to exile from the seats of power indicates clearly that Wolsey means to imitate Christ or at least to create the impression that he imitates Christ. The Cardinal frames his journey with announcements recalling Christ's words in Passiontide: "if . . . [my garments] may do you any good or pleasure/ I wold not stykke to devyde them among you" or, "my tyme drawyth nere that I must depart owt of this world" (108, 175).[6] The journey north is even marked by a betrayal dinner, during which "oon doctor Augusteyn," later to turn King's evidence against Wolsey, capsizes a cross, which strikes the head of the master of the Cardinal's "faculties and sperytuall Iurisdiccions." "**Malum Omen,**" the Cardinal intones soberly and therewith retires to lament and to pray (151–52). Most explicitly, of course, Wolsey's journey into the North takes place "in the begynnyng/ of the passion weke/ byfore Ester" (132).

The journey to York is Wolsey's passion play. It is real enough insofar as it really happened, but its relation to truth is not so certain. We can see symbolic penitence in hope of restoration, either political or spiritual, in the timing of the journey. We can see in it an act of self-pity or of aggrandizement, of sincerity or of pure theater. Wolsey's journey, regarded by his modern biographer A.F. Pollard as the ploy of a "consummate actor," does look in part like pure playacting;[7] but in the context of Cavendish's *Life*, where, after all, Pollard found it, Wolsey's journey also looks in part like a valid dramatization of injustice, suffering, and faith; and in part, much the largest part, it looks like a merely selfish appropriation, a possibly sincere but nonetheless self-serving use, of sacred meanings. We might recall for a moment the *imitatio Christi* of Bede's *Cuthbert;* in comparison, Wolsey's latest pattern, his imitation of the Passion, is not without meaning but is invested with meaning of a merely human and thoroughly ironic kind.

At the end of *The Life of Wolsey,* Cavendish himself at last defines the real nature of the awareness, indeed of the truth, that has grown in his work. Appropriately and dramatically he defines this awareness in an action. Having been present at Wolsey's deathbed, Cavendish has witnessed Wolsey's long, dying warning to the King of the rebellion likely to ensue if "this newe peruers sekte" of the Lutherans is tolerated in England (179). In Wolsey's eyes, Lutheranism is a resurgence of Wycliffite heresies that is bound to lead to another upheaval like the Peasants' Revolt in the reign of Richard II, and Cavendish intends to report Wolsey's stern warning faithfully to the King's Council. Before he can do so, he encounters an ominous sample of Henry's cynicism and greed: the King "examyned me of dyuers waytty matters concernyng my lord/ whysshyng that leuer than xx $M^{l\,li}$ [twenty thousand pounds] he had lyved/ than he asked me for the xv ^{Cli} [fifteen hundred pounds] (whiche master kingeston moved to my lord byfore his deathe)" (184). Next, as we have seen, Cavendish encounters Kingston, who counsels him to prevaricate to the Council, and, in order to preserve himself, Cavendish does so: this most loyal of servants flatly denies knowledge of his master's last words, indeed, of his last gesture. Thereafter he abruptly leaves the Court, though, in a literary sense, he returns to it many years later in writing *The Life* "accordyng to the trouthe": "trouthe," factual and objective truth, of course, but as Cavendish becomes progressively involved in *The Life,* also the more subjective "trouthe" that is loyalty. Like Wolsey's character and Cavendish's response to it, the meaning of *truth* alters and evolves in this biography.

In the context—and only in the context—of this *Life,* Cavendish's denial of Wolsey bears a resemblance to Peter's denial of Christ that even sober historians have noted.[8] The resemblance is quietly ironical. Cavendish neither identifies the too-human, fallen churchman with Christ nor satirizes the contrast between them. Instead, by the compliment of parallel, Cavendish dramatizes and elevates his human loyalty to and purely human affection for the great Cardinal, and by the criticism of parallel he suggests Wolsey's unworthiness and inability to evoke anything more self-sacrificing. Cavendish thus charges further with human and ironic significance the tradition of holy men and Christ-like martyrs that Wolsey's words and actions have evoked so strangely and, in comparison to Bede's *Cuthbert,* so anticlimactically.

We might pursue the comparison to *Cuthbert* for a moment. If we consider

The Life of Wolsey in terms of the reality and integrity of saintly patterns, terms that *The Life* itself pointedly includes, it is a degenerate work. Poor old Wolsey stages his passion, impresses his attendants by accurately prophesying his own death (on the basis, it turns out, of his considerable medical knowledge: 178, 181–82), and in his last moments delivers himself of an urgent message for the good of the King, and nothing comes of these resonating gestures but the belated loyalty, strong yet unillusioned, of his gentleman-usher.

But if we consider *The Life* in terms of its dynamic patterns, exploration of meaning, and complexity of character, it is a fascinating and an impressive achievement. Since it concerns a man who is a moral disappointment even to his loyal biographer, it is a representative landmark in the evolution of biographical truth. It is the *Life* of a human individual, which lacks the broader focus of a history, and it is larger, more real, and better than a moralized exemplum. *The Life of Wolsey* shows that truth—or at least biographical truth—might include the real *Lives* of sinners, as well as of saints.

Cavendish's ending, his denial of Wolsey and departure from Court, dramatically reasserts the importance of moral awareness, of conscience, to the concerns that emerge in *The Life*. Looking back from this ending to the pivotal event of Wolsey's *Life*, as in actual life the biographer had to look back, we find the lengthy presentation of Henry's divorce proceedings against Catherine. This event occurs in the center of the biography and might very well have inspired the deepening of Cavendish's thematic focus in the second half. In the speeches concerning the divorce, the question of conscience rings like a refrain: "I put it to your concyence . . . yt was a certyn Scripulositie that prykked my concyence . . . thes wordes ware so conceyved with in my scripulous concyence . . . Thus/ beyng trobled in waves of a scripulos concience . . . in the releafe of the waytie borden of scrypulous concience . . . to whos concyence and Iugement/ I haue commytted the charge . . . after I oons perceyved my concyence wondyd . . . it ware myche agaynst my concyence . . . I haue no suche respect to the persons that I woll offend my consience . . . my commyng . . . here is oonly to se Iustice mynystred accordyng to my Concyence."[9] These speeches raise explicitly the issue that reechoes throughout *The Life of Wolsey*—in the Cardinal's confusion of values, in his ambiguous self-knowledge, and in his own words. The "scripulous" bulk of them are King Henry's. In view of Cavendish's bitter disapproval of Henry's divorce, his inclusion of them in *The Life* without explicit editorial comment is likely to have been deliberated.[10]

Cavendish's editor, Richard S. Sylvester, suggests that Cavendish used Hall's *Chronicle* in order to refresh his memory of certain events he treats in *The Life* and cites as evidence a number of close verbal similarities between Hall's and Cavendish's reports of the speeches concerning the divorce trial.[11] It is likely that in turning to Hall as he wrote about the divorce proceedings and in brooding over Hall's report of them, Cavendish gained insight into the events through which he had lived and found his understanding of Wolsey's significance renewed and deepened. Certainly this account agrees with our impression in reading Cavendish that he does not merely impose meaning on *The Life* (though he does this) but also finds it in his materials as he shapes them.

In the Prologue to *The Life*, Cavendish mentions his sources: "some parte shalbe of myn owen knowlege And some of other persons Informacion" (3). In the body of *The Life* he usually comments on the credibility of such persons (e.g., Wolsey's chaplain, cited above), and several times remarks that direct conversation with Wolsey is his source (e.g., 10). His editor observes that "in many passages" Cavendish's "factual accuracy . . . is astonishing."[12] The presumption that Cavendish used Hall, especially for the divorce proceedings, does not seriously compromise his veracity. Hall, an apologist for Henry VIII, offers a particularly "credible" source for the King's speeches. Cavendish's distrust and eventual dislike of Henry are evident in *The Life*, and we can regard his turning to Hall to refresh his memory as a responsible action.

Nonetheless, Cavendish's inclusion of the speeches about the divorce proceedings has more to do with theme than with factual accuracy, more to do with a literary, than with a factual, motive. Cavendish groups the speeches together, especially Henry's, to make the repetition of the word "conscience" more insistent than it is in the Chronicles. Catherine's speech and one of Henry's at the trial in Cavendish come at an earlier date and in another location in Hall; and Hall claims to have witnessed the speech by Henry and hence to know its historical context and occasion firsthand.[13] Cavendish's grouping the speeches on conscience together ensures that Henry's occur in a context in which they sound less than straightforward and in which their tone becomes clearly ironical.

Cavendish's apparent suppression of evidence in *The Life* is a more serious fault than his possible rearrangement of speeches, yet it, too, points to a literary intention and helps further to define the nature of biographical truth in this work. As we have seen, such truth is both objective and subjective and partakes at once of historical fact and of the procedures and insight of fiction. We need to return to a passage in Cavendish's Prologue, cited in chapter 1: "in my Iugement I neuer sawe thys realme/ in better order quyotnes and obedyence/ than it was in the tyme of his [Wolsey's] auctoryte and Rule/ ne Iustice better mynestred with indifferencye" (4). This judgment is hard to square with lines given to Wolsey in Cavendish's *Metrical Visions*, another work written long after Cavendish's return to the country and substantially finished around 1554, presumably right before Cavendish began *The Life:*

> Syttying in iugement / parcyall ware my domes
> I spared non estate / of hyghe or lowe degree.

I preferred whome me lyst / exaltyng symple gromes
Above the nobles / I spared myche the spiritualtie
Not passyng myche / on the temperaltie /
Promotyng suche / to so hyghe estate
As vnto prynces / wold boldly say chekmate.[14]

To a modern reader, characterizations so disparate are bewildering. There is no way to reconcile their factual content. Yet consideration of the conventional nature and purpose of the *Visions* casts light on this disparity; within a few lines of those cited, the character Wolsey continues, "Who workyth fraude / often is disceyved / As in a myrror / ye may behold in / me" (169–70), and then he continues some more:

Nowe fykkell fortune / torned hathe hir whele
Or I it wyst all sodenly / and down she dyd me cast
Down was my hed / and vpward went my heale.

[190–92]

Numerous additional passages, similarly dreary, could be cited, but perhaps we can settle more mercifully for Cavendish's explanation of his purpose in the Prologue to the *Visions:*

The cause that moved me / to this enterprice
Specyally was / that all estates myght se
What it is to trust to ffortunes mutabylite.

[54–56]

The *Visions* are uninspired, wholly conventional examples of the Fall-of-Princes and Mirror-for-Princes tradition. In them Cavendish feels free to reduce Wolsey to a moral exemplum and may well for this purpose feel justified in using "hearsay" about the Cardinal that he rejects in *The Life.*

Of course Cavendish's version of truth in *The Life* has another side to it, one that might lead him to reject information inappropriate to his essential conception of Wolsey. For Cavendish, even a *Life's* truth—that is, biographical truth—has still about it something of Bede's truth: the essential truth and the essential pattern are truer than a discrepant or distracting detail. Nonetheless, the pattern in *The Life* remains more imperfect, less neat and less unambiguous, and, in short, more human than Bede's or the conventional pattern of the Fall-of-Princes.

What is clear is that the *Visions* and *The Life* offer us two different aspects of truth. In the *Visions,* Cavendish's purpose is *primarily* moral; in *The Life* it is moral, to be sure, but morality there has a less narrow meaning and certainly approaches equation with conscience, with moral awareness, and finally with self-awareness. *The Life* uses the Fall-of-Princes tradition but that is just the point: it *uses* tradition and deepens it, whereas the *Visions* use lives as exempla. As a matter of fact, in *The Life* when Cavendish most audibly echoes the Fall-of-Princes tradition in his lamentations about Fortune, we hear his conventional reflexes, his despair of meaning or his nervous attempts to impose some kind of order and control: "O madness/ O folyshe desier/ O fond hope/ O gredy desier of vayn honors, dignyties, and Ryches/ O what inconstant trust And assuraunce is in Rollyng ffortune" (188). These are the twitches of his conventional self, the wails of his gloom, and not the fineness and acuteness of his human and historical perception.

FOUR
ROPER
Deliberated Design and Designer

In *The Life of Wolsey* Cavendish gives the impression of coming to terms gradually and for the first time with the true significance of Wolsey's actions and his own relation to them. He seems to rejoin his former self as he rediscovers it. Except, perhaps, for the laments about Fortune, we have little sense in reading Cavendish of how long ago it was that these things happened, and even the laments, far from sounding like an older and wiser Cavendish, sound simply like another, emotional but not very thoughtful, one.

In contrast to Cavendish's practice, Roper takes care in *The Life of More* to remind us of the distance between his past responses and his present understanding. Roper's view of More is settled reasonably well even before he writes: "What he ment thereby I then wist not, yeat loth to seeme ignorant, I awneswered . . . But as I coniectured afterward*es*, it was for [that] the loue he had to god wrought in him so effectually" (73). His judgment of his own role, if also spontaneously felt, is likewise clear and certain: "I said: 'By my troth, sir, it is very desp*er*ately spoken.' That vyle tearme, I cry god mercy, did I geeue him" (35). Throughout *The Life of More* Roper's point of view is more controlled and stabler than is Cavendish's in *The Lifę of Wolsey*.

The distance between Roper's present and past responses has led to descriptions of his "fictional guise" as one that is "simple, direct, unsophisticated—Lemuel Gulliver in sixteenth-century dress."[1] Gulliver aside (young Roper is not so fully characterized), the phrase "fictional guise" is useful: young Roper surely is something of a straight man to More's wit and wisdom. Still, we must ask in what sense this guise is "fictional," since presumably it is also true. The guise appears to be fictional, first, because it is different from *present* truth; second, because it is consistent, hence controlled or manipulated; and third, because it is finished, closed or completed.

We might further ask how Roper's self-portrayal differs from his portrayal of More, how the fictional truth or truthful fiction of autobiography differs in this admittedly limited instance from that of biography.[2] Here the chief difference involves degree rather than kind of awareness. It lies in the explicitness of the writer's awareness of his image-making or image-presenting, in his pointed manner of manipulating his own image to deliberate effect. As we have already seen to some extent in the first chapter of this section, such awareness of control and even contrivance of the human image also becomes increasingly evident in the writing of biography in the Tudor-Stuart period: witness Walton.

Roper's artistry in *The Life of More* lies to a considerable extent in his genius for the selection and arrangement of material, for the timing of its presentation, and for the dramatic analysis of motive. All seem natural and yet could not be more deliberate: for example, the ironical counterpointing of More's realistic appraisal of the value of Henry VIII's affection for him—"if my head [could] winne him a castle in Fraunce . . . it should not faile to goe"—and the words of the Emperor Charles at the end of *The Life* when he hears of More's execution—"we wold rather haue lost the best city of our dominions then haue lost such a worthy councell*our*" (21, 104); or the pointed nature of More's leaving his family to answer the summons to Lambeth to take the oaths of succession and supremacy: "whereas he evermore vsed before, at his dep*ar*ture from his wife *and* children . . . to haue them bring him to his boate . . . Then wold he Suffer none of them forthe of the gate to followe him, but pulled the wickatt after him, *and* shutt them all from him" (72–73). Roper, it turns out, accompanies More to London and so looks back, like More, from the other side of the gate. The closing of that gate is More's symbolic gesture, but it is also Roper's recollection, selection, and "reading" of the incident.

Another familiar example takes our sense of Roper's artistry further, namely, the parable of the virgin who is the first to commit a capital offense from the penalty for which virgins alone are exempted but whose fate is subsequently sealed by a clever counselor: "Let her first be deffloured, *and* then after may she be devoured" (58–59). According to Roper, More tells this parable to several bishops and then remarks that, although he might well be devoured, he will take care not to be deflowered by compromising his views on Henry's divorce and remarriage. Like the closing of the gate, More's remarks to the bishops illuminate his motives not only in this incident but in others as well and do so dramatically. Once again, the dramatization and analysis of motive are More's own; in More's life, however, it is implausible that the parable stood out—isolated from daily events or indeed from other moments of wit—to the degree that it does in Roper's *Life of More*. In actual life, More's parable might not have served as so major a commentary on More's actions. Roper does not tell us that it did; instead, he lets us assume this fact or find it out for ourselves, as he evidently did. That is, the image of More we receive through More's own words is, to the extent that Roper's memory and honesty can be trusted, More's own, but it is also, perhaps equally, Roper's.[3]

The practice of Harpsfield is illuminating in this connection. Harpsfield knew Roper himself and had Roper's *More* open before him as he wrote his own biography of More. Like Roper's, Harpsfield's reputation for historical accuracy is fairly good and for truthfulness is excellent.[4] Yet at times in his biography of More, Harpsfield shifts into indirect discourse the words More speaks dramatically in Roper's *Life*.[5] At other times Harpsfield omits or alters words and phrases attributed directly to More by Roper, even when Roper is the immediate witness for the event. To take one example: "if my head could winne him a castle in Fraunce . . . it should not faile to serue his turne" (25–26); as cited earlier, the final phrase in Roper's *Life* is "faile to goe" (21).[6] Either Harpsfield did not regard More's speeches in Roper as verbatim records or else he did not always consider their accuracy important enough to preserve exactly. The demands of his own way of presenting More, in fact of his own image of More, took precedence. In either case, we are left with the fact and the importance of the biographer's invention.[7]

Although Roper is scrupulously accurate in quoting from More's last letter from the Tower to his daughter Margaret, he, too, can be shown to have taken liberties with More's words in the interest of an overall conception in *The Life*.[8] In at least one clear instance, Roper skillfully modifies a letter from More to Henry VIII. The letter refers to Henry's words to More when the latter resigned the chancellorship:

> It pleased your Highnes ferther to say vn to me, that for the service which I byfore had done you *(which it than lyked your goodnes far aboue my deserving to commend)* that in eny suit that I should after haue vn to your Highnes, which either should concerne myn honor (that word it lyked your Highnes to vse vn to me) or that should perteyne vn to my profit, I should fynd your Highnes good and graciouse lord vn to me.[9]

Aside from minor alterations in phrasing required by Roper's narrative and an arbitrary preference for *that* or *which*, the italicized parenthesis in the preceding passage indicates his only significant change. Its omission in *The Life* influences tone considerably:

> so pleased it his highnes [further] to say * vnto him, that for the * service that he before had done hym, in anye sute w*hi*ch he should after haue vnto him, that either should concerne his honor (for that word it liked his highnes to vse vnto him) or that should app*er*taine vnto his p*ro*fitt, he should find his highnes good and gratious Lord vnto him.[10]

With the omitted parenthesis, More's gratitude for Henry's goodness fades from view; Henry's hypocrisy and Roper's irony become perceptible; More's worth receives greater emphasis. The second parenthesis in the letter, as retained by Roper, intensifies these changes by the addition of that little word "for," which implies that Henry's reference to More's "honor" is amply justified.

Having traced Roper's alterations, however, I should note that he does not assign the passage in question directly to More, as he does the scrupulously quoted words from More's last letter to Margaret. He appears to distinguish sharply between an organizing and even overriding conception of More in *The Life* and untruth or deliberate falsification. His conception coexists persuasively (some might say sophistically) with a lawyer's sense of accuracy.

Terms like *arrangement*, *design*, *balance*, or *symmetry* are more fitting to describe Roper's structural practices than is the more rigorous term *pattern*. Roper's "arrangements" are so broad and general or so specific and unextended that they are not properly patterns, although his tendency to make such arrangements might itself be seen as a pattern in the work. Careful arrangement is evident in the long speeches which frame the main body of More's public life. More utters the first speech when he is chosen Speaker of Parliament and the second when he is tried for treason.[11] The first speech is almost the same distance from the opening of Roper's *Life of More*, as is the second speech from its closing, and they share eloquently a concern for the discharge and inviolability of conscience.

Even a casual attempt to outline *The Life* indicates a topical arrangement: youth, public and political involvement, private life, including family life and personal virtues; the problem of King Henry's divorce, withdrawal first from public and then from family life, imprisonment, and death. More's resignation from the chancellorship occurs in the middle of *The Life*, amid pressure from Henry to support his divorce and remarriage. The resignation is immediately preceded by no fewer than five concentrated references to conscience (50–51). In the course of them More tells Henry that he would willingly lose a limb to be able to find some way "with his consciens, safely" whereby he could satisfy Henry's desires and then reminds Henry of the King's own words to him when he first entered into royal service, namely, "to looke vnto god, *and* after god to him." To this apology the King replies, "that if he could not [therein] w*i*th his consciens serue him, he was content taccept his service otherwise; And vsing the aduice of other [of] his learned councell, whose consciences could well inough agre therew*i*th, wold neu*er*theles contynewe his gratious favour tow*ar*ds him, *and* neuer w*i*th that matter molest his consciens after." The word "otherwise" could simply mean "in another way" or "differently"; but even with (and even more without) the emendation "therein" from other manuscripts, it could mean "without his conscience" or "unscrupulously." Henry's subsequent reference to the more serviceable consciences of his Council is gratuitous, virtually parenthetical, defensive, and discomforting. The referent of "that matter" in the same sentence is just a little indefinite; it refers to the divorce surely but also suggests the more immediate syntactical possibility, Henry's "gratious favour," a favor with which Henry thought any conscientious subject should reckon as if his life depended on it: "*Indignatio principis mors est*," as Norfolk later reminds More (71).[12]

Henry's uses of the word "conscience," as Roper presents them here, introduce a divorce of another kind in the work, a divorce of moral and political meanings, of private and public roles. The ambiguity—perhaps, literally the duplicity—of Henry's conscience is sinister, rather than merely ironic. Where irony hints at the disunity of truth and, whether bitterly, cynically, or playfully, considers this disunity with some degree of detachment, Henry's ambiguity threatens. It is charged not simply with opposite meanings but, more ominously, with unclearly related ones. His conversation with More and More's decision to resign the chancellorship, which immediately and suggestively follows this conversation, is a carefully designed and controlled turning point at the heart of *The Life of More*.

Despite Roper's interest in design, there are surprisingly few traces of the pattern of a saint's *Life* in *The Life* of this saint. More has his prophetic moments—about Henry's treatment of him, about the coming success of the Reformation, about the future suffering of Anne Boleyn—but Roper treats them as moments of insight or wisdom that are human and, more often than not, shrewd and secular. More's "fervent prayer myraculously" recovers his daughter Margaret from the sweating sickness, but while he is praying, it turns out, he suddenly realizes that a "glister," or enema, is the only way to cure her; the remedy is administered, and she recovers (28–29). Miraculous the cure may be, but it is also practical.

Near the end of *The Life*, in reply to the passing of sentence upon him, More suggests an analogy between the condemnation of him and Paul's consenting to the death of St. Stephen and continues, "yeat be they [nowe] both twayne holy Sainctes in heaven, and shall continue there frendes for euer, So I verily [truste], *and* shall therefore right hartelye pray, that thoughe yo*ur* lordshippes haue . . . in earthe bine Judges to my condemnacion, we may yeat hereafter in heaven meerily all meete together" (96). The analogy is aimed essentially at More's judges, instead of at himself, and is notable for its ironical wit and immense generosity. More is not setting himself up as a latter-day Stephen so much as he is requiring his judges to become truer men, as did Paul.[13]

Perhaps it is finally too neat that Thomas More should die, as is his wish, on "St Thomas even, *and* the vtas of St Peeter," on the eve of a day honoring the martyred English saint named Thomas who resisted another King Henry's incursions into ecclesiastical power and in the octave of St. Peter, the first head of the Church; but as a matter of historical fact, this is when More was executed, an occasion, I hardly need add, quite beyond his control (99). In the seemingly providential date of More's execution we find a crucial difference between Cavendish's *Wolsey* and Roper's *More.* In Roper's *Life* such occurrences are not simply staged or put on by the historical actor, and they are not part of a traditional pattern evoked but deliberately unfulfilled by the writer. Instead of suggesting the irony of merely feigned patterns, their presentation suggests patterns beyond our own design.

To an extent unparalleled even in Cavendish, earlier passages foreshadow later ones in Roper's *More* and largely account for our sense of the consistency of More's character. We have already noted relevant parallels: More's first speech on conscience and his last one, his appraisal of his value to Henry and the Emperor Charles's appraisal of More's worth. Many slight echoes subtly but significantly enhance our awareness of design in *The Life*. For example, More's words to Roper after his initial examination before a committee of the Privy Council—"In good faithe, I reioyced, sonne . . . that I had geuen the divell a fowle fall"—recall his teaching to his family much earlier, namely, that "the divell of disposition" is so proud and envious that he fears to assault the persevering man a second time, "least he should therby . . . catche a fowle fall himself" and "minister to the man more matter of merite" (69, 27).

Again, the imprisoned More's conversation with Master Rich, who becomes the chief accuser of More, holds memories both of More's earlier reminder to the King of the King's own advice—"first to looke vnto god, *and* after god to him"—and of More's earlier response to the Duke of Norfolk's astonishment at finding Lord Chancellor More singing in a church choir with a surplice on his back: to Norfolk's "a p*ar*ish clark! you dishonor the king *and* his office," More answers, "the king, yo*ur* master *and* myne, will [*not*] w*i*th me, for servinge of god, his master, be offended, or therby count his office dishonoured" (50–51). In the later passage More replies to a sequence of moot cases Master Rich proposes: first, if an act of Parliament were to make Rich king, would More take him for king; second, if by such an act Rich were made Pope, would More take him for Pope. More replies affirmatively to the first proposal and to the second, with a moot case of his own: "Suppose the p*ar*liam*en*t wold make a lawe that god should not be god"? (85). Should we seek to rationalize Roper's memorial selection and thematic arrangement in all these passages, we might take as our basic text the biblical observation "No man can serve two masters" (Matt. 6:24).[14] With this text, other echoes increase in significance: for example, Henry's promising More upon his resignation that More would always "find his highnes good and gratious Lord vnto him" and, within a few pages, the conclusion of More's parable of the offending virgin: "they maye devoure me; but god being my good lord, I will p*ro*vide that they shall neuer deffloure me" (52, 59).

Nearly every detail in the opening of *The Life*—after Roper's prologue and before More's first long speech as Speaker—becomes charged with additional significance as we look back from later stages. Retrospective shading may be a better description of this technique than foreshadowing, although the two types of temporal shading are not entirely separate. Within the first two modern-size pages of Roper's work, we are given a sense of the potential for rich, complex, unified experience in More's life and, as we later realize, a sense of the potential for disunited realities and conflicting demands. Roper's narrative quickly notes More's tutelage in the household of the mighty John

Morton, then Archbishop and Lord Chancellor, and his flair for impromptu acting while resident there; his study of Greek, Latin, and then law; his public lectures on St. Augustine, his living for four years, without vow, in a strict community of monks; his first marriage.[15] Within two pages more, Roper relates in some detail and with emphasis how, as a member of Parliament, young More incurred the hostility of Henry VII by blocking his will and how he was then nearly trapped by the dishonest counsel of one of the King's bishops into putting himself into the King's vengeful power. The scenario of willful king, deceptive counselors, and puppet churchmen in More's later life is in retrospect evident already. In yet another two pages, with considerable expansiveness, Roper tells us how More was once appointed to assist the Pope's side in a case involving forfeiture of a ship and argued so effectively that the Pope's side won, at which point, of course, Henry VIII refused to forbear any longer More's entering into his service. Once again the scenario seems prophetic, this time of Henry's insistence that More's conscience should submit to serve royal supremacy in religion.

Seen retrospectively and in outline, the opening of *The Life* begins to look as prearranged as an allegory, and there is still one page to go before More is chosen Speaker. The marginal glosses in Hitchcock's edition suffice for most of the remainder: "His company sought by Henry VIII"; "His liberty thereby much restricted" (11). In order to get some time with his family, More has to feign an attack of dullness, "to dissemble his nature" and gradually from his former "myrthe to [disvse] himself" (12). Early in *The Life*, with favor and preferment still before him, this story is amusing, but later, More's need "to dissemble his nature" in the presence of royal attentions takes a more ominous twist.

Comparison of temporal shading in Roper and Cavendish clarifies the nature of design in each. Shading in Cavendish, the significance beyond the present with which incidents are invested, first suggests a kind of Nemesis and later, as we read on, suggests an order at best ironic and at worst irrational. One incident that stands out at the beginning of Cavendish's *Life* concerns an "officious country gentleman" who clapped Wolsey in the stocks when Wolsey was a schoolmaster and found some years later that Chancellor Wolsey enjoined him to stay in London for about six years.[16] Cavendish worries the moral of this incident at great length, seeing in it a warning to men in authority to remember the impermanence of their power and to be mindful of "god And ffortune" (6). The warning is obviously meant to apply to Wolsey himself and could be said to anticipate a change in his fortunes and even to forecast a reversal of the roles of persecutor and victim. But at the beginning of *The Life*, where Wolsey's power is in the ascendant, this application is incongruous; moreover, so explicit a forecast is forced and in fact too narrow for the life that follows. The difference between this beginning and Roper's is evident: in Roper, the significance of early incidents is richer and better suits what is to come; at the same time it is implied rather than imposed and becomes fully available only later in *The Life*. Again, Cavendish searches, sometimes fumbles, and gradually finds both his art and his meaning, but Roper knows from the outset where he is going.

Roper's temporal shading in the beginning and elsewhere results in a subtler, more pervasive, and more providential effect than is present in Cavendish. By contributing to our impression of the consistency of More's character, Roper's shading greatly influences our sense of stability, even of confidence, in *The Life*, despite flagrant royal injustice. Odd as it may sound, More himself, rather than Roper, seems in charge, or at least aware, of significant designs in his life, which foreshadowing and retrospective shading accentuate: "but god being my good lord, *I* will p*ro*vide that they shall neuer deffloure me"; or again, "to morowe is St Thomas even . . . *therefore* too morowe longe I to goe to god" (emphasis mine, excepting *ro*). In both cases More may be helped by other designers, namely Roper and God, but he, too, is actively helping. With Roper in writing and God in living, More is coauthor of his own integrity.

On the basis of a providential design in *The Life of More* and an ironic one in *The Life of Wolsey*, we cannot generalize absolutely about the world view of their respective authors. Either author's subject, on the one hand a sinner and on the other a saint, obviously influences the overall order effected. But we can see the choice of writing the *Life* of a subject and what is done with the *Life* itself, what is shaped out of its materials, as having in this period at least a direct and necessary relation and even a debt to the writer's own views, values, and experiences. The lawyer Roper's prologue, a detached deposition, comes again to mind, as does Cavendish's ending, where the true point of Wolsey's *Life* is dramatized in his own. In either case the writer is implicated in the work.

As Roper portrays More's character, it is consistent *amid* change, especially amid changing fortunes, and in this respect quite different from the consistency of Cuthbert's life, as from the inconsistencies of Wolsey's. In Roper's *More*, the credibility of rounded character, dramatized motives, real conflict, and developing plot—in short, the credibility of so many of the commonplaces of dramatic art—is reaffirmed, and with it the proximity of Roper's *More* to fiction. More's character is persuasively lifelike in Roper's work, and yet its consistency—its center and focus—suggests fiction. Since, in large part, human centers themselves are fashioned rather than given, it is entirely conceivable that the consistency Roper depicts, illuminates, and heightens so artfully is originally and essentially More's creation.

The coalescence of art and life, of fiction and persuasion, in Roper's *More* will bear momentary analogy with a fiction by Donne, coincidentally a poem that Walton believed directly related to an actual event in Donne's life.[17] The poem "A Valediction: forbidding Mourning," which begins with a deathbed scene and "end[s], where . . . [the poet] begunne," renovates the motto "in my end is my beginning." Both More's and Cuthbert's lives, as presented by Roper and Bede, might be said to reflect a similar circularity but to do so in significantly distinct ways. From the beginning of the written *Life*, Cuthbert's end is settled and known; More's is not. We see More's end in his beginning only in retrospect. Cuthbert's *Life* revitalizes a circular pattern by illustrating it, and More's *Life* refashions a circular pattern to the extent that it becomes nearly indistinguishable from a real life.

Roper's art is elusive because it is artfully hidden. Harpsfield's practices, by contrast with Roper's, again elucidate them. Very near the beginning of his biography, Harpsfield, like Roper, tells of More's trial period in a monastery but expands his report with incidents drawn from much later stages in Roper's *Life of More:* namely, More's remarking that he would never have meddled further with worldly affairs if his daughter Margaret had not been cured and his saying to Margaret when in prison that if it had not been for his wife and children, "he had voluntarily longe ere that time shutt him selfe in as narrowe or narrower a roome then that [*cell*] was."[18] Harpsfield's juxtaposing these remarks with More's early trial of the monastic life makes explicit the consistency of More's character that Roper's temporal shading dramatically implies. At the same time, Harpsfield's rearrangement of incidents in More's life rationalizes and radically limits their meaning. The same remarks in Roper's context are considerably more open-ended and humanly interesting. There they admit the pious meaning Harpsfield finds in them, but they also admit an aura of weariness and at least the temptation to withdraw, merely to retreat, from the arena. Judged by modern standards of completeness and decisiveness, Harpsfield's biography is better than Roper's, as R. W. Chambers judges it in his introduction to Harpsfield. But in the passage at hand, which is not atypical, Harpsfield voids the drama of Roper's version, excludes the reader's active involvement in meaning, and remakes More's life in the image of Cuthbert's simplicity—"a life of rigid consistency," as Chambers himself describes Harpsfield's version.[19]

Harpsfield's *Life of More* may be good biography—or at least good "modern" biography—but in comparison with Roper's version, it is less satisfactory art. The passage near the beginning of Harpsfield's biography that has just been described goes on, first to query More's decision not to become a contemplative, since the contemplative life is a higher calling; then to defend More's decision (not every man is bound to become a monk); and finally to justify and to judge More's decision: "God himselfe seemeth to haue chosen and appointed this man to another kinde of life, to serue him therein more acceptably . . . and more profitably for the wealth of the Realme and his owne soule also." Harpsfield, for all his virtues as a diligent biographer, would pluck out the heart of More's mystery.

Harpsfield has designs on us. Although his designs stop short of factual dishonesty or distorting omissions, they are explicitly hagiographical and even include, at the end of *The Life*, an extensive comparison of More to St. Thomas of Dover and St. Thomas of Canterbury that ends to More's advantage: "There is therfore in *Sir* Thomas More a deeper cause of martyrdome then in the other twaine" (216). There is nothing remotely comparable in Roper. Yet the designs Harpsfield has on us are not made one with the fabric of More's life. Most often, they alternate with Harpsfield's biographical raw materials, preceding or following them. In doing so, however, they bear mute testimony to another rent in the seams of unified truth in this century, and in this instance the truth rent is biographical.

In Harpsfield's *Life of More*, we meet a more careful separation of objective and subjective truths, of historical record and authorial interpretation, than is present in the other *Lives* so far discussed. From an artistic point of view this separation is regrettable, for as Harpsfield himself believed but perhaps failed fully and imaginatively to grasp, More died at once for the unity of Christendom and for the integrity of the individual conscience (213): for Harpsfield's More, these two truths, one historical and public and one individual and private, were not in principle at odds and ought not in fact to be so.[20] The presentation, the very form, of Harpsfield's *Life of More*, unlike that of Roper's *Life*, thus seems to work subtly against the unified truth that is, by both these accounts, the deliberately chosen theme of More's being and in this sense is untrue to More's life. Roper's profoundly artful presentation adheres more faithfully to the encompassing idea of unity More himself, by both accounts, embraced. Of the two, it is the more persuasive and, to me, the more truly biographical. It presumes to depict the fundamental principle of More's life—not without a strong sense of conflicting pressures but with an underlying sense of direction still stronger. Roper's *Life* is less nearly complete and more subjective than Harpsfield's, and yet, if it is an idea, an ideal, or a fantasy, it both is artistically and was actually a very real one. If it finally answers to a truth somewhat different from the modern biographer's, the impulse Roper takes to be central to More's life is imagined and reconstructed truly in it.

These comments return us to Roper's role, which is really the role of Roper's art, in *The Life of More*. Roper's sensitivity to the nuances of tone and his dramatic timing of events figure high among the distinctive literary features of his art and among the differences between it and Harpsfield's. The visit of Dame Alice, More's wife, to him in prison, for example, is rightly remembered by readers for its mixture of domestic humor and witty righteousness, for Alice's astringent tongue and More's astringent mind: " 'What the good yere, m*aster* Moore,' quoth she, 'I mervaile that you, that have bine alwaies hitherto taken for so wise a man, will nowe so play the foole to lye heare in this close, filthy prison, and be content thus to be shut vpp amongst mise *and* rattes, when you might be abroade at yo*ur* libertye. . . .' " Dame

Alice continues for some length in this and in a more appealing vein: when "you might in the company of me your wife, [your] children, *and* howshold be meerye, I muse what a gods name you meane heare still thus fondly to tarye." After More has, Roper points out, "a while quietly heard her," he speaks to her "with a chearefull countenaunce," and effectively shifts the grounds of argument:

> "I pray thee, good m*istris* Alice, tell me one thing."
> "What is that?" quoth shee.
> "Is not this house," quoth he, "as nighe heauen as my owne?"
> To whome shee, after hir accustomed homely fashion, not liking such talke, awneswered, "Tylle valle, Tylle valle!"
>
> [82–83]

Perhaps enough of this scene has been cited to suggest its human credibility, its true-to-life quality, and enough to suggest its dramatic art as well. Roper gives a realistic tirade, natural dialogue, stage directions ("quietly," "chearefull countenaunce"), and tonal analysis to boot ("homely," "not liking"). Without ruining the effect of Dame Alice's initial barrage by overexplaining it, he alerts us to its approach, telling us that she, "at her first cominge, like a simple ignorant woman, *and* somewhat worldly too, w*i*th this manner of salutacion bluntlye saluted him." Roper's warning is not intrusive because Dame Alice's speech justifies it and in fact overwhelms its strategic demurrer.

Another reason for the dramatic effect of this scene (and incidentally for Roper's warning) is the context in which it occurs, especially the sharpness of contrast between this scene and the two incidents it follows. The more striking of these begins with More's looking out a window in the Tower and chancing to see the Bridgettine Richard Reynolds and three monks of the Charterhouse, the community in which More once lived, on their way to a brutal execution for their opposition to the King's remarriage and supremacy in religion.[21] The rest of this incident, spoken to More's daughter, concerns his response to what he has seen. The second incident, even briefer than the first, is simply reported to us. The King's Secretary (Thomas Cromwell) comes to More to tell him that the King is "his good and gratious Lorde" and henceforth does not want More to have "any cause of scruple . . . to trouble his consciens" (81). Under a pretense of friendship, the Secretary's purpose, like that of the traditional tempter, is to beguile and deceive. Roper observes laconically that More expresses "what comforte he conceaved of . . . [*Master Secretary's*] word*es*" by writing a stanza on Fortune's deceptive appearances once the Secretary has departed. Roper's alert to the reader of Dame Alice's approach and her opening salutation follow immediately on the last verses of More's stanza:

> Truste I shall god, to enter in a while
> Hys haven of heaven, sure *and* vniforme;
> Ever after thy [*Fortune's*] calme looke I for [a] storme.

Enter Dame Alice in an attempt to persuade More to settle for another haven in Chelsea. In outline, at least, the unwitting but stormy Dame Alice—though hardly a Miltonic Dalilah—seems the next step in a dramatic series of very human temptations.

A glance at the same incidents in Harpsfield shows Roper's art to be doubly deliberate. Keeping the interview between More and Dame Alice intact as Roper wrote it, Harpsfield moves it into a new context, which could be labeled "collected anecdotes about Dame Alice" (93–99) and which follows other information about More's household and precedes an extended analysis of More's writings. Some of the anecdotes not to be found in Roper are amusing and valuable pieces of the record of More's life.[22] As we read Roper's interview between More and his wife in Harpsfield, however, we realize that because of its new context, its dramatic impact and memorability are gone. Even Roper's stage directions, though nominally present, have lost much of their force.

Without denying Harpsfield a notable achievement in his *Life of More*, which is worthy in its own comprehensive way, we can perhaps observe of his assembled anecdotes that any good playwright would have known better. Collected anecdotes abstracted from their ongoing, temporal context and then assembled by theme or character are made to *look* forced and lifeless, even if true. Like tales in a joke book, they fail to create a lifelike illusion and, from an artistic viewpoint, are unreal and untrue. Harpsfield's collected anecdotes suggest how much what seems lifelike partakes of art and indeed of illusion and how artistic a form good biography must be.

FIVE
WALTON
Likeness and Truth

With Walton's *Life of Donne*, we reach a biographical watershed, in part because of the artificiality—the artfulness—of *The Life* and in part because of its historicity. We can verify more of Walton's materials than in the earlier *Lives* or challenge his handling of them, often as a result of Walton's own identification of sources or marginal glosses.[1] Oddly enough, Walton's historical accountability makes it harder, rather than easier, to come to terms with his achievement. Our own standards for biographical interpretation keep intruding: "Walton's misuse of fact . . . create[s] an impression which is antithetical to the truth," as David Novarr, one of our best modern critics of Walton, has stated. I take "truth" in Novarr's statement to mean the "whole truth," as opposed to a partial truth, and objective, factual truth, as opposed to subjective, imaginative truth, the sort of truth that we sometimes call fiction.[2]

Novarr's judgment, while not wrong, is relative; it involves our looking at Walton's work through only one end of the telescope, from the large to the small end. What if we look from the other end, from Bede, Cavendish, and Roper forward to Walton, thus reading history forward rather than backward? From this point of view, Walton's use of documents, his awareness of the importance of narrative chronology, his care, when possible, to employ the phrases Donne created, instead of those entirely of his own invention, and his frequent indications of his own sources and procedures in composing a *Life* are responsible and impressive. Moreover, even if we grant—for the moment most conditionally—some licentiousness to Walton as a recorder of fact, we should ask, on the basis of *The Life* itself, what Walton thought he was doing. Did he give us a drawing or a finished portrait, an exact likeness or a more imaginative one? If his work is closer to a Nicholas Hilliard or an Isaac Oliver than to a Bernard Bachrach, should we not approach it differently?

Using the analogy of portraiture, we can clarify and extend the issues of objective and subjective truth in the depiction of human beings that the preceding paragraph raises. It is an article of popular faith that the camera does not lie: a factually detailed and accurate image, objectively and mechanically produced, is true. Yet almost anybody would recognize that this last statement is, if not untrue, conditionally and inadequately true—at least anybody who carries a passport would. Examination of identification photos soon leads to the discovery that one's own *idea* of one's appearance or of another's appearance can be very different from the camera's claims.

No image mechanically, objectively, or, indeed, anonymously produced is adequate or, to human eyes, true. The images of persons that satisfy us critically are likely to be artistic—suggestive, studied, and even posed, if only posed naturally—and the photographer who is really good is likely to have a style recognizable regardless of his particular subject. The problems that attend the making of a "likeness" in our own time are not entirely different from those of the past.

In a history of the likenesses of Thomas More, Stanley Morison concludes that the degree of variation in likenesses that can be identified as portraits of More is so great as to make it "difficult to select any single piece as a work of imagination"; they may all be this. The engraving of More by Jean Valdor (1590–1661), which is thought to be behind yet another engraved version of More that in 1626 appeared on the title page of the first edition of Roper's *Life of More*, is demonstrably imaginative, and certainly portraits of More by other artists, like Rubens (1577–1640), who never saw him, are bound to be imaginative to a great extent, even if they are based on earlier versions, now lost. Morison concludes that the "distinction between a faithful depiction and an imaginary likeness" was not in the foreground of sixteenth- and seventeenth-century concerns. In fact, it was hardly in the picture.[3]

Study of Renaissance portraiture has demonstrated a growing subjectivity both in the subject depicted and in the interpretative techniques of the artist.[4] This subjectivity is self-conscious, as the artist's self-portraits, from Dürer's many to Rembrandt's many more, bear witness.[5] Sometimes in Renaissance portraiture, exploration of an idea or a mood, such as melancholy, or of a condition, such as age or youth, combines in seeming paradox with greater human particularity and personality. In the case of melancholy, the Lothian portrait of John Donne, shadowed, brooding, and Byronic, which is reproduced in Gardner's edition of Donne's *Songs and Sonnets*, is an example ready to hand.[6]

Seeming paradox is also present in the increasing occurrence of an attitude at once highly posed or artificial and humanly dramatic. Again, it is convenient to refer for an example to a familiar portrait of Lucy, Countess of Bedford, reproduced in Milgate's edition of Donne's *Satires, Epigrams and Verse Letters*. In it, the Countess, seated, leans her head on one elegant finger and with a thoughtful and quizzical (or perhaps a sharper, more humorous) gaze engages the viewer's eyes directly.[7]

Some techniques of portraiture, especially in Elizabethan England, are "antique," but like Spenser's *Faerie Queene*, they are also self-conscious and bear further witness to a sophisticated subjectivity. It can be argued that even such emblematic, floodlit images as the Ditchley portrait of Queen Elizabeth (or rather of her costume) is for the artist a self-consciously subjective fabrication: a hieratic figure in Bede's time is found or discovered; it is given; in Elizabeth's and James' time, it is feigned and fashioned with careful deliberation. It could still be believed in, but not quite so literally.[8]

Surely the same is true of still another popular form of Renaissance portraiture, the donor with or else the subject as St. John the Baptist, St. George, St. Benedict, St. Thomas, St. Jerome, or the like.[9] In the Bodleian Library there is a portrait inscribed "Nicholaus Harpsfeldus" that is described as a bust, leaning to the left, with a bald head, some "greyish hair; lanky brown beard and long moustache; the face thin and distressed, mouth open; apparently represented as Saint Jerome or some other ascetic saint, beating his breast with a stone held in his r[ight] hand."[10] Whether a portrait or not—the learned cataloguer is unsure, significantly enough—this picture illustrates the uncertain "distinction between a faithful depiction and an imaginary likeness."[11] It also serves to illustrate the fashion of staged or costumed portraiture, of which there are countless uncontested Renaissance examples. This fashion is perhaps the most curious of all to a modern viewer, and it is one for which we have already noted remarkable analogues in the written *Lives* and shall later have occasion to note further in Walton's *Life of Donne*.[12]

Walton's introduction to this *Life*, as the reader will recall from my own introduction, promises us the "*best plain Picture*" that his "*artless Pensil*" can "*present.*" This is the reading of the third and fourth revised editions of *The Life* in 1670 and 1675, respectively. Except for omission of the word "plain," the first version of *The Life* in 1640 has the same phrasing. In the second edition (1658), however, Walton changed "best picture" to "best narration" and "artlesse Pensil" to "artlesse pen."[13] What is more interesting in view of the care Walton spent revising is that in 1670 he changed "narration" back to "picture" (now "*best plain Picture*") and "pen" back to "Pensil" and reaffirmed this act of restoration by retaining it in the fourth and last revision of 1675.

In 1675 Walton also added to *The Life* the discussion of a picture of Donne as a young man known to us as the Marshall engraving, although probably based on a lost original by Hilliard.[14] This discussion, following almost immediately on Walton's description of Donne's deathbed portrait, puts additional emphasis both on it and on Walton's concern with pictures in this *Life*. Walton wants us to understand that he has "seen many Pictures of . . . [Donne], in several habits, and, at several ages, and in several postures" (79).

Walton indeed may know the difference between "a picture and a narrative," as Novarr notes, but that knowledge makes his restoration of the word "picture" to its original place in the introduction all the more striking.[15] Although Walton implies that he is simply reproducing the original introduction in the later editions, his practice in general and his specific changes in 1658 rule out historical authenticity as his motive for the restoration. Walton does not hesitate to change a word—anyone's word—if he thinks he can make a passage clearer, less ambiguous, or better—that is, truer. Walton revises habitually, but virtually never does he restore earlier readings. The word "picture" must have seemed to him the more fitting choice.

The frequency with which critics of Walton revert to pictorial analogies —more often, incidentally, than is the case with the earlier *Lives* we have considered—is suggestive. These analogies may differ in detail, but they point consistently to Walton's manipulation of appearance and effect: "In painting a glowing picture an artist selects a point of view, and to what is visible from that point subordinates all else. So Walton works." Or again, Walton's "diminution of light and shade in favor of a heightening by one shadow tended to produce, in biography, a too even picture."[16] Critical practice thus lends additional relevance and even some credence to an analogy with portraiture.

If we ask what kinds of portraits Walton knew, for our present purpose we can hardly do better than to turn to his own careful description of one in *The Life of Donne.* There, shortly before Donne's death, "a choice Painter" is got in "to draw his Picture" in his winding-sheet, "so tyed with knots at his head and feet, and his hands so placed, as dead bodies are usually fitted to be shrowded and put into their Coffin." Donne poses for the painter on an urn, newly made for this occasion according to Donne's own specifications as to height and circumference. He stands on the urn " 'with his eyes shut, and with so much of the sheet turned aside as might shew his lean, pale, and death-like face, which was purposely turned toward the East, from whence he expected the second coming of his and our Saviour.' In this posture he was drawn at his just height," and when the picture is completed, Donne has it set by his bedside, where it becomes "his hourly object till his death" (78).

The winding-sheet, carefully arranged to show the face, the closed eyes, the head *purposely* facing the East—all is posed, significant, artificial. The deathlike thinness and pallor of his face, his own winding-sheet, his exact height—all is real and particular. Walton's presentation of Donne's funerary picture raises one more question: with a subject, an admired subject, whose own behavior is so studied and so significant, so contrived and so dramatic, so real and so much an act, which kind of *Life* will be true; what type of Picture will make clear its guidance "*by the hand of truth*"? Not, I should think, a loosely managed, artless, or merely natural one, untrue to Donne's true nature.[17]

It is enough to recall the divergence between Cavendish's presentation of Wolsey in *The Life* and in the *Metrical Visions* to suggest the possibility that the demonstrable purpose of *The Life of Donne* might be material to our assessment of it, and other evidence enhances this possibility. In Walton's own elegy on Donne, which he appends to *The Life* in 1670 and 1675, Walton places considerably more emphasis on Donne as a poet and on his own relation to Donne, referring to the facts that he himself was "*lov'd*" by Donne and was "*his Convert.*" In slightly variant form, this elegy, along with elegies by other hands, was originally published with the 1633 edition of Donne's poems. It is therefore fitting that Walton's elegy should dwell on Donne's poetry and, since published only two years after Donne's death, on Walton's personal closeness to the poet whose loss still freshly affects him. The omission of such personal emphasis in *The Life* and a lessening of emphasis on and coverage of Donne's poems indicate less a change of heart or an altered judgment than a different purpose on Walton's part.

Walton's aim, as manifest in his portrait of Donne in *The Life*, is to be more formal and less personal than in the elegy. As artist, Walton is not about to picture himself in a corner of the portrait proper (in any case, certainly not in a simplified "fictional guise") but he is eager to let us into his studio to see how he works. And when he has finally finished the *Donne*, his picture will not present Donne after the Romantic manner of the Lothian portrait—with collar unlaced carefully to signify carelessness—but instead it will show the life "Thus *variable*, thus *vertuous*" and the death "thus *excellent*, thus *exemplary* . . . of this memorable man" (82). It will be true to Donne's own ending, an artificial monument to his life.

Walton's work on Donne is life-writing and should not be confused with the demands and purposes of modern biography, for which the English term was coined only after the Restoration.[18] Life-writing, historically a more accurate description of earlier *Lives*, should be regarded as a precursor of modern biography or, if regarded as a form of it, as a more open, ambiguous, and potentially more artificial form than the modern one. Historically, however, life-writing is the more inclusive term, and modern biography should actually be regarded as a form of it.

Charles Cotton, whose poetical address to Walton the latter thought fit to affix before the collected *Lives* of 1675, had considerable insight into the purpose of Walton's biographical efforts, as we have noticed before. Referring to the collected *Lives*—Wotton, Herbert, Hooker, and Donne—Cotton observes that each of these men "*rais'd unto himself, a Monument / With which Ambition*" might rest contented. Yet, he continues,

> *. . . their great works, though they can never dye:*
> *And, are in truth superlatively high,*
> *Are no just scale, to take their vertues by.*

Cotton then explains that the works of these men are an incomplete measure of their virtues because they fail to show "*how th' Almighties grace*" by various ways "*Brought them to be the Organs of his praise.*" It is Walton's *Lives* that reveal God's way in each individual case. Bede preferred his cases more generic, but otherwise I think he would have approved.

In Cotton's view, *The Life* is not merely a comment on Donne's work, such as his poems and sermons, but a supplement to them. Walton's role in *The Life* is interpretative, and it is also openly inventive. Working with the materials of Donne's life, Walton is not, in Cotton's view, creating ex nihilo fancifully and presumptuously, but he is being truly and responsibly creative. Thus artificial, *The Life* he writes is also historical, and it is true.

Elsewhere in the prefatory verses to Walton, Cotton refers to the monument of Donne, for which the funerary picture of Donne was drawn. This monument, described by Walton as "*a kind of artificial Miracle*," was damaged by the Great Fire of London in 1666, a fact to which Cotton alludes in calling Walton's *Life of Donne* "*a place / More faithful to* . . . [Donne], *than his Marble was*," a place that no fire "*shall e're deface.*" Cotton next praises Walton's *Life* as "*A Monument! that, as it has, shall last / And prove a Monument to that defac't.*" The very fact of Walton's three revisions suggests that his purpose in *The Life of Donne* evolved, becoming sharper and clearer over a period of about thirty-five years. His finished portrait of Donne, as his contemporary Cotton recognizes, is an honorific memorial and, quite literally, a monumental work of art.

In the "Advertisement To *the Reader*" at the beginning of Donne's *Psevdo-Martyr*, a work Walton uses in *The Life*, Donne has a few words to say about his own method of using sources:

> And in those places which are cited from other Authors (which hee shall know by the Margine) I doe not alwayes precisely and superstitiously binde my selfe to the words of the Authors . . . sometimes I collect their sense, and expresse their Arguments or their opinions, and the Resultance of a whole leafe, in two or three lines . . . This is the comfort which my conscience hath, and the assurance which I can giue the Reader, that I haue no where made any Author, speake more or lesse, in sense, than hee intended, to that purpose, for which I cite him.[19]

Like Donne, Walton employs marginal glosses, and it would be an understatement to say that Walton does not always bind himself to the author's own words. But this passage might have caught Walton's eye for another reason, namely, Donne's assurance to the reader that his selective quotations and summary paraphrases do not distort an author's actual statements about the subject for which he is cited: "to that *purpose,* for which I cite him" (my emphasis).

I doubt that Walton would have understood this last assurance by Donne quite as we might, namely, as a promise to be "true" to the total context of an author's statements when citing them. Donne's words admit of this meaning but just as readily admit of another, more limited one. For example, if a writer speaks in a letter of his despondency or of his business plans or enlivens his painful description of illness with a few choice conceits or a passing witticism, Walton could use only the painful statements to illustrate the writer's melancholy state of mind, melancholy being the purpose of his citation in this case. In other words, Walton could omit the livelier and homelier portion of the letter, be true to the letter-writer's "sense" respecting melancholy, and comfort his conscience about his own honesty—trust-worthiness, as Walton's introduction to *The Life of Donne* has it. Walton could even congratulate himself for his historical responsibility in using the writer's own words on a subject instead of simply making them up, as many an earlier biographer had done. Of course I offer this description of Waltonian procedure in the spirit of pure speculation, although the following paragraphs will endeavor to bring it to bear more seriously on Walton's actual conduct of *The Life*, first on a fairly faithful version of a passage in Donne's Preface to *Psevdo-Martyr* and then on a very much freer version of Donne's letters.

In the Preface to *Psevdo-Martyr*, Donne explains how he wrestled with choosing between the Anglican and the Roman Catholic churches:

And although I apprehended well enough, that this irresolution not onely retarded my fortune, but also bred some scandall, and endangered my spirituall reputation, by laying me open to many mis-interpretations; yet all these respects did not transport me to any violent and sudden determination, till I had, to the measure of my poore wit and iudgement, suruayed and digested the whole body of Diuinity, controuerted betweene ours and the Romane Church. In which search and disquisition, that God, which awakened me then, and hath never forsaken me in that industry, as he is the Authour of that purpose, so is he a witnes of this protestation; that I behaued my selfe and proceeded therin with humility, and diffidence in my selfe; and by that, which by his grace, I tooke to be the ordinary meanes, which is frequent praier, and equall and indifferent affections. [B3r]

Walton makes a good number of relatively insignificant changes in transposing this information to *The Life*, and it can be granted, with Novarr, that they tend to elevate Donne's language (e.g., deletion of "*behaued my selfe*" in the middle of the second sentence), to emphasize his piety (e.g., omission of the reference to "*fortune*" in the beginning of the first sentence), and to imply his seemingly destined allegiance to the Anglican Church (e.g., deletion of "*equall*" at the end of the second sentence).[20]

In assessing these changes, however, one should also remember that Donne's Preface is explicitly addressed to "The Priestes, and Iesvits, and to their Disciples in this Kingdome," as Walton's work is not, and that the passage in question is an apology, a polemical confession, again as Walton's is not. The Preface was published in 1610, thirty years before Walton's first version of *The Life* and sixty-five before his last. A change in the purpose for which information in the passage is used—now a *Life*, written by another person—and a change, equally important, in the audience to which the work is addressed, and finally a change in the historical context, from pre- ultimately to post-Cromwellian England, render many of Walton's changes not only understandable but also responsible (e.g., insertion of "then" before "*controuerted*" at the end of the first sentence, and substitution of the theologically more tactful "*safest way*" for "*ordinary meanes*" at the end of the second sentence).

Walton transposes the passage from Donne's Preface to *Pseudo-Martyr* as follows. To rectify his scruples with respect to particular churches, Donne

> lay aside all study of the Law: and, of all other Sciences that might give him a denomination; and, begun seriously to survey, and consider the Body of Divinity, as it was then controverted betwixt the *Reformed* and the *Roman Church*. And as *Gods blessed Spirit did then awaken him to the search, and in that industry did never forsake him*, (they be his own words) *so he calls the same holy Spirit to witness this Protestation; that, in that disquisition and search, he proceeded with humility and diffidence in himself; and, by that which he took to be the safest way; namely, frequent Prayers, and an indifferent affection to both parties.* [25]

Worth noting is the care with which Walton specifies that "they be his own words" when he is especially close to Donne's own phrasing. Walton appears to distinguish these words from his freer paraphrases. The words, of course, are not quite Donne's own, but we grasp this fact without hesitation since they are transposed to a third-person form. Walton's practice here is more careful than Harpsfield's but is otherwise reminiscent of that earlier writer's.

Two additional points should be observed of this passage: first, that a marginal gloss in *The Life* identifies the Preface to *Pseudo-Martyr* as the source for Donne's "own words"; and second, that Walton sets the passage into a narrative frame or an interpretative context, as we can see in the first two lines which immediately follow it: "and indeed, truth had too much light about her to be hid from so sharp an Inquirer; and, he had too much ingenuity, not to acknowledge he had found her." These lines positively glow with Waltonian approval. The artist's presence as interpreter is quite open in them.

Walton's handling of two letters attributed to Donne in *The Life* is considerably harder on the modern critical digestion. These letters concern the depression of Donne's mind, body, and fortune when he is living at Mitcham, but they dramatize especially the darkness of his mood. At moments in reading them we are reminded of Donne's poetry: for example, "A Nocturnall upon S. Lucies Day"—"*and now I am become so little, or such a nothing, that I am not a subject good enough for one of my own letters*"—or perhaps, by contrast, "Loves Growth"—"*tis now Spring, and all the pleasures of it displease me; every other tree blossoms, and I wither*"—and more generally and repeatedly motives in Donne's religious poems and *Devotions*—"*I have often suspected my self to be overtaken* . . . with an over earnest desire of the next life" or "*to be no part of any body, is as to be nothing*" (37).[21] George Saintsbury's comment on the second of the letters would gain the assent of most readers: "The earlier part of this [letter] can scarcely be surpassed even in the Sermons, as an example of that long-drawn, echoing, melancholy music which so often lends an almost uncanny charm to its author's prose." Such music, Saintsbury adds, contrasts effectively "with the harmonious but not in the least mysterious simplicity of Walton's" prose.[22]

A modern reader is startled at first to discover that both letters are a synthesis of quotation and paraphrase drawn freely from a number of Donne's letters. As R. E. Bennett has shown, the first letter uses material written by Donne after his gloomy period at Mitcham, and the second letter is a tissue of selections extracted from five different letters whose total contexts exhibit a greater variety of interests and less unrelieved gloom.[23] What is amazing upon reflection, however, is not the boldness of Walton's technique but the success of it. The letters sound, not like Walton, but like Donne. They may not be a faithful depiction of Donne, but they are a likeness, an imaginative and a perceptive one. They portray a truth about Donne's character and especially about his period at Mitcham that is essentially, if not completely, valid.

Walton's synthesizing letters out of the real epistolary materials of Donne's life is deliberate art rather than deliberate deception. The modern reader's indignation, if aroused by Walton's method of portrayal, is likely to be based on assumptions about total context that have no place in *The Life of Donne;* once these assumptions are made, it becomes difficult to credit Walton's explanations and other indications of the method he is using. Walton introduces the first letter by stating explicitly that he is presenting "an extract collected out of some few of his many Letters" and several sentences later he introduces the second letter, "Thus he did bemoan himself: And thus in other letters" (36). Right after the second letter, Walton comments, "By this you have seen, *a part of the picture* of his narrow fortune, and the perplexities of his generous mind" (38: my emphasis). Apparently even Walton knew that the picture was not in every respect whole.

Other considerations are pertinent. The letters from which Walton drew his extracts had already been published in *Letters to Severall Persons of Honour, 1651*, and were therefore available to those who presumably would be especially interested in Donne's *Life*. Walton himself had reprinted four of these letters at the end of his revision of *The Life* in 1658. As Bennett has noted, his reprint is "remarkably faithful," even reproducing some "typographical peculiarities." Like Walton's own elegy in later editions, the letters reprinted in 1658 are external to the narrative frame, or interpretative context, of *The Life* and beyond its shaping influence. Walton's moving portions of these and other letters inside this frame actually constitutes an advance in his biographical documentation.[24] It also signals an artistic advance, in its own way equally significant, toward the epistolary novel. Once again we encounter the heightening yet the curiously tense coexistence of historicity and artistry in Walton's *Donne*.

The main difference between Walton's use of letters that, despite his framing disclaimers, *appear* to be real and the letters used in a novel by Richardson is that Walton's are drawn directly and closely from the actual letters of a real person. The function of the letters in Walton's *Donne*, like those in Richardson's novels, is largely to provide psychological insight. As Walton's own statements also show us, he uses Donne's letters in *The Life* to portray "the then present Condition of . . . [Donne's] mind and fortune" (36).

My purpose is not to defend Walton's accuracy but better to understand his achievement in *The Life of Donne.* From what we have seen already, Walton does not quote correctly by the standards we require of an historian, and he takes one liberty more extravagant still, changing the reference to a date in one of Donne's letters by somewhat more than a month (from "before Christmas" to "*Candlemas*") in order to sharpen dramatically the outlines, essentially true, of his picture of Donne's dedication to God in the months before his death. This, in my view, is the most licentious modification of fact Walton perpetrates.[25] But once having recognized what *The Life* is—a monument, a portrait, primarily a work of art—we should be little more shocked by this license than we are when Shakespeare puts Margaret of Anjou in *Richard III* to participate in events that occurred after her death. When even a portrait photographer softens a wrinkle or smooths out a wart, we ordinarily do not pass moral judgments on his procedures; we may prefer our faces with warts but we nonetheless grasp the conventions in which he works.

Looking for exact, factual historicity in Walton, we can underestimate Walton's art—the perceptive truth of his synthesis and, indeed, of his fiction. Like Cavendish in *The Life of Wolsey,* Walton spends much more time on the end of his subject's life than on the earlier years, although Walton is chronologically better balanced than Cavendish, spending roughly half *The Life* on the last, priestly quarter of Donne's life, to Cavendish's half on the final year of Wolsey's. As this instance suggests, in assessing Walton's portrait of Donne, we should remember not only the conventions in which Walton operated but also the formal title he gave to his work: *The Life of Dr. "John Donne," Late Dean of St. "Paul's" Church.* Thinking in terms of the "wrenched . . . chronological proportions" of Walton's *Donne* rather than in terms of its artfully conceived shape, we can misjudge another resemblance among Walton, Cavendish, and Roper as artists, namely, their own involvement, or presence, in what they write.[26]

Walton may blend his facts with his point of view but the resulting image is one we should recognize as artificial, contrived, or even fictional. We are not aware of these qualities equally at every moment in *The Life,* and we do not recognize them while in the act of reading every letter from Mitcham. If we did, the illusion of lifelikeness in *The Life*—the miracle of its art, to paraphrase Walton's description of Donne's monument—would be gone. But often in *The Life* Walton makes his role, which is really the role of his art, obvious: "And now, having brought him through the many labyrinths and perplexities of a various life: even to the gates of death and the grave; my desire is, he may rest till I have told my Reader . . ." (79). Walton is so obviously in charge. Here he does not even write having watched or followed him but "having brought him" and indulges his pronounced taste for artificially balanced, sonorous doublets not once but twice: "labyrinths and perplexities," "death and the grave."

Walton alerts us often enough to his presence to have earned the reputation of having a quaintly mannered style, and only a conviction that Walton is artless can keep us from seeing the self-exposure of his art. Ironically this conviction, where it exists, is probably based on Walton's own artful and disarming words to the "dear reader." If we are deceived by Walton's art, we are simply not being alert enough to its presence. For example, Walton praises Donne's preaching in extravagant terms but calls our attention to his own extravagance: "A Preacher in earnest; weeping sometimes for his Auditory, sometimes with them: alwayes preaching to himself, like an Angel from a cloud, but in none; carrying some, as St. *Paul* was, to Heaven in holy raptures, and inticing others by a sacred Art and Courtship to amend their lives" (49). Walton's perception of the "sacred Art and Courtship" of Donne's style in the sermons is affective but also sophisticated; we have but recently recovered this insight in our own time. If we question Walton's awareness of his own art in the passage just quoted, we have only to read his self-conscious comment on it: "There may be some that may incline to think (such indeed as have not heard him) that my affection to my Friend, hath transported me to an immoderate Commendation of his Preaching" (49). This comment at once confirms and disarms our awareness of Walton's extravagant praise just before.[27]

In *The Life of More* Roper in fact may be as much in charge of his subject as Walton is in *The Life of Donne*, but he is not so obviously in charge. Instead of entering the work in a "fictional guise," like that of the young Roper, Walton might be said to have cast such a guise over his subject: "At the hearing of this, Mr. *Donne*'s faint breath and perplext countenance gave a visible testimony of an inward conflict" (33). Our attention to Donne's response is increased by Walton's dramatic rendering of it, or to characterize the effect more exactly, our attention is prolonged: not only "countenance" but also "breath" and, further, breath "faint" and countenance specifically "perplext"; testimony "visible," a description gathering up "breath" and "countenance" and preparing for the complementary adjective "inward." "Mr. Donne's countenance testified to his conflict"—my reductive paraphrase clarifies the extent to which Walton implies an audio-visual dimension (breath, visible). Once more in Walton's narrative art, we detect the strokes of the novelist's pen.

Walton's fictional "guising" of Donne, like Roper's "fictional guise," is perceptively true in vital ways, although not true in every way, and is contrived self-consciously. We have one more indication of this contrivance in the last example cited. I doubt that the reader was much bothered by my omitting the context of this example, namely, the Bishop of Durham's offering Donne a benefice if Donne could be persuaded to take holy orders. It was possible to discuss Walton's studied version of Donne's response without identifying what Donne was responding to. The response, as response, is both interesting and conspicuous. This fact testifies to the interior quality of Walton's concern with Donne and to the substantiality of Walton's artistic presence in *The Life.* In other words, Walton's subject matter, as he conceives it, and his techniques are notably subjective.[28]

The subjectivity of Walton's picture of Donne illuminates a central paradox of *The Life*, the fact that it both is dramatic and again is not. Donne's major conflicts, though reported affectively ("faint breath"), are not performed by Donne himself, except perhaps in quotations from his own poems or in the synthetic letters from Mitcham attributed to him by Walton. His conflicts are not acted out, dramatized objectively. Such matters as Donne's preaching, grief, perplexity, resolution, and generosity are reported dramatically but not performed dramatically. In this sense we could say that their drama is Walton's. His own response or interpretation of Donne's is affective, even to the extent (as we have noted) that he uses a kind of ventriloquism in *The Life*, presenting the reader's response dramatically, as he imagines it: "my Reader [might have] occasion, to ask himself with some amazement, *Lord! How much may I also . . . be chang'd*" (80). The reader is even directed to imagine a tone of amazement.

At moments Walton seems to be imagining Donne's responses to a situation by projecting his own. "*Now,*" he exclaims when Donne takes holy orders, "the *English Church* had gain'd a second St. *Austine,*" and continues,

> And *now* all his studies . . . were all concentred in Divinity. *Now* he had a *new* calling, *new* thoughts, and a *new* imployment for his wit and eloquence: *Now,* all his earthly affections were changed into divine love . . . and *now,* such a change was wrought in him, that he could say with *David, Oh how amiable are thy Tabernacles, O Lord God of Hosts!*[29]

Repetition of the word "now," reinforced by the sound and sense of the thrice recurring word "new," lends increasing immediacy to these announcements. In the excitement of Walton's rhetorical moment we might overlook the fact that this rendition of Donne's renewal, in all its melodrama, is clearly Walton's. There is really nothing to make us think otherwise. Walton does not even make up a speech for Donne but openly assimilates Donne's responses to David's.

Walton's interjection of opinion and aphorism into *The Life* invites comparison in another way with Harpsfield. Like Harpsfield, Walton holds firm opinions about the subject he treats and states them at times quite plainly, as when he opens his reflections on Donne's life with the following blunt judgment: "His marriage was the remarkable error of his life" (60). Frequently Walton is as aphoristic an assayer as Francis Bacon or, again, as the essay-interjecting novelists of the next century: "It hath been observed by wise and considering men, that Wealth hath seldom been the Portion, and never the Mark to discover good People"; and a paragraph later, "God hath been so good to his Church, as to afford it in every age some such men to serve at his Altar as have been piously ambitious of doing good to mankind" (31). But Walton's incursions also go beyond Harpsfield's to become one with the fabric of Walton's *Life of Donne*. If we stop to look, we can actually see Walton interpreting the facts, visibly shaping his image: "This was his present resolution; but, the heart of man is not in his own keeping; and he was destined to this sacred service by an higher hand . . . of which I shall give the Reader an account before I shall give a rest to my Pen" (35). The fact of Donne's "resolution," Walton's reflection on it ("heart . . . of man"), and his interest in the larger pattern he perceives in Donne's life ("destined . . . hand") blend together in a single sentence, at the end of which we notice Walton's presence explicitly.

Oddly enough, most readers tolerate Walton's interpreting presence, whether with interest or amusement or a slightly stifled yawn. Harpsfield's asides and lectures to the reader are likely to prove more offensive. Harpsfield tells us directly, with an objectivity and openness that are admirable but are also heavy-handed. As the last example suggests, Walton enters *The Life* smoothly, gradually, tactfully. Both examples preceding it introduce new paragraphs, the first of which soon ends this way: "Which I mention, for that at this time there was a most generous offer made him for the moderating of his worldly cares; the declaration of which shall be the next employment of my Pen" (31). The second example, initially digressive, likewise brings an explanation within a few lines: Walton tells us he has referred to God's gift of pious priests to mankind "because I have occasion to mention one of them in my following discourse" (32). Walton treats us reasonably. Once we are led to see the purpose of his aphoristic essays, they no longer strike us as digressions or, rather, as impositions. Our recognition of their propriety is stronger, I expect, because we have to revise an aesthetic judgment that in retrospect appears hasty and unfair.[30]

Walton induces our assent, using methods considerably less straightforward than Harpsfield's, yet such inducement is not deception. As Walton's apology for his praise of Donne's preaching confirms *and* disarms our response to that praise, as the praise therefore is and is not excessive; as Walton does and does not trust fancy's shaping power, so his art hides and exposes itself, is and is not deceptive, is and is not open.[31] In the aphoristic essays at issue we find smoothness and subtlety in blending viewpoint and fact and, as our own pronounced awareness of them as essays shows, we find conspicuousness, visibility, exposure. We might miss or misjudge this exposure when it appears for the first or second time, but only as it builds, even occurring in consecutive paragraphs, does it become truly important and at the same time unmistakable.

Walton's art in *The Life of Donne* is all of a piece, even to his handling of detail and to the pacing of his story.[32] In this *Life*, for instance, we do not often meet what I might call focal objects, the equivalent of Cuthbert's half-gnawed onion, Wolsey's red buckram bag, or More's wicket, the gate he closes on Chelsea. With the notable exception of the deathbed portrait, conceived and posed by Donne himself, Walton's medium, like the essayist's, is more abstractly verbal than phenomenal, and it is fitting that his finished work should also be more consistently, self-consciously interpretative than any of the *Lives* earlier discussed.

The pacing of *The Life* is similarly geared to Walton's tight control of Donne's image. Walton's is the most continuous exposition of a life met so far. Consider, for example, representative openings of three consecutive paragraphs: "And [in order] that," "Immediately after," "For [i.e., because] this bitter Physick" (28–29). Through countless little touches—a conjunctive expression, reference to a progressive temporal sequence, a causal explanation, a demonstrative adjective rather than an article—the reader's attention is moved smoothly along. Walton's control of the perspective directs our eyes where he wants them. When he wishes to redirect our gaze radically or abruptly, he enters *The Life* to apologize for digressing, to anticipate or disarm the reader's reluctance to change direction: for example, Walton trusts that "*thou wilt not think it an impertinent digression to look back with* . . . [him], *upon some observations of* . . . [Donne's] *life*" (60).

In the other *Lives* discussed, we have observed numerous analogies between the subject's life and the lives of the patriarchs, apostles, and saints. Walton's employment of such analogies in *The Life* further defines the relation of this work to the conventions of those preceding it. The frequency and explicitness of Walton's references to the lives of the Bible and the saints are striking, especially in the second half of *The Life of Donne*. If we count from Donne's taking holy orders, shortly before the midpoint of *The Life*, through his death, more than thirty-six such references occur in as many pages (46–81). There is more than one analogy with Moses, St. Stephen, Job, and St. Augustine, but Walton's favorites by far for this *Life* are St. Paul, David, and Jacob. Statistically, at least, we have seen nothing quite like the quantity and variety of these sacred analogies since Bede.

Walton's analogies are reasonable and deliberate, fitting and heightening the features of Donne's *Life* that, in his perception, are essential. Discussion of Donne's election and of his marriage and family brings mention of Jacob (29, 47, 54–55, 80). As religious leader and psalmist, David relates to Donne's position in the Church and much more, to his art as a holy poet and preacher (47–48, 51–52, 55, 66). Variously Donne's humility, mindfulness of death, conversion, exemplary role as priest, and especially his preaching are prefigured for Walton in the life of St. Paul (46, 49, 52–54, 60).[33] The reader similarly recognizes the relevance of other analogies to Walton's conception of Donne: the religious leadership of Moses, St. Stephen's holy death, the conversion, introspection, and religious vocation of St. Augustine, Job's family and his patience in suffering.

In comparison to Bede's, Walton's analogies are more exclusively biblical and are less farfetched; they are moral, ethical, or religious rather than miraculous and magical. At first glance, the observation may seem odd that they are also more literary—that is, less direct and literal. Here it might help to recall again that curious Renaissance fashion of portraiture in costume as (or with) a famous saint or as a hieratic figure. As I had occasion to remark earlier, such analogies could still in some ways be believed, but no longer so literally as in Bede's time. Surely the effect of the Reformation on the standing of the sainted Fathers of the Middle Ages partly accounts for Walton's far greater reliance on biblical holy men, but I suspect that there is another reason for it as well. Walton also prefers the biblical holy men because they are more generic figures. Walton posits his analogies on a less complete, exact, and particular correspondence than does Bede and therefore usually employs figures who are more distant and more legendary. If Walton makes an exception, the analogy refers to a figure such as Augustine, whose life, like Job's or Paul's, has mythic stature.

Describing Donne's death, Walton makes a connection with the death of St. Stephen: "Being speechless, and, seeing heaven by that illumination by which he saw it; he did, as St. *Stephen, look stedfastly into it, till he saw the Son of man, standing at the right hand of God his Father*" (81). We are likely to be struck by this comparison because the first reference to Stephen has occurred only a few pages before. The first reference, like the second, relates Donne's death to Stephen's: "Being full of joy that God had enabled him" to preach, as it were, "*his own Funeral Sermon,*" Donne "hastened to his house; out of which he never moved, till like St. *Stephen, he was carried by devout men to his Grave*" (75). A modern reader, perhaps not so well versed in the Bible as Walton, is likely to think first of the stoning of Stephen and to wonder what his martyrdom has to do with Donne's quiet death in the deanery. But the story of Stephen in Acts 6:5–8:1 offers a better basis for Walton's analogy. Answering his accusers at length, Stephen, like Donne, preaches what is in effect his own funeral sermon. As his answer draws to an end, his accusers cast him out of the city and stone him. Walton might also have found the character of Stephen relevant: "a man full of faith and of the Holy Ghost" who "did great wonders and miracles among the people" and disputed with people unable "to resist the wisdom and the spirit by which he spake" (Acts 6:5, 8, 10).[34] As preacher, Stephen sounds very like Walton's conception of Dr. Donne. Moreover, in a Lenten sermon, Donne himself had recommended the contemplation of Stephen's martyrdom as a pattern and an example of holy dying, and Walton might well have found therein his initial warrant for alluding to Stephen.[35]

Yet there is also something conspicuous, almost a little gratuitous, about the references to Stephen's death as they occur in Walton's *Donne*. We *are* likely to think of the stoning and, having consulted Acts, to notice other loose ends or discrepancies: Paul's (Saul's) consent to Stephen's martyrdom; the subject of Stephen's last speech, namely, Jewish rejection of those inspired by the Spirit; and the audience, "stiffnecked and uncircumcised in heart and ears." Stephen, after all, looks "up stedfastly into heaven," right before the mob rushes him, and Donne's own funeral sermon can more appropriately be seen as a figurative comment on Stephen's death, than Stephen's on his, since Donne preaches on the outcomes of, judgments on, and kinds of death and specifically treats of violent death and of the need not merely to scourge but to crucify, utterly to kill, "that sinne that governes thee."[36] On the one hand, then, Walton's analogy between Donne's death and Stephen's, though not without basis, is limited and inexact. On the other, it is rather fanciful, even imaginative. We might recall how literal the perception of resemblance between Cuthbert and the saints was in Bede. Most often the analogy *is* the episode and the essential point in Bede; with Walton, the analogy is more submerged and likely to be, in the Renaissance sense, highly artificial.

Walton's handling of quotations from the Bible in his analogies further indicates the degree to which his own image of Donne took precedence over literal accuracy and, incidentally, shows again that Walton's view of the accuracy required of quotations, even of the sacred words from Holy Writ, was considerably freer than ours. Walton does not hesitate to conflate, invert, paraphrase, or otherwise modify scriptural quotations, although to my knowledge he never modifies them beyond easy recognition; if he did, we should have no way to check on him. When Donne repairs the chapel of the deanery, for example, Walton observes Donne "suffering, as holy *David once vowed, his eyes and temples to take no rest, till he had first beautified the house of God*" (55). The King James version of Psalm 132:4–5 reads as follows: "I will not give sleep to mine eyes, or slumber to mine eyelids, / Until I find out a place for the Lord, an habitation for the mighty God of Jacob." Like Harpsfield, Walton alters the words and perhaps more consistently changes the person of quotations in order to accommodate them to *his* composition, his perception of the subject's life.

A more complex instance of Walton's adaptation of Scripture to his own purposes occurs when he writes of Donne, "So . . . he came to ask *King Davids* thankful question, *Lord, who am I, that thou art so mindful of me?*" (47). Walton conflates the famous line from Psalm 8:4, "What is man, that thou art mindful of him," with one or more of four other passages spoken by David, I Samuel 18:18, II Samuel 7:18, repeated in I Chronicles 17:16; and I Chronicles 29:14. Both passages in Chronicles are "thankful": "Who am I, O Lord God, and what is mine house, that thou hast brought me hitherto?"; "But who am I, and what is my people, that we should be able to offer so willingly after this sort? for all things come of thee, and of thine own have we given thee." Walton's conflated version of these texts comes as he imagines Donne's thoughts just before the latter takes holy orders. In his version of these thoughts, Walton includes a reference to King James I that may make even the passage in I Samuel imaginatively relevant. Walton refers to God's having inspired "the learned'st of Kings, to descend to move . . . [Donne] to serve at the Altar." The relevant verse in I Samuel presents David's question to King Saul: "Who am I? and what is my life . . . that I should be son in law to the king?"[37] Walton's conflation of the various passages cited is free but not, I think, irresponsible or accidental.

The same conflation *("Lord, who am I, that thou art so mindful of me?")* is in context characteristic of Walton's methods in another way. A few lines before it occurs, Walton has twice supposed that Donne, before heeding the call to the priesthood, had asked God "with *Moses, Who am I?*" (46–47). The conflation at issue, attributed by Walton to King David, appears to have been for Walton triggered by and associated with Moses' question to God, "Who am I, that I should go unto Pharaoh?" in Exodus 3:11. The lines that immediately follow the conflation make Walton's association of David's "thankful question" with the earlier, humbler question of Moses self-evident. The lines read, "So mindful of me, as to lead me for more then forty years through this wilderness of the many temptations, and various turnings of a dangerous life." Here Moses' forty years in the wilderness seem suggestively to touch Christ's forty days of trial, self-discovery, and deepening commitment to His mission; and sure enough, a very few lines later occurs the more explicit reference to Christ that Walton's associations have led us to expect: "and so," Walton continues with Donne's supposed thoughts, "*blessed Jesus*, I do take the cup of Salvation, and will call upon thy Name, and will preach thy Gospel" (47). Walton's deployment of Scripture is skillful and imaginative.[38]

The quotations we have been considering for the last two paragraphs are part of a larger passage of about three pages treating Donne's "conversion" to a holy calling. This amazing passage epitomizes many of the characteristics analyzed in this section and much of Walton's technique in the *Donne*, beginning with a brief, generalized essay (46) and ending with the assimilation of Walton's Donne to the community of holy men (48). In the middle of the passage, Walton tries, as Bede never does, to penetrate Donne's mind with the insight provided by his own imagination.[39] But not quite all by his own: here Walton uses the lives of the saints and especially of the Bible to assist, to direct, and indeed to validate the workings of his imagination. We might suppose the Bible to have been in Walton's view a responsible and reliable "source" for a *Life* of Donne. Using it, he might imagine Donne's thoughts and emotions in a situation generic to the Bible—acceptance of God's calling—without feeling that he had simply invented them. He could also feel that he had again alerted us more than sufficiently to his method by first explicitly qualifying the directness of the interior discourse he gives to Donne: "and doubtless, considering his own demerits, [he] did humbly ask with St. *Paul*, *Lord*, *who is sufficient for these things?*" The word "doubtless" guides our understanding of Walton's assigning the Pauline statement to Donne. Of course, even without the recurrence of such qualifying guides, Walton must expect us to recognize the italicized biblical quotations and to allow the force—occasionally the shock—of recognition to heighten the drama and significance of Donne's conversion. And just to be sure that our recognition of the pertinence of his quotations is not frustrated by our own memory or ignorance, Walton usually directs us more explicitly to his source in St. Paul, the story of Moses or Stephen, and the like.

Should we ask, one last time, whether such biographical methods leave us with a sense of Donne or really of Walton, we would have to conclude that they leave us with Walton's picture of Donne, a real seventeenth-century view of a real life lived in historical time; that is, they leave us inextricably with both. Seen as a skillful contemporary portrayal of a late Renaissance person, Walton's *Life of Donne* is valuable, irreplaceable even by a greater, more accurate body of facts, and within the frame of its own vision, it is true.[40]

Each of the Renaissance *Lives* in this section is, while explicitly historical in subject and detail, selective, partial, artful, and deliberate. Markedly, even radically, each employs the techniques of fiction. The author of each exhibits significant awareness both of his own presence in the work and of its bearing on his interpretation of materials. He shows an additional awareness—tentative at first in Cavendish and pronounced in Walton—of his own creative shaping of another's life.

These works might tell us as much about biographical fiction as about biographical truth in the period. Yet the fact remains that the works themselves claim to be truth, and their claims have the nature neither of pretense nor of greed but of conviction.[41] Further, for most readers, these works are examples of the best *Lives* written in the period, and unlike less fictive works such as Hayward's *Life and Raigne of King Edward the Sixt* or less historical works such as Drayton's *Legend of Great Cromwell*, they could not conceivably be designated something other than biography, or, again more accurately, other than life-writing.[42] *Lives* like Cavendish's, Roper's, and Walton's represent, if any do, the purer and defining form of the Tudor-Stuart *Life*.

Biography itself is a mixed form, having always a tendency to merge on the one side with fiction and on the other side with history. But in Tudor-Stuart times this tendency has a special meaning, which is, if not unique to life-writing, most sharply expressed in it.[43] In *Lives* of this period, fiction and history, creative invention and objective truth, are presumed to be complementary and even inseparable rather than opposed. As we have seen, *Lives* themselves make untenable the commonly held view that this presumption results simply from the author's lack of awareness of fiction in the *Life*. It results more likely from the absence of the Enlightenment suspicion and the post-Enlightenment persuasion that fiction and factual truth really are total opposites.[44]

In the essay "The New Biography" (1927) Virginia Woolf wrote that "Truth of fact and truth of fiction are incompatible; yet . . . [the biographer] is now more than ever urged to combine them." She added prophetically, "For it would seem that the life which is increasingly real to us is the fictitious life."[45] If not a prophecy of quite recent developments, such as metahistory, Woolf's latter remark might be thought to describe a much earlier period. With her latter remark, Renaissance life-writers might well have agreed, although they would have tended to assume an educational, if not necessarily always a moral, purpose in the fiction. But I doubt they would have agreed so easily with Woolf's first sentence. When writers of the twentieth century say biography overlaps with fiction and with history, they usually take as given (as does Woolf) the absolute primacy of what has come to be known as the rules of evidence and the standards of factual accuracy.[46] While the relation of truth to fiction in Renaissance *Lives* moves toward these rules and standards, it remains both closer and freer; measured only by them, it would appear merely confused and licentious.

There is no denying that Renaissance *Lives* overstep the bounds of accuracy we now acknowledge necessary, and they may do so in large part because their authors do not have our sense of the point at which a fiction that answers to fact becomes a fiction that tampers improperly with fact, as in the one instance of Walton's dating. But these *Lives* overstep not because they are simply naive or because they espouse license but because they credit—and sometimes overcredit—the truth of fiction. The convergence of fiction and historical truth in Tudor-Stuart *Lives* is less unconscious or unthinking than it is deliberate, and it expresses a conception of biographical truth—as procedure, purpose, and product—somewhat different from what our own century conceives this to be.

Recent studies of autobiography—often as a form wholly distinct from biography—illuminate this conception of truth and may, in turn, be enlarged by it. The convergence of the biographer's experience in actual life with his subject's generates, in Paul Murray Kendall's words, "the chief ornaments of biographical composition" until the twentieth century. Accordingly, Kendall suggests the useful term "life-relationship biography" for all such "ornaments" as Cavendish's, Roper's, and Walton's *Donne*.[47]

If, as a number of theorists find, autobiography is a still freer, more subjective, more poetic form than biography, the convergence of autobiographical and biographical activity in many of the best early life-writings further conditions the nature of their truth.[48] The conjunction of life-lived and *Life*-written, past events and present telling, character and author, is present to some extent in all biographies, but in "life-relationship" biographies, its actuality has a kind of double existence: the writer constructs the life through his own memory, as well as through historical evidence and literary art. His involvement is thus at once historically real and doubly mind-made.

PART II

SIX
MORE'S *RICHARD III*
History and Biography

Thomas More's *History of King Richard III* enlarges our conception of truth in the depiction of historically real persons in Renaissance literature. More's biographical history or historical biography is a generically mixed work and a virtual touchstone for the extension of biographical truth beyond a single form or genre. It opens a way to tracing the transformations of such truth in history and drama, the two major forms that border and overlap biography in the period.[1]

More's *Richard* raises many of the issues about the relation of history to literature, of factual truth to fiction, that we have already encountered discussing the *Lives*. Predictably, it also provokes disagreement about the nature of this relationship, on which the following excerpts each comment:

"More was working as an artist and a teacher rather than as a scholar. The result was not necessarily truthful, but it was instructive and effective since everything was organized into an intelligible and moving whole"—Leonard F. Dean.

More's "history is literary art, and not historical science"; and in a second article, "if More's *Richard III* is primarily dramatic, the question of its fidelity to historical fact hardly arises"; still, "It is clear that much of More's information is authentic, and there is historical truth in his *Richard III* as there is in Shakespeare's historical plays"—A. F. Pollard.

"More's own statements" prove "that he did indeed conceive of the *Richard* as 'history' in some sense of the word"; "Yet the judgement of the modern historians remains pertinent: More's . . . *Richard III* is just as surely literature as it is history"—Richard S. Sylvester.

"The structure of this work is essentially founded upon a dramatic conceit"; and again, its "literary techniques and intentions . . . are so prevalent as considerably to overshadow any historical value it may have and should disqualify it as much from unquestioned acceptance as a historical source as the dramatic medium disqualifies Shakespeare's play"—Arthur Noel Kincaid.

More "allowed his satiric instincts full play in the work, so that in some important respects it forms a Lucianic, and so irreverent, comment on the whole craft of history. . . . Like Shakespeare's history plays, his work . . . is an expounding or interpretation—an imaginative reconstruction"—Alison Hanham.[2]

As is not the case with the *Lives*, commentators overwhelmingly grant that More's *Richard* is literary and more specifically dramatic. In fact, the *Richard* is defined and lauded as art to the extent that its pretensions as history are slighted or rejected. Reading modern discussions of the *Richard* we might find it hard to remember that this *History* is not, as a matter of record, a stage play, whether a five-act play, a morality play, or a mock-morality play.[3] No one denies that More's dramatic talents and contacts with playwrights were considerable, but we might for these reasons assume that he could have written the *Richard* as a play if he had wished to do so and that his choice of another form, one more mixed and less dramatic, is significant.[4]

In More's own century the *Richard* had the status of a valid historical source. The chronicle-historians Grafton, Hall, Holinshed, and Stow appropriate More's work nearly whole, with few changes and without demurrer. More's *Richard* is also described by Queen Elizabeth's tutor, Roger Ascham, as a work that "doth in most part . . . of all these points" advisable in history-writing of the highest order "content all men." The "points" to which Ascham refers are familiar but still worth detailing: first, "to write nothing false" and "next, to be bold to say any truth." "Then," Ascham continues, "to mark diligently the causes, counsels, acts, and issues in all great attempts" and to observe the presence or absence of justice, wisdom, or courage in them. The historian is also to note in the outcome of each endeavor "some general lesson of wisdom and wariness," a lesson apparently practical rather than merely philosophical, "for like matters in time to come." He is to keep truly "the order of time" and to describe in lively terms both sites and the "nature of persons, not only for the outward shape of the body, but also for the inward disposition of the mind, as [do] Thucydides . . . and Homer . . . and our Chaucer." Ascham concludes that the historian should write in such a way that "a man shall think [himself] not to be reading, but present in doing of the same."[5] Thus the true historian does not use a dramatic medium, but he does write vividly, affectively, and dramatically. He notes and in fact imagines what occurs in other men's minds. The methods of life-writing—variously of Cavendish, Roper and Walton—appear highly relevant to his art.

Although the long, explanatory title of *The History of King Richard*, as Rastell printed it, cannot be More's, twice in this work More uses the word *history*, once when referring to the *Richard* itself—"this hystorye" (9)—and again when referring to the "history" of Perkin Warbeck, a pretender to the throne of Henry VII, which, More explains, he does not have place to treat in this present work but might treat later on (83).[6] His explanation implies that the *Richard*, like the projected work on Perkin, is a history. Seeking to discount this implication, Pollard notes that More also refers to the *Utopia* as a "history" in the prefatory letter to Peter Giles, but he seems to forget More's recurrent irony in this letter.[7] Indeed, More's letter refers not to his own narrative as "history" but to the imaginary Hythloday's Utopian tale, making the reference doubly ironic because it is twice removed from historical fact.[8]

Like Pollard, Hanham associates the *Richard* with the "history" of Utopia and discounts the crucial distinction that the *Richard* corresponds to historical reality in a way the second Book of *Utopia*, for all its satiric relevance to England, simply does not. She accepts but also goes beyond the sense of the word *history*, namely, "just a story" or "only a tale," that Pollard would attribute to More when she finds the *Richard* essentially tongue-in-cheek, a satire on the "craft of history."[9] Her views render More's work both radically unhistorical and radically modern, since his failure to meet modern historical standards is interpreted as his recognition and deliberate satire of the methods of other contemporary historians, notably Polydore Vergil. While Hanham's views of More's work profitably redress an excessively moral reading of it, they themselves are extreme and unbalanced. To a great extent, however, this is a literary argument that concerns the tone and coherence of More's text, one properly belonging to the closer examination of it in subsequent pages.

Ascham's description of the requirements of a true history is very likely nearer More's sense of the word *history* than are the meanings Pollard and Hanham would assign to More. Like the notion of "untruth" in the *Lives*, even Ascham's stricture on falsehood cannot be taken to refer exclusively to imprecision or factual inaccuracy, let alone to considered viewpoint or literary invention of the sort present in the *Richard: true* history, as Ascham describes it, is inventive.

In fact, although More does not claim that the *Richard* is truth, his referring to it as history appears on the surface to align it with the leading historical commonplace of his time, namely, that a written history subserves a higher truth. The wedge had not really been driven between moral instruction and historical fact, or rather, in the early decades of the sixteenth century most writers who considered the nature and purpose of history had not faced the reality of this wedge. For them, history was not only a serious business; it was moral and Christian.[10] Machiavelli is an obvious exception to this rule, and, as I shall argue, to an extent so is More. For the present, however, we might conclude simply that the meaning of *history*, whether in the *Richard* or applied to it, is problematical and, to judge from the evidence cited so far, perhaps in modern terms somewhere between historical fact and historical fiction, the creative action of the imagination on the actual materials of history.

Readers have had as much trouble deciding whether More's *Richard* is history or biography as they have had deciding whether it is history or literature, and their comments suggest that these problems are related.[11]

George B. Churchill, for example, observes that "More's account is not a chronicle, but a biography of Richard," and later, "its feeling is throughout aroused by and directed toward the central figure of the story." More, he points out, is the first writer to make Richard not only "the chief and central figure, but the moving impulse." Richard is made a dramatic character and essentially the work is about him, including his motivating effects on those around him: in essence, then, More's work is both art and biography. Similarly for Stauffer, the *Richard* offers "the finest instance of royal biography in English during the sixteenth century," and it is throughout "more than an objective and impersonal chronicle." Stauffer approves More's irony, detachment, and especially the "dramatic and psychological skill" of his treatment. A. R. Myers, who, like Pollard, regards the *Richard* as dramatic art rather than history, simply assumes the propriety of referring "to More's biography." Each of these citations thus aligns an artistic, and more exactly a dramatic, intention in the *Richard* with a biographical one.[12]

Dean, who sees the *Richard* as the work of an artist and teacher, suggests that we find in it a "stage in the history of . . . the biographical or historical example."[13] The moral emphasis of his description leads us to a final alignment of an essentially historical intention in the *Richard* with an exemplary or devotional one: an alignment of truth with moral efficacy. Making this alignment, R. W. Chambers grants that the *Richard* "might be claimed as biography," first because of More's own statement that "this Dukes demeanoure ministreth in effecte all the whole matter whereof this booke shall entreate" (6), and second because "More's interest in the character of Richard is what gives unity to the whole book"; still, Chambers doubts that the *Richard* really can be called biography:

> the book covers only the history of four months, and much of it is not immediately concerned with Richard himself. *Richard III* is rather the first modern treatment of a limited period of English history. With it begins modern English historical writing of distinction.

Clearly Chambers once again has in mind the tight focus and the chronological proportions of modern "realistic" biography rather than those of the Renaissance *Lives*—for example, of Cavendish's thematic excursion on Henry VIII's divorce trial or of Walton's brief generalizing essays or of half of Cavendish's work on Wolsey's last year and half of Walton's on Donne in Orders. His objection is telling but it tells equally against the argument that the *Richard* is history. Precedents for "the first modern treatment of a limited period of English history," as Chambers knew, are not easy to come by. If guided by Chambers' own description of the biographical claims of the *Richard*, namely, More's subject matter and "interest in the character of Richard," we might think most readily of Suetonius' *Lives of the Caesars*—a work known to More and arguably closer to biography than to history.[14]

Having held that the *Richard* is history, however, Chambers adds that "More, like Harpsfield, is in the devotional tradition." In the moral sense, Chambers then argues, More's *Richard* belongs with Harpsfield's biography of More: though the *Richard* may be our "first great piece of modern English history," it is also "a sermon against ambition," important to the historian of prose "both as history and as sermon." If in other descriptions biography finds an alignment with dramatic art and thereby with fiction in the *Richard*, here history somehow finds its alignment with truth, if not factual, then moral.[15]

When we deal with More's *Richard*, as earlier with the *Lives*, our unspoken assumptions about the presence of truth and fiction in various genres and the associations among genres we make as a result of them are persistent and perplexing. And it may well be, as it was in the *Lives*, that the *Richard* perplexes our categories because it was never meant to be aligned with them and that, as it is in some sense both truth and fiction, so it combines history with life-writing and drama as well. While I do not deny the pertinence of dramatic form to the *Richard*, I shall concentrate on the biographical and historical features of the work, both to balance an exaggerated alignment of it with drama (prophetically including Shakespearean drama) and to suggest what is, in my view, the more fundamental, conceptual influence on portrayal and structure in it.

Although history converges with biography in More's *Richard*, the characteristic emphases of these two forms can be distinguished for the purpose of discussion. History has its share of fiction, to which Ascham's choice of model historians attests, as does the rhetoric of history-writing. Nonetheless history, as concept and term, provides the objective pole or factual point of reference for biography. History must deal with actual events and facts, whereas life-writing must have in it a considerable element, not of untruth, but of fiction. This distinction in the priorities of the forms implies a correlative distinction in the relation of writer to subject and audience. The life-writer tends both to participate in his subject's *Life* and to imagine his audience more fully and consistently than does the historian.

Life-writing is primarily and essentially committed to the portrayal of persons and, virtually by definition, is therefore more personal in scope and more subjective or interior in focus than history is. At least in the Renaissance, a period lacking reams of accurately recorded psychological data and objectively reliable methods of assessing them, "more subjective and interior" implies "more intuitive and inventive, more imaginative and fictional." In addition to the strong, explicit ties of life-writing to the historical reality of living persons, its association with the fictionalizing imagination is pronounced and necessary. The resulting tension between living person and fictive character distinguishes the finest achievements in this form.

In More's *Richard*, as subsequent pages will argue, we are dealing with the subject matter and methods of life-writing when, for example, we encounter More's artful and fictional version of Richard's nature, personality, and motives as essential cause of historical actions, of "the course of this hystorye," as More puts it (9). More's *Richard* expresses the kind of truth and the awareness in depicting historical persons that we have found in the *Lives* earlier discussed. This is not to say that the *Richard* is an inverted or a somehow parodic version of Bede's *Cuthbert* or that in defiance of chronology it was influenced by Cavendish's *Wolsey*.[16] But it is to say that the *Richard* shares fundamental, characterizing features of method and vision with the single-minded portrayal of the historical saint's *Life*, with the frustration of deliberately evoked saintly patterns in the *Life* of the worldly prelate, and more generally with the "truthful" depiction of historical figures in biographies of the Tudor-Stuart period. What I would emphasize is the nearness of studied fiction in the *Richard* to the tradition of literary portraiture or life-writing in the Renaissance, and I would urge its classification as such. This tradition—more objective and factual than Tudor drama, more subjective and fictional than chronicle-history—proves highly relevant to the later fortunes of More's *Richard*, to its longevity both in history and in art.

More's *Richard* begins with the death and character of Edward IV—with a finished life and an idealized portrait of the man who lived it: "Kyng Edwarde of that name the fowrth, after that hee hadde lyued fiftie and three yeares, seuen monethes, and sixe dayes, and thereof reygned two and twentye yeres, one moneth, and eighte dayes, dyed at Westmynster the nynth daye of Aprill, the yere of oure redempcion, a thowsande foure houndred foure score and three, leauinge muche fayre yssue" (3). More's first sentence exhibits a notorious lack of factual accuracy: Edward died at the age of forty, when, incidentally, More himself was a child of six.[17] Still, the opening of the *Richard* has a tone of certainty, dignity, and significance. Its momentum is far more authoritative than would have been a simple statement of fact, such as "Edward IV died when he was fifty-three," not to mention the less ripened age of forty. If More's work were not in some sense a history, we should have to say that its beginning alludes to the manner of one as unmistakably as the beginning of Roper's *Life of More* alludes to a legal document.[18]

In Robert Fabyan's *Chronicle*, to instance a work More probably knew, passages similar to the opening of the *Richard* occur consistently enough to be considered formulaic:

> This yere, that is to meane of the mayer, and begynnyng of the. xxiii. yere of the kynge, at Westmynster, vpon the. ix. day of Apryll, dyed that noble prynce Edwarde the. iiii. late kynge of Englande . . . when he had reygned, to rekyn his beynge out of the lande, with all other tyme, full. xxii. yeres, and asmoche as from the. iiii. daye of Marche vnto the. ix. day of Apryll, leuynge after hym. ii. sonnes, that is to say prynce Edwarde his eldest sone and Richarde duke of Yorke, and. iii. doughters, as Elizabeth that after was quene, Cecyle, and Katheryne.[19]

The death of Henry IV affords another typical example: "and so after he made hymself redy, and dyed shortly after, vpon the day of seynt Cuthbert, or the. xx. day of Marche, when he had reygned. xiii. yeres. v. monthes, and. xxi. dayes, leuynge after hym. iiii. sonnes . . . and ii. doughters. . . .[20] Most passages in Renaissance histories noting the death of a king proceed to an enumeration of his children and their conditions and then comment, often at fair length, on one or several aspects of the king's character—political, religious, and personal.

Likewise More, having enumerated Edward's children at the outset of the *Richard*, next characterizes Edward, first as a prince and then as a person. The *process* of idealization is progressively evident in More's description of the dead King. Initially the description, though highly laudatory, maintains a careful balance with qualifying facts: King Edward had "suche gouernaunce and behauioure *in time of peace* (for in war eche parte muste needes bee others enemye) that there was neuer anye Prince of this lande *attaynynge the Crowne by battayle* so heartely beloued" (3: my emphasis). Edward's conduct of war and his path, by war, to the crown are less than ideal here. As More's description of Edward's princely character progresses, however, it becomes thoroughly idealistic: "of hearte couragious, politique in counsaile, in aduersitie nothynge abashed, in prosperitie, rather ioyfull then prowde, in peace iuste and mercifull, in warre, sharpe and fyerce, in the fielde, bolde and hardye" (4). The adjectives become predictable.

More's description of Edward's person shows how deliberate his idealization of the dead King is. Actual facts embarrass More's claims that Edward's "fleshlye wantonnesse" was "in hys latter dayes: lessyd and wel lefte" and that at his death "He hadde lefte all gatherynge of money." Contemporary documents indicate that these claims are incorrect.[21] The suspicious-minded might even entertain the possibility that More made Edward older in the opening sentence of the *Richard* in order that the King might more credibly be beyond the fleshly and financial temptations of power and that his life might appear more nearly closed and completed. Giving rein to suspicion, one might contrast with the sense of fulfillment characterizing More's initial depiction of Edward's life the reflection on the untimeliness of Edward's premature death in *The Great Chronicle* of London, another document contemporary with More: "thus was This noble and victorious prynce Sodeynly to speke of, takyn ffrom the Unstabyll Glory of this world whan he passid not the age of xlvj yeris."[22]

Besides modifying fact for his idealized portrait of King Edward, More suppresses the sort of detail that might make the forthcoming contrast between good King Edward and wicked King Richard less sharp. More implies that Edward has left nothing unfinished that he had intended to achieve, for he had obtained his tribute money from France, "And the yere foregoynge hys deathe, hee hadde obtayned Barwycke" (5). More does not mention that it was Richard's troops who captured Berwick, and thus that Richard has contributed to the finished wholeness of Edward's life, or rather to that of More's idealized portrait. We have had occasions earlier to observe that a finished and completed life has in it some elements of fiction—in King Edward's case, a substantial quantity of them.

The phrasing of the description of Edward's person is by itself enough to alert the reader to More's idealizing of Edward: "He was of visage louelye, of bodye mightie, stronge, and cleane made: how bee it in his latter dayes wyth ouer liberall dyet, sommewhat corpulente and boorelye, and nathelesse not vncomelye" (4). A contemporary of Edward notes that the King habitually took emetics "for the delight of gorging his stomach once more," but even without this information, we can see that More is doing his best to reduce the dimensions of Edward's gluttony.[23] He uses euphemism ("ouer liberall" for gluttonous or intemperate) and qualification ("sommewhat corpulente").[24] Next he mounts a postpositive—or in this case, postnegative—retrieval operation ("nathelesse") and settles for a negative assertion ("not vncomelye").

More apologizes for Edward's excesses, for that "fleshlye wantonnesse: from whiche healthe of bodye in greate prosperitye and Fortune, wythoute a specyall grace hardelye refrayneth." He then goes beyond apology to excuse and virtually to defend Edward's "faute [which] not greatlye gryeued the people: for neyther could any one mans pleasure, stretch and extende to the dyspleasure of verye manye, and was wythoute violence," and now More adds, moving into pure fiction, "in hys latter dayes: lessyd and wel lefte." In the text of the *Richard*, the quotations in this and the preceding paragraph are sequential, concentrated in a few lines. Their rhetoric is conspicuous; it not only reveals but also briefly exposes the fact of More's idealization of Edward.

But More's purpose in idealizing Edward is neither to satirize the King nor to deceive the reader. More frees himself from strict accuracy, from the realism of an un-illusioned judgment of Edward, and, perhaps most important, from an unimaginative assessment of truth. He takes fictional license with fact and most notably with biographical data—facts about Edward's person, or facts "*in homine*," as the Croyland chronicler puts it. Yet More also alerts us to what he is doing.

Still, he does not want seriously to compromise his idealized portrait of King Edward, so he restricts the exposure, keeping it only slightly visible except for one conspicuous moment. He thus maintains the conceptual proportions of the *true* King Edward IV without losing sight of the failings of the actual one. The ties to historical reality in the portrait remain strong and particular but do not short-circuit the process of idealization. The end of More's portrait of Edward, like the dominant tone throughout, is most persuasively laudatory: "hee was wyth hys people, soo benygne, courteyse and so familyer, that no parte of hys vertues was more estemed: yet that condicyon in the ende of hys dayes . . . meruaylouslye in him grewe and increased" (5). The truth about More's Edward is that he was essentially a good king. Unlike satire, which assumes or implies a norm, More's *Richard* thus asserts one.[25]

More is the most sophisticated writer we have discussed so far in this book, and he is also the most deliberately artful. I have already implied that his error regarding Edward's age at death in virtually the first words of the first sentence of the *Richard* is not accidental. It is an error stated in loving detail and with unqualified assurance, where uncertainty or conflicting information as to his age, which was likely to have been available to More, would have called for a different approach.[26] Although we can speculate that More might have been following an erroneous source no longer extant, this speculation is substantiated only by the manner of More's opening or by an overall judgment about the historicity of his work. We are thus left with the fact of the originality of More's presumed mistake and without a source to rationalize it.

If the age More attributes to Edward is another instance of idealization, as I am inclined to argue, in view of our modern knowledge of chronology it has also at some level to be recognized as an historical error. The question is at what level, at one that is purposeful and artistic or at one that is uncontrolled and totally unwitting? To readers, like Pollard, who accept the date that Gairdner proposes in the *DNB* for the marriage of Edward's parents, namely 1438, the increased age More assigns Edward would make Edward a bastard and invalidate the right of his sons to the crown.[27] Only what More presents as slander in the *Richard* supports this suggestion (59, 66, 73). Pollard is aware that his presumption of a marriage in 1438, together with an increase in Edward's age of thirteen years and seven months, implies conclusions either wholly contradictory to More's meaning or absurdly ironic in relation to it. Pollard wisely chooses not to pursue their implications, yet by raising them, he suggests More's incompetence rather thoroughly.

To begin with, More is less likely to have known the date when Richard of York, Edward IV's father, married Cecily Neville than the more public fact of a recent King's age at death, and a mistake with respect to the marriage is therefore more likely to have been inadvertent. Thus inadvertence regarding the date of marriage need not negate the likelihood that More deliberately exaggerated Edward's age. But inadvertence in this case assumes not only that More might have been privy to York's date of marriage but also that the date 1438 is accurate, as I suspect it is not. A date of marriage as late as 1438 for these principals—an unmarried heir of York and an unmarried Neville—would be at best surprising. Born in 1415, Cecily was "married," or at least contracted in marriage, to Richard in 1424, when she was about nine, and he about thirteen.[28] (The date in 1424 was apparently unknown to Gairdner in the *DNB* article.) Presumably the marriage was formalized or consummated some years later, although fourteen years later, or 1438, the "probable" date of marriage Gairdner derives from Richard's most recent whereabouts and the birth of Richard's and Cecily's first child in 1439, flatly challenges credibility.[29] If a marriage date of 1438 is incorrect, as seems likely, then Pollard's doubts about More's control of the implication regarding Edward's legitimacy at the outset of the *Richard* provide a very red herring. In view of the evidence we have, our choice in interpreting More's careful statement of Edward's age as 53 years, 7 months, and 6 days in 1483 is between straightforward inaccuracy and purposeful idealization. The idealizing context of More's initial portrait of Edward and the deliberated manner of the opening of the *Richard* argue that the increase in Edward's age is strategic, a possibility I shall subsequently assume to be the case.

The likelihood that More deliberately opened the *Richard* with an incorrect fact is a little shocking, but is it our allegiance to fact—or More's—that makes it so? We might recall the flat contradictions between the factual content of *The Life of Wolsey* and that of the *Metrical Visions*, both by George Cavendish, for much of his life More's contemporary. For Cavendish, form could take priority over fact. The period Richard S. Sylvester, More's most recent editor, assigned to the composition of the *Richard* (1514–18) partly overlaps and otherwise follows that customarily assigned to the *Utopia* (1515–16).[30] The writer who produced the *Utopia* and in the letter to Giles engaged in the further spoofing of unimaginative readers by referring factually and geographically to its reality might well have been capable of such bold experimentation with fact. In making this suggestion, I am not concurring with Pollard's view (and more recently Hanham's) that More attaches the same meaning to the word "history" when used to describe the *Richard* and when used ironically to describe Hythloday's Utopian story. Hythloday is a purely imaginary figure; Edward and Richard were real people, historical figures, if you will. The *Utopia* and the *Richard* are quite different, as well as significantly related, works. The *Richard* engages recent history more directly.

Alluding to the manner of a history so conspicuously and employing fact so licentiously in the opening sentence of the *Richard*, More indicates the historical nature of his work *and* limits its claim to literal, exact historicity. His opening signals that he treats historical fact but that he treats it very much as subject rather than as inviolable object. He primarily masters its essential truth, whether ideal or otherwise, rather than primarily recording its data. If this is his meaning, his choice of a biographical approach in the *Richard*—that is, his choice of a relatively more subjective form than straight history takes—is wonderfully apt.

More's "error" at the beginning of the *Richard* does not destroy the authenticity of his engagement with history. The exaggeration of Edward's age is in context a carefully controlled inaccuracy: it does nothing to influence our impression of Edward that the immediately succeeding character sketch does not do more fully, and without this sketch, which clearly reveals More's idealizing methods and purpose, it would be simply meaningless. A reader with enough knowledge to recognize the inaccuracy will suspect More's purpose the sooner; one without enough should perceive that purpose within a few pages. More's exaggeration is a fairly innocuous outrage that invites us to notice his deliberate idealization of Edward rather than to reject his right to an imaginative and searching interpretation of actual history, in fact, of the recent past.

In the sentence that follows the initial character of Edward but continues to pay tribute to "this noble king," More begins to draw Richard into the picture. Appropriately, he introduces Richard with two contrary-to-fact constructions. The love between Edward and his subjects "hadde bene . . . a meruailouse forteresse" to his children, More explains, "if deuision and discension of their frendes, hadde not vnarmed them . . . and the execrable desire of souerayntee, prouoked him to theire destruccion, which yf either kinde or kindenesse hadde holden place, muste needes haue bene theire chiefe defence" (5–6). The kind of fact to which the destruction of the young princes is contrary is thematically important: love, friendship or amity, and nature ("kind"), including kinship and generosity; in short, human "trouthe"—integrity, loyalty, and truth.

Equally important is the manner of the introduction of Richard, a mere pronoun in the phrase "prouoked him to theire destruccion." The pronoun reluctantly introducing Richard suggests his anonymity, his lack of integrity, of wholeness and real identity—the lack of truth and of form in his being. Noting the pronoun, as we must because identification of its referent is delayed, we might again recall the introduction of Edward just three pages before: "Kyng Edwarde of that name the fowrth, after that hee hadde lyued fiftie and three yeares, seuen monethes, and sixe dayes, and thereof reygned two and twentye yeres, one moneth, and eighte dayes. . . ." More might have had still another reason for sounding so certain about Edward's age; if his introduction of Edward had been less finished, less secure and definite, he would have been hard pressed to define Richard's anonymity. After all, as any Renaissance writer knew, one defines a negative by the absence of a positive; one defines the *fact* of anonymity or formlessness, then, by contrast. But More also knew that such a fact was historical in Richard's case and, in the historical sense, real—as real, in fact, as Richard's name in the genealogical tables.

After insinuating the anonymity of Richard's unnatural presence, More names him: "For Richarde the Duke of Gloucester, by nature theyr Vncle, by office theire protectoure, to theire father beholden, to them selfe by othe and allegyaunce bownden, al the bandes broken that binden manne and manne together, withoute anye respecte of Godde or the worlde, vnnaturallye contriued to bereue them, not onelye their dignitie, but also their liues"

(6). It is as if More would from the beginning master and, if possible, control the historical reality he acknowledges in and as Richard of Gloucester. In the sentence just quoted, Richard is simultaneously granted his identity, both noble and familial, and stripped of it as a consequence of his own villainy, his own cancellation of his human truth or human "kinde"—nature, kin, and kindness. One is reminded by More's rhetorical strategy of a description John Foxe gives of the actual degradation of the monk Richard Bayfield during More's tenure as Chancellor. Bayfield is first fully vested and then methodically divested of his ecclesiastical garments.[31] The strategy of More's sentence describing Richard thus observes a familiar pattern: Richard is not only identified by name but also indicted, found guilty, and divested of his identity. More seems to want to have Richard's reality both ways—as something and as nothing.

More's conception of Richard's behavior is made perfectly clear to us at the start. For the second time, in consecutive sentences describing Richard, the same theme appears: "al the bandes . . . that binden manne and manne together," the bonds of nature, law, and love, of God and of the world, and in short, the bonds of "trouthe." Once again More's contrast between Richard and Edward is sharp: the description of Edward has employed a cognate of the word *love* three times ("beloued," "louynge," "loue," 3–5), as well as related words like "fauor," "affection," and "courtesy," to describe the bond between the King and his people.

At this point More announces that Richard's "demeanoure" is the "whole matter" of his book and that he therefore wishes, "sommewhat to shewe you ere we farther goe, what maner of manne this was, that coulde fynde in his hearte, so much mischiefe to conceiue" (6). Thus Richard is not to be defined entirely or even primarily by his historical actions; he is primarily More's subject rather than primarily an objective sequence of acts. Richard's demeanor may be the "matter" of More's book, but it is not its shaping form. Conceptually, at least, the *Richard* is Renaissance life-writing.

More now begins to flesh out and to give depth to his picture of Richard. He starts with Richard's background, recounting the claims to the throne of Richard of York, Richard III's father; York's uprising and death, the accession of his son, Edward IV; and the execution of George of Clarence, brother of Edward and Richard, at Edward's command. He then focuses his attention directly on Richard, "in witte and courage" equal to his brothers but in appearance and strength much their inferior: little, ill-formed, crook-backed, lopsided, ill-featured, belligerent—or probably just rapacious and cruel—in expression; and as for the inward disposition of his mind, "malicious, wrathfull, enuious, and from afore his birth, euer frowarde" (7).

More sheds further light on this surprising prenatal datum, which he uses wittily here to heighten our impression of Richard's unnaturalness, momentarily his almost comic monstrosity. "It is for trouth," More begins but carefully adds, "reported," that Richard's mother required "cutting" (surgery) in order to be "deliuered of hym"—freed of him, as the phrasing suggests—

and that hee came into the worlde with the feete forwarde, as menne bee borne outwarde, and (as the fame runneth) also not vntothed, whither menne of hatred reporte aboue the trouthe, or elles that nature chaunged her course in hys beginninge, whiche in the course of his lyfe many thinges vnnaturallye committed.

Baby Richard with fangs is a hard fact to chew, let alone to swallow. Further, More knows it. His phrasing shows that he does not accept these tales uncritically ("reported") and hesitates more pointedly to credit some of them as literal facts ("as the fame runneth"). But the careful arrangement of facts from more to less credible—cutting, to breech birth, to teeth—and the cumulative impact of so many striking facts suggest that More would like to believe them or, rather, would like his readers to be inclined to do so.

The steady increase of figurative meaning in the passage is further evidence of this intention: first the suggestive phrasing, "deliuered of hym," next the attribution of deadly significance to the breech birth ("as menne bee borne outwarde"), and then the exploitation of the symbolic possibilities of the least credible detail, the infant's teeth. More does not let us linger over this dental anomaly but defuses our skepticism by immediately admitting that the report he has heard might be "aboue the trouthe," phrasing which just happens to echo the first words of the sentence, thereby reinforcing our association of the rest of the sentence with truth and sandwiching together the three facts of cutting, birth, and teeth into a single, reliable assertion of Richard's monstrosity. When we finally reach More's alternative explanation of little Richard's teeth, seen now as the result of nature's cooperative expertise in unnatural symbolism ("or elles . . . course"), we are predisposed to assent to its plausibility. To help our assent along, More adds a last subordinate clause ("whiche . . . committed") that explains and effectively rationalizes nature's thoughtful symbolism.

With each fact the reports of Richard's birth become less credible, and with the explanation of each fact they become more plausible, of greater significance, and more fully symbolic. The reports become less literal and more figurative, less true and more so, and in this way More proceeds in giving real symbolic dimension to his portrait of Richard. The fact about Richard's teeth may be fabulous, but the idea it illustrates is, for More, the truth about him.

More charges Richard's figure with additional symbolism in these early pages through the continuing use of recurrent thematic words and through allusion and association of ideas and images. Whereas the description of King Edward employed cognates of *love* three times, for example, that of Richard thrice uses cognates of *hatred* (7–8). As the recurrence of these words twelve times in the seventy-odd lines of Edward's deathbed speech will suggest, love and hate are the basic antitheses in the work, their cognates being reinforced by numerous related pairs of words, notably "trust" and "mistrust."

More also alludes repeatedly but naturally, unobtrusively, to such generic contexts of love and hatred as the Redemption or the Fall. Richard is "close and secrete, a deepe dissimuler, lowlye of counteynaunce, arrogant of heart, outwardly coumpinable where he inwardely hated, not letting to kisse whome hee thoughte to kyll: dispitious and cruell, not for euill will alway, but ofter for ambicion, and either for the suretie or encrease of his estate" (8). This allusion to Judas' kiss of betrayal is later counterpointed by the words of Elizabeth, Edward's Queen, to her younger son, as he is led away from her, "let me kis you ones yet ere you goe, for God knoweth when we shal kis togither agayne" (42); the contrapuntal echo is fulfilled, as it were, a few lines later when Richard takes his nephew "in his armes and [then] kissed him."

The allusion to ambition in the initial portrait of Richard—"ofter for ambicion"—likewise finds an echo just a few pages later in Edward's dying speech: "Suche a pestilente serpente is ambicion and desyre of vaineglorye and soueraintye, whiche amonge states where he once entreth crepeth foorth so farre, tyll . . . hee turneth all to mischiefe" (12). The serpent of ambition in the garden of the noble heart—More's imagery places Richard's failing in a time-honored moral context. To take another example of More's figurative shading of Richard's figure, one with a general proverbial resonance, we might note his laconic reflection on Richard's having "sodainelye fallen in soo greate truste" as to have been appointed Protector of the young King Edward V and his realm: "so (that were it destenye or were it foly) the lamb was betaken to the wolfe to kepe" (24–25).

More's handling of fact and rumor in his expansion of the "maner of manne" Richard is further indicates both the versatility of his methods of persuasion and the consistency of his conception of the usurping Duke. After considering Richard's birth, More finds his next specific fact about Richard's behavior in the death of Henry VI: "where his aduauntage grew, he spared no mans deathe, whose life withstoode his purpose. He slewe with his owne handes king Henry the sixt, being prisoner in the Tower, as menne constantly saye, and that without . . . knoweledge of the king" (8). The fact, "He slewe," follows from the generalization, "he spared no" man, instead of preceding it and does so with maximum certainty. Only later, almost buried in a long sentence, comes the qualification, "as menne . . . saye," a qualification whose force is diminished by the word "constantly." More's timing in introducing the qualification overwhelmingly implies Richard's guilt and, to judge from contemporary sources, accurately reflects a commonly held view.[32]

But the rest of More's sentence works more subtly and perhaps even more effectively to degrade Richard's character: if Edward IV had intended the murder of Henry, More continues, undoubtedly he would "haue appointed that boocherly office, to some other then his owne borne brother." More's reasonable and decent objection is expressed in conditional terms. If this objection stood by itself, it would argue for the unlikelihood of Richard's butchery, but it is attached as a subordinate clause ("whiche woulde vndoubtedly yf he had entended that thinge") to the initial assertion of the sentence, "He slewe with his owne handes" and without Edward's knowledge. In the light of its attachment and subordination we might paraphrase as follows: If Edward had intended the murder of Henry, but he didn't, he surely would never have appointed the butcher's office, which Richard appointed himself, to his own brother. The seemingly conditional construction becomes in the reality of its full context contrary to the fact of Edward's wishes and of Richard's bloodthirstiness. More's seemingly reasonable objection to the likelihood of Richard's savagery becomes the outcry at it of a reasonable man. More's narrative voice, like the voices of the other life-writers, also has its moments of drama and fictional projection in the *Richard.* In time we shall return to More's role in the work more explicitly.

The next sentence and the next specific fact in More's depiction of Richard after King Henry's murder concern the death of Clarence: "Somme wise menne also weene, that his drifte couertly conuayde, lacked not in helping furth his brother of Clarence to his death: whiche hee resisted openly, howbeit somwhat (as menne demed) more faintly then he that wer hartely minded to his welth" (8). More is careful to distinguish the more limited authority for this report—"Some . . . menne"—from that for Henry's murder, and he even reminds us a second time that he is dealing with supposition.[33] Yet we notice that the report of Richard's complicity in Clarence's death comes after we have all but assented to his agency in Henry's murder and comes as an entry under the generalization two sentences earlier: "where his aduauntage grew, he spared no mans deathe." We also note that the men who credit Richard's complicity in his brother's death are characterized as "wise." Their opinion gets strong support in the two following sentences, which give the plausible reason behind it, namely Richard's plot, hatched during Edward IV's life, to be king if Edward died while his children were young, as seemed the likely result of Edward's "euil dyete." If Richard were to succeed Edward, it was to his "aduauntage" not to spare the death of Clarence, his older brother. The sequence of More's argument has first led us to believe that Richard, the butcher of a king, at least would be capable of complicity in fratricide and, now, that he had a powerful motive for seeing his brother dead.

Having rationalized Richard's complicity persuasively for us, More then adds, "But of al this pointe, is there no certaintie," and continues with breezy detachment, "whoso diuineth vppon coniectures, maye as wel shote to farre as to short." The self-aware reference to conjecture loosens the tension of the argument, a relaxation that makes the opening of the next sentence all the more striking. "How beit," More begins, drawing our attention up sharply, "this haue I by credible informacion learned" and relates how "one Mystlebrooke" came to "one Pottyer dwellyng in reddecrosse strete without crepulgate" on the night of Edward IV's death, and when Potter heard the news he replied, "then wyll my mayster the Duke of Gloucester bee kynge" (9). More speculates as to the reasons behind Potter's statement but has no doubt as to its meaning that Richard purposed to be king. Both Mistlebrook and Potter, the one Edward's servant and the other Richard's, can be identified in contemporary records with reasonable confidence, and it is entirely plausible that their conversation took place.[34] As Pollard notes, the Louvain edition of the *Richard* identifies More's "credible informacion" as his own memory of the report made of this conversation to his father approximately at the time of its occurrence.[35] Be that as it may, More's placing Potter's statement at the end of his initial portrait of Richard makes its incrimination of Richard ominously clear.

When More finishes depicting the "maner of manne" Richard is at the time of Edward IV's death, our impression of Richard's evil and unnatural character is strong, clear, and lasting. In analyzing Richard's nature, More uses speculation, symbolism, myth, rumor, fact, and above all, Richard's past. Richard is, as it were, stopped in his tracks—or plots—while the narrator shapes meaning out of his past. To echo Shakespeare, past is prologue. More's treatment of Richard's past during a pause in the main narrative adds depth to his larger picture and greatly contributes to the sense of purpose and significance, of latent design, with which we approach it. In other words, we approach the rest of the *Richard* with assumptions about both its artistry and its conception of history.

More, in interpreting Richard's past, is essentially showing Richard's nature, which stands to what follows in the work as cause to effect. Sylvester observes that "analysis of the causal relationships among events . . . was to be one of More's major contributions to the writing of history in English."[36] Yet at the outset of his work, More bases his view of causation on his view of human nature in general and on his conception of the particular nature of Richard. We therefore might say equally well that More's analysis of character and thence of motive is his major contribution to biography and, perhaps beyond it, to drama.

Having unfolded Richard's character, More simply remarks, "But nowe to returne to the course of this hystorye" (9), and begins to describe Richard's scheme to seize the throne. In the first sentence of this description More keeps his distance from Richard, standing outside him to pronounce on his actions. Whether Richard had long since or newly purposed to be king, More writes, "certayn is it that hee contriued" the destruction of the princes, "with the vsurpacion of the regal dignitye vppon hymselfe." The second sentence is long and involved, consisting of 117 words in nine clauses, at least one of which is parenthetical. This sentence is positively serpentine in its phrasing. It starts formally and logically—"And for as muche"—and has time for expansive, overlapping doublets—"well wiste and holpe," "long continued grudge and hearte brennynge." Its end, in comparison, is clipped, almost abrupt and colloquial: "and those that coulde not bee wonne, myght be loste ere they looked therefore [i.e., for it]" (10). Toward its middle, the sentence shifts from what Richard had done in the past to what he "nowe thought" the general ground of "al his building" should be, and next to a specific plan with two distinct stages: "yf he might firste vnder the pretext of reuengynge of olde displeasure, abuse the anger and ygnoraunce of the tone partie, to the destruccion of the tother: and then wynne to his purpose as manye as he coulde. . . ." On the firm basis of the character he has established for Richard, More now recounts not simply what Richard did ("certayn is it that hee contriued") but begins to imagine and indeed to realize what Richard probably thought as he viewed the historical situation.

Finally, in the third sentence after the passage in which he establishes Richard's character, More penetrates Richard's thinking and does so succinctly: "For of one thynge was hee certayne, that if his entente were perceiued, he shold soone haue made peace beetwene the bothe parties, with his owne bloude." In three sentences More has moved from "certayn is it that hee contriued" to "For of one thynge was hee certayne," from an external and objective perspective to an internal and subjective one. This movement is typical of More's treatment of Richard and is the reason that most of Richard's actual speeches, unlike most other speeches in the work, begin in indirect discourse and end in direct. As More himself has told us, Richard's demeanor is "in effecte" focal (6).

In the shift from an objective to a subjective perspective just examined, we can actually see Richard coming alive for More. He does so first in these sentences *because* immediately prior to them More has established Richard's character firmly enough to enable himself to enter when appropriate into Richard's spirit. Here More enters that spirit for a moment, and Richard becomes More's subject in a less static sense than was the case in the fangs-to-fratricide character of him. In pictorial terms Richard is first framed by More in the character and then—in the "course" of events, or indeed of "hystorye"—he is led out of the frame and into action.

More now follows his subject into situations more clearly and strictly delineated by objective, historical fact: the arrest of Rivers, Grey, and Vaughan; the Queen's flight into sanctuary, the execution of Hastings, Richard's coronation, the death of the princes, Buckingham's defection, Richard's death "in the fielde, hacked and hewed of his enemies handes" (87). But Richard remains More's subject, not in the sense that More shapes him without regard to his objective reality, not in the sense that he re-forms

Richard either morally or historically, but in the sense that he imagines, enters, and inevitably shapes Richard's thoughts and motives, in addition to interpreting or commenting in a variety of less immediate ways on their significance. More explores a Richard of real history and of his own conceiving. His method continues to combine biography with history and factual truth with fiction.

Before turning to the less immediate ways in which More reflects on Richard's behavior, we should assent to the utility of a stage metaphor once Richard starts acting, and indeed at an especially appropriate moment, right after Richard stages from an upper gallery his bashful acceptance of the crown, More introduces a familiar, ironic comparison: "these matters bee Kynges games, as it were stage playes, and for the more part plaied vpon scafoldes" (81). If we insist on extending a stage metaphor to the description of the whole course of the *Richard,* however, we should also have to add that at each intermission, as we move toward the lobby, More beckons to us from the side door, urging that we pause to look at his collection of pictures from productions of the past: too trustful Hastings, Fortune's plaything; Edward IV at the time of his marriage, the same Edward in the attitude of the dying king; Shore's wife, merry concubine, withered old woman, victim of human ingratitude and unkindness, Fortune's cruel jest (49–52, 60–65, 11–13, 54–57). Catching our eyes in a lull in the action near the end of this theatrical rendering of the *Richard,* More also shares with us his sketches of future productions: the fates of Miles Forest, John Dighton, and Sir James Tyrell, conspirators in the murder of the princes; King Richard's posture in death, a somewhat fuller drawing of Richard as usurper, "wyth feareful dreames"; and even a likeness of John Morton, then Bishop of Ely, a man of "depe insighte in politike worldli driftes"—incidentally, the man in whose household young More was tutored (87, 91).

For variety, during one particularly extended intermission, More even offers to play us a couple of very long speeches about sanctuary—a hot issue in his own day—which he recorded at a rehearsal of the *Richard.*[37] We can listen to his recording, he explains, without being distracted by any dramatic action at all, so we can attend to the important issues it presents, too easily missed on the stage. But then he can't find the tape, because, as it happens, his recording has been taken for use in our hypothetical play itself when all those characters—Dukes, lesser lords, a Cardinal, and a Queen—are just standing there, as if in tableau, silhouetted against the larger issues of nature, law, and God—the bonds of truth and trust—to which the speeches about sanctuary give focus. These issues, our play thus hopes to show, have become a vital part of their own lives, as well as an extension of those vital to Richard's. These are the collective issues that bind character to character, life to life, and finally supersede individual actions. As Edward IV's Queen states her right to shelter her son in sanctuary: "mans law serueth the gardain to kepe the infant. The law of nature wyll the mother kepe her childe. Gods law pryuelegeth the sanctuary, and the sanctuary my sonne, sith I fere to put hym in the protectours [Richard's] handes" (39). In the work of Cavendish and Roper the question of conscience has a focal, thematic relation to the lives of Wolsey and More analogous to that of the bonds of "trouthe" and trust in More's *Richard*, but in the *Richard* thematic focus is even stronger, more conspicuous, more deliberate.

It is amazing how large a portion of More's *Richard* is not a single or an immediate action. In it there are striking dramatic scenes—the arrest of Hastings or Richard's performance in the gallery—but there are surprisingly few of them. There are more brief moments of drama—for example, Richard's kiss of betrayal for his nephew—but there are many more orations, narrations, digressions, characterizations, and authorial reflections. It is amazing, in short, how great and how visible a role, especially in those intermissions between present acts, More's artistic conception and at times his own voice play. "These matters bee Kynges games . . . for the more part plaied vpon scafoldes" (81): for a fleeting moment one wonders whether More could have intended a pun on his own name ("more part"), as well as the pun on "scafoldes" (platforms for stage plays and for executions).

Had More written the *Richard* as an objective history, he himself could have had no part, and if as a stage play, his own part would have to have been either behind the scenes or external to them, a commentator from another century and another medium or literary form. More's part, analogous to those of the other life-writers, instead intersects with Richard's. To speak more specifically, his art interacts conspicuously with the facts and issues of Richard's life.

The Holbein portrait of the More family group provides an image and a pictorial metaphor for the *Richard* as appropriate in its own way, if also as partial, as the metaphor of the stage. More is known to have had an interest in portraiture and to have commissioned portraits by Holbein of himself and his family, the best likenesses we have of him. Stanley Morison speculates that More himself might have been the moving spirit behind the famous portrait of the More family group, said to be "the first example of an intimate group portrait not of devotional or ceremonial character to be painted this side of the Alps," of which Holbein's original is lost but of which his pen and ink drawing and versions by other hands survive.[38]

Holbein's portrait of the More group implies relationships among the figures, not least through "the revolutionary method" of grouping but also through attitude, size, and position in the composition. More himself sits in the center of the picture and the other figures radiate out (not entirely symmetrically) from him. Margaret Roper, More's favorite daughter, dominates the right foreground. Dame Alice, his second wife, by whom he had no children, kneels, apparently on a prie-dieu, behind Margaret and far to More's left, her tame monkey by her side. More's fool, Henry Patenson, flanks More's son John, who stands beside and slightly behind More himself. On More's other side, slightly forward of him, More's father sits on the same bench with Sir Thomas, nearly as important in mass and focus as his respectful son.[39] Above and between More and his father is a clock with hanging weights. Although there are four other important figures in the portrait (More's other two daughters, his ward, and, of minimal size, his son's betrothed), these examples suffice to illustrate its relational grouping.

Like the Queen, Cardinal, and other lords grouped around the issue of sanctuary in the *Richard*, the figures in the More family portrait are grouped thematically as well as spatially. This portrait embodies the bonds of "trouthe" and trust, as in a darker sense does the *Richard*. Five women and More's son hold books in the portrait (of which four are open and two closed, one because the woman is removing a glove); More's ward, Margaret Giggs, leans toward the two More patriarchs, seeming to consult regarding the selection about to be read. Cecily, More's daughter, fingers what may be a braided belt or, perhaps, a rosary upon a closed book. The portrait evidently catches the More household in one of those moments of communal prayer reported by Roper.[40] Morison suggests that Holbein's model (as distinct from More's idea) for the grouping of several portraits might have been an Adoration and therefore an example of the "adaptation of a religious formula to a secular purpose." Although the purpose of the group portrait may not be entirely secular, and its character not entirely nondevotional, we can see in it an adaptation of a primarily religious formula to a primarily human purpose, one both biographical and historical or, rather, familial and factual. We also find such adaptation frequently in the Renaissance and markedly in life-writing, as we have seen from Bede, variously through Cavendish and Roper, to Walton.

As earlier observed, a pictorial metaphor for the *Richard*, like that of the stage, is partial. *Ut pictura poesis* or rather *ut pictura vitae scriptura* has limitations prominent since the Enlightenment. Renaissance writers also knew there were differences between poems and paintings, but they appear to have been more interested in the conceptual similarities between them. Repeatedly they found the analogy of literary with pictorial artifice an enlightening one. For our purposes, the kind of relational and thematic conception evident in the More group portrait pertains also to the grouped lives of the *Richard*, of which the execution is More's own. More's grouping, relating, and pointing of human figures in the *Richard* comprise an important function of his role in the work, which is clearly illustrated in his deployment of Hastings' death, Shore's Wife, and Edward IV's marriage. Each of the figures in these espisodes, as placed and treated by More, is caught in an attitude that reflects and reflects on the behavior of Richard.

More's introduction to Hastings' end is indirect and general, present in the implications of his remarks about the "muttering amonge the people" that mysteriously began when to all appearances plans were going forward to crown Edward V but secretly counter plans were being laid to make Richard king. The people mutter "as though al should not long be wel, though they neither wist what thei feared nor wherfore: were it that before such great thinges, mens hartes of a secret instinct of nature misgiueth them. As the sea without wind swelleth of himself somtime before a tempest: or were it" otherwise (44). More models his speculation on a passage in Seneca's *Thyestes* but significantly alters Seneca's diction to work the word "nature" (lacking in Seneca) into the passage.[41] "Nature," as More refers to it, is instinct with warning, charged with meaning, almost sentient. Whether in the human breast or in the ocean, nature anticipates a threat to form and stability. More's reference to nature here implies an underlying rational order.

There follow the onset of Lord Stanley's "mistrust" of Richard and Catesby's betrayal of Hastings by operating as a counterspy for Richard. "No man," More tells us, was "so much beholden" to Hastings as Catesby, and in none did Hastings put "so special trust," but Catesby betrayed him "much the rather, for that he trusted by his deth to obtaine much of the rule that the lorde Hastinges bare in his countrey" (45–46). Urged by Catesby, Richard then arrests and executes Hastings on charges of treason because Richard cannot trust him to conspire to usurp the throne.

With Hastings summarily beheaded, More begins to reflect on this precipitate action. He relates at length four omens of ill by which the unsuspecting Hastings was either warned or, if destined for destruction, at least prepared: namely, Stanley's dream that a boar, Richard's heraldic device, would gore both himself and Hastings; the stumbling of Hastings' horse two or three times as he rode to his fatal appointment with Richard; Hastings' meeting with a priest on the morning of his arrest and his treacherous companion's double-edged jest—"whereto talke you so long with that priest, you haue no nede of a prist yet . . . as though he would say, ye shal haue sone"; and finally, Hastings' meeting that same Friday morning with the very messenger, also named Hastings, whom he had met before in the same spot when he was in such royal disfavor as to endanger his life, a situation opposite, so he thinks, to his present one, since the "quenes kindred," his known enemies, were that day to be beheaded (50–52).

It is at this juncture that More himself as teller breaks into his tale forcefully and abruptly: "O good god, the blindnes of our mortall nature, when he most feared, he was in good suerty: when he rekened him self surest, he lost his life, and that within two howres after" (52). For a moment More's part in the work is explicit and outspoken. With Chaucerian finesse, his outcry at our blindness redirects our attention to the four omens and especially to the last of them, which it follows directly.[42] Hastings has failed to heed these omens, including the least superstitious, most Christian, and most ironic of them, the possible similarity of his enemies' fate to his own. This warning is embodied in the final omen, Hastings' meeting with Hastings, factually, perhaps, a messenger of the same name but figuratively himself. It is hard to be certain whether Hastings the pursuivant is a true fact with symbolic potential or a fiction as true to Hastings' life in its own way as a fact.[43] As so often in Roper's *More* or Cavendish's *Wolsey*, truth of fact and truth of fiction prove simultaneous here.

The meaning of the final omen Hastings encounters is the most and least hidden of them all—least obvious in appearance, most plain to thought and reflection. In its context, which is finally the context of Hastings' life for More, we understand the "blindnes of our mortall nature" to be the blindness of our fatal folly, our failure to heed the "secret instinct of nature" (44) and to see our own fate reflected in that of others. In More's outcry there is something of the blending of nature with folly that Erasmus celebrates so ironically in *The Praise of Folly* but nothing of Erasmus' joy in the disordering energy of this blend. The folly that physically and perhaps spiritually is fatal to a human being as real as our historical records, namely "the lorde Hastynges," can no longer be fun.

It is worth observing, however, that More uses the word "nature" to mean folly instead of using the word "folly" itself or another equivalent. In the phrase "secret instinct of nature" More implies an order stretching all the way from elemental disturbance and human fear—in the ocean, in the human breast, and again in the first two of Hastings' omens, the stumbling horse and Stanley's dream, interpreted by Hastings as merely fancied fear (50)—to fellow feeling, brotherly love, and charity in the final omen, the meeting of Hastings with the pursuivant Hastings. In the phrase "the blindnes of our mortall nature" More implies the opposite of nature's "secret instinct": disorder, foolishness, self-betrayal, hatred, and death. These two uses of the single word "nature," however modified, are symptomatic of a nagging concern and a possibly real contradiction in the *Richard*, in which the major concepts—nature, truth, trust, love, hatred—all are involved. The *Richard* questions which meanings of such words are true, negative or positive ones, naturalistic and phenomenal or idealistic and conceptually absolute ones.

More explores natures and values is this work, including those of biographical and historical truth. Progressively in the *Richard* the usurper's presence and effects on others make their weight felt. Progressively Richard's kind of nature—not instinct with order and love but with chaos and hatred—becomes more of an experienced reality, and if more real, then, how not more true? After all, More's outcry on "mortall nature" carries special emphasis because it comes sharply and in his own voice.

Following this outcry, More continues in a manner more formal yet still clearly authorial: "Thus ended this honorable man, a good knight and a gentle" (52). He proceeds to a brief character of Hastings and concludes it by describing him as "eth to begile, as he that of good hart and corage forestudied no perilles. A louing man and passing wel beloued. Very faithful, and trusty ynough, trusting to much." This is high praise on the whole. Yet in the context of Hastings' life the reality of love is more limited than ideal, for it excludes the "quenes kindred"—those bound by "kind" or nature to the Queen—and more generally excludes Hastings' enemies. In a deathbed speech heard by Richard, Hastings, and some of the Queen's kindred, More's idealized king, Edward IV, earlier had mentioned as a cause of love both "That we be al men" and "that we be christen men" and had implored his listeners "to remember, that the one parte of you is of my bloode, the other of myne alies, and eche of yow with other, eyther of kinred or affinitie [the "spirytuall kynred" of the sacrament of marriage], whiche . . . shoulde no lesse moue vs to charitye, then the respecte of fleshlye consanguinitye" (12). Reading later that Hastings is a "good" man—and he is one—we might wonder with More what goodness means in a real and public life.

More's final words on Hastings—"Very faithful, and trusty ynough, trusting to much" (i.e., too much)—suggest meanings less limited than perverse. In the treacherous, unstable, unnatural world of a Richard, such trust as Hastings' is self-betrayal and therefore unnatural. In the course of More's exploration of grouped lives in the *Richard*, his vision darkens—not cynically or hopelessly but perhaps realistically. His ideals persist conspicuously but they become harder to locate naturally in the historical record. Looking back, we might recall his control over the initial character of Richard and indeed his comic distance from that newborn infant's teeth. In comparison, his concern—perhaps even a fearful misgiving in his own breast—at the spread, ease, and plausibility of Richard's evil effects noticeably increases. It does so in his reflections on Hastings' death and more markedly once Richard has actually been crowned. In the interludes, or rather "ludes," between More's reflections, digressions, and the like, Richard's behavior before the murder of the princes can still be made to look comic and even farcical by More. But even this comedy becomes grimmer, and More's asides on Richard become so heavily ironic as to be sarcastic, as in his observing that the public humiliation of Shore's wife was caused by Richard "(as a goodly continent prince clene and fautles of himself, sent oute of heauen into this vicious world for the amendement of mens maners)" (54).

More's reflections on Hastings give way to present action, to a few quick performances by or ordered by Richard. (It should be noted that these performances, rendered in narrative, receive slightly less than equal time.)[44] First Richard masquerades with Buckingham in rusty armor to prove that he had no time to choose proper arms against Hastings' alleged treason; next comes the proclamation, equally faked and unpersuasive, concerning Hastings' alleged crimes; and there follows the despoliation of Shore's wife for her alleged complicity in Hastings' alleged treason, her imprisonment, and finally the enforcement of her "open penance" for her sexual affairs, notably with Edward IV and, after his death, with Hastings.

In their actual lives, Shore's wife, Edward IV, and Hastings were triangularly related. More's lengthy depiction of Edward when the King is about to marry follows his character of Shore's wife (55–57), separated from it, as it in turn is separated from Hastings' death, by references to Richard's present behavior, this time merely to Richard's plans for his next performance during Shaa's sermon. (The sermon itself directly succeeds the depiction of Edward IV's proposing to marry.) Thus as in life, so Hastings, Shore's wife, and Edward are grouped by More near the center of his *Richard.* Thus also, all three lives are related to Richard's action and to one another. As we shall see, the three are related thematically as well as by arrangement, or spatially, to use a pictorial term. To sum it all up, we might say that they are thus related by history (fact), morality (theme), and art (arrangement), and that More's depictions of them thus inter-act with Richard's performances.

More's interest in people, in the lives of people, is especially clear in the case of Shore's wife. This woman, the wife of "an honest citezen" before Edward IV "required her," does not belong in a history of King Richard, and More knows it: "I doubt not," he allows, but "some shal think this woman to sleight a thing, to be written of and set amonge the remembraunce of great matters" (55, 56). Perhaps Shore's wife no more belongs in the *Richard* than Henry Patenson, More's fool, belongs in the family group portrait from which "sonne [in-law] Roper" appears to be missing.[45] And yet it could be argued by standards less narrowly decorous, more eclectic, and less purely classical than we often attribute to a humanist of More's repute that Mistress Shore does belong in the work which gave her legendary stature.

More's recognition of anomaly in Mistress Shore's presence is Tacitean, but neither Tacitus nor any other classical historian alone accounts for her part in the *Richard* or fully represents the mixture of traditions that underlie it.[46] The combining of life-writing with history traditional in England (and on the Continent) both before and during More's time approaches his presentation of her more nearly. More combines these forms not only in the portrayal of Richard himself but also in the number of compact, highly individualized portraits of lesser characters his work contains. The tradition of religious history he inherits is not uniquely, but is remarkably, mixed in this way, perhaps because it embodies a sense of human value and achievement that is more personal and interior than that of the classical historians. Bede's *History,* for example, consists in large part of exemplary lives and briefly sketches a number of simpler lives, such as Owine's or, to take one well known, Caedmon's.[47] These less public, less political lives give anecdotal texture and human breadth to a thematically unified whole. For that matter, the Bible, the truest history of all for most Renaissance writers, has a still more obvious relevance to the writing of history. Individual lives abound in the Old Testament, and particularly in reference to More's Mistress Shore, one thinks of the life of another whore, Mary Magdalen, in the New. Like the Holbein sketch of the More family, that of Mistress Shore might be said to adapt a mainly religious model to a mainly secular purpose. The adaptation, moreover, is a natural one, since the model itself is biographical and historical, as well as religious, to begin with.

More's *Richard* assimilates elements of a religious tradition to a developing secular form, the process we have already observed in Cavendish's *Wolsey*. The subsequent absorption both of the *Wolsey* and of the *Richard*—the latter virtually whole—into chronicle-histories in turn illustrates forcefully the convergence of biographical and historical conventions. In these histories the life of a Richard or a Wolsey, central in an earlier and more truly biographical form, is swept either into a wider pattern of meaning with many human centers, as long ago Cuthbert was swept into Bede's *History*, or else into a mere collection of faces and events with no center at all. In a history a life loses some autonomy and hence some identity, but its very presence embodies the juncture of portrayal and perception in history and life-writing. More's depiction of Shore's wife is a life in a history that derives from both religious and secular traditions and, in small, exemplifies all these developments.

Having reported Richard's hypocritical harassment of Shore's wife, More proceeds to depict the character of her life at considerable length: first her birth, upbringing, and marriage; then the King's passion for her, her succumbing to it, her husband's prudent abandonment of her, and Hastings' liaison with her after the King's death. As earlier in describing King Edward, More explains and as best he can excuses her wanton record: she was married before she was "wel ripe," and so "she not very feruently loued, for whom she neuer longed." He adds to this reason her respect for the King, the hope of high living, and the vulnerability of her "softe tender hearte" (55).

There follows the rightly celebrated description of her person, which indicates more clearly the extent to which the perception and portrayal of Shore's wife have engaged More's imagination. Its first sentence, though evidently not based on More's own memories of her, imitates in the successive development of its three clauses the process and the very rhythm of human portrayal: "Proper she was and faire: nothing in her body that you wold haue changed, but if you would haue wished her somewhat higher" (55). Like a Chaucerian sketch of Criseyde, this description suggests the way an artist with a pencil or simply an engaged onlooker might size a woman up: the initial statement is positive and definitive, if also general, in its assessment; the second clause is hyperbolically, but negatively, appreciative—"nothing you would change," rather than "she is perfect"; the final clause is refined, tentative, subordinate. More continues the description of Shore's wife:

> Thus say thei that knew her in her youthe. Albeit some that now se her (for yet she liueth) deme her neuer to haue ben wel visaged. Whose iugement semeth me somwhat like, as though men should gesse the bewty of one longe before departed, by her scalpe taken out of the charnel house: for now is she old lene, withered, and dried vp, nothing left but ryuilde skin and hard bone. And yet being euen such: whoso wel aduise her visage, might gesse and deuise which partes how filled, wold make it a faire face. [55–56]

Shore's wife may still be living in More's London ("yet she liueth") but More's description of her figure, taken in its entirety, is hardly what a casual or merely objective observer of her would have seen. As often happens in the *Richard*, More sees fact but at the same time imaginatively perceives potential.

More turns next to Mistress Shore's "plesant behauiour," a greater delight to men, as he tells us, than even her beauty (56). He admires her native wit, literate intelligence, and above all her merriment in company, "redy and quick of aunswer, neither mute nor ful of bable, sometime taunting without displesure and not without disport." Then, after a merry anecdote about this merriest of women, More first slips and then positively plunges into praise of her human decency and generosity to others—in a word, her kindness, her truly human nature ("kynd").

He first touches on her kindness gingerly, almost as an afterthought, complete with a self-consciously merry jest: "For many" concubines Edward "had, but her he loued, whose fauour to saithe trouth (for sinne it wer to belie the deuil) she neuer abused to any mans hurt, but to many a mans comfort and relief." If this were the extent of More's praise, we might simply conclude that he was admitting the facts about Edward's licentiousness only to suggest its benefit to the realm—counting the concubines, as it were, in a privileged context. But this is by no means the whole case. More's compliment to her kindness, which at first seems wrung out of him, is subsequently expanded emphatically: "where the king toke displeasure, she would mitigate and appease his mind: where men were out of fauour, she wold bring them in his grace. For many that had highly offended, shee obtained pardon. Of great forfetures she gate men remission" (56). This litany continues: More adds that she was of assistance even in weighty suits "for none, or very smal rewardes, and those rather gay then rich," and finally speculates as to her motives: "either . . . she was content with the dede selfe well done, or . . . she delited to be suid vnto . . . or . . . wanton women and welthy be not always couetouse." Anyone who has read much Chaucerian, Erasmian, or Spenserian literature is likely to respond to More's list of motives, "all three."

More now points his portrayal of Shore's wife, explaining that she is not the less but the more worthy of memory because she is at present so utterly destitute, where before she had wealth, royal favor, influence, and respect, "as many other men were in their times, which be now famouse, only by the infamy of their il dedes" (57). Our suspicion that Shore's wife is in this work because, despite her wanton failings, her nature contrasts sharply with Richard's, is confirmed in the next sentence's reaffirmation of the preceding one: "Her doinges were not much lesse [than those of famous men], albeit thei be muche lesse remembred, because thei were not so euil." The final sentence of this portrayal epitomizes the significance of her life, as More perceives it: "For men vse if they haue an euil turne, to write it in marble: and whoso doth vs a good tourne, we write it in duste which is not worst proued by her: for at this daye shee beggeth of many at this daye liuing, that at this day had begged if she had not bene." More depicts the life of Shore's wife in the *Richard* because he manifestly wants to write as Christian a history as history will let him. But I doubt that a writer capable of the calculated repetition in the last sentence ("at this day") could have missed the fact that in this sentence, if it is indeed the last word on Shore's wife, Richard's unkind nature seems to have won. His nature had carried the day, as a rueful but still ironical More might have written, and with the day, perhaps, the reality that is historical time.

With the portrayal of Edward IV's choosing a queen, the next of the intermissions between present acts, More reaches backward in time beyond Richard's dominant influence in history. Although this intermission is justified to explain Richard's present behavior, namely, his causing Shaa to preach a sermon showing that the illegitimacy of Edward's children should bar them from the succession, More's lingering for six pages over it is unnecessary for the purpose he states and, if merrily recreative, is also plainly digressive. Starting his explanation, More is brisk and businesslike: "The coloure and pretext wherof cannot be wel perceiued, but if we first repete you some thinges longe before done about king Edwardes mariage" (59–60). Ending it, he knows that he has lingered and, with repetition a little pre-Waltonian, apologetically explains it again: "I haue rehersed this busines about this mariage somwhat the more at lenght [*sic*], because it might therby the better appere vpon how slipper a grounde the protector [Richard] builded his colour, by which he pretended king Edwardes children to be bastardes" (66). The effect of two such formal explanations—uncommon in the *Richard*—is to frame More's final portrait of Edward, setting it off from the present plotting of Richard that surrounds it. In his final appearance in the *Richard*, Edward becomes a Utopian island in the midst of Richard's slough, and yet he is more than Utopian because as finally depicted, once, "long before," he really existed.

More has already presented a full character of Edward in maturity at the outset of the *Richard*, so now, rather than give us another character of Edward when about twenty years younger, More develops Edward's personality more dramatically, both through indirect discourse and through actual dialogue: to quote a valiantly witty King to his incensed mother in defense of his Queen-to-be, "That she is a widow and hath alredy children, by gods blessed Ladye I am a batcheler and haue some to: and so eche of vs hath a profe that neither of vs is lyke to be barain" (64). Edward is attractive and credibly moral in the exchange with his mother, which expansively occupies the center of More's explanation of the King's marital affairs and most indulgently exercises More's art. In this way, for a time at least, Edward's reality vies directly with Richard's.

More does not make Edward's enamorment of "hys enemies wife," the widow Elizabeth Woodville Grey, overly sentimental, despite its potential for treatment of the rags-to-riches and rake-to-regenerate types. While presenting the enamorment in the best possible light, he manages to keep it entirely persuasive. Chronologically, of course, the enamorment is out of order in More's work because it follows rather than precedes Edward's affair with Shore's wife, thus reversing the order of actual fact. In relating Edward's enamorment of the widow Grey, More at once keeps Edward in the character of a Lothario and, for our final impression of this King, makes him in love an honest man. For this purpose More does not violate explicit dates but quietly places his flashback to Edward's marriage as the last Edwardian scene in the *Richard*.

Elizabeth Grey first catches King Edward's ready eye when she comes to plead with him to restore to her the property her dead husband gave her. In the course of one sentence, Edward beholds her and waxes enamored of her, and in one more, "taking her . . . secretly aside, [he] began to entre in talking more familiarly" (61). The virtuous lady denies him but in so wise a manner that his enamorment waxes some more. Meetings, promises, and further royal waxing ensue, until the King will not turn back, at which point the lady "shewed him plaine, that as she wist herself to simple to be his wife, so thought she her self to good to be his concubine." Astonished by rejection, impressed by virtue, and urged by desire, Edward determines to marry the lady "in al possible hast." More does not tell us, as Mancini does, that in the course of wooing, Edward even "placed a dagger at her throat, to make her submit to his passion,"[48] but he does convey to us the directness of Edward's approach and the explicit sexuality of his wishes before her virtuous resistance and Edward's impetuous desire hurl him headlong into marriage. More may gloss over a few sharp edges but his version of the wooing is realistic rather than merely sentimental.

Having determined to marry, however, Edward had to contend with the unyielding opposition of his mother, the Duchess of York, who "diswaded the mariage asmuch as she possible might alleging that it was his honor, profite, and surety also, to mary in a noble progeny out of his realm"; "that it was not princely to mary hys owne subiect"; and that it was "highe disparagement, to the sacre magesty of a prince . . . to be defouled with bigamy in his first mariage" (62). The all-too-real opposition of the disagreeable

Duchess offers More a credible opportunity to develop the engaging wit and earnest principle of the King's character.

The King reminds his mother that marriage ought "to be made for the respecte of God where his grace enclineth the parties to loue together" rather than for temporal advantage. Yet he also maintains that the marriage he proposes is advantageous, "For he reckened the amitye of no earthly nacion so necessari for him as the frendship of his own. Which he thought likely to beare him so muche the more herty fauor in that he disdayned not to marye with one of his own land" (63). As the upholder of love and holy wedlock and the true prince of all the people, Edward has come a long way through his wooing of the widow Grey. He now embodies the bonds of "trouthe"—truth and, quite literally, plighted troth.

The rest of Edward's reply to his mother is both more personal and more personable. He avers that he would never wed where he did not love, adding, "I wold not be a kyng with that condicion, to forbere mine own lyberty in choise of my own mariage" (64). Finally, rejecting his mother's objection to the fact that Elizabeth Grey is not an unwed maiden, the King concludes merrily, "as for the bigamy, let the bishop hardely lay it in my wai, when I come to take orders" (64). So much for the Duchess. Edward has won hands down.

But the Duchess has not conceded. She next connives to disrupt Edward's plans to marry by trying to persuade a noble woman Edward had earlier gotten with child to claim that she had been betrothed to him and therefore was his wife before God. But when the Lady is sworn to tell the truth, she denies the betrothal, thereby removing this obstacle to the King's marriage to Elizabeth Grey. The Duchess has posed a real threat to true love and marriage, but she is again defeated. The marriage of young Edward IV thus does not afford a picture of love without the threats of selfishness or malice, but of love finally triumphant.

Before More returns to present time and Richard's behavior, he digresses still further to treat the rebellion of Warwick against Edward IV, in More's eyes caused by Warwick's indignation at the King's marriage to Elizabeth Grey (65). Again More admits into his picture a real danger to the endurance of his happy King and again the danger is roundly defeated. Edward returns to England, from which he had been forced to flee, to slay Warwick, and "so stably . . . [to attain] the crowne againe, that he peassybly enioyed it vntil his dieng day" (66). The history of England under Edward does not present an ideal realm without war, but in the wars that do occur, Edward ultimately wins, and finally civil war itself ceases. Or so it seems until we read the words and grasp the implications of the coda More attaches to his portrayal of the happy King, namely, to the phrase "vntil his dieng day." More simply adds, "and in such plight [Edward] left it [the crown], that it could not be lost, but by the discorde of his verye frendes, or falshed of his fained frendes." Returning from Edward's past to Richard's present, More and his readers know that it was lost. In Richard III the happy King and his happy kingdom come to a very dead end.

After the murder of the princes the *Richard* presents not unrelieved gloom but history unrelieved by idealism, by efforts to perfect or to modify history's message.[49] This distinction is an important one, and More's own summary comment on the murder of the princes suggests it: "god neuer gaue this world a more notable example, neither in what vnsuretie standeth this worldly wel, or what mischief worketh the prowde enterprise of an hyghe heart, or finally what wretched end ensueth such dispiteous crueltie" (86). The final clause alone offers a limited vindication of historical time, and More pursues it, recording the ends of the murderers: "Miles Forest at sainct Martens pecemele rotted away. Dighton in dede yet walketh on a liue in good possibilitie to bee hanged ere he dye . . . sir Iames Tirel dyed at Tower hill, beheaded for treason. King Richard himselfe . . . slain in the fielde . . . haryed on horsebacke dead, his here in despite torn and togged lyke a cur dogge" (87).[50] An order of harsh, vengeful justice can be perceived in history but certainly not, in these acts, an order of love. We also note the loose end in the order of retribution, Dighton yet living, and conclude that, while expressing his view that Dighton in time will face a reckoning, More sticks here to the colder comfort of actual fact.

In detailing the torments of Richard's conscience before his death, More gives greater rein to his imaginative insight, but he asserts nothing more positive than the effects of disorder. If an expression of idealism in any sense, the tortures of the damned are a negative, destructive one. There is some warrant for Richard's bad dreams in the historical record preceding More's *Richard*, but no picture of Richard's "feare anguish and sorow within" so concentrated as the one More gives us.[51] More might be said to intensify Richard's disturbance of mind, which history elsewhere suggests, and, with Polydore Vergil, to attribute it specifically to Richard's consciousness of his abominable deed.

More's evil usurper is never at peace and never secure. His eyes whirl about, his hand touches his dagger, he is sleepless at night, or, if fitfully sleeping, troubled with fearful dreams from which he suddenly wakes to leap from his bed, "so was his restles herte continually tossed and tumbled with the tedious impression and stormy remembrance of his abominable dede" (87). Richard's breast is not instinct with natural fear at the approach of disorder; it is instinct with the unnatural fear whose origin is disorder itself, the outrage and denial of nature. There is an assertion of order in the torment of Richard's mind, but as this assertion stands—memorable, vivid, realistic—it is profoundly limited and negative, a far cry from the order of love More idealistically posits in Edwards IV's speech as a dying King and again, more positively, in his love for Elizabeth Grey. An order of love asserted by negation is not historically real. More's powerful picture of Richard's inner torment, like his depiction of the justice done to the actual murderers, further suggests a darkening of historical vision in the course of this work.

More's *Richard* ends suddenly when Bishop Morton, arrested by Richard the day Hastings was executed and now in the custody of Buckingham, clearly hints to this Duke that he ought to advance his own claims to the throne. Morton has already detected that Buckingham, formerly Richard's right-hand conspirator, has fallen out with Richard and suspects that he is ripe to rise in open rebellion against the Crown:

> Wherupon the byshop said: in good faith my lord, as for the late protector, sith he is now king in possession, I purpose not to dispute his title. But for the weale of this realm, wherof his grace hath now the gouernance, and wherof I am my self one poore member, I was about to wish, that to those good habilities wherof he hath already right many, litle nedyng my prayse: it might yet haue pleased Godde for the better store, to haue geuen him some of suche other excellente vertues mete for the rule of a realm, as oure lorde hath planted in the parsone of youre grace. [93]

On this devious note, the body of Morton's temptation of Buckingham opens, and More's experiment in historical life-writing ends.

Two major ways of explaining More's ending, one essentially political and one moralistic, have dominated discussion of it.[52] Pollard's explanation, illustrative of the first way, is that More suddenly remembered there was in his own time a third duke of Buckingham "with the same claims to the throne as the second duke of Buckingham whose temptation he was depicting." At the terminus a quo Sylvester proposes for the writing of the *Richard,* Henry VIII had no heir and at the terminus ad quem still no male heir (1514–18). The third Duke of Buckingham—in fact executed for treason in 1521—was the next male in line for the throne in these years. "Incitement to treason was no safer in 1514 than in 1483," Pollard observes, evidently seeing Morton's incitement itself as treasonable and More's position as writer in 1514 parallel to Morton's position as inciter in 1483.[53] A second political explanation frequently advanced, surprisingly enough, is quite the opposite of Pollard's, namely, that More gradually realized his work could be taken (as Hall, for example, evidently took it) as an apology for the Tudor dynasty, which he himself did not entirely trust, and that he therefore broke the work off.[54]

The moralistic reading of More's conclusion is well illustrated by Kincaid's remarks: "In the final pages before the work breaks off, we are led to see, through the introduction of Morton, the triumph of the rational mind over the confusions and alienations created by Richard's selfish pursuit of ambition"; and again, more pointedly, the ending introduces "the rational man's [Morton's] incipient moral victory over the tyrant's minion [Buckingham]."[55] Leonard Dean takes a similar tack for another reason: because More has earlier described the fate of the murderers of the princes, Dean feels that we "read the unfinished account of the conspiracy between Buckingham and Morton in the light of its conclusion." He adds, "thus . . . we see More to the very end writing history as a Christian humanist, using intelligently the methods of ancient rhetoric in order to make persuasive his conception of the life of faith and reason in a world complicated by the presence of evil and irrationality."[56]

I suppose that either of the speculations I have termed "political" regarding More's reasons for ending the *Richard* could be valid, although I prefer Pollard's. The moralistic readings, however, seem simply wrong, at odds with the entire tone of the work from Richard's coronation to Morton's last speech. The effect of that speech is oddly circular and sinister; it sounds so familiar that we almost think we have seen or heard something like it before. And if we had not, we should be unable to agree—as we all do—that Morton means by it that Buckingham should put forward his claims to the throne. After all, Morton does not state this meaning; he hints it, however plainly. The fact that the *Richard* ends with his words heightens their sinister, circular effect. Morton's words are not sweetly or triumphantly rational; they are expedient, taken at their best "politike [and] worldli" and, at their worst, treacherous and unnatural (unkind). They are a compromising means to an end that is as desirable as Henry Tudor, the father of Henry VIII, turned out in time to be.[57]

Reading the end of Morton's speech, we realize that the wheel has begun to come full circle, to reinstate or rather to continue the untrue, trustless, loveless ways of a Richard. In Morton we see the correction of Hastings' fault of "trusting to much," but the rationale of Morton's behavior is posited on the nature of Richard, to which it answers in kind and in this way assents. The present ending of the *Richard* appears to have been designed by More both for maximum artistic effect and for maximum expression of moral concern.

With the perception that an historical cycle of compromise and corruption is endless, More's history is complete, even though it is paradoxically also unfinished. The Rastell edition of the *Richard* contains six gaps, thought to reflect spaces left by More in the text for the later insertion of missing names, dates, or geographical distances and therefore thought to show that the work is unfinished. In the course of the *Richard*, More also signals his intention to continue the work beyond its present ending by writing a fuller account of Richard's death.[58] The gaps have no bearing on the "rightness" of the present ending, and, while our expectations of a fuller account may qualify the present ending's finish, they pale into insignificance before the impact of its irony. We have already observed how More's vision darkened in the course of the *Richard* and how his confidence in the moral content of history lessened. His plan appears to have developed progressively as he wrote and to have done so dramatically and definitively near the end of the work, where he carefully develops the encircling effect of Morton's words to Buckingham and thereby the ironical truth of the present ending.

Morton's is the last character More depicts in the *Richard.* In Morton we see something of a life that really touched More's own, certainly when More was resident in Morton's household and thereafter when More was placed by Morton in Oxford and probably also through other channels, such as More's own father, by whom so desirable a residence as the Lord Chancellor's was doubtless obtained for his son.[59] Like More's portrayal of Edward IV as a young man, that of Morton moves from description and narrative to dialogue. It moves as well from principles to political expedience and from past time to present action. Indeed, the very end of the *Richard* is couched in direct discourse without any narrative presence or frame and might be said to exist directly in the presence of the reader. In small, the character of Morton encapsulates the movement of the entire *Richard.* It becomes the final reflection of and reflection on the issues embodied in Richard's life.

Introducing Morton in Buckingham's custody, More quickly tells us that Morton "waxed . . . familier" with the Duke and through his "wisedom abused" Buckingham's pride, thereby delivering himself and destroying the Duke (90). Although Bishop Morton is not exactly turning the other cheek, it seems unfair not to see his behavior as natural, perhaps even prudent, in his position of enforced residence at Buckingham's castle. After all, More has termed the Bishop's behavior wise, and he continues in the next sentence to identify the Bishop as "a man of gret natural wit, very wel lerned, and honorable in behaueor, lacking no wise waies to win fauor." If for an instant we worried about More's infelicitous choice of the word "abuse" to describe the action of Morton's wisdom, even though the abuse was only of Buckingham's pride, and thought we detected a slight odor of self-interest in Morton's aims, this second sentence is momentarily reassuring: it restricts —or, perhaps, ironically contains—the ambiguity of its predecessor quite effectively.

Descriptions of Morton's former loyalty, first to Henry VI, and only when Henry was utterly defeated, to Edward IV, reinforce a high estimation of the Bishop's "trouthe." In fact, after Henry's defeat it was for Morton's "faste faith and wisedom" that his former enemy, Edward IV, welcomed the Bishop to his "secret trust and very speciall fauor" (91). Having outlined the subsequent deeds and high offices of the Bishop, More concludes his portrait: "Thus liuing many dayes in asmuch honor as one man mighte well wish, [he] ended them so godly, that his death with gods mercy wel changed his life." Morton's character appears unimpeachable and unalterably so, since More has got the good Bishop safely to heaven.

We almost do not notice that More returns to Morton's character in the sentence that follows its consignment to heaven: "Thys man therfore as I was about to tell you . . . hadde gotten by great experience the verye mother and maistres of wisdom, a depe insighte in politike worldli driftes" (91). After the flight to heaven, the logic of More's "therefore" is somewhat embarrassed, and his explanation—"I was about to"—tacitly admits his digression in treating the events of Morton's life that are subsequent to his temptation of Buckingham. This Duke, we next hear, Morton "craftelye sought . . . to pricke . . . forwarde taking alwaies thoccasion of his comming . . . that he rather semed him to folow hym then to lead him." Even More's pronouns, blurring the identities of tempter and temptee, imitate Morton's skillful confusion of the roles of leader and follower and of appearance and reality. The Bishop leads Buckingham on to destruction with wit, cunning, and the craft of a consummate Machiavel until More puts an end at once to his historical role and to the *Richard*.

Looking in retrospect from the later stages of More's treatment of Morton to the earlier ones, we now find these tarnished with ironical ambiguity: Morton's natural wit—but with which meaning of nature, Richard's or an ideal one; Morton's great learning—but in what and to what end; Morton's honor in behavior—but perhaps only in behavior and not in his heart; Morton's wisdom in the ways of courting favor—but his wisdom in ways not limited to the serving of time? Once the stain is noticed, it seems to spread. Morton's "faste faith" is either his "fixed" or his "speedy, unprincipled" faith and syntactically is either to Henry VI or to Edward IV (91). The wisdom that recommends Morton to Edward in retrospect cannot with assurance be distinguished from mere pragmatism and cannot be dissociated from the more ominous "politike worldli driftes" (91). Not even the phrase that consigns Morton to heaven is untouched: "wel changed his life" means "went from this life to a heavenly one" but, in this tainted context, could also mean "reformed his life, not in all respects unimpeachable, for the better." More's portrait of Morton, at first laudatory, then stained by Morton's temptation of Buckingham—that is, by his action in present time—suggests strongly that involvement in history is itself compromising.

In comparison to Richard's minion, Buckingham, Bishop Morton does represent a more rational power and therefore an improvement, but he does not, as More depicts him, by any stretch of the imagination represent a moral ideal. More may have had other reasons for ending the *Richard*, but I think that he had seen enough of the reality of ideals in history and in real political lives and saw no reason to continue. Truth of fact had too nearly overwhelmed the more rational and Christian truth of his fiction.

When More began the *Richard* he could not have known that he would be Wolsey's successor as Lord Chancellor, but before finishing it, he presumably knew that a successor to Morton's office as Chancellor was eventually Wolsey.[60] The man who saw in Hastings' meeting with the pursuivant Hastings a figurative meeting with self and punned with Erasmus about the meaning of his own name in Latin (*Morus* or fool) might also have noticed the auditory and visual repetition in such a phrase as "More's portrait of Morton," the man of law whose character—witty, learned, honorable, wise in the ways of winning favor—resembles Roper's account of More's.[61] Be that as it may, More's artistic vision and all the lives of the *Richard* interact to combine history with fiction and to produce the interpenetration of subjective and objective, of imagined and exterior truth, and finally of self and other, that is characteristically biographical in the Renaissance.

SEVEN
SHAKESPEARE'S *RICHARD III*
The Metamorphosis of Biographical Truth to Fiction

Shakespeare's *Richard III* suggests the metamorphosis that biographical truth undergoes as it is moved into a form primarily artificial and into a truly dramatic medium. Shakespeare's *Richard*, by comparison with More's, is more radically fictive and more self-reflective about the process by which a human fiction is shaped and the elements that make it credible, compelling, or whole. The poet's dramatization of Richard's story thus brings to center stage the fictive elements and potencies characteristic of life-writing in the Renaissance period. It magnifies and openly assays not just the historical King or the shape-shifting Vice or the power-mad Machiavel, but also the striking biographical fiction that *is* Richard, the truth about Richard, in More and the chronicles that mainly derive from his work.[1]

Shakespeare's *Richard* uses the story matter of the chronicles extensively, but its form, from blank verse to near mythic characterizations, unambiguously declares it to be a work of the creative imagination. Through the chronicles of Hall, Holinshed (1587), and possibly Grafton and Stow, Shakespeare's *Richard* is based on the accounts of Polydore Vergil and, above all, of Thomas More.[2] In the stage play, however, we are not tempted automatically to conclude "the author forgot" or "failed to check the archives" or "must have been joking" or—the ultimate panacea—"meant it ironically" when he alters historical facts or chronology, modifies character, invents meaning, or charges implausible rumor with symbolic truth. Our formal assumptions about *Richard III* play a formidable role in our response to it.

As Herbert Lindenberger has observed, however, historical dramas "make a greater pretense at engaging with reality than do writings whose [basic] fictiveness we accept from the start." Such dramas heighten "the transactions between imaginative literature and the external world."[3] In *Richard III* the historicity of much of Shakespeare's material is conspicuous, and the play draws our attention to its importance. While Shakespeare magnifies the fiction of Richard's identity, he also makes historical time more centrally and conceptually thematic than it is in More's work.[4] In both ways the playwright heightens the tension between life and art, living person and created fiction, that we have seen to exist in the best *Lives* of the period. In comparison to More and to the chronicles, in Shakespeare the biographical and historical poles of meaning are alike strengthened.

A. P. Rossiter's remark, in an otherwise admirable and influential essay, that it is "derisible naïvety" to think "we are seeing anything like sober history" in *Richard III* ridicules the limitations of taking the historicity of the play too literally but itself displays the limitations of discounting its reality and real pertinence.[5] The historian's familiar complaint that Shakespeare's image of Richard's character—derived mainly from More's but better known than his—should have interfered so tenaciously with an assessment of the historical King is worth pondering in this connection.[6] Perhaps Rossiter's remark can be squared with such interference, but more likely it is itself prone to isolate too neatly the power of fact from the power of imagination. If *Richard III* did not create the illusion that it is somehow real history, we could not take Richard—"a monstrous being incredible in any sober, historical scheme of things"—seriously.[7] The play would lose its distinctive power, its sustained and boldly strained tension between fiction and fact.[8]

Richard III is conventionally regarded as a history play because it draws primarily on post-Conquest chronicle material rather than primarily on the material of folklore and legend, romance, or other "literary" sources; because it appeared to the editors of the First Folio to be an historical or a chronicle drama; and because a clear majority of arbiters has not as yet agreed that its many persons and actions, its characterizations and plot, and its preoccupation with English chronicle-history conform to our notions of tragedy, comedy, or some other form. Although much debated, the conventional classification of *Richard III* appears chiefly to depend on its chronicle-matter.[9]

As we have seen, however, the materials of the chronicles—More's *Richard*, for a prime example—are themsleves of mixed origin and mixed form, combining fact with fiction and history with life-writing. To the editors of the First Folio, Shakespeare's *Richard* was also a mixture, for they classified the play as a history, entitled it a tragedy, and used as an alternative title and a running-head, *The Life and Death of Richard the Third*, a heading more properly biographical than historical in Renaissance writing.[10] If our formal assumptions about Shakespeare's *Richard* do in fact carry substantial (if not always stated) weight in assessing it, the nearness of life-writing to it is important as well. The reverse, the nearness of Shakespeare's history play to life-writing, is equally revealing with respect to biographical form in the Renaissance.

As I have suggested, Shakespeare heightens and thereby modifies both the historical and biographical traditions that come to him in the depiction of Richard's reign in the chronicles. Since the historical tradition is the more intractably factual—ipso facto less potentially artful and dramatic—Shakespeare's handling of it casts a direct light on the character of truth in his play as a whole. As earlier observed, a *Life* loses some of its identity in a chronicle-history. The chronicles have a sweep of persons, actions, and issues (though not necessarily of themes) greater than that of an individual *Life*, even of the relatively less narrowly focused *Lives* of the Renaissance, such as Cavendish's *Life of Wolsey*. Despite Shakespeare's artistic selection and focusing of detail, his *Richard III* exhibits this wider sweep to a greater extent than does More's, even though More's *Richard* is itself a hybrid of history and biography. Shakespeare's historical pattern is larger and more representative than More's, a fact evidenced by the chorus of lamenting and cursing women, old Margaret of Anjou, Queen of the Lancastrian Henry VI; Cecily, Duchess of York and mother of Edward IV, Clarence, and Richard III; and Elizabeth, Queen of Edward IV and mother of his two young sons.

Margaret, whose bloodcurdling curses stand even smooth Buckingham's hair on end (I.iii.303), is important enough to the play to appear in defiance of historical fact, since she died in France in 1482, the year before Edward IV's death. Like the Duchess of York, Margaret exists in the play to allude recurrently to the sweep of time past and present. Crimes past are her specialty; she lives only in desire of vengeance:

> Long mayst thou live to wail thy children's death,
> And see another, as I see thee now,
> Deck'd in thy rights as thou art stall'd in mine!
>
> [I.iii.203–05]

Her vengeful thirsts are slaked in the play. She and the Duchess, both old women, are joined by Queen Elizabeth, newly displaced from power and embittered by the loss of husband, brother, and sons in the present action of the play, as Margaret and the Duchess were earlier displaced and embittered by the loss of husband and son and as the latter is now embittered more deeply by the loss of more sons and grandsons.

The circularity of time—justice or vengeance, providence or mere fate—that is only gradually manifest in More's *Richard* is from the start one of Shakespeare's major themes. The relatively numerous and conspicuous children of this play—the princes Edward and Richard and the children of Clarence, Edward and Margaret—belong to this theme, as symbols both of the future and of the presence of the past. The laments of the orphaned children of Clarence chorically join those of the Duchess and Queen Elizabeth in Act II (ii.72–79), uniting three generations in loss. Prince Edward's precocious reflections on the antiquity of the Tower in Act III (i.68–78) resonate ironically when his mother addresses its walls in Act

IV—"Pity, you ancient stones, those tender babes" (i.98)—thus extending our awareness of historical time still further.

Like the living women and children, the ghosts who haunt King Richard the night before Bosworth Field also belong to the temporal theme, though they have a psychological function as well. The ghosts might be said to internalize the temporal theme in Richard's conscience, thereby uniting history and biography. At the end of the play, the major function of Richmond's final speech—and indeed of Richmond—is to point to the future as a blessed time that will be free of the cursed circularity of the past. Richmond is to replace his semihomonymic opposite, Richard, as in the later tragedy of *Lear* Edgar will replace the semihomonymic Edmund; ironically, in the history play, however, no challenge to moral justice as brutal as the hanging of Cordelia will be allowed to spoil the tidy symmetry.

At the end of Shakespeare's *Richard,* the sweep of time's hand breaks out of a closed circle to a view that is apparently far brighter than the one at the end of More's. Yet as many other readers have felt, in the terms the play so emphatically uses and therefore makes real, Richmond's last speech seems rather unreal, far more idealistically than actually and dramatically true. Neither in this play nor in any other by Shakespeare is Richmond's character or reign made real for us on stage. His hopeful vision stands apart from the massive forces of history and personality that inform the play. Such vision, as I shall subsequently argue, never comes close to realization until much later plays by Shakespeare that are more fully and inclusively symbolic in form and, in Lindenberger's phrase, make a lesser "pretense at engaging with [historical] reality."

We do not know for certain that Shakespeare ever saw the sudden termination of More's *Richard* as printed in Rastell's 1557 edition or that his critical perception detected in the chronicle version of More's *Richard* the gradual darkening of vision or the more pronounced change in style and outlook after Richard's coronation. But we do know that Shakespeare used Holinshed and possibly Stow as well, and both are markedly closer to Rastell's edition than Hall is: both note marginally the point at which More's *Richard* ceases, indicate additions by Grafton and Hall to More's text, and set off translations from More's Latin text by an asterisk.[11] Whether betraying knowledge of More's ending or not, Shakespeare's own bright ending of *Richard III,* like the pitiless vision that dominates four earlier acts, insinuates his awareness that an ideal movement in history might not be real or lasting.

If Shakespeare heightens the historical significance of Richard's reign, he also heightens the character of Richard. Shakespeare's Richard of Gloucester, like the play's historical patterns, also looms larger than More's and, as Gloucester is often described, larger than life. Shakespeare's Richard is wickeder than More's: his hand in the deaths of Henry VI, of Prince Edward, Henry's son, and of his own brother George is a certainty; his wooing of the murdered Prince Edward's widow and his intention to wed his brother's daughter, the sister of the little princes whose lives he has taken, are dramatized on the stage before our eyes. Besides being wickeder, Richard is more focal in Shakespeare; there is simply more of him, as the long wooing scenes, neither to be found in More's *Richard*, suggest: first the wooing of Anne and later the vicarious wooing of Elizabeth, Richard's niece, through her mother Queen Elizabeth. These parallel scenes are the most outrageous, humanly offensive, unnatural, and sustained exhibitions of Richard's character actually staged in the play, and aside from the chronicle-facts that Richard married Anne Neville and cast a matrimonial leer at his niece, they are Shakespeare's inventions.[12]

In Shakespeare, Richard is also more inward, from his first soliloquy, which opens the play—"Dive, thoughts, down to my soul"—to his last soliloquy, right after the ghosts of his victims curse him mind, soul, and body with the incantation "Despair and die." The absence of an authorial or a narrative voice like More's is one reason Richard becomes a more conscious and autonomous character in Shakespeare. For example, the change in More's style and outlook after Richard's coronation becomes in Shakespeare's play a change in Richard's own mind and behavior. As Richard begins to lose control of others, such as Buckingham, and then of himself, his opportunism turns to instability and his quick wit to irrationality. The scene in which Richard, having learned that Richmond is on the seas, urges Catesby to "fly to the Duke" but neglects to tell him why and meanwhile orders Ratcliffe to "Post to Salisbury," only to forget that he has so ordered him, has the mindless energy of farce (IV.iv.442–56). This energy is real enough but it is frenetic and formless. In the final stages of More's *Richard*, change is mediated by More's own role as reporter and interpreter; in the final stage of Shakespeare's play, change is dramatized primarily in Richard.[13]

If by comparison either More's or Shakespeare's Richard seems more real than the other, he is so in a different way. It is well documented that Shakespeare takes greater liberties with historical fact than does More—the most notorious instances being the conflation in Act I of Henry VI's death in 1471 and the presumed date of Richard's wooing of Anne Neville in 1471–72 with the execution of Clarence in 1478, the life of Margaret of Anjou, which ended in 1482, and the death of Edward IV in 1483.[14] But other reasons weigh even more heavily in making More's Richard look surprisingly more historical and surprisingly less literary than Shakespeare's. It is the latter's Richard who is characterized—in his own words—as "the formal Vice, Iniquity" and who, with the exclamation "Hoy-day, a riddle! neither good nor bad!" for a moment rules to the tune of the cow jumping over the moon (III.i.82, IV.iv.459). Richard's exclamation immediately succeeds his farcical flurry of empty and abortive orders to Catesby and Ratcliffe and similarly belongs to a world of chess games ("fly to the Duke," "Post to Salisbury"), theatrical roles (the Vice, Iniquity), and holiday entertainments ("Hoy-day, a riddle!"). The Richard of More and of the chronicles is also an actor but not to an extent so great, self-conscous, or incorrigible.

In Shakespeare, even Richard's greatest moment of introspection on waking abruptly from ghost-ridden sleep is artificial in the extreme. Its internal and end-rhymes positively jingle:

> What do I fear! Myself? There's none else by.
> Richard loves Richard, that is, I [am] I.
> Is there a murtherer here? No. Yes, I am.
> Then fly. What, from myself? Great reason why—
> Lest I revenge. What, myself upon myself?
>
> [V.iii.182–86]

This is verbal solitaire—or better, bridge with a solitary player. Making a bid from one side of the bridge table and then rushing to another side to parry it, Richard tries to fill the resonating emptiness in the center of his being.

If more literary, however, Shakespeare's Richard is also more susceptible to the insights and techniques of character analysis than is his predecessor in More. In his wickedness Shakespeare's Richard, while finally larger than life, is more nearly whole and coherent. He has an active role as a son, a wooer, and a military commander in the play, in addition to his roles in More, and he also has an acute awareness of his own deformity. This awareness, which is *his* awareness, not his narrator's as in More, dominates our first and lasting impression of him in the soliloquy that opens the play. Richard's own deformity is the keynote of this soliloquy. Here, as elsewhere in aside and soliloquy, Richard's attitude toward his unnatural shape is essentially sardonic and contemptuous:

> Why, I, in this weak piping time of peace,
> Have no delight to pass away the time,
> Unless to see my shadow in the sun
> And descant on mine own deformity.
>
> [I.i.24–27]

Richard cloaks the deformity he cannot deny and cannot accept in flagrant contempt, an attitude based on the assumption of his superiority to the cheats of "dissembling nature" (19) and one entirely subject to his Thespian control. Later, however, when Richard's nephew taunts him painfully about his shape—"Because that I am little, like an ape, / He thinks that you should bear me on your shoulders" (III.i.130–31)—Richard's totally ignoring his taunts is not only ominous but also revealing. It suggests his vulnerability in the face of contempt that he neither initiates nor directs. Such vulnerability is merely negative, however; it falls far short of the ironic yet effectually more positive yearning of an Edmund clutching for humanity between the stirrup and the ground: "Yet Edmund was belov'd! . . . Some *good* I mean to do, / Despite of mine own nature."[15]

Through Richard's asides and soliloquies, Shakespeare embodies in the person of Richard himself the increasingly heavy irony and eventual sarcasm of More's authorial observations and parenthetical remarks. Or rather, it is as if Richard had internalized these for his own consumption.[16] When Richard's nephew scorns his uncle, it is, moreover, as if the voice of contempt Richard had internalized thus to control had got loose outside him.

Even Richard's last words with himself in his final soliloquy display a similar psychological pattern of control and self-consumption. They move from a desire for pity stated in a negative, self-canceling form—"there is no creature loves me, / And if I die no soul will pity me"—to a self-enclosed rejection of the possibility of pity—"And wherefore should they, since that I myself / Find in myself no pity to myself?" (V.iii.200–03). Then they subside into flat, tired statement in whose first word we already see Richard planting the seeds of disbelief:

> Methought the souls of all that I had murther'd
> Came to my tent, and every one did threat
> To-morrow's vengeance on the head of Richard.
>
> [V.iii.204–06]

Spontaneous emotion yields to the distancing mechanism of rational control and the possibility of internal reform is aborted, as it probably must be in a play about to make a "pretense at engaging with [the historical] reality" of the Tudor dynasty.[17]

The susceptibility of Shakespeare's Richard to realistic analysis is pronounced enough to have attracted the attention even of Freud.[18] This susceptibility makes Richard both more engaging and more disturbing by moving him closer to the human terms that are inadequate in the end to account for him. Moody Prior's description of "the chasm" that separates Richard from "ordinary wicked humanity" could hardly be bettered: "Every detail about Richard is believable as having its counterpart in human experience, but what makes him fascinating is that he combines these qualities and capacities in a degree of consistency and magnitude that places him outside the usual human scale of measure and judgment." Continuing, Prior compares Richard to "some absolute zero which nature seems to be approaching as a limit but which escapes realization" except in the imagination.[19] The condition Prior describes goes beyond the mere heightening of human qualities; it is so different in degree that it has become a monstrous difference in kind. Like a psychological paradigm magnified beyond human proportions, Richard's nature finally seems to mock both itself and the fictions of identity out of which it is constructed.

Richard's "wholeness"—his consistency and magnitude—is an empty one. He is in actuality an inversion of human wholeness, a parodic black hole, an absolute space in the center of his own being. Credibly human in every detail and credibly historical in fact and setting, he is at once a reality and an absolute fiction. Moreover, he is the misshapen product of nature and time and also, as we watch him in the play, the product of his own making.

In Richard, Shakespeare takes the tension between the historical King and the mythic monster, the living person and the imagined fiction, to its limit. Compared to the Richard of More and the chronicles, Shakespeare's is both more real as a psychological entity and more imaginary. He is, by his own choice, more clearly and consistently a type—be it Vice, Machiavel, Senecan Tyrant, or all three—and he is also more insistently a symbol, the vicious, subhuman, murderous boar; in mythic terms, chaos, hatred, winter, and death.[20] He is, in addition, more self-conscious about his own shape and more consciously a player of roles and a shaper of his own identity. Aberrant but unmistakable both as a work of nature *and* as a work of art, more whole in his wickedness *and* more fictional than his predecessors, the figure of Shakespeare's Richard thus magnifies for our scrutiny a tension that informs the Renaissance *Lives* we have earlier examined and specifically characterizes the life of More's Richard. In Shakespeare's Richard the fact and operation of fiction in the wholeness of an identity—the biographical fiction so pervasive in the *Lives*—become matters of explicit concern and deliberate experimentation. Shakespeare not only finds the fiction in biographical truth in More's portrayal of Richard but also exploits its implications for human identity.

Shakespeare experiments with biographical fiction, the fiction in human wholeness, repeatedly in his plays, at various times finding in it both hope for humanity and despair. *Hamlet*, sometimes coupled as a "disguise play" with *Richard III*,[21] is a case in point, as are *Lear*, *As You Like It*, *The Tempest*, and indeed all the plays in which disguise, whether primarily psychological or physical as well, has a vital role. In *Richard III* the dissembling performances of Richard form an obvious part of this theme, as do the performances of his supporting cast, for example, the counterfeit "deep tragedian" Buckingham or Queen Elizabeth, who, if relenting in her response to Richard's suit, is a "Poor painted queen" in truth (III.v.5, I.iii.240). The fiction in human identity is one of the two central themes explored in the play, time's circularity being the other.

In embryonic form, however, there is in the play an even broader and equally familiar Shakespearean theme related to both the biographical and historical ones and in later plays bridging them, namely, the transmutation of human suffering to art and beyond that to a state of renewal imagined and imaged in art. Ariel's famous song in *The Tempest* has long been considered the touchstone of this theme:

> Full fadom five thy father lies,
> Of his bones are coral made:
> Those are pearls that were his eyes:
> Nothing of him that doth fade,
> But doth suffer a sea-change
> Into something rich and strange.[22]

The same theme is anticipated in Clarence's dream of death by water, but, like the possibility of Richard's internal reform in his last soliloquy, it is aborted:

> Methoughts I saw a thousand fearful wracks;
> A thousand men that fishes gnaw'd upon;
> Wedges of gold, great anchors, heaps of pearl,
> Inestimable stones, unvalued jewels,
> All scatt'red in the bottom of the sea:
> Some lay in dead men's skulls, and in the holes
> Where eyes did once inhabit, there were crept
> (As 'twere in scorn of eyes) reflecting gems,
> That woo'd the slimy bottom of the deep,
> And mock'd the dead bones that lay scatt'red by.
>
> [I.iv.24–33]

Fear and death and art are here, but here is no renewal.

The transmutation of suffering to art and renewal occurs more explicitly in Richard's words to Queen Elizabeth when he seeks her daughter's hand in marriage. To Elizabeth's bitter rehearsal of the fates of her slaughtered sons, Richard replies that when he is married to her daughter, "The liquid drops of tears that you have shed / Shall come again, transform'd to orient pearl" (IV.iv.321–22). In other words, her sorrow will "suffer a sea-change / Into something rich and strange." Elizabeth's subsequent reminder, "Yet thou didst kill my children," Richard counters with an image of renewal, which, however pointedly it alludes to physical generation, would be absurd if taken literally:

> But in your daughter's womb I bury them;
> Where in that nest of spicery they will breed
> Selves of themselves, to your recomforture.
>
> [IV.iv.423–25]

The boar would root in the Garden of Adonis. It is as if he would break from his tomblike cave beneath the Mount to riot in the place of mythic fertility, of imagination and renewal. In Richard's offer of renewal, the echoes of Spenser's Garden of Adonis are explicit and powerful.[23]

Although Richard's image of the Garden, "that nest of spicery," belongs primarily to the realm of myth and imagination, in his mouth it is viscerally offensive. His hypocrisy and essential un-truth pervert the words of renewal, as his acting and feigning pervert imaginative power. They also make the connection between biographical fiction and the larger, more visionary theme of transmutation and renewal explicit. The imaginative potential for reform, like the words and images of renewal, is Richard's alone in the play. Misused by him, the power to renew and to fulfill the self touches and subverts even the possibility of a better vision.

In Shakespeare's late plays, the fiction in human wholeness is often a vital but subsidiary expression of the larger, more visionary theme of transmutation and renewal. Perhaps in Shakespeare's very movement away from the marked engagement with chronicle-history we find in *Richard III* to the still more artificial forms of high comedy, tragedy, and romance, we can see an assimilation of the historical theme of *Richard* to this larger theme as well. This assimilation is also anticipated, if again abortively, in *Richard III* when Richard pays suit to Queen Elizabeth for her daughter's hand. He counsels the Queen to "drown the sad remembrance of those wrongs" in "the Lethe of thy angry soul" thus to liberate the possibility of sea-change and swears, for lack of anything else he has not defiled, by "The time to come" (IV.iv.251–52, cf. 321–22, 387). But Elizabeth perceives the hypocrisy of his proffered reform and renewal and answers with a little sermon on the circularity of time:

> That [time to come] thou hast wronged in the time o'erpast;
> For I myself have many tears to wash
> Hereafter time, for time past wrong'd by thee.
>
> Swear not by time to come, for that thou hast
> Misus'd ere us'd, by times ill-used [o'erpast].[24]

As old Queen Margaret knows when the play opens and Queen Anne learns too late, to drown wrongs past, indeed to lose the imagination and image of them, is to lose one's self and one's identity in Richard's world. It is at best to drown, to find oblivion instead of renewal. Vengeance and hatred, not love and transcendence, stir imagination in this play, and as a result, time's circle is vicious.

Although the transmutation of suffering to art and to renewal is embryonic in *Richard III*, its frustrated potential is everywhere present. Such a theme is hardly what we find—or should expect to find—in More's *Richard*. Its presence in Shakespeare's *Richard* further shows that if the playwright accentuates the historical and biographical traditions in depicting Richard's reign, he also heightens the fictional one. *Richard III* not only is a more imaginative and fictional work than its historical sources but is also more consciously, thematically concerned with biographical fiction, with its origin and power in human lives and history. The play explores both the inescapability of fiction in human identity and its implications for destruction or renewal of self and society. In this play the negative implications dominate: the figure of Richard suggests intense fascination with the role of the fictionalizing imagination and fearful distrust of it.

The sources and resources of the imagination are primarily destructive in *Richard III*, as they are not, for example, in *The Tempest*. Whether in the presence of Ceres, beneficent but still mindful of Dis, or in Ariel's song about sea-change, the imaginative association of birth and death, womb and tomb, is vital and regenerative in *The Tempest* (IV. i. 86–91, 110–17). The same association, which is as evident in Rabelais and Spenser as in the ancient myths of fertility and redemption (e.g., Adonis, Ceres, Isis/Osiris) so dear to the Renaissance, degenerates in Richard's world to a perverse image of denied potential.[25] I have touched already on Richard's use of the association of womb and tomb in his suit to Queen Elizabeth for her daughter's hand ("But in your daughter's womb I bury them") and should now emphasize its thematic persistence. The same association occurs more than once in Richard's suit and may help to account for the great length of the second wooing scene in the Folio text. In an intense, if disturbing way, this scene occupied the poet's imagination.

About midway through his suit, Richard informs Elizabeth, "If I have kill'd the issue of your womb . . . I will beget / Mine issue of your blood upon your daughter" (IV.iv.296–98). Soon again, in stichomythic fencing, he objects to her, "Your reasons are too shallow and too quick," only to hear the rejoinder, "O no, my reasons are too deep and dead— / Too deep and dead, poor infants, in their graves" (361–63). Like Richard, Elizabeth refers to her reasons for resisting his suit, but in the context of the scene her words, falling between Richard's two explicit linkings of womb and tomb, pun on this association as well. Elizabeth's reasons echo hollowly the Augustinian commonplace of the *rationes seminales* (seminal reasons), "the germs of those things which were to develop in the course of time" or, alternatively, the potentialities implanted by God in the Creation to develop by temporal unfolding.[26] Copleston, explaining this familiar theory, borrows an analogy from Bonaventure that reads like an ironic epitaph on Elizabeth's young sons, the buds of the white rose of York. Bonaventure compares the *ratio seminalis* to the rosebud, "which is not yet actually the rose but will develop into the rose, given the presence of the necessary positive agencies and the absence of negative or preventive agencies" (76). Associations with growth and renewal are imaginative and strong in *Richard III*, but they always seem to lead to pitiless irony and negation.

Whereas magic in *The Tempest* is also regenerative, the related forces and forms of imagination in *Richard III* are destructive. Rossiter and countless others have directed our attention to the insistent, sometimes grating ritual of the scenes of female cursing and lamentation:

I had an Edward, till a Richard kill'd him;
I had a [Harry], till a Richard kill'd him:
Thou hadst an Edward, till a Richard kill'd him;
Thou hadst a Richard, till a Richard kill'd him.

[IV.iv.40–43]

In these lines old Queen Margaret might as well be sticking verbal pins into a voodoo doll. Her lines are not really unlike Richard's verbal solitaire.

Enumerating the symmetries of emptiness and death, they give her being. They *are* the fiction of her identity.

Margaret cursing—recognized by Richard as a "Foul wrinkled witch"—is demonic; she is an imaginative force and form. No one, not even Richard, can ignore her cursing, and no audience forgets it, however much, like Richard himself, an audience might try to distance or to make fun of the excesses of her inhuman hatred. The horrid ritual of Margaret's incantations does not make her "unrealistic" except to a naively historical judgment. Instead, it relates her to the perverted imaginative power and the deathly realm of the usurping boar.

At her first appearance in the play, in terms of explicitly staged symbolism, Margaret comes out of the depths. Coming from behind the other actors, she comments on their words seven times in asides unheard by them and then thrusts herself into their midst: "Hear me, you wrangling pirates, that fall out / In sharing that which you have pill'd from me!" (I.iii.157–58). Ironically, Margaret's presence soon succeeds in uniting the rival factions in hatred (187–89).

Margaret's relation to Richard in her dramatic first appearance is especially marked. Five of her seven asides directly succeed his words, and he is the first to respond to her outspoken presence, initially by trying to turn away from her and then by confronting her as a witch and expecting her to vanish (162–63). Some of the words Richard speaks before Margaret intrudes into his awareness could as easily have been spoken by Margaret herself. They interact with the temporal burden of her words and virtually introduce her open presence; for example,

> Let me put in your minds, if you forget,
> What you have been ere this, and what you are;
> Withal, what I have been, and what I am.[27]

Richard quickly becomes impatient with Margaret's persistently audible curses—"Have done thy charm, thou hateful with'red hag" (214)—and he is far from immune to them until he deflects the aim of her worst vituperations, substituting her name for his own at the climax of her curse: "Thou rag of honor! thou detested," she cries, and quickly Richard adds, "Margaret" (232–33). Redirecting Margaret's verbal venom, Richard's reply is gamesome, almost childish, and, above all, magical. To name—in childhood, in superstition, and in magic—is to possess. It is also, for an adult, to recognize and to acknowledge, as Richard acknowledges his kinship to Margaret in the exchange of names. After this exchange, Richard's serious involvement in the scene ceases. For him Margaret's charm is dissolved, not by resistance but by appropriation.

Old Queen Margaret is an autonomous, objective, historical figure in *Richard III*, but like the witches in *Macbeth*, she is also a correlative to the elemental and emotional depths in the play: the "deep" of ocean and of

Clarence's dream, of his fearful and futile prayers, of the sin in which his brother is as "deep" as he (I.i.4, iv.32, 35, 69, 214); the "deep disgrace in brotherhood" that touches Richard "deeper" than his brother can imagine, the "deep" of Richard's intent and the depths of his soul; the "deep" of his vice and the "deep enemies" that disturb his sleep (I.i.111–12, 149, 41; II.ii.28; IV.ii.72–73); the "deep" of cursing and lamentation that fill the earth, the "deep" of treachery and tragedy, of suspicions and designs (I.ii.52, iii.223; II.i.38; III.v.5, 8; vii.67; IV.ii.42, 119); "the fatal bowels of the deep," "the swallowing gulf / Of dark forgetfulness and deep oblivion," the "reasons" of Queen Elizabeth—"Too deep and dead, poor infants, in their graves" (III.iv.101, vii.128–29; IV.iv.362–63). The association of the deep with the primitive, irrational, and subconscious is overwhelming. Margaret is part of this symbolism, as her entrance from behind the other actors suggests. Her bitter incantations and historically allusive presence—together the sum of her identity—extend this symbolism to history, the depths of time.

In *Richard III* the elemental, historical, and psychic depths are the source and center of corruption rather than of release and renewal.[28] They are destructive and deathly, not fertile and truly creative. They are the origin of hate and deceit rather than pity and vision. At the same time, however, there is nothing so powerful and real in the play as what rises out of them. They can no more be ignored or simply replaced than the elements or emotions, than history or the subconscious, or indeed than their major symbol in the play, the sea itself. They are the same depths out of which the potential for forming and re-forming human wholeness must come, as it does in the most compelling or efficacious characters in Shakespeare's later works. The biographical fiction that ignores these depths is as deceitful as the one that misuses them in the Thespian manner of a Richard. Such a fiction is merely theatrical rather than true.

Near the end of the play, some effort is made to associate the figure of Richmond *ex machina* with the depths of nature, history, and personality, but the effort is not a persuasive one. It is evident, for example, in the fact that the ghosts of Richard's victims appear to Richmond, as well as to Richard, if only to wish him good health and happy fighting. It may also be present—though I doubt it—in the repeated statement that Richmond is "on the seas," in touch with their surface at least (IV.iv.462–63, 473). But efforts to counter or simply to replace the depths of the play are more conspicuous, and even symbolically, the figure of "shallow" Richmond, as Richard describes him, does not satisfy (V.iii.219). The association of Richmond with the sun is insistent, evidently meant to counter that of Richard with darkness, rather than to include, recover, or redirect its demonic energies: in a real world, however, night is as natural as day, the deep of ocean as real as its surface. Richmond's concluding speech, a vision of forgiveness, fidelity, hope, and harmony sharply opposes the evils of Richard's reign. Yet the redemptive Richmond neither appropriates nor cancels Richard's real influence. Richmond does not re-possess Richard's imagination or, as a dramatic figure, his power. Richard, Clarence's dream, and Margaret are what we remember.

In terms the play itself has developed, Richmond's nature lacks depth. He is a Tudor blazon without fully human dimension. He is not realized as a character in and of the play. He is moral and fictional but neither whole nor quite credible: the illusion of biographical truth is not in him.[29] Returning to an earlier statement in this chapter, I might make this point another way: Shakespeare's image of Henry VII's character has not interfered with our assessing the historical King and did not even interfere significantly with Francis Bacon's assessment of Henry three decades or less after the play was written. Bacon's *Historie of the Raigne of King Henry the Seventh* even opens with the legendary tyranny of Richard and the relative insignificance of his opponent: "Richard . . . king in fact only, but tyrant both in title and regiment, and so commonly termed and reputed in all times since, was by the Divine Revenge, favouring the design of an exiled man, overthrown and slain at Bosworth Field."[30] In both our own time and Bacon's, however, the image of Richard III in Shakespeare's play and its sources has persistently influenced appraisals of him. Despite ourselves, we believe it.

EIGHT
SHAKESPEARE'S *HENRY VIII*
The Changing Relation of Truth to Fiction

Shakespeare's *Henry VIII* looks back to Cavendish's *Life of Wolsey*, upon which it draws via the chronicles, and evokes comparison with the incidental treatments of Henry in Cavendish and in Roper's *Life of More*. It also invites comparison with Shakespeare's *Richard III*, one of his earliest history plays, simply by being—whether Shakespeare's in whole or in part—his last. Equally important for the present study, *Henry VIII* anticipates later treatments of historical figures like those of Henry VII and Henry VIII by Francis Bacon and Herbert of Cherbury, respectively. In these two histories and in Shakespeare's *Henry VIII*, the relation of truth to fiction differs from that we have witnessed in earlier Tudor writings. In these later works, there either exists a sharper distinction or else an increasingly self-conscious relation between history and life-writing and more generally between fiction and truth, subjective and objective modes of portrayal, than typically exists before. We have already noted the self-consciousness of this relation in Walton's *Life of Donne*. In Bacon the sharpness of distinction is first more noticeable, if finally more equivocal, than in Walton. No chronicler, Bacon writes about a single king, but his subject is specifically *The Historie of the Raigne*, rather than the *Life*, of Henry VII. His goal is truth, specifically historical truth, and the method he embraces specifically rejects the poet's fictions.

Comparison of passages from Bacon's *Advancement of Learning* and Sidney's *Defence of Poetry* will clarify the changing relation between fiction and truth, poetic feigning and history, which, I shall subsequently argue, is central to the concerns of Shakespeare's *Henry VIII*. In *The Advancement*, Bacon explains,

> because the acts or events of true history have not that magnitude which satisfieth the mind of man, poesy feigneth acts and events greater and more heroical; because true history propoundeth the successes and issues of actions not so agreeable to the merits of virtue and vice, therefore poesy feigns them more just in retribution, and more according to revealed providence; because true history representeth actions and

events more ordinary and less interchanged, therefore poesy endueth them with more rareness, and more unexpected and alternative variations.[1]

This passage has been taken to suggest the proximity of Bacon's view of the relation of poetry and truth to Sidney's or, to rephrase in accord with Sidney's *Defence*, the relation of fiction (feigning) to truth.[2] In a limited sense Bacon's and Sidney's views of this relation are similar, but their differences are more definitive and mutually more illuminating. Sidney, like Bacon, finds history less morally edifying than the poet's feigning: "to that which commonly is attributed to the praise of history, in respect of the notable learning is got by marking the success, as though therein a man should see virtue exalted and vice punished—truly that commendation is particular to poetry, and far off from history."[3] Yet Sidney's references to history, compared with Bacon's, are slighting and scornful, for example, when Sidney observes that "the history, being captived to the truth of a foolish world, is many times a terror from well-doing, and an encouragement to unbridled wickedness" (90).

Conversely, Sidney idealizes the true poet. Such a poet, whether writing in verse or prose, "with the force of a divine breath" brings forth a golden world and grows "in effect another nature, in making things either better than nature bringeth forth, or quite anew" (78–79). Sidney's "right poet" stands apart from "the meaner sort of painters, who counterfeit only such faces as are set before them"; instead he resembles "the more excellent [sort], who having no law but wit, bestow that in colours upon you which is fittest for the eye to see" (80). Thus described, Sidney's poet sounds like the painter of an Elizabethan court portrait, who embodied an Idea rather than simply depicting a person. Sidney's poet perfects nature and idealizes history.

As the preceding quotations suggest, Sidney's view of the relation of fiction to truth also differs significantly from Bacon's. To Sidney, poetic fiction is without qualification superior to history and "truer" than history; in Bacon's view, poetry is more edifying and pleasing than "true history" but is also less truthful. Its pleasure looks more like an anodyne than an inspiration. Bacon's view reflects the weighting of truth toward palpable fact, experience, and objectivity that we used to call "modern." As I have suggested, the same weighting is fundamental to the ambivalence of Shakespeare's *Henry VIII*.

In the First Folio the title of *Henry VIII* is *The Famous History of the Life of King Henry the Eight*. A contemporary account of the play, important for establishing its date, entitles it *All is True*, which, as R.A. Foakes remarks, might well have been the play's alternative title.[4] Thrice in thirty-two lines, the Prologue to the play mentions "truth" explicitly. First those members of the audience who "hope they may believe" receive assurance from the Prologue that they "May here find truth too." The assurance is tentative—"may find," rather than "shall" or "will." The Prologue next elevates the seriousness of "our chosen truth," thus remarking a connection between the truth of the play and the process of selecting or interpreting—choosing. Then it declares the intention of play and players to present nothing but the truth: "the opinion that we bring / To make that only true we now intend." Again this declaration is slightly guarded, an intention or opinion being a lesser guarantee than an accomplished fact or unqualified truth.

The Prologue continues, "Think ye see / The very persons of our noble story / As they were living," and thereby invites us to "think" (suppose? imagine? pretend?) for the duration of the play that we are seeing human truth, real people as they really were. Seemingly in the same vein, the Prologue adds, "think you see them great, . . . then, in a moment, see / How soon this mightiness meets misery." The repetition of the phrase "think you see," followed by a collapse of greatness that we "see" without the possible illusions thinking produces, makes the original invitation to "Think ye see" human truth ambivalent and potentially ironic. Having read the Prologue, we are likely to find the alternative title of the play, *All is True*, at face value the most extensive and unqualified claim made for the authority of the play's contents, unless, of course, it turns out that we find these contents to be truly contradictory or truly ambiguous and the very notion of objective truth thereby subjected to examination. In this last case the claim that "all is true" becomes not false, but ironic, as indeed I take it truly to be.[5]

Divorce is more than an historical problem and event in *Henry VIII*. It is a theme in a broader and more conceptual way, involving the disjunction of inner and outer and private and public lives. It is a disjoining of the aspects of reality, a displaying of the torn seams of truth. Like truth in the play, divorce is an issue everywhere present but explicit references make its centrality pointed. Before Henry's divorce from Catherine is even mentioned, Buckingham asks those "few that lov'd" him to accompany him to the block:

> And as the long divorce of steel falls on me,
> Make of your prayers one sweet sacrifice
> And lift my soul to heaven.
>
> [II.i.76–78]

This passage is charged with metaphor. The sword is to sever head from body, soul from flesh, dignity of spirit from dignity of worldly rank and estate, eternity from time.[6] This matrix of associations is reconfirmed when Anne Boleyn expresses pity for Catherine, wishing the Queen had never "known pomp;"

> though't be temporal,
> Yet if that quarrel, fortune, do divorce
> It from the bearer, 'tis a sufferance panging
> As soul and body's severing.
>
> [II.iii.13–16]

Catherine's own defiant rejection of divorce when Wolsey interviews her echoes the same associations:

> My lord, I dare not make myself so guilty
> To give up willingly that noble title
> Your master wed me to: nothing but death
> Shall e'er divorce my dignities.
>
> [III.i.139–42]

It is hardly coincidental that the scene witnessing Catherine's defiant rejection begins with a song about Orpheus, that Renaissance favorite for the evocation of ideas of harmony, inspiration, and perfection. In the first stanza of the song, Orpheus lives up to his reputation, plants and flowers spring to his music, "as sun and showers / There had made a lasting spring." In the second stanza, however, we hear an enervating Orpheus, in whose "music is such art, / Killing care and grief of heart / Fall asleep, or hearing die." These lines suggest Bacon's anodyne more than Sidney's inspiration and renewal. Killing care and heart-grief fall asleep and die in lines whose syntax could be read to make "Killing" a participle modifying "art" or more ambiguously to make "Fall" and "die" verbs in the imperative mood. The conspicuous personification of the lines in question (fall asleep, hear, die) draws notice to these syntactical possibilities. Composing this song, the playwright might have remembered another "long divorce" of soul from body, the severance of Orpheus' head as the result of the Bacchantes' unbridled passions.[7]

Another reference to Henry's divorce of Catherine, which at first seems merely factual, reinforces the opposition of divorce to a unifed truth in this play, as well as the association of divorce with disharmony and disjunction in the broader sense. Norfolk reports to his peers as "true" the fact that "In the divorce his [Wolsey's] contrary proceedings / Are all unfolded" (III.ii.25–27). By "contrary proceedings" Norfolk evidently refers to the contradiction between Wolsey's apparent support for the divorce and his secretly advising the Pope to defer judgment on it. In the quotation, however, normal syntax is inverted—reading "in the divorce his proceedings" rather than "his proceedings in (with respect to) the divorce"—and consequently the meaning of it is suggestively ambiguous. The quotation as readily means that in the very concept of the divorce is the unfolding of Wolsey's contrary proceedings, the revelation of all his self-opposing actions and the distillation of his contradictory career.

As analogue to Wolsey and example of another Renaissance commonplace alive in *Henry VIII*, one thinks of Spenser's Ate, source of discord and "mother of debate,"

> And all dissention, which doth dayly grow
> Amongst fraile men, that many a publike state
> And many a priuate oft doth ouerthrow.[8]

Like her lying tongue, Ate's heart is divided and "neuer thoght one thing, but doubly stil was guided." She hears as well as speaks double ("Fild with false rumors and seditious trouble"), and even her feet are odd, one long, one short, "And both misplast; that when th'one forward yode, / The other backe retired, and contrarie trode" (IV.i.27–28). Wolsey is no allegorical Ate, but his lifelike figure embodies discord and divorce, ideas that exercised Renaissance imaginations, and within the play, he is thematically focal.

The question of conscience and specifically of King Henry's conscience relates in an obvious way to the fact of Henry's divorce from Catherine and is itself evidence of a divorce of values and truths in the play. As in Cavendish's and Roper's handling of Henry's divorce, the word "conscience" punctuates the action of the play repeatedly with ambivalent meanings. The greatest concentration of references to conscience comes in the King's divorce trial, as we should expect by now. To a reader of earlier chapters in this book, the refrain is familiar: "My conscience first receiv'd a tenderness, / Scruple and prick"; "This respite shook / The bosom of my conscience"; "thus hulling in / The wild sea of my conscience," "I meant to rectify my conscience" (II.iv.168–69, 179–80, 197–98, 201). But our crediting the King's words and our sympathizing with his troubles are seriously impaired by what we have heard about conscience already in this play, for example, from Buckingham, who has been legally condemned for treason: "And if I have a conscience, let it sink me, . . . if I be not faithful" (II.i.60–61). Discrepancy between the external judgments of the law and of one's own conscience was common enough in Tudor-Stuart England, but dramatically in its opening acts, the play makes this discrepancy an issue.

Because irreverent, Suffolk's jest about King Henry's conscience, which follows hard on Buckingham's execution, compromises Henry's long-suffering but valiantly impartial posture at the divorce trial still more. To the Lord Chamberlain's explanation that Henry's "marriage with his brother's wife / Has crept too near his conscience," Suffolk offers this gloss, "No, his conscience / Has crept too near another lady" (II.ii.15–18), and thereby wittily equates conscience with desire, convenience, and self-interest. The King's own use of the word "conscience" is yet more disturbing. Having just ordered Wolsey to make arrangements for the divorce trial, Henry continues,

> O my lord,
> Would it not grieve an able man to leave
> So sweet a bedfellow? But conscience, conscience;
> O 'tis a tender place, and I must leave her.
>
> [II.ii.140–43]

J. C. Maxwell tells us that these lines are "certainly not as Pecksniffian" as they tend "to seem to a modern reader."[9] Actually, it is hard to know how to characterize them. Presumably the King refers in them to Catherine rather than to Anne, to "So sweet a bedfellow" ejected rather than anticipated, yet his specific reference to himself as an "able man," rather than as a faithful or moral man, seems inappropriate to this reading. Despite his concern to neutralize the Pecksniffian aroma, Maxwell, too, must have wondered about the use of "able," for he glosses this common word, as here meaning "vigorous" or "lusty."[10]

"But conscience, conscience," Henry intones, and we might feel that the duplicity—the doubleness literally present in his repetition of the word—is somehow very apt, if not really pre-Pecksniffian. "O 'tis a tender place," he adds, presumably referring to conscience but in a way so suggestively sensitive ("tender") and physical ("place") that, in a play peppered with sexual quibbles, the reader who does not take rigorous precautions to ignore such hints of Pecksniffery might dimly sense an association between "So sweet a bedfellow" and "a tender place." (The reader who has taken precautions might test the effect of any of the following substitutions on the lines in question: "So loving a woman" for "So sweet a bedfellow"; "painful place" or "tender thing" for "tender place." The associations in the playwright's lines depend on subtle and deliberate diction and syntax, and even slight tampering dispels them.) The least the "tender place" can mean here is a bed.[11] In the final clause of the quotation, the woman—"her"—Henry must leave is again presumably Catherine, but with Henry's doubled use of "conscience, conscience" sounding still from the line preceding, we cannot be sure that both the King's consciences would choose Anne. It would appear that Henry intends to divorce one of his consciences, one kind of moral awareness, and thus to leave the type of truth (or plighted troth) it entails. The effect of this action would therefore be to reject the possibility of a seamless truth and indeed to tear the seams wide open.[12]

In the scene which immediately follows this confusion of Henry's conscience in Act II, scene ii, the Old Lady, Anne Boleyn's friend, teases Anne about the capacity of her "soft cheveril conscience," that is, about its ability to accommodate or stretch, as does the leather *(cheveril)* in a kid glove (II.iii.32). Disquietingly, perhaps, the image of the "soft cheveril conscience" recalls Henry's tenderness of conscience and summarizes most fittingly the impression of conscience that dominates the first two acts of the play. We approach Henry's speeches at the divorce trial with the convenient and merely accommodating aspects of conscience fresh in our minds, and the rest of the trial scene, especially the contradictory claims about Wolsey's and Henry's own responsibility for initiating the divorce action, does not make it easier for us to locate either the truth or the relation of Henry's conscience to it.

Nor does the ambivalence of conscience cease after the divorce is accomplished. One of the gentlemen who watch the coronation procession of Anne Boleyn observes admiringly,

> Our king has all the Indies in his arms,

> And more, and richer, when he strains that lady;
> I cannot blame his conscience.
>
> [IV.i.45–47]

His remark equates the royal conscience with the King's good taste in women. Another ironically resonant use of the concept of conscience occurs when Wolsey learns that Sir Thomas More has replaced him in the office of Lord Chancellor. Generously Wolsey wishes that More might continue

> Long in his highness' favour, and do justice
> For truth's sake, and his conscience; that his bones,
> When he has run his course and sleeps in blessings,
> May have a tomb of orphans' tears wept on him.
>
> [III.ii.396–99]

While altering the chronological relation of Henry's marriage to Anne (1533) and Wolsey's fall and death (1528–30), the playwright appears also to have extended Wolsey's prophetic powers, so that Wolsey foresees More's execution after refusing to take the oaths of succession and supremacy (1535). In this play a reference to More's unaccommodating conscience cannot be innocent of irony, although it need not imply unqualified approval of his choice: the failure to accommodate can prove self-destructive, if also, to borrow Wolsey's prophetic term, blessed. Catherine of Aragon's conscience in the play has much in common with More's.

For the present, perhaps, the best we can say of conscience after the divorce trial is that it tends to correlate increasingly with a heightened, though also more nearly solipsistic and sectarian, subjectivity, with a greater privacy in the self and greater claims for this privacy. The worst we can say is that conscience has become merely sensuous or ornamental—like a cheveril glove or the riches of the Indies—and is no longer essential. Clearly, however, the troubled question of conscience and of the truth to which it answers lies at the core of this play. Disjunctive truths and ambivalent moral attitudes are not what the play commits but what it studies, perhaps too truly. Yet a play in which "all is true" ought to be true to life in a special way.

Truth-to-life is at once the problem and the fascination of *Henry VIII*. This play is a controlled and possibly cynical experiment. It may not be artistically great, but it is artistically interesting. Its structure and resolution may be "flawed" by ambivalence, divorce, and disjunction, but as we have seen to some extent already, these "flaws" are patterned and full of meaning, controlled and deliberate. They comment on human truth and art, exploring how literally, objectively true to life great art can be, or rather, suggesting how fictional it must be.[13]

The nature of meaning and of art in *Henry VIII* must wait a final consideration until the end of this chapter, but reference to it raises questions about the authorship of the play (Shakespeare and Fletcher or Shakespeare alone) and about my own artistic assumptions, which should be addressed before proceeding. To find an artistic work problematical is not necessarily to find it of multiple authorship, artless, or disunified. (Book V of Spenser's *Faerie Queene*, the Book closest to a treatment of actual history, is another case in point.) Artistic form need not be ideal, beautiful, and closed; it can be irregular, open-ended, and imperfect.

Formal judgments—debatable to begin with—have no necessary authority in questions of authorship and at least in theory the reverse is also true: authorship does not guarantee formal quality. In practice, however, most editions of *Henry VIII* proceed logically, as well as in format, from the question of authorship to critical evaluation (single authorship = fine play; multiple authorship = inferior play). There is no external evidence concerning the authorship of the play beyond the fact that the editors of the First Folio attributed it to Shakespeare, and there is no significant textual problem in the play that doubts about authorship hinder us from resolving. It therefore appears more reasonable to proceed from a reading of the play itself to deductions about its author, if we feel compelled to make any, instead of the reverse, which is likely to prejudice our reading and to provoke assumptions about its unity before we have understood it fully. For convenience, I shall refer to the author as Shakespeare, the fact, if not the precise quantity, of whose part in the writing of *Henry VIII* I take for granted.[14]

Editors and interpreters of *Henry VIII* customarily remark its closeness to its sources in the chronicles—Holinshed (1587), in striking particular; possibly Hall and Speed, and, as I shall argue, very likely Stow (1592).[15] *Henry VIII* is commonly regarded as being more "historical" than is typical of Shakespeare's major history plays. Many passages in it seem versified Holinshed. Yet even a play like *Richard III* is also very close to its chronicle-sources, for instance, in the extensive treatment of Hastings or in Richard's coy acceptance of the crown from the upper gallery; and once we make allowances for Shakespeare's shifting many of More's observations to the mouths of the characters themselves, *Richard III* is nearly as close to its sources as *Henry VIII*. Moreover, the two plays are alike nearly as far from their sources in one important historical respect, chronology. There is not a great deal to choose on grounds of historical accuracy, for example, between the conflation of the deaths of Edward IV (1483), Henry VI (1471), and Clarence (1478) and the resurrection of Margaret of Anjou (d. 1482) in *Richard* and the conflation of the weavers' rebellion against excessive taxation (1525) with Buckingham's execution (1521) and the reversals of Henry's marriage to Anne Boleyn (1533) with Wolsey's fall and death (1528–30), of the birth of Elizabeth I (1533) with the death of Catherine of Aragon (1536), and of the christening of Elizabeth I with Cranmer's narrow escape from commitment to the Tower (1543).[16]

The distinction between *Henry VIII* and Shakespeare's more universally admired history plays is, perhaps, not that it is more historical but that it is less fictional. If we turn again to the example of *Richard III*, we find that the nature of Shakespeare's source in the chronicles correlates suggestively with this difference. The treatment of the characters of *Richard III* in the chronicles Shakespeare used is more fictive than is that of the characters of *Henry VIII*. The former is closer to More's original *Richard* than is the latter to any extra-chronicle, literary source, such as Cavendish's *Life of Wolsey*.

Insofar as Cavendish's *Wolsey* survives in the chronicles, it is less personal and less fictional than the *Life* Cavendish wrote. During the reign of the Tudors, the life of the Cardinal who served as Henry VIII's Lord Chancellor is a more dangerous subject than is the arch-villain and anti-type of Henry Tudor, Richard III. The chroniclers therefore snip and slash Cavendish's work to a much greater extent than they do More's. Their excisions make Cavendish appear disinterested and more purely historical than he is in the original form. Whereas More's authorial interpretation and participation in the *Richard* are largely retained in the chronicles, for example, Cavendish's opinions and, more striking, his own role in the *Wolsey* are largely omitted, even in the 1592 Stow's *Annales,* which more fully and faithfully renders Cavendish's work than does Stow's earlier *Chronicles* of 1580, Holinshed's edition of 1587 (dependent on Stow 1580 for its rendition of Cavendish), or Speed's first edition in 1611 (the only edition of Speed to precede the performance of *Henry VIII* in 1613).

It is not the presence of fact or chronicle-matter in *Henry VIII* but the restraint of the imagination's transforming power that is distinctive. Extravagant dramatic performances like Richard III's wooing or his gallery scene are virtually absent from *Henry VIII,* and the play even lacks a single, clearly focal protagonist. Poetic elaborations—Clarence's dream, for example—which at least distract us from a simple level of historical action and at best modify and enrich its significance, are limited and contained through irony, opposition, or isolation in *Henry VIII*. If given any scope, as in Catherine's dream or Anne's coronation, they are made pathetic or ironic by echoes and juxtaposed events. The relation of their art to truth, an encompassing truth, is called frankly in doubt. In Buckingham's exit and in the divorce trial, we have historical spectacles of power and order with an uncertain relation to justice; in Wolsey's dinner and Henry's masque, we have historical spectacles of pleasure with an uncertain relation to licit possession and licit desire. Aside from such visual and ambiguous effects, the texture of *Henry VIII* is spare in a way reminiscent of that other troubled historical work of the Renaissance, Book V of *The Faerie Queene,* much of whose later cantos consists of straightforward, unelaborated narrative. Indeed, the structure of Spenser's fifth Book, oscillating between moments of romance and parodic realism in the beginning, then between emblem and narrative, ideal age and history toward the end, raises issues of interpretation analogous to those in Shakespeare's play.[17]

The sheer amount of informative recounting by anonymous gentlemen is telling about the nature of *Henry VIII*.[18] Whether we find the gentlemen's exchanges lively and realistic or woodenly artificial, they are plain and pointedly newsy:

1 Gent. Sir,
You must no more call it York-place, that's past;
For since the cardinal fell, that title's lost,
'Tis now the king's, and call'd Whitehall.
3 Gent. I know it;
But 'tis so lately alter'd that the old name
Is fresh about me.
2 Gent. What two reverend bishops
Were those that went on each side of the queen?
3 Gent. Stokesley and Gardiner, the one of Winchester,
Newly preferr'd from the king's secretary;
The other, London.

[IV.i.94–103]

The gentlemen's conversations are objectively, rather than subjectively or imaginatively, referential. Their effect (205 lines of it) is cumulative, and the sharper gossip of the courtiers reinforces it. Norfolk, for example, complains of Wolsey's conduct:

How holily he works in all his business,
And with what zeal! for now he has crack'd the league
Between us and the emperor (the queen's great nephew).

[II.ii.23–25]

Norfolk adds that Wolsey counsels a divorce, and the Lord Chamberlain replies,

Heaven keep me from such counsel: 'tis most true
These news are everywhere, every tongue speaks 'em,
And every true heart weeps for't. All that dare
Look into these affairs see this main end,
The French king's sister.

[II.ii.37–41]

Most characters in *Henry VIII* lack innerness or, like Henry, Wolsey, and Buckingham, have an ambiguous innerness, disjunctive rather than conjunctive with their outer, public roles. In varying degrees, they lack fictional coherence. When a character seems both truly inward and coherent, as Catherine does and as each truly penitent figure could become, then this character is isolated, eliminated, and in short, divorced. The naive and innocent Cranmer may alone conjoin inner and outer realities, but if he escapes elimination he is aided by the ambivalent Henry, and if Cranmer's innerness is true in some sense, it is achieved too easily in the play to be entirely convincing, that is, to be true in dramatic terms. The figure of Cranmer may have coherence, but such coherence seems unreal and *merely* fictional in the context of this play.[19]

Buckingham and Catherine frame the inner circle of the play; Cranmer is outside it. We have seen that Buckingham pits a worldly reality—tangible status, public honor, legal truth—against an inner reality—personal loyalty, integrity, and conscience—when he is executed near the opening of the play. Near its end, Catherine's heavenly vision of figures wearing white and crowned with garlands, who hold a spare garland symbolically over her head, even more radically juxtaposes an otherworldly reality to her worldly one: "Spirits of peace, where are ye? are ye all gone? / And leave me here in wretchedness behind ye?" (IV.ii.83–84). There is poetic recompense for Catherine's wretchedness in the invitation to a banquet given her by the "blessed troop . . . whose bright faces / Cast thousand beams upon" her "like the sun" and promise her "eternal happiness" (87–90); but there is also an ironic recollection of her earlier declaration, "nothing but death / Shall e'er divorce my dignities" (III.i.141–42). Combining poetic recompense and actual divorce, the play gives us cause to wonder whether Catherine's vision is just another anodyne or is true inspiration. In the context of this play, her vision is appealing but is at the very least ambivalent.

Historicity strongly and intimately affects the portrayal of King Henry and Cardinal Wolsey, the two figures who, with Catherine, are the most prominent in the play, or rather, through selection and omission, pacing and emphasis, it is made to affect them and thereby to become an issue in the play, part of the larger issue of truth. Both figures pointedly and tellingly reflect the ambiguities, contradictions, and imperfections of their chronicle sources and in this way are made to look "too human" and "too historical." They are certainly fictional to a considerable extent, talking in blank verse and to the agreed-upon topics, coordinating their concerns and significant gestures closely with those of others in the play, and thoughtfully repeating "divorce," "conscience," "truth," but making sure they do so in varied but purposeful ways. Fictional as Henry and Wolsey may be, however, they are neither idealized enough nor coherent enough to satisfy our expectations of art. They are too true.

We have already seen much of the ambivalence and indeed the incoherence of Henry's conscience: his responsibility in and motives for divorce, his attitude toward Catherine, and his awareness of himself. As Madeleine Doran has noted, the "fundamental moral ambiguity" of Henry in the divorce is inherent in the chronicles as well.[20] But instead of taking this ambiguity "over into the play without examination," Shakespeare turns a spotlight on it, highlighting it artificially and examining it. He emphasizes it not only in verbal and thematic ways but also by structuring Henry's appearances in seriatim fashion. We get a number of different shots of Henry—being gracious to Catherine, judging Buckingham, falling into love at the mere touch of Anne's fair hand, bemoaning his tender conscience, speaking with love and high praise of Catherine in the courtroom, expressing his eagerness to preserve this marriage, if legal, and seconds later expressing his hope of dissolving it; discovering Wolsey's deceptions, saving Cranmer—but the procession from one of these shots to the next is usually sudden, surprising, and *non*-persuasive. Moreover, we view Henry's changes from the outside and, in this sense, objectively. With one possible exception and that unlikely—the address beginning "O my lord" and proceeding to "conscience, conscience; / O 'tis a tender place" (II.ii.140–43)—even Henry's references to conscience are made to others and most of them in a well-witnessed courtroom. If Henry grows in stature, we do not see it happen. The changes he undergoes are credible *as facts* on stage, but their true meaning is ambivalence.

Although the immediacy of Henry's concern with conscience subsides after the divorce, his ambiguity persists, most insistently as the result of Catherine's affecting presence in the play. In addition to Catherine and to passing ironic reflections on Henry's conscientious choice of Anne as wife and More as Chancellor, however, we still have to reckon with Henry's promotion of the notorious Stephen Gardiner to Bishop of Winchester (IV.i.101–02) and his royal sulk upon learning that Anne's child, the Princess Elizabeth, is a girl.[21] The Old Lady who brings Henry the good tidings of the Princess' birth expects an ample reward and is indignant at what she gets: "An hundred marks? By this light, I'll ha' more. . . . Said I for this the girl was like to him?" (V.i.171, 174). Her sense of personal offense is amusing in context, but Henry's attitude to the birth is ominous and is the more so for being expressed indirectly in his failure fully to acknowledge and generously to reward the news of it. Such indirection causes additional concern for the King's self-awareness. Even at the end of the play, Henry's interceding for Cranmer and for a justice that lies outside mere law is unlikely to make an audience easy. The higher justice Henry institutes exists essentially in the royal conscience and is only as reliable as we have found that conscience to be in the play.

Henry is at once too much a king and too imperfect a man in this drama; he is too much and too little a figurehead. Had he been more purely a symbol or more simply a fact or had he been either more imperfect or less so, his figure would not have been so uncompromisingly problematical. In a real, historical sense, Henry is credible; indeed, he is close enough to his chronicle-sources that he almost has to be. Yet a truly historical Henry is not quite credible in art, and the author of *Henry VIII* is at pains not merely to show us this fact but also to probe its meaning.

Starting to discuss Cavendish's *Life of Wolsey*, I remarked the extent to which it is characterized by ambiguity and irony, developing understanding, mixed motives, changing roles, and even some inconsistency of attitude, perhaps the unavoidable result of Cavendish's avowed effort to present a complex and self-contradictory life "accordyng to the trouthe." Cavendish's *Life of Wolsey* is at the heart of the treatment of Wolsey in *Henry VIII*, and to a greater extent than is usually recognized, Shakespeare's treatment of Wolsey is a conceptual paradigm of the play's ambiguity and fundamental ambivalence. If Buckingham and Catherine frame the inner circle of the play, the figure of Wolsey encapsulates the problem at its center. Although he himself disappears from stage at the end of Act III, nearly one-third of Act IV is devoted to discussion of him.

There is no evidence that Shakespeare knew Cavendish's *Wolsey* directly. It is usually assumed that whatever Shakespeare had of Cavendish's work he found in Holinshed's second edition, 1587, which in turn depends closely on Stow's *Chronicles* of 1580 for what it includes of Cavendish. Even in the "sparse pages" of Stow's 1580 edition, however, it is worth noting that "the *Life of Wolsey* stands out like a series of purple patches," and Stow's 1592 edition includes considerably more of Cavendish's *Wolsey*, a borrowing Paul L. Wiley has described this way: "by thus clearing a wide place for the insertion of what amounted to a separate biographical sketch of the cardinal . . . [Stow] set a fashion which many Renaissance historians were to follow." Its effect "was to make Wolsey the most prominent figure in the period of Henry VIII and to contribute to history a new brief biography or 'character.' "[22]

Stow's rendition of Cavendish in the 1592 edition differs significantly from the second edition of Holinshed, and Shakespeare's knowledge of it would illuminate both the historicity and the ambivalence of *Henry VIII*. The most important difference between Stow 1592 and Holinshed 1587 is that the former preserves more faithfully the essential ambiguity of Wolsey's awareness that we find so forcefully present in Cavendish. In fact nearly all the passages I used earlier in this book to demonstrate the ambiguity of Wolsey's awareness are preserved, almost verbatim, in Stow, 1592.[23] In comparison, there are just hints of this ambiguity in Holinshed.

While Stow did excise portions of Cavendish's work, his excisions do not seriously affect the bearing of his history on *Henry VIII*. Presumably his motive for the excisions was political-religious. Although Stow acknowledges "Georgius Cauandish" in his table of authors in 1592 and clearly had access to a manuscript of Cavendish's *Wolsey*, he does not acknowledge Cavendish as its author in the body of the work and, as earlier noted, greatly depersonalizes the *Wolsey*, excising Cavendish's own role amost completely, deleting many of his opinions, and omitting or replacing most of his first-person pronouns.[24] Stow removes Cavendish's generally unflattering references to Anne Boleyn (mother of the Queen ruling England in 1592) and Cavendish's ironic glances at Thomas Cromwell. He also deletes passages in Cavendish critical of the Protestant position, though he does not suppress such a passage touching Henry Tudor as Wolsey's sharp reminder to the King: "howbeit shew his highnes from me, that I most humbly desire his maiestie to cal to his most gratious remembrance, that there is both a heaven and hell."[25] A more ambivalent and relatively more sympathetic Wolsey, it should be noted, requires a more ambivalent and puzzling portrayal of Henry VIII, such as we find in Cavendish's *Wolsey* and to a considerable extent in Stow.

In the absence of a Tudor printing of Cavendish's *Wolsey*, the undoubted influence of this work on *Henry VIII* would ordinarily suggest Shakespeare's knowledge of Stow, whose 1592 version of the *Wolsey* was the fullest in print available to Shakespeare; but many of Shakespeare's borrowings—the more striking ones often among them—occur in both editions of Stow and are copied from Stow's earlier edition by Holinshed 1587. Since there is no question of Shakespeare's familiarity with Holinshed's second edition, these borrowings are therefore usually taken to show another instance of it. The logic of this conclusion is more economical than necessary, but even allowing it, we find strong indications in Shakespeare's treatment of Cromwell's interview with Wolsey after the latter's fall that Shakespeare knew Stow's edition of 1592.

Cromwell, Wolsey's servant, finds Wolsey alone right after Wolsey's famous soliloquy, "Farewell? a long farewell to all my greatness" (III.ii.351). His interview with Wolsey provides the culminating scene of the Cardinal's career. Cromwell is the one figure in the play who directly offers Wolsey comfort and loyalty, in effect playing part of Cavendish's role, as well as most of his own, as we find these roles in *The Life of Wolsey*. Eventually, at Wolsey's own request, Cromwell reluctantly takes leave of the Cardinal's service to enter the King's but leaves with the tearful promise of continued devotion to his old master and with the Cardinal's tearful blessing and designation of him as his best student. Wolsey tells Cromwell, "where no mention / Of me more must be heard of, say I taught thee," and he continues, "Say Wolsey . . . Found thee a way (out of his wrack) to rise in, / A sure and safe one, though thy master miss'd it" (III.ii.433–38).

Annotating this interview, Foakes concludes that "Cromwell's faithful attentions here are expanded from . . . [a] mere hint in Holinshed."[26] In toto, this hint reads, "But at this time diuerse of his seruants departed from him to the kings seruice, and in especiall Thomas Crumwell one of his chiefe counsell, and chiefe dooer for him in the suppression of abbeies" (913). Foakes also remarks the appropriateness to the full interview of Cavendish's stronger observation that Cromwell "was estymed to be the most faythefullest seruaunt to his master of all other" but adds that Cavendish's observation was not taken over into the chronicles and consequently dismisses it.[27]

As a matter of fact, Cavendish's observation and other relevant passages surrounding it were taken over into Stow's 1592 edition. Stow prints this observation and its immediate context as follows: "Insomuch that there was nothing alledged against my L[ord] but that he [Cromwell] was ready to make answer therto: Insomuch that at the length his honest estimation, and earnest behauour in his masters cause, grew so in euerie mans opinion, how that he was the most faithfull seruant to his master of all other, wherein hee was greatly of all men commended" (927). A few pages later, Stow enforces this point: Cromwell "was had in great estimation for his behauior therein, and also for the true and faithfull demeanor towards his lord and master."[28]

The tearful scene of farewell between Wolsey and his servant, and the closeness of their relationship in the play also have their origin in Stow, who in his turn found them in Cavendish.[29] Stow describes Wolsey's farewell to his faithful servants: "beholding the goodly number of his seruants, . . . [he] could not speak vnto them vntill the teares ran downe his cheekes, which fewe teares perceiued by his seruants, caused the fountaines of water to gush out of their faithfull eies in such sort, as it would cause a cruell hart to lament" (924). Regretting the past and his present inability to reward his servants as they deserve, Stow's Wolsey vows, "I will neuer during my life, [again] esteeme the goods of [*sic*] riches of this world any otherwise" than as reasonable necessities (924). Like Cavendish's, Stow's Wolsey turns surprisingly moral in the face of his faithful servants, and Shakespeare's Wolsey does so too: "Cromwell, I charge thee, fling away ambition" (III.ii.440). In Stow, Cromwell leaves Wolsey more willingly than in Shakespeare, where he has virtually to be ordered away ("Go get thee from me Cromwell, / I am a poor fall'n man": III.ii. 412–13), but the suggestions for Cromwell's devotion in Shakespeare are unmistakably present in the *Annales*:

> some [servants of Wolsey] determined to go to their friends, and some would not depart from my lord, until they might see him in better estate. My lord returned into his chamber lamenting the departure from his servants, making his mone to master *Cromwell*, who comforted him the best he could. [925]

Cromwell next asks Wolsey's permission to go to London, "wheras he would either make or marre" his own fortune; he then communes a while in secret with Wolsey and departs promising faithfully, "yee shall heare shortly of me, and if I speede well, I will not faile to be heare againe within these two daies" (925).

In Cavendish and Stow, as in Shakespeare, Cromwell is Wolsey's best student, who, on Wolsey's advice, finds "a way (out of his wrack) to rise in," albeit in the two earlier works the course in which Wolsey's student excels is distinguished less by morality and more by worldly profit than in Shakespeare. In both the earlier works, Wolsey coaches Cromwell on how to answer the charges brought against the Cardinal in Parliament, and these very answers are what initially bring Cromwell the commendation of all men and identify him as a paragon of fidelity.[30] Later, Wolsey and Cromwell put their heads together in a scheme, to the success of which their cooperation is necessary, to advance Cromwell's fortunes in order not only that he might be in a better financial and political position but also in a better position to help his old master, Wolsey. By prior arrangement with Wolsey, Cromwell becomes the means of solicitation to him for those whose fees and annuities, granted by the King out of Wolsey's attached revenues, had for legal reasons to be confirmed by Wolsey in order to be considered truly binding.[31] In such ways, while remaining conspicuously loyal to Wolsey, Cromwell quite literally finds the way to rise out of Wolsey's ruin. If Shakespeare found Cromwell's closeness and loyalty to Wolsey in Stow, as is likely, it is conceivable that he found there as well the suggestion for Wolsey's teaching of Cromwell and transposed onto it the increasingly moral awareness which, in Cavendish and Stow, Wolsey develops more gradually and fitfully. Dramatic form, after all, demands compression and sharpness of impact.

A newsy interruption in Stow's version of Cavendish's account of the support given Wolsey by Cromwell soon after the Cardinal's fall also has a curious parallel in Shakespeare. Early in the interview between Cromwell and Wolsey, the Cardinal assures his anxious servant that he is happier in his fall and newly quiet conscience than ever before and that he is inwardly stronger

> (Out of a fortitude of soul I feel)
> To endure more miseries, and greater far
> Than my weak-hearted enemies dare offer.
> What news abroad?
>
> [III.ii.388–91]

Wolsey's final question comes abruptly and indicates a decidedly ambiguous shift in his attention. Wolsey suddenly changes the subject, perhaps to display his new-found fortitude, but certainly the effect of his question is also to express his real interest in the larger world outside him—he does care still about it. Cromwell, ever solicitous of the Cardinal in this scene, reports first that the worst news abroad is Wolsey's own disfavor with the King; "The next is, that Sir Thomas More is chose / Lord Chancellor in your place" (III.ii.393–94). Cromwell then adds that Cranmer has been installed as Archbishop of Canterbury and that Henry has already married Anne Boleyn.

Cromwell's news bulletin in the play goes back in a circuitous way to Cavendish. In the midst of recounting Cromwell's assistance to the fallen Wolsey, Cavendish digressively relates a prophecy concerning a cow and a bull told him by Wolsey, which Cavendish later realizes must signify the marriage of Henry and Anne Boleyn (the cow being one of the King's beasts pertaining to his Earldom of Richmond and the bull being in the "Bullen" coat of arms).[32] Stow excises Cavendish's digression, doubtless because of its personal, anecdotal nature and its uncomplimentary reference to Anne Boleyn. But instead of sewing either side of the excised digression together, as he might perfectly well have done, Stow, the conscientious antiquarian, replaces the excision with a substitute. Simply announcing that this is a good place to speak briefly of other matters, Stow reports that at this time peace was made between the Emperor and the King of England, that Thomas More was made Chancellor, that Tyndale's English New Testament was conveyed into England (1530), that ambassadors had been sent to the Emperor and the Pope, but that suit to Rome had been forbidden because of Rome's procrastination in Henry's divorce, Henry's displeasure at reports of him made to Rome, and the urging of Henry's counselors that he follow the German example and break with Rome (931–33).

While not wishing to press the parallel too far, I should suggest that —excluding Cromwell's reference to Wolsey's own fall, a remark generated directly by the relationship of the two characters in the play—there is a notable similarity between the news Cromwell reports to Wolsey in the play and the news recorded briefly by Stow in the midst of his account of the mutual concerns of Cromwell and Wolsey. More's Chancellorship is obviously the same in both reports. For the religious and marital concerns (Pope, Tyndale, divorce, Germany) contemporary with Wolsey's fall, the playwright substitutes the later and more crucial events to which that fall is relevant, namely, Henry's marriage to Anne and elevation of Cranmer, a major architect of that marriage. These later events, of course, could not have been found in Stow or in any other chronicle treating a period prior to Wolsey's death in 1530, since Cranmer was elevated to Archbishop of Canterbury in 1533, the same year Henry married Anne. By virtue of his poetic or, rather, his chronological license, Shakespeare offers a news flash that is at once fuller of significance and briefer than Stow's, yet it is more than possible that his timing and conception are here inspired by what he found in Stow's *Annales*.

A final modification of actual history (or biography) that Stow, again following Cavendish, invites is Shakespeare's transposition of Wolsey's most famous lines from his deathbed to his final appearance after his fall from favor, where he laments,

> Had I but serv'd my God with half the zeal
> I serv'd my king, he would not in mine age
> Have left me naked to mine enemies.
>
> [III.ii.455–57]

In Cavendish and in all the pertinent chronicles, which here derive from his work, the same lines come in variant but unmistakably similar forms only with Wolsey's death, for example, in Stow: "but if I had serued God as diligently as I haue done the king, hee woulde not haue giuen mee ouer in my graie haires."[33] Previously in Stow, however, on the same page that tells us Cromwell was esteemed "the most faithfull seruant to his master of all other" and therein "greatly of all men commended," Wolsey speaks to the King's emissaries as follows:

thus much you may saie to his highesse, that I am wholie under his obeysance and will, and doo submit my selfe to al things that shall bee his princelie pleasure, whose will and commaundement I neuer disobeyed or repugned, *but was alwaies contented, and glade to please him before God, whom I ought most chiefely to haue obeyed*, the which nowe mee repents: notwithstanding, . . . I do and will during my life, pray to God to sende him much prosperous honor and victory ouer his enimies.[34]

Here is much the same regret, still divided loyalty, and ambiguity present more poignantly in Wolsey's dying words. While not presenting Wolsey's death on stage, Shakespeare transposes the words spoken shortly before it to an earlier stage in Wolsey's fall, where it is in a sense—and a source—already present.

One other incident in Wolsey's fall seems curiously to relate the play to Cavendish's *Wolsey* but without Stow's *Annales* as an intermediary. In *Henry VIII*, just before Wolsey is left to himself and then to Cromwell's company, he is taunted for his faults by the noblemen in Henry's court. Eventually the Lord Chamberlain breaks into their taunts to caution them, "Press not a falling man too far; 'tis virtue." He adds that laws, not private malice, should deal with Wolsey's transgressions and adds, "My heart weeps to see him / So little of his great self." Wolsey's chief reviler answers, "I forgive him" (III.ii. 332–36). In a portion of *The Life of Wolsey* that Stow excises, Cavendish reports the deliberations of the King's Council on Wolsey's request, delivered by his emissary Cromwell, for funds adequate to retire to his benefice of York. The Councilors are at odds over the request, but some argue that it would be "a great slaunder . . . to the kyng and his hole councell to se hyme want that latly had so myche/ and nowe so lyttill" (130–31). One of the Councilors even offers his own plate as a pledge to raise the funds for Wolsey and warns, "lett vs do to hyme as we wold be don vnto consideryng his small offence and his [formerly] in estymable Substaunce . . . lett not malice cloke thys matter wherby that pitie and mercy may take no place/ ye haue all your pleasures fulfillyd whiche ye haue long desired/ And nowe suffer concyence to mynester vnto hyme some liberalitie" (131). The relevance of this passage to the themes of forgiveness and growth of conscience in *Henry VIII* is conspicuous. Unfortunately, however, Stow fails to include the passage in his *Annales*, presumably because other parts of it are highly critical of the King's Council and of royal justice.

Yet it is conceivable, given the more sympathetic picture of the fallen Wolsey that Stow finds in Cavendish and alone of contemporary chroniclers prints, that Shakespeare might have been inspired by Stow to invent the Chamberlain's charitable reflections without benefit of the excised passage. In other words, I should hesitate to argue without additional evidence that Shakespeare knew Cavendish's work directly, and in fact the absence from the play of Cavendish's occasionally ironic attitude toward Cromwell suggests he did not know it. Equally significant respecting Shakespeare's probable sources, moreover, is the fact that this irony is carefully removed by Stow from Cavendish's account of Cromwell.

Summarizing this discussion of Shakespeare and Stow, I find it most unlikely in the presence of an accessible, a familiar, and a pointedly relevant source that Shakespeare should have invented virtually out of thin air the singular importance of Cromwell to Wolsey, the close nature of their relationship, and the rather tearful circumstances of their farewell. In view of these similarities, the coincidence of the "news abroad" that Shakespeare's Cromwell gives Wolsey and Stow's interrupting his running account of Cromwell and Wolsey with a comparable news bulletin is notable, as is Shakespeare's transposition of Wolsey's dying words to an earlier context, which Stow makes inviting. Returning now to *Henry VIII* and specifically to Wolsey's role in the play, I am assuming that Stow's true or at least "historical" Wolsey, a figure essentially ambiguous rather than merely corrupt, was most likely crucial for Shakespeare's conception of him.[35]

Wolsey's and Henry's roles in the play are complementary. Like Henry, Wolsey is a little too human and too historical—too true—to satisfy the expectations of purity of conception and coherence that we bring to dramatic art. His figure, too, realizes a moral ambiguity present in the chronicles, including Holinshed, but most clearly and provocatively present in Stow. Again like Henry's, Wolsey's role in and attitude toward the divorce is strongly ambivalent in both the play and its sources, and when he exits from stage, we cannot quite get him to cooperate with our interpretative categories—quite to fit either symbol or human sufferer, villain or victim, arch-tempter or scapegoat. Wolsey's figure refuses to be either credibly great or credibly monstrous. As a result, his exit does not wash clean the sins—and still less the ambiguities—of Henry's world.

Wolsey's figure is in some ways distinct from Henry's, as well as similar to it. His appearances do not seem to occur in so disjointed a fashion because his presence until the final acts of the play is pervasive even in his absence from the stage, because his character is until his fall more externalized even than Henry's, and because his actions are for the most part required by his official posts as Chancellor, chief counselor, and Cardinal-legate. Wolsey usually operates in another's business in the play, albeit with a constant eye to his own advantage. It is not his conscience but the King's that is thrust to the foreground early in the play, and it is Wolsey's power, not his morality, that really sets the hornets' nest of Henry's courtiers buzzing. To a considerable extent Wolsey is just a leading political functionary, at worst an ambitious schemer and at best an officious administrator.

Perhaps to a greater extent, however, the odd combination of pervasiveness and externality in Wolsey's role has an opposite effect. Wolsey seems more mysterious than Henry VIII, whose conscience gives us more than one irreverent pause. Until quite suddenly at the end of his career, Wolsey seems to have almost no inside at all. Aside from his conspicuous, externalized ambition, until his last scene Wolsey seems wholly oriented to the world outside him. Buckingham and Norfolk, hardly trustworthy witnesses in this case, imply contemptuously that Wolsey's lowly beginnings might be responsible for his ambition, but its source fails to engage the playwright's interest—a situation opposite to that in *Richard III*, where the playwright probes the connection between Richard's own contempt for his deformity and his ambition for power. Yet the reality of Wolsey's power, attested as much by the courtiers' outraged, fearful, envious obsession with it as by Henry's reliance on Wolsey, suggests what a Tudor-Stuart writer might have called a subtler or deeper nature. For all the externality of Henry's conscience, for all the publicity of his private scruples and the incoherence of his behavior, we see him for the most part head-on, acting openly on stage. Wolsey, however, we see more often and more crucially through a maze of gossip, speculation, and innuendo. This maze of mediation contributes essentially to the ambiguity of the Cardinal's figure.

Wolsey is touched by ambiguity from the outset of the play. The ambiguity is minimal at first but develops and grows more difficult to resolve neatly as the play continues. In the first scene of the play our initial impression of Wolsey is filled with silence and significant looks as he makes his way past Buckingham and other noblemen to the King; we see him next in scene ii with the King and Queen, doing his best to wriggle out of responsibility for excessive taxes levied in the King's name and presenting for the King's examination the key witness against Buckingham. We hear a great deal about the Cardinal from his enemies before he ever speaks on stage: his arranging the Field of the Cloth of Gold, his ambition, pride, poor judgment, failure to value the nobility, his greed, malice, potency, and vengeance. Nearly the whole of scene i is fixed on the Cardinal, and while the lively tone of the discussants—Buckingham, Norfolk, Abergavenny—both catches and demands our attention, it is hardly temperate or disinterested. At the first mention of the Cardinal's name, Buckingham bursts out, "The devil speed him: no man's pie is freed / From his ambitious finger" (I.i.52–53). Referring disdainfully to the Field of the Cloth of Gold, Buckingham asks with rhetorical scorn, "What had he [Wolsey] / To do in these fierce vanities?" He continues without pause,

> I wonder
> That such a keech can with his very bulk
> Take up the rays o'th'beneficial sun,
> And keep it from the earth.
>
> [I.i.54–57]

Norfolk, having caught the scent of scorn, rejoins,

> There's in him stuff that puts him to these ends;
> For being not propp'd by ancestry, whose grace

> Chalks successors their way, nor call'd upon
> For high feats done to th'crown, neither allied
> To eminent assistants, but spider-like,
> Out of his self-drawing web. . . .
>
> [I.i.58–63]

No audience is likely to trust these overheated descriptions of Wolsey entirely, and however crafty and conniving Wolsey's behavior in the next scene is, he fails to live up to them. He is a little too petty, too reasonable, and too credible in scene ii, and he disappoints any hopes we might cherish of seeing Satan in scarlet clericals.

Critical history indicates that the noblemen's complaints do have an impact, however, one that can lead to exaggeration of Wolsey's part in condemning Buckingham in the next scene. That part is actually slight and too easily rationalized to suggest convincingly that Wolsey wishes to delude the King about Buckingham's intentions. During the Surveyor's testimony Wolsey twice interrupts him officiously, but it is the King himself who skillfully questions the Surveyor—"What was that Henton . . . How know'st thou this?"—and repeatedly urges him to "Speak on," "Go forward," and "Proceed" (I.ii.148, 150, 143, 177, 188).

The Surveyor triggers Wolsey's first interruption when he testifies that Buckingham not only had designs on the throne but also had vengeful intentions toward the Cardinal—intentions an audience might well credit after listening to Buckingham's wrath in scene i. Wolsey's interruption at this moment is about as deft as what we might expect from a Polonius. "Please your highness note / This dangerous conception in this point," he explains superfluously and then gets to what is really bothering him, namely, that Buckingham's malignant will, as he puts it, "stretches / Beyond you to your friends" (I.ii.138–42). Catherine rebukes Wolsey's uncharitable and obvious self-interest, and he falls silent until nearly the end of the Surveyor's testimony, when the latter claims that Buckingham had threatened to kill the King if the King tried to send him to the Tower. With righteous concern, Wolsey asks the Queen, "Now madam, may his highness live in freedom, / And this man out of prison?" (I.ii.200–01).

Before going beyond recognition of a triumphant note in Wolsey's righteousness, we ought to consider what Wolsey should have done if he had indeed uncovered rather than inspired the Surveyor's allegations. To ignore or to conceal them from Henry would have been treasonous. Bringing them to Henry's attention is safe, convenient, and ostensibly just. Henry leaves Buckingham to the laws and to the legal judgment of his peers, among them notably Norfolk, Buckingham's companion in scene i and historically lord high steward for Buckingham's trial; and Buckingham's peers condemn him for treason.[36] Of course the distinct possibility exists that Wolsey has bribed Buckingham's disaffected Surveyor to talk; this certainly is Buckingham's view, but we have only Buckingham's word for its validity—the word of a rash man whose seeming prescience about the source and nature of the charges against him is itself disturbing: "My surveyor is false," he suddenly realizes and quickly adds, "the o'er-great cardinal / Hath show'd him gold" (I.i.222–23). Moreover, as Lee Bliss has observed, we never learn whether Buckingham thinks Wolsey's gold has led the Surveyor to reveal "harmful truths" or to "fabricate lies" about him.[37] When the Surveyor is examined in the next scene, we may want to think that Wolsey is coaching him and thereby deceiving the King, but if we actually *see* any deception, we see the King deceiving himself.

The eagerness—which I share—to find something heroically wicked in Wolsey's first appearance tends to make us concentrate on Wolsey's part in examining the Surveyor rather than on his part in the less exciting business of taxation, which immediately precedes the Surveyor's testimony. Catherine's charges against Wolsey concerning the taxation are well informed, substantiated, and persuasive:

> The subjects' grief
> Comes through commissions, which compels from each
> The sixth part of his substance, to be levied
> Without delay; and the pretence for this
> Is nam'd your wars in France. . . .
>
> [I.ii.55–60]

She cuts easily through Wolsey's equivocation regarding his part in these exactions, commenting, for example, on his role in the King's Council:

> No, my lord,
> You know no more than others; but you frame
> Things that are known alike, which are not wholesome
> To those which would not know them, and yet must
> Perforce be their acquaintance.
>
> [I.ii.43–47]

Wolsey's demeanor in the face of Catherine's accusations is conspicuously guilty, as it is not when Catherine rebukes his lack of charity in responding to the Surveyor's testimony and he simply falls silent. Here he squirms, equivocates, and speaks a blue streak of irrelevant but resonant generalizations:

> If we shall stand still,
> In fear our motion will be mock'd or carp'd at,
> We should take root here, where we sit;
> Or sit state-statues only.
>
> [I.ii.85–88]

It is amazing at times how much Wolsey shares with Polonius.

Wolsey's words to Gardiner at the end of the taxation incident cap our impression of him in it. The King has revoked the excessive taxes, which the people had loudly laid to Wolsey's charge. Wolsey therefore whispers to Gardiner that in addition to publicizing the King's revocation and general pardon he should let it be known, untruly, that both come through Wolsey's intercession with the King (I.ii.102–08). Wolsey's aside to Gardiner is the worst we get from him in the whole scene. It is unambiguously corrupt, but it is also disappointingly petty—routinely historical, if you will.

First the noblemen's violent criticisms of Wolsey in scene i invite our expectations of evil on a grand scale, and then, at the very end of this scene, we anticipate the outcome of Buckingham's dramatic arrest. The placing of the Surveyor's testimony about Buckingham after the duller business of taxation ensures our hurrying over the earlier incident to concentrate on the later one, which seems at once more urgent and more intriguing and in which Wolsey's part is more ambiguous. Significantly, the play does not attribute this *sequence* of incidents to Wolsey's machination; he is unprepared for Catherine's introducing the issue of taxation and fumbles in the face of it. Rather, the playwright stages a sequence of incidents calculated to make our assessment of the wicked Wolsey more realistic, to diminish his legendary stature and to increase his human, historical one. That Wolsey is corrupt at the beginning of the play is not surprising; what is surprising is that he is not more simply and monstrously so.

After Wolsey's first full scene, the ambiguity of his figure increases, until it is realized dramatically in the central divorce scenes: the trial itself and Wolsey's subsequent interview with Catherine. After the Surveyor's examination, for example, we see the Cardinal next as the genial, solicitous host of the banquet at which King Henry is smitten—to Wolsey's ultimate confusion—by love for Anne Boleyn. We also hear more street rumors and court gossip about Wolsey and increasingly about his responsibility for Henry's seeking a divorce. We see Cardinals Wolsey and Campeggio come to Henry at night to arrange the divorce proceedings but wonder why in the play it should be Wolsey who tells the King,

> I know your majesty has always lov'd her [Catherine]
> So dear in heart, not to deny her that
> A woman of less place might ask by law,
> Scholars allow'd freely to argue for her.
>
> [II.ii.109–12]

We then see another instance of collusion between Wolsey and Gardiner, the latter now the King's secretary but ready to assist his old patron, Wolsey, at the latter's command.

At the divorce trial itself, Catherine vehemently accuses Wolsey of being her most malicious foe and of having "blown this coal" between her and Henry (II.iv.77). Wolsey denies his responsibility and later calls upon the

King to declare whether he initially broached or later encouraged the possibility of divorce or ever spoke against the Queen's estate or person (II.iv.141–53). "My lord cardinal," the King replies, "I do excuse you; yea, upon mine honour / I free you from" this charge, and he adds more emphatically a few lines later,

> y'are excus'd:
> But will you be more justified? you ever
> Have wish'd the sleeping of this business, never desir'd
> It to be stirr'd, but oft have hinder'd, oft
> The passages made toward it; on my honour,
> I speak my good lord card'nal to this point,
> And thus far clear him.
>
> [II.iv.159–65]

The King's utter clarity on this point, to which Shakespeare's sources likewise attest, increases the Cardinal's ambiguity still further.[38]

In the interview of Catherine by the two Cardinals after the divorce hearing, it is difficult to fault Wolsey for anything he says.[39] With Campeggio, he professes to be a peacemaker and a friend to the Queen, ready to do his best to help her. Until her passion dissipates at the end of the scene, the Queen is forceful, but considered dispassionately, she is also haughty, suspicious, and sharp-tongued with her visitors. Her position—"nothing but death / Shall e'er divorce my dignities"—is historically hopeless, and in view at once of this fact and of her integrity, we sympathize with her. We admire her strength of spirit and principle in the face of her own realistic appraisal of her position, and probably we share some of her suspicion that the Cardinals mean her no good.[40]

But many readers, while sympathetic to Catherine, also notice the difference between her control in the trial scene and in this interview, between her dignified vehemence there and her bitter sarcasm here. Her anger at the Cardinals persistently seems excessive, its object not *clearly* justifiable. We remember Henry's emphatic denial of Wolsey's responsibility for the divorce only a short space before, and we may even remember Catherine's intervention for Buckingham in Act I and wonder for a complicating and unwelcome moment whether the spirited Queen has ever shared anything of Buckingham's contempt and hatred for the ignoble Cardinal and whether in the context of *Henry VIII* we can rely wholly even on her word.

As a result of the divorce trial and the interview of Wolsey with Catherine, we might begin to entertain the possibility that Wolsey has a shred of altruism in him and that his elusive motives have a firmer center than expediency and ambition. Just as we do, however, King Henry reveals his discovery that Wolsey is now secretly advising the Pope to postpone action on the divorce and has given as his reason not moral opposition to the divorce or friendship to Catherine but opposition to the King's marrying Anne Boleyn.

If this discovery were not disorienting enough at this point, Wolsey then complicates his contrary proceedings in the divorce some more. In an aside he shows that he objects to Anne because she is "A spleeny Lutheran, and not wholesome to / Our cause" and because her station in life is insufficiently elevated: "The late queen's gentlewoman? a knight's daughter / To be her mistress' mistress? the queen's queen?" (III.ii.99–100, 94–95). He objects, in other words, because Anne is a threat to influence and an affront to power—Henry's and England's to an extent, perhaps, but more obviously Wolsey's own.

Political opportunism is an expression rather than a cause; it is an external and a centrifugal dissipation of human character. As before Wolsey's fall in the chronicles, so in the play we still find no inner, emotional, or moral center to hold Wolsey's contrary proceedings and contradictory attitudes together. Contrariety—the principle, as it were, of opportunism—can satisfy our artistic expectations as the center of an allegorical abstraction like Spenser's Ate, who is so contrary that she not only thinks and talks but also walks in two different directions at once, but it frustrates them as the center of a dramatic character, often present on stage and as often discussed. As the center of a dramatic character, contrariety is ambiguity, inconsistency, and perhaps even incredibility. The figure of Wolsey found in the chronicles can elicit a similar frustration, and Cavendish's impulse to pattern, to structure, and to fictionalize Wolsey's life testifies yet more directly to the riddle of its meaning, which Cavendish finally resolves in terms of his own.

Even if Stow had not almost excluded from the *Annales* Cavendish's personal role in Wolsey's *Life,* Shakespeare's dramatic medium would have excluded Cavendish as authorial commentator and interpreter, as it had earlier excluded More's authorial voice from *Richard III.* In the text of *Henry VIII,* the first approach to a resolution of Wolsey's ambiguity, or doubleness, that is in any way analogous to Cavendish's comes in Wolsey's sudden change when he is left alone on stage after Henry's exposure of him and thereafter joined only by Cromwell. Suddenly Wolsey develops an inside and in fact a conscience: in Wolsey's own words, "A still and quiet" one (III.ii.380). Wolsey's change is moving, not to say startling, and the strength of its expression goes far to make it persuasive. Yet the Cardinal's last scene is not entirely unambiguous in itself and is still less so in relation to the rest of the play. Ordinarily we think conscience an opposite of opportunism, but in the world of Henry VIII the truth of such a proposition is no longer quite so clear.

Wolsey's mood progresses swiftly in the soliloquy that precedes Cromwell's entrance, from a long farewell to his greatness, to reflections on the general instability of the human condition ("The third day comes . . . a killing frost"), and then to a more personal realization of his own littleness, foolishness, and presumption:

I have ventur'd
Like little wanton boys that swim on bladders,
This many summers in a sea of glory,
But far beyond my depth: my high-blown pride
At length broke under me. . . .

[III.ii.358–62]

From this realization Wolsey plunges to a revulsion from his former life and rises again in renewal: "Vain pomp and glory of this world, I hate ye; / I feel my heart new open'd" (365–66). Like Henry VIII's metamorphoses, Wolsey's sudden renewal is *in itself* a credible conversion, but what has it to do with the Wolsey who preceded it; what has prepared for it? Upon consideration, however, Wolsey's conversion is hardly more sudden than what begins unmistakably to happen to the Cardinal the moment he falls from favor in Cavendish's account of him and in the account of Stow that derives from it. In the play, Wolsey's conversion is more complete and self-conscious, but given the demands of dramatic compression and of direct rather than indirect or narrative characterization, his conversion is also "true" to the best contemporary historical account of Wolsey. In being so it forces our questions about the incredibility of historical life and the credibility of good fiction.

After Wolsey's soliloquy Cromwell enters and hears from Wolsey that the Cardinal is

Never so truly happy, my good Cromwell;
I know myself now, and I feel within me
A peace above all earthly dignities,
A still and quiet conscience. The King has cur'd me,
I humbly thank his grace. . . .

[III.ii.377–81]

Like Wolsey's hairshirt in Cavendish and Stow (but not in Holinshed), this is almost too good to be true, and we could take Cromwell's response to it—"I am glad your grace has made that right use of it"—as the ultimate in ironic restraint as easily as we could take it to be dumbfounded admiration. Perhaps if King Henry were more of a white knight or conquering hero in the play, Wolsey's gratitude to him would not sound so specious. Or if Catherine's words—"nothing but death / Shall e'er divorce my dignities"—did not still echo in the play, perhaps we should not find the divorce of dignities Wolsey so readily accepts a little too easy. Yet Wolsey's acceptance is only a little too easy: as the rest of the scene shows, half of him means what he says here to Cromwell, while half of him still does not. Even a penitent Wolsey remains ambivalent.

Wolsey speaks a few more lines in the hairshirt tradition before his attention shifts back to the external world even more suddenly than it converged on his conscience: "What news abroad?" (391). Wolsey's next long speech follows immediately on Cromwell's telling him that Henry is already married to Anne Boleyn and expresses his realization that his earthly dignities are now really and irrevocably gone: "all my glories / In that one woman I have lost for ever" (408–09). By the tone of this speech we can measure the ambiguity, the *half*-heartedness, of the renunciation that went before and, incidentally, prepared for this one. The speech moves quickly and naturally from realization—"There was the weight that pull'd me down. O Cromwell, / The King has gone beyond me"—to regret:

> No sun shall ever usher forth mine honours,
> Or gild again the noble troops that waited
> Upon my smiles.
>
> [III.ii.410–12]

The elevated rhetoric of Wolsey's regret, complete with regal imagery, is not yet renunciation, but at this point it seems honest and in character. From it, Wolsey moves to a reasonable appraisal of his own status and advises Cromwell to seek the service of the King.

Wolsey's last long speech to Cromwell is essentially moral. Calling on Cromwell to "fling away ambition," Wolsey becomes a fervent spokesman for truth:

> Love thyself last, cherish those hearts that hate thee;
> Corruption wins not more than honesty.
> Still in thy right hand carry gentle peace
> To silence envious tongues. Be just, and fear not;
> Let all the ends thou aim'st at be thy country's,
> Thy God's and truth's.
>
> [III.ii.443–48]

It is as if Cavendish's moral reflections on Wolsey and on his own role in *The Life*, along with Wolsey's own increasingly moral statements there after his fall, had all been compacted in this speech into Wolsey's own greater morality.

Excepting a few early rhetorical lapses—"Say Wolsey, that once trod the ways of glory, / And sounded all the depths and shoals of honour" —Wolsey's last long speech is increasingly plain and "honest." Like the chronicles that derive from Cavendish, however, it does not fully resolve the ambiguity of the Cardinal's awareness. In it Wolsey continues his sermon to Cromwell:

> Serve the king: and prithee lead me in:
> There take an inventory of all I have,
> To the last penny, 'tis the king's. My robe,
> And my integrity to heaven, is all
> I dare now call mine own. O Cromwell, Cromwell,
> Had I but serv'd my God with half the zeal

I serv'd my king, he would not in mine age
Have left me naked to mine enemies.

[III.ii.450–57]

Wolsey's nakedness takes final precedence over his robe and his integrity and yet seems strangely contradicted by them. His confusion of roles also lingers in the still-wavering referent of the pronoun "he" in the penultimate line, but it is neither so prominent there nor in the chronicles as it is in Cavendish, where Wolsey's confusion of masters—God or Caesar, the King—is a more pronounced theme. Yet the Cardinal's ambiguous awareness of himself and his own values remains unmistakably present in his final appearance. The play is thereby as "true" to its chronicle-sources as a competent dramatization could be.

Wolsey's last scene on stage is not the end of him. The next Act presents, as it were, his epitaph, an appropriately double image of him in the words first of Catherine and then of her gentleman-usher, Griffith. A better epitaph to Wolsey's ambiguity than the twin characterizations, one critical and one laudatory, that they speak of him would be hard to imagine. Having heard that Wolsey has died full of penitence and sorrow, Catherine describes him as a man of unbounded ambition, unprincipled, opportunistic, self-willed, unfeeling, and untrue: "He would say untruths, and be ever double / Both in his words and meaning" (IV.ii.38–39).[41] Griffith in turn notes the Cardinal's humble birth and considerable scholarly attainments despite it and proceeds to his behavior:

Exceeding wise, fair-spoken and persuading:
Lofty and sour to them that lov'd him not,
But to those men that sought him, sweet as summer.
And though he were unsatisfied in getting
(Which was a sin) yet in bestowing, madam,
He was most princely.

[IV.ii.52–57]

Like the gentleman-usher Cavendish, Griffith has no illusion about Wolsey's love of worldly riches, but he remains impressed by the Cardinal's "virtues" despite the Cardinal's vice (IV.ii.45–47), and he stresses the importance of the Cardinal's growth in awareness after his fall from power:

His overthrow heap'd happiness upon him,
For then, and not till then, he felt himself,
And found the blessedness of being little;
And to add greater honours to his age
Than man could give him, he died fearing God.

[IV.ii.64–68]

Griffith is more enthusiastic about Wolsey's regeneration and perhaps more naively confident of it than Cavendish, but his positive emphases resemble Cavendish's avowed effort to report Wolsey truly.

Catherine's response to Griffith's character of Wolsey suggests her generosity, both to Wolsey and to his defender. Reading it in conjunction with the chronicle-sources for the play's version of Wolsey, we might suspect that it openly alludes to the ambiguity present in these sources and in effect comments on them:

> After my death I wish no other herald,
> No other speaker of my living actions
> To keep mine honour from corruption,
> But such an *honest chronicler* as Griffith.
> Whom I most hated living, thou hast made me,
> With thy religious truth and modesty,
> Now in his ashes honour.
>
> [IV.ii.69–75: my emphasis]

Catherine's response notes the relevance of personal motive, of belief ("religious truth") and affection ("Whom I . . . hated") to chronicle-account. It surely increases the likelihood that the play examines deliberately the ambiguity of Wolsey's figure and the conflicting judgments of it to which the chronicles attest.[42]

At the end of *Henry VIII* Cranmer's prophecy of the happy reigns of Elizabeth Tudor and James Stuart seems to relate poetic vision to historical fact, yet in doing so it invites our asking how vision itself relates to the rest of the play and how the play's ending relates to history. Cranmer prophesies that the infant Elizabeth promises "Upon this land a thousand thousand blessings, / Which time shall bring to ripeness" (V.iv.19–20). He foresees that Queen Elizabeth will be a pattern to princes, the nursling of Truth, a joy to her own people, and a terror to her foes. His vision, like Catherine's compensatory vision of heavenly bliss in Act IV, echoes the Bible, but the peace he envisages belongs to this world, as much as to another one; he sees that good will grow with Elizabeth:

> In her days every man shall eat in safety
> Under his own vine what he plants, and sing
> The merry songs of peace to all his neighbours.
> God shall be truly known. . . .[43]

By a transposition to outright myth, Cranmer's vision transcends even the divorce of diginities death makes inevitable: the maiden phoenix Elizabeth will from

> Her ashes new create another heir
> As great in admiration as herself,
> So shall she leave her blessedness to one
> (When heaven shall call her from this cloud of darkness)

Who from the sacred ashes of her honour
Shall star-like rise. . . .

[V.iv.41–46]

The evident contradiction between the "merry songs of peace" in Elizabeth's godly reign and the parenthetical and quite unnecessary reference to "this cloud of darkness" is a caution, but at the end of a play as historically truthful as *Henry VIII*, conspicuous poetic vision itself is one.[44]

Looking back from Cranmer's vision to the rest of the play, even in the absence of an intentional signal from the playwright, we should have difficulty not wondering whether so nice a vision is not merely rhetorical like Wolsey's lies and dodges or ornamental like Bacon's anodyne or like the Lady Anne's conscience and a cheveril glove. If an audience is neither drugged nor ecstatic (hardly the case at the end of this troubled but highly intellectual play), can it succeed in *not* remembering history: Anne Boleyn, Elizabeth's mother, and Thomas Cromwell beheaded by Henry VIII; Cranmer burned by Catherine's and Henry's daughter Mary, Queen Elizabeth's death, James Stuart's immoral court, and the very recent death of Henry Stuart, the popular Prince of Wales, which by itself lends an odd resonance to Cranmer's prophesying that James will flourish "And like a mountain cedar, reach his branches / To all the plains about him" (V.iv.53–54)?

In quantity and lyric quality, however, the emphasis of Cranmer's vision falls on Elizabeth's reign, which came to an end ten years before this play was first performed. The dramatic occasion of the prophecy, Elizabeth's christening, enforces her importance further, in fact to the point that a non-Stuart audience could overlook the specificity of allusion to James I. It is not, perhaps, Elizabeth's death but the symbolism, the promise of peace, however passing, in her reign that really matters in 1613 or in any later century.[45]

The alternative interpretations that Cranmer's prophecy invites, symbol or fact, spirit or history, truth or anodyne, suggest a description of conscience's role in the play offered earlier, namely, that it tends to correlate increasingly with a heightened subjectivity, with greater claims for private, self-referential, or sectarian vision or, viewed conversely, with the merely ornamental, unimportant, and unreal. These interpretations also reflect on the interpretative process itself, on the roles of belief, affection, and predisposed commitment in it. Cranmer's prophecy, nearly as persuasive as lyrically attractive, raises again the question of the credibility of fiction and the incredibility of fact—of Elizabeth's reign as a lasting promise of peace and of the end of her reign, irrevocable and nonregenerating. I should qualify my earlier suggestion that *Henry VIII* is a controlled and possibly cynical experiment: the play may be difficult and troubled, but it is also deliberate and provocative, and it need not be cynical unless, in contradistinction to all the characters in the play who suddenly find a deeper vision, we choose to take it so.

***

Both More's history of Richard and Shakespeare's historical dramas of Richard III and Henry VIII exhibit their authors' awareness of the fiction in biographical truth: the fiction in any wholeness of identity, whether sinner's or saint's, and, indeed, in any final *human* truth, whether Catherine's heaven, Cranmer's New Jerusalem, or Richard's hell. Shakespeare's dramas, going beyond More's highly conscious art, show an explicit, additionally self-conscious concern with the nature and varieties of truth in the portrayal of historical persons in art and in chronicle. The disjunction between fact and credibility and the tie between fabrication, or perhaps deception, and insight become subjects he explores and, in the characters of *Henry VIII*, examines.

Henry VIII is not an isolated instance of these concerns in the Stuart period. Ford's *Perkin Warbeck* provides another, radical examination of similar issues—one that is just on the other side of the following chapters on Bacon and, for reasons of space, of this book. In *Perkin*, Ford confronts the relative claims of pure fiction with those of factual truth and those of an imagined with those of an objective identity. In the terms of Bacon, with which we began this chapter, he pits poetic feigning against historical truth, or in the terms of another contemporary work, John Donne's "Canonization," he pits sonnets against chronicles:

> And if no peece of Chronicle wee prove,
> We'll build in sonnets pretty roomes;
> As well a well wrought urne becomes
> The greatest ashes, as half-acre tombes.[46]

In Ford's play, Perkin might well have endorsed these lines, but in Shakespeare's *Henry VIII*, only Cranmer while in prophetic flight might have done so—or possibly Catherine, before she wakes up to the indignity of a saucy messenger and then to the humility of her own death.

PART III

NINE
BACON'S THEORY OF LIFE-WRITING
"True History" and Equivocal Truth

Studies of Bacon's *Historie of the Raigne of King Henry the Seventh* have given short shrift to the contemporary practice and the tradition of life-writing to which, by Bacon's own definition, the *Henry* must chiefly belong. Those that do touch on the tradition indicate considerable disagreement, if not confusion, about its nature and bearing on the *Henry*, as the following three examples will demonstrate. Each of the three comes from an important and influential discussion of Bacon's history-writing, and each makes assumptions or explicit claims about the relation of a biographical tradition to the writing of history in Tudor-Stuart times. None of them is simply wrong, yet all three cannot be entirely right.

Classifying Bacon as one of several writers of "politic history," F. J. Levy explains how in Bacon's lifetime "the new enthusiasm for history as an illustration of politics" brought "a devaluation of the purely biographical approach to historical thinking"; he continues, "the raw material" of the Tudor history "was usually biographical: that is, the center point was the deeds of some monarch or great man." Later, however, Levy qualifies this view, granting that "Personality was still an issue" in politic history and then adding, "if anything, more power was given to the individual ruler" in it.[1] In contrast to Levy's major premise, George H. Nadel stresses how important biography was to Bacon and yet how Bacon's view of it differed from everyone else's: "the subject of biography, 'the characters of persons,' was to him [Bacon] both object and validation of history studied as a science. [Yet] the conventional position, accepted by everyone [else], that we improve ourselves morally by drawing the appropriate lessons from reading about the lives of others was too vague for Bacon, however much he agreed with its [general] sentiment."[2] Nadel and Levy thus agree that Bacon's approach to history differs from everyone else's, but they disagree on exactly how it differs or how it is related to life-writing, about which they hold variant and elusive assumptions.

Analyzing Bacon's rhetoric in *Henry VII*, Edward I. Berry develops

Nadel's views: "The extent to which Bacon funnels all of our concern for causation into questions of character—at the expense of the social and economic causes preferred by the modern historian—is revealed in his treatment of Henry, who as monarch is conceived of as the chief cause of the events of his reign."[3] Berry later adds that "Unlike humanistic historians, whose tendency is to simplify character, to chisel away all but the essentials, Bacon tends to complicate, to add a variety of important and sometimes relatively trivial psychological traits." Under the rubric "humanistic historians," Berry appears to include virtually all historians, except Machiavelli and Guicciardini, from the time of More until the advent of Bacon.

Aside from the fact that my understanding of More's *Richard III* differs from Berry's, I wonder whether Berry would have described the practice of the life-writers in just the same terms. Cavendish and even Harpsfield come to mind; likewise Mancini, who mentioned Edward IV's emetics, and Stow, who carefully did not excise Wolsey's hairshirt; then, too, one thinks of the numerous other *Lives,* in whole or in part, that found their way into the chronicle-histories. Berry attributes the excellence of *Henry VII* to Bacon's "imaginative grasp of a new approach to reality." I think it would be more accurate to say that the *Henry* shows his imaginative grasp of the possibilities inherent in an old approach, historical life-writing, and the usefulness of this form of writing for proponing what he considered true: a reality more political than providential and more psychological than moralistic.

Despite the difficulty, not to say the futility, of defining *Lives* narrowly, few of us would be stymied if asked to cite examples of them in the Tudor-Stuart period. As a phenomenon in the period, life-writing is easily located, but lacking a conveniently regular shape, it is also easily ignored or else pushed into one. Reduction to rules is peculiarly apt to violate this body of writing because it is so unstable a blend of life and art, of fact and invention. Still, the *Life* was recognized as a form of composition in the period itself, and examples of life-writing exhibit at least one characteristic beyond the focus on an individual who existed in historical time and its inevitable corollary, a substantial measure of historically factual content. This is a fictional component whose proportion rises as the *Life* is to a greater extent "shaped." Although the shaping is shared—again to a variable extent—by subject and author, a seemingly inevitable corollary of it in its turn is a functional and therefore significant authorial presence, whether disguised or open.

Without reference to life-writing, even the meaning of Bacon's own theoretical statements about the writing of history is needlessly obscure. With it, the oft-celebrated inconsistency of Bacon's theory with his practice of history is greatly diminished. This is the case in large part because it becomes less tempting to simplify or to tighten Bacon's theoretical statements and then, having done so, to marvel at the distance between his theory and practice.

In *The Advancement of Learning* (1605), Bacon classifies "Just and Perfect" civil (human) history into three kinds, the chronicle or history of a period, the *Life* or history of a person, and the narration or relation of a single action, such as the Peloponnesian War or the conspiracy of Catiline.[4] Since he develops his explanation of these kinds as a continuing process of analysis rather than as a single finished pronouncement on each, the only way to gloss his argument accurately is to follow its interlocked stages instead of considering them as a series of detached fragments. Although Bacon considers the chronicle "the most complete and absolute kind of history" and distinguishes it by the formality and compass ("the magnitude") of its actions, he finds its relevance to human conduct superficial and its purpose somewhat aimless and shapeless. *Lives* therefore excel chronicles "in profit and use," and narrations excel chronicles "in verity and sincerity." Then *Lives* must be better for instruction, whatever the specific nature of it, and narrations must be more authentic—"truer" in content and more ingenuous, franker, less artful in feeling. *Lives* evidently have more human depth, shape, and purpose: whereas chronicles "set forth the pomp of business," *Lives* present "the true and inward resorts thereof."

As the definitions of these three kinds of perfect history continue, each kind mutually illuminating and progressively defining the others, it becomes increasingly clear that, while chronicles have surface and breadth, narrations are more factual, closer to raw material, and *Lives* have *true* humanity and more artful shape. Thus if *Lives* are "well written" and "represent" a person in whom are mixed "actions both greater and smaller, public and private," they "must of necessity contain a more true, native, and lively representation" than do chronicles. In context, "more true" means not simply "inward" but generally "more human"—truer to the wholeness of life as we actually live it. Paraphrasing "more true, native, and lively," I should suggest "fuller, more natural, and more lifelike."[5] My paraphrase, like Bacon's own terms, would have a notably different meaning for Bede—or for that matter, for such writers as Cavendish or Walton—from that it has for Bacon himself.

Although Bacon's definitions are investigative rather than "magistral and peremptory," his awareness of different kinds of truths in the *Lives* and in other forms of perfect civil history-writing is evident.[6] Whereas *Lives* are "true, native, and lively," narrations "cannot but be more purely and exactly true," because their scope is limited, specific, and presumably contemporary (190). "More purely and exactly true" apparently means true by virtue of yet fuller and more detailed information. In a subsequent passage Bacon recommends that more "narrations and relations" be compiled so "particularity of actions memorable" might be "reported as they pass." Such reports might then provide the basis for "a complete History" of an entire period: "the collection of such relations might be as a nursery garden, whereby to plant a fair and stately garden" (195–96).

De Dignitate et Augmentis Scientiarum (1623), the next work to which Bacon turned after writing (1621) and publishing (1622) *Henry VII*, enlarges and refines his definitions of the various kinds of civil history-writing. While most of his revisions are relatively minor, the purpose of life-writing is made more specific and didactic, and the partisan bias frequently present in narrations is now acknowledged. In *De Augmentis*, *Lives* are held to excel more concretely "in profit and examples" rather than merely "in profit and use," and they are said to "contain a more lively and faithful representation of things and one which you may more safely and happily take for example in another case" than a chronicle.[7] If *Lives* become more exemplary, narrations become still more clearly factual and also less reliable. Now Bacon himself explains why narrations are "more purely and exactly true" than chronicles: "because they may choose a manageable and definite argument, whereof a perfect knowledge and certainty and full information may be had." Still, "the sincerity of Relations [or narrations], must be taken with reservation; for . . . relations . . . especially if published near the time of the actions themselves (being commonly written either in favour or in spite), are of all other histories the most to be suspected." But he again concludes that even crude or biased reports can become "no bad materials and provision for a more perfect history" in the hands of a prudent historian. As Bacon is well aware, experience itself is no more exemplary than thought is natively a highly honed Baconian aphorism.[8] Even a sincere relation is likely to be too close to undigested experience to afford the "profit and examples" available in the "more lively and faithful representation" and, it is increasingly clear, in the more artful representation that is life-writing.

At times Bacon refers to "simple" chronicles—as above to narrations but not to *Lives*—as the relatively rawer material for richer, fuller, and wiser histories. In what is thought to have been the prospectus for a "History of the reign of K. Henry the Eight, K. Edward, Q. Mary, and part of the reign of Q. Elizabeth" (written sometime before 1603), Bacon expresses his appreciation, albeit concessive, for original sources but reveals his preference for them in pre-packaged form: "finding no public memories of any consideration or worth," he complains, "the supply must be out of the freshness of memory and tradition, and out of the acts, instruments, and negotiations of state themselves, together with the glances of foreign histories; which though I do acknowledge to be the best originals . . . yet the travel must be much greater than if there had been already digested any tolerable chronicle as a simple narration of the actions themselves, which should only have needed out of the former helps to be enriched with the counsels and the speeches and notable particularities."[9] Citing this passage, Leonard F. Dean remarks Bacon's failure to realize fully the continuum between researcher and historian and the inseparability of valid historical facts and the validity of the interpretation that makes use of them. His conclusion could hardly be bettered: "Bacon wished the historian to work with facts, as many as can be accumulated;" yet his "emphasis is always on the proper treatment of facts rather than on their collection. . . . [For Bacon] the most glaring lack is the skillful interpretation of the facts already available."[10]

Yet even Dean's balanced views leave me with occasional reservations. While Bacon's preference for received research is evident in the passage at issue, his limited regard for the Tudor chronicles is equally so. The logic of the passage implies that a "tolerable chronicle" does not exist because no one has properly recorded and organized the facts. My second reservation concerns those "counsels" and "speeches" with which Bacon would enrich such a tolerable chronicle. We cannot assume that Bacon would treat a fact or a source quite as we might and thus that he means only counsels and speeches actually expressed and recorded rather than those derived more freely from relevant documents by the historian himself or composed by him on the basis of what is known about an occasion. One cannot be sure exactly what Bacon means by "counsels" in the passage, but the words "advice," "judgments," and "purposes" and the phrases "inmost counsels," "counsels *of* princes," "wise counsels," "counsels *for* princes" are alike available as glosses.[11] The only even remote equivalent to "counsels" among the original sources mentioned by Bacon is "negotiations of state," but they sound more formal in the context cited and more likely to have become matters of record in numerous ways.[12] Given Bacon's statements elsewhere on the writing of history and his own practice in *Henry VII,* I strongly suspect that a significant portion of the enriching counsels the Baconian historian would contribute to a tolerable chronicle, in fact, would be his own. The same would be true of the "speeches" to which Bacon refers if we were to judge from his practice in *Henry VII,* where speeches are loosely derived from approximate sources (e.g., Perkin's Proclamation as source for his initial speech to James IV of Scotland) or more often are freely invented.[13] Despite Bacon's relatively advanced awareness of the "help" to be gained from original sources in the passage cited, we must acknowledge the likelihood that in it he *aims* at an historical truth less purely factual and more fictive than ours would be, and, as a result, that the gap between this passage and Bacon's practice in *Henry VII* is not very great.[14]

Both the materials of history and the treatment of them offer more than one puzzle in Bacon's theory and practice of perfect history-writing. Moreover, they offer them together. Much as Bacon does respect fact and much as the *Henry* has a "solid core" of it, he essentially transforms the raw material of Tudor-Stuart chronicle to a highly artful *Life;* in his statements on history and particularly on *Lives,* he again and again expresses an awareness of the artifice proper to them.[15] In a letter to Lord Ellesmere (like *The Advancement* dated 1605) Bacon speaks of a projected "tomb or monument" for Queen Elizabeth and proposes a truer "Representative" or history of her.

He writes that he has been "put in mind, by [the monument,] this Representative of her person, of the more true and more firm Representative, which is of her life and government. For as Statuaes and Pictures are dumb histories, so histories are speaking Pictures." He then adds, "if Plutarch were alive to write lives by parallels, it would trouble him for virtue and fortune both to find for her a parallel amongst women."[16] The kind of history Bacon has in mind here is clearly a *Life* and, to judge from that favorite Machiavellian combination "virtue and fortune" (*virtù/fortuna*), one that is "true, native, and lively" in the words of *The Advancement*.[17] Just as clearly, however, Bacon not only associates this proposed *Life* with art forms, namely, pictures and statues, but also describes it in a phrase, "speaking Pictures," that is a commonplace in the Renaissance for describing poetry.[18] As we shall see when we turn to the *Henry*, the statement on life-writing made to Lord Ellesmere is close in spirit and actual words to the way Bacon refers to his own history in the dedicatory letter that precedes it and again at its end. At present, however, I should return to descriptions of history by Bacon and his interpreters that are external to the *Henry* itself.

In his edition of the *Henry*, Spedding, a staunch defender of the historical value of Bacon's work, praises it in terms appropriate to life-writing and to Bacon's own view of "*true* and *perfect* Civil History." Spedding admires Bacon's ability "to educe a living likeness of the man and the time" and continues, "The portrait of Henry as drawn by . . . [Bacon] is the original, more or less faithfully copied, of all the portraits which have been drawn since." Sounding like Ascham, who considered the characterizations of Thucydides, Chaucer, and More alike historical, and sounding even more like Bacon himself, Spedding adds that "the proper object of history is to reproduce such an image of the past that the actors shall seem to live and the events to pass before our eyes" (15, 20). When Spedding thus defined the objective of history, he probably recalled Bacon's description of the historian's task in *De Augmentis;* namely, "to carry the mind in writing back into the past, and bring it into sympathy with antiquity; diligently to examine, freely and faithfully to report, and by the light of words to place as it were before the eyes, the revolutions of times, the characters of persons, the fluctuations of counsels, the courses and currents of actions, the bottoms of pretences, and the secrets of governments" (421). Though drawing heavily on historical fact, a task conceived so vividly and affectively, not to say so omnisciently, is certainly not devoid of art or, indeed, of fiction.

"I consider history and experience to be the same thing," Bacon wrote in *De Augmentis,* thereby offering a position at once clear-cut and open-ended (408). It maintains that history treats real-life experiences, that history is objective and realistic; but it also implies a continuum between experience past and present and opens the door to the interpreter's active presence in a written history. A more outspoken description of the historian's concerns by the poet-historian Samuel Daniel can clarify what is implicit in Bacon's position. Daniel proposes in *The Civil Wars* (1609) that the writer of history should focus particularly on character, inventing speeches when appropriate, much as Bacon does in *Henry VII*. Daniel explains that *"many of these Images are drawne with the pencil of mine owne conceiuing: yet I knowe, they are according to the portraiture of Nature; and carrie a resemblance to the life of Action, and their complexions whom they represent. For I see, Ambition, Faction, and Affections, speake euer one Language, weare like colours (though in seuerall fashions) feed, and are fed with the same nutriments; and only vary but in time."*[19] Human nature and experience, conceived as constants, become the justification for poetic, or, more accurately in this case, for historical, license.

Bacon's reasoning is again not entirely dissimilar to Daniel's when he argues that "monks or closet penmen" are not qualified historians—"no faithful witnesses as to the real passages of business"—and then explains, "It is for ministers and great officers to judge of these things, and those who have handled the helm of government, and been acquainted with the difficulties and mysteries of state business."[20] The writing of history is thus not for isolated scholars who understand nothing of the real world, that is, of experience, but for great officers like Francis St. Alban himself: it is not the recording of fact but the perspective brought to it that matters most. Indeed, if the center of "these things" and "mysteries" to which Bacon refers is the character of the Queen herself, as it is that of the King in *Henry VII*, there would appear to be no genuine difference between Daniel's sentiments regarding the true source and usefulness of the historian's insight and Bacon's.

Bacon's remarks on the treatment of historical materials and more particularly on the role of the historian himself bring us progressively closer to his equivocation regarding the relation of truth to fiction and objective to subjective modes of portrayal, as I described it in beginning the previous chapter. In the following quotation from *De Augmentis*, Bacon is more clearly than ever trying to have his historian's role both ways: "for a man who is professedly writing a Perfect History to be everywhere introducing political reflexions, and thereby interrupting the narrative, is unseasonable . . . For though every wise history is pregnant (as it were) with political precepts and warnings, yet the writer himself should not play the midwife" (433).[21] Bacon does not argue for objectivity here, at least in a modern sense. He argues against an intrusive role that interrupts the narrative and preempts the reader's act of judgment. He also argues that a "wise" history does not need such authorial intervention or midwifery. But a "wise" history—seemingly well on its way to personification—can have been written only by a "wise" historian, one of Bacon's ministers or great officers, perhaps. And so wise a history—indeed, historical matter so wise, to borrow Bacon's pregnant image and the almost unavoidable Renaissance pun on matter (*mater-ia*) and *mater* that underlies it—has been impregnated (as it were) by the wise historian's precepts and warnings. No unnatural or unhistorical distortion, no untruth whatever, is caused by such an historian's penetrating insight or by his artful method of expressing—or representing—it. He makes the material of civil history fertile; in fact, he perfects it.

Bacon no more argues entirely objectively in the passage at hand than he argues entirely for objectivity. His prose is alive with art, and to ignore its presence would be to violate his meaning. It is a subsumed, an understated, and, to my mind, an equivocal art, but like Bacon's own image of the impregnation of matter by wisdom, it is also true to his sense of the relation between art, whether rhetorical, political, or historical, and nature.[22]

What is perhaps Bacon's best-known pronouncement on historical matter and the historian's role has also been read too uncritically: "History of all writings . . . holdeth least of the author, and most of the things themselves."[23] Bacon's two qualifications, however obvious, should first be noted: "least" rather than "none," and "of all writings . . . least" rather than simply "History holdeth least." The second of these qualifications carries additional weight when one recalls Bacon's awareness of the potential distortions, as well as the potential profit and use, of written discourse—"*For men believe* that their reason governs words; *but it is also true* that words react on the understanding."[24] In view of the examples I have cited above, it should also be evident that the phrase "least of the author" refers as much to explicit authorial role, namely, decorous respect for the integrity of the narrative, as to the selection and nature of materials. Successive stages of Bacon's argument further indicate that the same phrase—"least of the author"—includes manner, as well as content, for he contrasts readers of history, who find useful knowledge, with readers of poetry, who become "conceited" (overly ingenious in manner and content), and with readers of philosophy, who become "stiff and opinionate" (magistral and peremptory in manner and content) or else "perplexed and confused" (complicated and obscure in manner and content). The concluding phrase of Bacon's sentence, "most of the things themselves," by now should give us further pause. "The things themselves" may not be exactly the same for us and for Bacon here, even though it is often assumed that they are. The "things themselves" means not objective reality but reality as Bacon conceives it, which is to a considerable extent objective but includes invented speeches, inner thoughts and hidden motives of historical characters, political wisdom, and the like. It means history "perfected," not distorted by falsehood, faction, or morality, but made pregnant, profitable, and useful for real life through human wisdom.

Returning again to Sidney's and Bacon's disparate views of the relation of poetry to history will enable us to take Bacon's equivocal awareness of the historian's perfecting art one step further. Briefly, to encapsulate my earlier discussion, Sidney considers poetry "truer" than history because more nearly perfect or ideal, and Bacon distinguishes sharply between "true history" and untrue history, which he denominates poetry.[25] Both the nature of truth either writer has in mind and the relation of truth to poetic feigning or fiction differ. Bacon's definition of poetry is deliberate and reductive: poetry "is nothing else but *Feigned History*," whether in prose or verse. Read in the larger context of Bacon's thought, the effect of his definition is negative in whole as in part; for example, poetry, "being not tied to the laws of matter, may at pleasure join that which nature hath severed, and sever that which nature hath joined, and so make unlawful matches and divorces of things."[26] The diction could hardly be more damaging. Poetry sounds not merely unnatural but downright ungodly—a far cry from the relation of the Baconian scientist or historian to the nature of God's creation. No matter how soothing poetry so defined might still prove to savage breasts, Bacon sees it as unbridled fantasy, escape, and untruth.[27]

While I do not agree that Bacon's view of poetry has anything but a most superficial resemblance to Sidney's, I could not agree more with the suggestion that Bacon probably had Sidney in mind when he so carefully limited the province and value of poetry.[28] Bacon's reason may not be far to seek. Sidney, almost as skeptical of the historian's claims as Bacon is of the poet's, curtly notes the kinship between the two arts: "Many times" the historian "must tell events whereof he can yield no cause; or, if he do, it must be poetically." The word "poetically"—equated with "fictionally" in the *Defence* —is here closer to meaning "conjecturally," "hypothetically," or simply "imaginatively" than to meaning "ideally." Its extension to meanings other than "ideally" is precisely what Bacon's reductive definition of poetry seeks to prevent. Surely Bacon would have resisted substitution of the word "poetry" for the phrase "by wit and conjecture" ("*ingenio et conjectura*") in this passage from *De Augmentis:* history "(especially if it be of a period much before the age of the writer) is sure . . . to contain empty spaces which must be . . . supplied at pleasure ["*licenter*": freely] by wit and conjecture" (425).

Both Bacon and Sidney are aware of the interpretative aspect of the historian's craft and of an element of conjecture in it. To Sidney, this element is fiction. In the hands of the prudent, experienced historian, it is to Bacon wisdom or, more simply, truth. Albeit in different words and with different attitudes, both writers refer to a point at which the method of the historian touches that of the poet.

Although I think Leonard Dean mistaken in denying Sidney's perception of kinship between poetry and history to Bacon, he glosses the implications of this perception acutely: "Bacon [failed to] perceive that emphasis on the interpretation of hidden causes and motives opens the way to the introduction of fiction, no matter how plausible, into ostensibly factual histories."[29] Rather than failing to perceive it, Bacon was aware of the element of fiction in the historian's perfecting art and included but subsumed it in his theory. In particular, he carefully distanced this fictive element from the word "fiction" and never did so more than when he so narrowly and emphatically defined poetic feigning as the exact opposite of historical truth. Bacon knew that words—certainly loaded words like "fiction"—matter, especially if one is trying to redefine the historian's task: for "whenever an understanding of greater acuteness or a more diligent observation would alter those [commonly understood] lines to suit the true division of nature, words stand in the way and resist the change."[30] The word "fiction," though not the fact, might well have been too dangerous in Bacon's eyes, too misleading with pronouncements like Sidney's still in the air. It might have encouraged the misconception that poetry is relevant to real life or that history is not truly objective.

So it might. Yet, as we have seen, part of the fiction Bacon puts out the front door when he defines poetry as untruth, he lets in the back door when he describes the nature and treatment of perfect civil history and especially of life-writing. Evidence of Bacon's real position is strongly present not only in the quotations already discussed but also in recurrent themes of his more general philosophy that concern the relation of mind and matter and, in his discussions of natural history, the relation of nature and perfecting art.

At its best and most efficient, the human mind works on and according to nature, yet it *works* on matter rather than the reverse: "For the wit and mind of man, if it work upon matter, which is the contemplation of the creatures of God, worketh according to the stuff, and is limited thereby." As famous as anything Bacon wrote, the same passage goes on to contrast such working on matter with the mind's working on itself and like the spider bringing forth "cobwebs of learning . . . of no substance or profit."[31] Bacon's distrust of the mind, like his distrust of language, is considerable, but even while he counsels limitation and verification of thought by matter, he describes the mind's relation to matter as active and operative rather than as merely passive or receptive. Consider the change in meaning effected by substituting the word "fact" or even the phrase "historical fact" for the italicized phrases of the following quotation, another of Bacon's enumerations of learning's illnesses: namely, "a kind of adoration of the mind and understanding of man; by means whereof men have withdrawn themselves too much from *the contemplation of nature and the observations of experience*, and have tumbled up and down in their own reason and conceits."[32] The substitute, "fact," is more sharply and simply opposed to "reason and conceits" than are Bacon's own phrases. "Fact" is more purely inert than "contemplation" and "observations," and it carries a more specific, objective meaning than do "nature" and "experience." The basic opposition in this quotation is neither between the mind's action and inaction nor even between one kind of mental process and another but between *something* outside the mind itself *and nothing* except the mind itself.

Likewise in *De Augmentis*, when, distinguishing poetry from history, Bacon explains that poetry accommodates "the shows of things to the desires of the mind, not (like reason and history) buckling and bowing down the mind to the nature of things," the basic opposition is between desires and nature or reality, as Bacon conceives the latter.[33] The opposition is not between history and poetry as such or even between fact and fiction as such but between truth and a fiction specifically ideal, namely, poetry defined as a flight from the nature of history and a refusal to face the nature of things. Bacon's reductive definition of poetry denies the tie that Sidney assumes (not altogether consistently) in the *Defence* between method and content, between any sort of fiction and an idealized one. Thus Bacon limits the province and value of poetry in an effort to separate history from the poet's truest or most purely imaginative role, the creation of a golden world. More exactly, he endeavors to separate the fiction in history, which he thought of as wisdom and truth, from an ideal history—from what Spenser, Sidney's and Bacon's Tudor contemporary, called an "antique Image" in his *Faerie Queene* (II.Pro.4). In view of my own concern with fiction in the present book, I cannot stress too strongly that Bacon's position does reflect the weighting of reality toward fact, experience, and objectivity and an effort to tie art, even fiction, more closely to these things. Nonetheless, the probability remains in his theory that an historical fiction, preferably derived from historical facts or at least faithful to historical reality, would not be, in Bacon's view, a distortion of nature or a violation of truth.

Bacon's understanding of the relation of mind to matter and more specifically of human art to nature is nowhere more evident than in his discussion of one type of natural history, that of "nature altered or wrought," which he also denominates repeatedly the "history of Arts."[34] By arts, Bacon means mechanical and experimental arts, yet in his discussion of these we find the most significant analogy to his conception of the historian's art, as well as further indication why he never stated this conception less equivocably. In *De Augmentis,* with one essential difference, namely, the role granted nature, Bacon speaks of the mechanical and experimental arts much as Sidney speaks of poetry. Their province is to constrain and to mold nature, making her "as it were new by art and the hand of man; as in things artificial." Explaining more fully, Bacon first apologizes for including the history of arts as a category under natural history, because it is commonly held "that art is something different from nature, and things artificial different from things [merely] natural." This opinion he rejects in the context of experimental arts, although, like Sidney, he maintains it elsewhere in regard to poetic art. Then Bacon continues, noting a more pernicious error, "that of considering art as merely an assistant to nature, having the power indeed to finish what nature has begun, to correct her when lapsing into error, or to set her free when in bondage, but by no means to change, transmute, or fundamentally alter nature."[35] Sidney, too, speaks of art's or, rather, of poetry's transmuting and perfecting power to make "things either better than nature bringeth forth, or, quite a new" and again of its power to make "forms such as never were in nature."[36] Whereas Sidney emphasizes the power of poetry to overgo nature, however, Bacon now defines the radical art that can transform and fundamentally alter nature somewhat flatly as "nature with man to help." The nature that Bacon designates is for Sidney "mere nature" above which man as poetic maker rises, utilizing the higher nature God has given him alone out of all earthly creatures.[37] Thus for Sidney the art of poetry is truly natural to man's "true" or higher nature, as well as distinct from physical nature. Both the similarities in Bacon's and Sidney's conceptions of a fundamentally transforming art and the differences in their conceptions of the relation of such an art to the material nature of things are striking. For Bacon, the subject of true art must be the nature of things; once it is, nature can profitably be subject to art and, indeed, to the perfecting action of human wisdom.

In *De Augmentis*, Bacon draws what he terms "the operative part of the liberal sciences" into the category of "mechanical or experimental arts."[38] While he does not place civil history per se in this category, it is significant that he discusses natural and civil history under the single rubric of history (as we should not) and therefore associates them. Moreover, his various descriptions of perfect civil history, which "possesseth the mind of the conceits . . . nearest allied unto action," tend to converge with his notion of arts operative.[39] As Bacon describes such arts in *The Advancement*, they are "of all others the most radical and fundamental towards . . . such natural philosophy . . . as shall be operative to the endowment and benefit of man's life" (187).

Arts operative—affecting action, having practical consequences, being relevant to real life—are good arts, and the art of the wise historian is in effect really one of them, if, as Bacon hoped, history might provide the foundation for a science of human behavior.[40] Arts operative are not poetry in Bacon's limited sense of the word, because they engage real life directly. They operate on nature; yet they are artificial, and if they are transferred from "one art to the use of another"[41]—for example, from a mechanical art to an historical one, and thus from one experimental art to another—we see how easily they become fictional; that is, they become hypothetical at the least and, if represented as truth, they could also become in Sidney's sense "poetic."

The true historian, the writer of *Lives* in particular, is, then, for Bacon a perfecter of raw experience and raw fact who imparts the shape of wisdom to them. He is essentially a synthesizer and an interpreter, not a recorder. He is realistic, telling not what men ought to do but what they do or, rather, what they *really* do, because he gets at inner springs and secret causes. He is essentially a revealer and an expounder of human truth and human reality. In Bacon's own word, equivocably poised among rhetorical, imaginative, and scientific meanings, he is an *Inventor* of truth as it inheres in human "individuals . . . circumscribed by place and time."[42] The truth he invents is radically different from that of life-writers like Bede or Walton, but not in every respect are his methods and the commitment to fiction underlying them.

TEN
BACON'S *HENRY VII*
"*WHAT is Truth?* said jesting Pilate"

To a reader of Bacon's historical theory, the letter of dedication to Charles, Prince of Wales, prefacing *The Historie of the Raigne of King Henry the Seventh* is significant but not surprising in its assessment: "I have not flattered him," Bacon writes of King Henry, "but took him to life as well as I could, sitting so far off, and having no better light."[1] As we have seen a pictorial metaphor is never far from Bacon's mind when he considers historical life-writing, and his choice of one here to describe the *Henry* again reveals an artistic point of view. Bacon's claim to have rendered a portrait faithful to life has distant analogies with Bede's promising "a plain, dependable account of the truth" or with Walton's assuring us of "*the Authors Picture in a natural dress,*" or a "*plain Picture*" of Donne.[2] Like the Venerable Bede's or the contemporary Walton's claims, of course, Bacon's own assessment of his achievement cannot be taken uncritically. What is lifelike, natural, and true, as well as what is artificial, differs for each of these writers.

A reader familiar with Walton's *Donne* and with the tradition of life-writing to which its conclusion alludes will be struck even more by the conclusion to Bacon's *Henry*. There Bacon observes that Henry lies buried "in one of the stateliest and daintiest monuments of Europe . . . So that he dwelleth more richly dead, in the monument of his tomb, than he did alive in Richmond or any of his palaces." Then, referring to his own *Historie* of Henry VII, Bacon adds, "I could wish he did the like in this monument of his fame" (365). In the memorable passage at the end of Donne's *Life* treated earlier, Walton describes Donne's monument as "A Statue indeed so like Dr. *Donne*, that . . . *it seems to breath faintly*," upon which "*Posterity shall look . . . as a kind of artificial Miracle.*" No more than Walton does Bacon parody tradition at the end of the *Henry*, but he, too, revises and renews it. His *Henry* has a different shape from a Bede's or a Walton's; his monument, as he conceives it, is *truly* lifelike, its biographical truth reliable.

As with the other life-writers, however, Bacon's handling of fact in the

Henry is fundamentally revealing with respect to his aims, assumptions, and methods and shows his attitude toward the relation of fiction to truth to be as equivocal in practice as in theory. His tracks are readily traced, essentially to the chronicle-historians Hall and Speed. As Wilhelm Busch reported nearly a century ago, "the real original authority forming the ground-work of Bacon's narrative, is Polydore Vergil" and, more exactly, Polydore, as Englished by Hall.[3] To a lesser extent, Bacon consulted other published histories, such as those of Fabyan and Stow and, among foreign histories, those of Commines and Guicciardini.[4] For Cabot's explorations, he drew on Richard Hakluyt's *Principall Navigations, Voiages and Discoveries of the English Nation*.[5] At some point, Bacon must have encountered in the Cotton collection a manuscript of Bernard André's *Henrici Septimi Historia* since this work is his source on two occasions; in the main, however, Bacon gets from Speed whatever of André he uses.[6] Since Cotton's library included printed books, it may also have provided to Bacon Fisher's *Mornynge Remembraunce*, in which the story of Margaret Beaufort's vision, recounted at the end of the *Henry*, is to be found.[7] From Cotton, Bacon obtained several other original manuscript sources, including *Vitellius* Ms A XVI, a London chronicle; a few reports, pamphlets, or other "negotiations of state"; and at least two letters, of which one is a letter from Henry to the Lord Mayor and aldermen of London.[8] In a marginal notation in *Henry VII*, Bacon acknowledges his debt to Cottonian manuscripts and implies that he has seen Cotton's copy of Perkin's Proclamation. Since Bacon's immediate source for much, though not quite all, of the Proclamation is Speed, Spedding's suggestion that Bacon had indeed encountered this document but lacked a copy of it when writing *Henry VII* is tenable.[9] Again relying on his own memory, Bacon refers to an account book kept by Empson and signed "almost to every leaf" by Henry VII, which he remembers having seen "long since."[10] Finally, in addition to such sources as these, Bacon drew fairly extensively on the books—or copies—of statutes.[11]

As Bacon's sources suggest, he constructs the *Henry* around a respectable core of factual information, albeit mainly derived from histories already in print, and to this core he brings the perceptions of an experienced lawyer and politician and a shrewd observer of human conduct. At the same time, however, Bacon mistakes and manipulates fact, engages openly in conjecture, and less openly but more pervasively employs the techniques of fiction: thematic structuring and rigorous selectivity, coherent patterns of words and images, dramatized, fictitious speeches; interior perspectives on character and causation, and complex but firmly conceived characterizations.

The opening paragraph of another history roughly contemporary with Bacon's, *The Life and Reign of King Henry VIII* by Edward Lord Herbert of Cherbury, sets in clearer focus Bacon's assessment of *Henry VII* in his dedication. Like that assessment, Lord Herbert's opening alludes to the aims and assumptions of traditional life-writing:

It is not easie to write that Princes History, of whom no one thing may constantly be affirmed. Changing of Manners and Condition alters the coherence of parts, which should give an uniforme description. *Nor is it probable* that contradictories should agree to the same Person: so that nothing can shake the credit of a Narration more, than if it grow unlike it selfe; when yet it may be not the Author, but the Argument caused the variation. *It is unpossible to draw his Picture well who hath severall countenances* [my emphasis].[12]

On the threshold of *Henry VIII,* Lord Herbert sounds quite different from Bacon on the threshold of *Henry VII.* Lord Herbert is more interested in truth here—objectively verifiable truth—than in probability. The portrait he projects will be neither perfected nor whole, and by Tudor-Stuart standards it will turn out to be minimally fictional—life-writing in little more than name. It will be significantly different from the complex but coherent, firmly drawn portrait of Henry VII that Bacon gives us.[13]

Bacon starts the *Henry* with a brief character of Richard III and his short but bloody reign, which serves to present the troubled historical context that Henry now enters as King. With barely a break and that not a fully logical use of the adversative conjunction, the conclusion of Richard's character introduces King Henry close-up for the first time in *The Historie:*

And as for the politic and wholesome laws which were enacted in his [Richard's] time, they were interpreted to be but the brocage of an usurper, thereby to woo and win the hearts of the people, as being conscious to himself that the true obligations of sovereignty in him failed and were wanting. But King Henry, in the very entrance of his reign and the instant of time when the kingdom was cast into his arms, met with a point of great difficulty and knotty to solve, able to trouble and confound the wisest King in the newness of his estate; and so much the more, because it could not endure a deliberation, but must be at once deliberated and determined. [47–48]

The conjunction "But" indicates contrast but defies rational paraphrase in this context. With its use, King Henry's situation and more exactly the problem of establishing his title to the throne and thereby his dynasty rather suddenly dominate our attention. The pressure of time is emphatic—"in the very entrance . . . and the instant of time . . . the newness . . . could not endure . . . but must be at once"—but it is also the situation, the urgent problem, that is emphasized and not just the King. The conspicuously paired terms in these sentences suggest contrast in meaning to an extent ("failed and were wanting"/"deliberated and determined"), but stylistically they also suggest the possible continuity of one reign with the next, of Richard's with Henry's, a continuous context of failure not as yet securely broken—or, indeed, rationally broken, to judge by the irrational use of the word "But."[14]

The immediacy of Henry's problem leads to analysis of it. Bacon explains that there were three ways in which Henry might claim the throne: "The first, the title of the Lady Elizabeth, with whom, by precedent pact with the party that brought him in, he was to marry. The second, the ancient and long disputed title (both by plea and arms) of the house of Lancaster, to which he was inheritor in his own person. The third, the title of the sword or conquest. . . ." The analysis could hardly be more systematic and less dramatic, hardly more detached and impersonal. Then, in much the way More originally set Richard acting, the setting of Bacon's account becomes relatively more interior: "But then it *lay plain before his eyes,* that if he relied upon that title . . . And though he should obtain by Parliament to be continued, yet *he knew* there was a very great difference . . . On the other side, if he stood upon his own title of the house of Lancaster, inherent in his person, *he knew* it was a title condemned . . ." (48–49; my emphasis). Berry is right in comparing this presentation of alternatives to "an internalized debate . . . which dramatizes the difficulty of choice," though I should append a few qualifications to his statement that will prove important in assessing the nature of Bacon's *Henry*.[15]

First, to use Bacon's own term, the "representation" of thought as an interior process is very much in the tradition of historical life-writing. We have observed it already in More's *Richard,* and it is conspicuous in Hall's *Chronicle*, one of Bacon's main sources. Examples from Hall's chapter on "The Politique Gouernaunce of Kyng Henry the VII" demonstrate at once Bacon's use of tradition and the extent to which he makes it more streamlined and deliberate. Like Bacon, Hall suggests a process of decision, at times even compacting the syntax of a complete sentence to do so:

> And surely not without a cause [was Henry "afflicted with no small feare"] for he wisely considred that he had neither a competent army ready prepared, nor harneys nor weapons for them that were present. And also he was now in such a doubtfull place, where he nether might nor could conueently gather an hoost together, consideryng that in the same cytie, the memory of kyng Richard his mortall enemy was yet recent and lyuely. . . . [427]

Again like Bacon, Hall interpolates royal mood or motive between subject and verb. In the following instance, Hall even displays nervousness (a kind of nascent consciousness, I suppose) about what he is doing and awkwardly reassures us of the subject: "The kyng not slepynge his matters, but mystrustyng and smellyng the storme that folowed, before the enemies arryued, he dispatched certeyne horsemen . . ." (433). A final example is useful to show Hall, his prolixity notwithstanding, beginning to structure the steps of a mental procedure, a method Bacon refined and developed. Hall explains that Henry, "hauyng both the ingenious forcast of the subtyl serpent, and also fearyng the burning fire like an infant that is a litle synged with a small flame: and farther vigilantly forseyng and prudently prouidyng for doubtes that might accidentally ensue: *deuysed, studyed and compassed* to extirpate" all seditious intentions (422: my emphasis).

Whereas my first qualification of Berry's seminal analysis concerns tradition, my others concern critical balance. Throughout the *Henry*, Bacon's internalizing of debate and decision is intermixed, indeed virtually interlineated, with remarks and whole sentences that are more clearly externalized, interpretative, and even editorial. These offset an interior perspective and in the long run encompass and direct it. As example of this intermixture in the short run, let us take the lengthy sentence that intervenes between Henry's knowing "there was a very great difference" and his knowing "it was a title condemned" in the initial passage of internalized debate, cited above:

> Neither wanted there even at that time secret rumours and whisperings, (which afterwards gathered strength and turned to great troubles) that the two young sons of King Edward the Fourth, or one of them, (which were said to be destroyed in the Tower,) were not indeed murdered but conveyed secretly away, and were yet living: which, if it had been true, had prevented the title of the Lady Elizabeth. [49]

Even aside from the parenthetical and, in the case of the first, the prophetical remarks, there is more of authorial exposition than of dramatic debate in this sentence. This point leads right into the next one: in *Henry VII* internalized debate does not become direct discourse or immediately dramatized action, as it does in More's *Richard*, where the first-person words of the character Richard evolve directly out of More's analyses of him. Whatever reservations we might have had about calling a history like More's dramatic are greatly increased in Bacon's *Henry*.

Qualifications in hand, we now should turn to the final stage of Bacon's internalized representations of Henry's decision to claim the title in his own Lancastrian right. This stage is the heart (but not the whole body) of Bacon's initial depiction of the King and is itself properly extensive:

> But the King, out of the greatness of his own mind, presently *cast the die;* and the *inconveniences appearing* unto him on all parts, and *knowing* there could not be any interreign or suspension of title, and *preferring* his affection to his own line and blood, and *liking* that title best which made him independent, *and being* in his nature and constitution of mind not very apprehensive or forecasting of future events afar off, but an entertainer of fortune by the day, *resolved* to rest upon the title of Lancaster as the main, and to use the other two, that of marriage and that of battle, but as supporters, the one to appease secret discontents, and the other to beat down open murmur and dispute; *not forgetting* that the same title of Lancaster had formerly maintained a possession of three descents in the crown; and might have proved a perpetuity, had it not ended in the weakness and inability of the last prince. [50–51: my emphasis]

Berry's analysis of the rhetoric in this sentence is accomplished, but he goes too far in concluding that "The sentence as a whole seems to mirror the perplexities of actual experience rather than order them, to plunge the mind, in fact, into . . . a 'very Tartarus of turmoil and confusion' " (291). This is to exaggerate the mimetic realism, the psychological drama, of the sentence, which is interiorized in focus and is in a sense mimetic but is also too rationally constructed for the realism of turbulent thought. The sentence is, in fact, analytically constructed.

The two decisive actions, the main verbs "cast" and "resolved," in themselves imply a structure and more exactly a Machiavellian point of view. Henry's response to his situation is framed here by those virtual emblems of a Machiavellian reading of reality, *fortuna* and *virtù*. His response exists within the framework of an inescapable element of chance or fortune and the firm exercise of will, without which the ruler's success is impossible and with which it may still prove elusive; it exists within the game of chance and decisive action, "casting the die" and resolving. An allusively Machiavellian frame is anachronistic for Henry, but not, of course, for Bacon, whose appreciation of Machiavelli is well known.[16]

In the same sentence the motives and reasons—"counsels," perhaps, as Bacon might have called them—between "cast" and "resolved" also belong to an analytic structure. The first two participial phrases—"inconveniences appearing" and "knowing"—indicate a responsible and realistic reading of the only sure realities of Henry's situation: no ideal or foolproof course of action exists, yet decisive action has urgently to be taken regarding the title. The next two participial phrases—"preferring" and "liking"—frankly and realistically express the emotional elements in Henry's decision, but the sequence of reasoning here makes a difference: they express these elements only after recognition of the impossibility of an entirely rational decision, founded in the objective realities of the situation, has been reached (participial phrases one and two).

The last of the participial phrases—"being"—stops short of intrusively disrupting the process of thought we could attribute until this point (if rather unrealistically) to Henry and instead blends with it: one can "be" habitually in a condition of political improvidence. Yet "being" properly and more obviously belongs not to Henry as thinker but to Bacon as interpreter. The phrase in which "being" occurs is proleptic, if not again downright prophetic, in a way that Henry himself could not possibly be, for it alludes to the "future events afar off" that will result from Henry's decision, not even as yet quite taken. In fact, Bacon here implants an important trait of Henry's character, shortsightedness, and prepares for development of a major theme in the *Henry*, namely, Yorkist dynastic identity and ambition.

And little wonder that Bacon, at least, should have vision so proleptic in this passage, since both theme and trait alluded to here were embryonically present in the earlier character of Henry VII, which Bacon wrote before 1603 in the prospectus for a history of the other Tudor monarchs: "and yet such a wisdom [Henry had] as seemed rather a dexterity to deliver himself from dangers . . . than any deep foresight to prevent them afar off." Even the wording of Bacon's proleptic vision in the *Henry* more than fifteen years later is notably similar. Bacon has a "fore-conceit," not only a clearly conceived view but also a written form of Henry's character as King before he writes the *Henry*, and practical man that he is, he utilizes it.[17] As we might almost have expected, the early prospectus also contains another version of the Machiavellian twins, *virtù* and *fortuna*, this time understood as "wisdom and fortune": Henry "was assailed with many troubles, which he overcame happily; a matter that did no less set forth his wisdom than his fortune," even if, as the sentence then continues, his wisdom was somewhat myopic.[18]

"Not forgetting," the final participial phrase that follows Henry's resolve —or Bacon's, since we can no longer be sure whose it is—does not violate the realistic political analysis, or what Bacon might have called the wisdom of the passage. In this phrase, Henry is represented (hardly literally) as saying in effect to himself, "Taking the title in my own Lancastrian right could work well enough after all, I imagine." Henry thus cheers but does not delude himself on the Lancastrian score. To be sure, he might be said here to rationalize his resolve, but he does so tentatively and only after his resolve has first been taken.

Bacon's interiorized representation of Henry's decision has the structure of objective analysis, not of subjective thought. It has the rhythm and syntax of the observer rather than of the actor. This point is a crucial one: it means that *Henry VII* is less a dramatic work than an analytic one and that there is more of Bacon—perhaps even more than of Henry—in it. Berry has noted "a distinctive syntactical pattern" in *Henry VII* that is used to render Henry's thinking, namely, the separation of subject from verb, most often by participial phrases.[19] But this pattern renders Bacon's, not Henry's, thinking, and the mental process it reflects is several removes from dramatic action. In this light, Levy's comment that Bacon's *Historie* "is a source only for what it reveals of the mind of its author" becomes more significant; and the observation of S. B. Chrimes, Henry VII's modern biographer, becomes almost ironic: "If we wish to get as near as we can to the real man, we must avoid being mesmerized by seductive Baconian phrases." Of course by "the real man," Chrimes means Henry.[20]

A few pages after his initial depiction of Henry, Bacon writes of the King's first Parliament, speedily summoned upon his arrival in London and actually meeting within a week of his coronation. The actions of this Parliament, in Bacon's view, are meant by Henry to signal the legal and consultative nature of the new government and thus to have symbolic significance.[21] Describing the bills of attainder enacted by this Parliament, Bacon remarks the "wisdom, stay, and moderation of the King's *spirit* of government" (62: my emphasis). This "spirit," although not invariably so wise and moderate, is the keynote and, as such, the real subject of Bacon's *Henry*. The spirit of Henry's government is clearly Henry himself, and yet this spirit is more nearly essential and timeless, more useful and exemplary, than the mere temporal phenomenon of Henry and the merely specific acts of his reign. The word "spirit" is exactly right to define the subject of a work that is personal in focus and yet aspires to a condition of impersonality.

This spirit, essentially the idea or foreconceit of the *Henry*, is realized both in large questions of structure and in the more detailed, more psychological analyses of Henry himself. More than any other phenomenon in the *Henry*, Bacon's handling of his sources and especially his introduction or elaboration of factual errors enable us to document his presuppositions and organizing themes. Relating Bacon's work to its sources, we repeatedly catch him in the conjectural or imaginative act.

The best known mistake in the *Henry* is Bacon's rendition of André's description of Henry's triumphant entry into London. André describes Henry as entering joyfully *(laetanter)*: "Rex ipse Richemundiae comes Saturni luce, quo etiam die de hostibus triumpharat, urbem Londinum magna procerum comitante caterva laetanter ingressus est."[22] Bacon's account is presumably based on Speed's misreading of André, whom Speed (unlike Bacon) identifies as his source. Further, Speed, evidently uneasy about the unlikely presence of the word *latenter* ("covertly"), which he apparently misreads for *laetanter*, in André's description, identifies *latenter* as his reading in the margin of his *History* and makes it clear that his understanding of *latenter* in the context of Henry's entry is conjectural: "But Henry staied not in Ceremonious greetings and popular acclamations, which (it seemes) hee did purposely eschue, for that (*Andreas* saith) hee entred couertly, *meaning belike*, in an Horse-litter or close Chariot."[23] Speed's conjectures become Bacon's facts in the *Henry*:

> with great and honourable attendance . . . he entered the City; himself not being on horseback, or in any open chair or throne, but in a close chariot; as one that having been sometimes an enemy to the whole state, and a proscribed person, chose rather to keep state and strike a reverence into the people than to fawn upon them. [53]

Bacon not only endorses Speed's misreading but also rationalizes it according to his own conception of Henry's natural secrecy and political strategy.

Even more, the "close chariot" becomes for Bacon a perfectly plausible expression of the larger "closeness" of Henry's character; his "fashion" of creating doubts rather than assurance, his "loving to seal up his own dangers," his "closeness" regarding Perkin's designs and connections, his "closeness" to confederates, such that "they stood in the light towards him, and he stood in the dark to them;" his "secret fears touching his own people," his infinite suspicions, his being "full of thoughts and secret observations; and full of notes and memorials of his own hand, especially touching persons"; his financial "nearness" in poring over even petty accounts, his covetousness in accumulating treasure, even the nearness of "the sight of his mind . . . rather strong at hand than to carry afar off."[24] Eventually Henry's "closeness" extends from secrecy, suspicion, strategy, and vision to avarice. It is his close-keeping of things—his guarding, protecting, possessing, and finally his hoarding of things, including himself. It is both strength and weakness, finding expression in Henry's carefulness, circumspection, and calculation and paradoxically inviting precisely those dangers from the envy, self-interest, and ambition of others that it most fears.

Such meanings are implicit at the outset of *Henry VII* in Bacon's adoption of Speed's "close chariot," and some are explicit in Bacon's rationalization of Henry's choice—or in a real sense of his own choice—of conveyance. There is not just an essentialist streak in Bacon's writing of history, there is a latently allegorical one as well. Henry in a close chariot is truly a representation of this King: literally an image or a picture of him and figuratively an encapsulation of much in his character.

The images in *Henry VII* are often inspired by Bacon's immediate sources, especially Hall and, still more noticeably, Speed.[25] There is a kind of authenticity in Bacon's using the imagery of his sources instead of inventing strange new ones, but it is an interpretative authenticity rather than a strictly historical one. The sources offer an origin for imagery external to the historian's own imagination and a specific point of reference for its play. They also offer an invitation to the historian further to point and to pattern their images—or what Bacon seems to have regarded as their imagistic raw material.

The relation of Bacon's patterns of imagery to their sources highlights the distinctive care with which he deployed them. Bacon's patterns are typically pervasive rather than conspicuous, almost subsumed rather than intrusive. They are decidedly present in the text but quotation of them in isolation proves peculiarly distorting. So quoted, the greater number of them are made to seem undeveloped or merely casual and a small number to seem flashier and more focal than they are in context. With the exception of one large group of images and associations, including "idols," counterfeit jewels, stageplays, enchantments, superstitions, poetry, and other things artificial, Bacon's patterns of imagery are largely natural, derived from the weather, the tides, animals, plants, growth and harvest, drink and bread (lees and leaven).[26] The King's enemies specialize in things artificial, the King in things natural, although the obvious moral is not quite so simple, since not all in the nature of the King and his reign is unambiguously benign. Nor all in nature, for that matter.

One of Bacon's major patterns of imagery derives from the action of sea and storm, and it would be difficult to think of a pattern more natural for England. Predictably, Bacon's sources are full of this imagery (as, indeed, was More's *Richard*), and his proximity to them is evident in specific borrowings. In Speed, Henry is "carefull vpon what coast this wandring clowd [Perkin] would at length dissolue it selfe" (II, 740), and in Bacon, Henry has "a careful eye where this [same] wandering cloud would break" (243). Bacon's handling of the imagery of sea and storm has distinctive point, however. As Berry has shown, Henry VII is beset by external storms and rough seas for much of his reign, but once they cease and his throne is finally secure, this imagery turns inward, beginning "to take place in the King; carrying as with a strong tide his affection and thoughts unto the gathering and heaping up of treasure."[27]

The imagery of artificiality—of unreality, untruth, and "poetry" —constitutes another important pattern which has thematic force. This pattern revolves upon the deceptions and self-deceptions of appearance. The material for it is again in Bacon's sources and most striking in Speed, who describes the impostors Lambert Simnell and Perkin Warbeck as "Idols and Counterfeits," and compares them singly to "a Puppet, or property" in a "tragicall motion," and to *"an imaginary and Stage-play Prince."*[28] Prior to Speed's work, of course, Bacon already had referred to Simnell and Warbeck as "idols and counterfeits" in the prospectus written before 1603, but if Speed gets this phrase from Bacon, he develops its associations and use substantially before Bacon gets it back. In Speed, for example, when France and England make peace, the sprightly Perkin and his colleagues are "smoakt out of *France* with the first graine of incense sacrificed vpon the Altars of Peace at Boloign," and in Bacon's *Henry*, "upon the first grain of incense that was sacrificed upon the altar of peace at Bulloigne, Perkin was smoked away." Or again, Speed, having compared Perkin to a false diamond, conjectures how, if only graced by "some great Princes" wearing, such a stone would have been taken for real; Bacon likewise speaks of Perkin as "a finer counterfeit stone than Lambert Symnell; better done, and worn upon greater hands."[29]

There is no tangible evidence that Speed, who notes his sources with unusual care, was able to make use of any material from Bacon about Henry VII except the early prospectus, which Speed duly acknowledges when he refers to it. There is plenty of evidence, however, that Bacon used Speed, and, to all appearances, Bacon let his mind play over Speed's images, as over the whole of Speed's treatment of Henry, probing their wit, developing their wisdom, ordering them into more coherent and meaningful patterns. On grounds of internal evidence alone, the relation between Bacon's and Speed's histories makes it inconceivable that Speed should have disordered Bacon's images, instead of Bacon's ordering Speed's. The relation thus gives us additional insight into the method of the Baconian historian, who, like a wise counselor, attends not only to other men's facts but also to their perceptions and interpretations of them. Such an historian evidently weighs even imaginative perceptions *of things*, refines what truth is in them, and finally conforms their shape to his own wisdom.

Characteristically Bacon develops the images and associations of sources by sharpening or even reducing them locally yet by weaving them more generally and deliberately through the whole text. Like Speed some ten years earlier, for example, Bacon particularly associates Margaret of Burgundy, a Yorkist by birth, with the creation of spirits, idols, and other counterfeit figures. But in Bacon this association is so persistent and often so witty that Margaret becomes a veritable Morgan le Fay, constantly plaguing King Henry with impostors, who should be unlikely but are not quite, and on the whole creating a nuisance that it ought to be reasonable but is actually dangerous to ignore. This Morgan—or Margaret—le Fay remains solidly real, the second sister of Edward IV of England, wife to Charles, Duke of Burgundy; childless herself but a rich and loving patron of her husband's grandchildren. At first even Margaret's motivations may seem real enough: "This Princess (having the spirit of a man and malice of a woman) . . . made it her design . . . to see the Majesty Royal of England once again replaced in her house . . . And she bare such a mortal hatred to the house of Lancaster and personally to the King, as she was no ways mollified by the conjunction of the houses in her niece's marriage; but rather hated her niece," namely, Elizabeth of York, eldest living child and therefore heir of Edward IV (83). Yet it must be granted as well that Margaret's motives quickly sound irrational, excessive, larger-than-life, and reminiscent of the more unreal and poetic ladies of myth like Morgan or Juno, the latter a name (as Bacon via Speed, via André, reports) actually given to Margaret by Henry VII's friends (200).

Subsequent references to Margaret heighten her mythic potential and realize her resemblance to an enchantress. The first impostor Margaret fosters, Lambert Simnell, is regarded by Henry "as an image of wax that others had tempered and moulded" and, once captured, is kept alive as "a continual spectacle, and a kind of remedy against the like inchantments of people in time to come" (91). When Margaret next produces Perkin Warbeck, Bacon explains, "At this time the King began again to be haunted with sprites; by the magic and curious arts of the Lady Margaret; who raised up the ghost of Richard Duke of York . . . to walk and vex the King" (199). And when this ghost is finally laid, Bacon adds, "though the King were no more haunted with sprites, for that by the sprinkling partly of blood and partly of water he had chased them away; yet nevertheless he had certain apparitions that troubled him: still shewing themselves from one region, which was the house of York" (315). This latest apparition also applies to Margaret for help, though it turns out that the failure of her earlier sprites has cooled her enthusiasm for conjuring.

Bacon's conception of Margaret of Burgundy as an ineffectual parody of the mythic enchantress may well illuminate his later association of a mythic "wall of brass" encompassing the kingdom with the text of an actual letter that Henry VII wrote to the City of London (353). Referring to this letter, Wilhelm Busch observes indignantly that its real text, which Bacon reproduces in substance, lacks "the saying he here ascribes to the king, that he had built 'a wall of brass' round his kingdom."[30] Busch's observation assumes that Bacon has written—or has tried to write—history as we should, rather than as he actually wrote it. Bacon does not ascribe the disputed saying to the

King but writes that Henry "expresseth himself *as if* he thought he had built a wall of brass about his kingdom" (my emphasis). In associating a "wall of brass" with the security of Henry's kingdom at his death, Bacon alludes to the brazen walls by which such magicians as Greene's Friar Bacon or Spenser's and Drayton's Merlin sought to surround and forever to protect a British kingdom.[31] Like many of Bacon's images, these allusions to myth and magic are subsumed and yet, with the unlikely assistance of Busch's indignation, they are readily available.

The story of Perkin Warbeck affords an example of Bacon's relation to his sources that is still more thematic in development than Bacon's patterns of imagery. As a result, it indicates dramatically the extent to which Bacon answers to plausibility rather than to fact and even in apparent disregard of fact. Speed, referring to Perkin as an "artificiall creature"—Hall's "poeticall . . . inuencion"—then comments on Perkin's beginning to believe his own lies: "and as it is so obserued of some, that by long using to report an vntruth, at last forgetting themselues to bee the Authors thereof, beleeue it in earnest."[32] Despite a notably poetic analogy to Speed's observation that Spedding finds in *The Tempest*, Bacon's immediate source is clearly Speed.[33] Bacon's version reads, "Nay himself with long and continual counterfeiting and with often telling a lie, was turned (by habit) almost into the thing he seemed to be, and from a liar to a believer" (210–11). In Perkin's figure, Bacon further develops the theme of the deceiver's self-deception—his no-win relation to reality—that Speed, too, associates with Perkin but does not so fully exploit. When Perkin is finally arrested and shown in his true role of juggler or prize-player in a May-game, Bacon remarks drily that now "Perkin could tell better what himself was, [and so] he was diligently examined" (292). Bacon's Perkin has earlier been said by Henry's agents to need "any good poet . . . to write his life," presumably instead of any true historian, and now his life is restored to its reality of falsehood (220). Perhaps the fascination of deception, self-deception, counterfeit forms—the idols of human experience—led Bacon to make Perkin so focal a character in the *Henry* and to relate his adventures at length, even giving him a major speech, an imaginative effort ordinarily reserved by Bacon for figures of such stature as Cardinal Morton, King Henry, and, just once, an ambassador of the French King.[34]

The thematic importance of Perkin in the *Henry* helps to account for Bacon's otherwise inexplicable errors in recounting Perkin's background and early life. These errors make the surprising success of Perkin's impersonation of Edward IV's second son, Richard of York, one of the princes who died in the Tower, less bizarre and more plausible, more profitable, and more exemplary. Their genesis winds back by way of Speed to André. Speed relates that Perkin "(by reason of his abode in *England* in K. *Edwards* dayes) could speake our language"; he continues, "This youth was borne (they say) in the City of *Tornéy*, and called *Peter Warbecke*, the son of a conuerted Jew, whose Godfather at Baptisme King *Edward* himselfe was." Speed claims Polydore and André as sources for his knowledge of Perkin, but Polydore adds nothing of importance here to André, who claims not that Perkin was the Jew's son, but only that he was brought up by him: "Petreyum autem quemdam Tornacensem ab Eduardo quondam Judaeo, postea a rege Eduardo sacro levato fonte, in hac regione educatum, regis Eduardi Quarti minorem filium effinxerunt." Later, André has Perkin speak of his youth: "Eduardi quondam Judaei ac antememorati regis Eduardi filioli in Anglia servulus eram . . . erat enim ille patronus meus regi Eduardo ac suis liberis familiarissimus."[35]

Bacon not only accepts Speed's statement that Perkin was the Jew's son but also elaborates on it, trying to align it with some facts in Perkin's confession following arrest but chiefly engaging in invention:

> There was a townsman of Tournay . . .whose name was John Osbeck (a converted Jew,) married to Katheren de Faro, whose business drew him to live for a time with his wife at London in King Edward the Fourth's days; during which time he had a son by her; and being known in court, the King either out of religious nobleness, because he was a convert, or upon some private acquaintance, did him the honour as to be godfather to his child, and named him Peter [i.e., Perkin]. [202–03]

In making Perkin, rather than the converted Jew Edward, the godson to Edward IV, Bacon apparently misconstrues Speed's none-too-clear syntax, taking its final clause ("whose Godfather . . .") to refer to "son" and not to "Jew," its immediate antecedent. Of course if Bacon had only Speed open before him, he might have forgotten that the Jew supposed by Speed to be Perkin's father was named Edward in André and was therefore the more likely godson of a King named Edward. Whereas, from Perkin's confession, reported in Speed and Hall, Bacon would have learned that Perkin's father was John Osbeck.[36]

If some of Bacon's extravagances in the matter of Perkin can be rationalized, however, some cannot. Having apologized for Bacon's mistaking the relation of Perkin to the Jew Edward and the King on the grounds that he lacked a copy of André, one encounters reluctantly Bacon's claim that the same mistake is to be found in André: "Lastly, there was a circumstance (which is mentioned by one that writ in the same time) . . . which is, that King Edward the Fourth was his godfather" (201). Since the writer contemporary with the matter of Perkin is André, Bacon has presumably taken his authority from Speed's annotations. Incredibly by modern standards, Bacon follows this invocation of André's authority with even freer invention; he reflects on his own notion that Edward IV was Perkin's godfather:

> Which, as it is somewhat suspicious for a wanton prince [i.e., Edward IV] to become gossip in so mean a house [as Perkin's], and might make a man think that he might indeed have in him some base blood of the House of York; so at the least (though that were not) it might give the occasion to the boy, in being called King Edward's godson, or perhaps in sport King Edward's son, to entertain such thoughts into his head. For tutor he had none (for ought that appears), as Lambert Symnell had, until he came unto the Lady Margaret who instructed him. [201–02]

What may be incredible by the standards of factual accuracy is entirely credible by the standards of human plausibility and fictional coherence or, to put the matter another way, by those of character and of theme, namely deception, including that of the self. If only for a Baconian moment, one wonders whether the richly imagined psychological possibilities of Perkin's being King Edward's godson did not make Bacon less attentive to Speed's syntax than he might otherwise have been.

There is other evidence of Bacon's eagerness to enhance the plausibility of Perkin's imposture in order to ensure that he is a phenomenon worth pondering rather than merely an oddity. In the passage we have been examining, which introduces Perkin, Bacon emphasizes the suitability of Perkin's person and manner for the role. Perkin's "favour and shape" are "fine," but more important, he has "a crafty and bewitching fashion both to move pity and to induce belief, as was like a kind of fascination and inchantment to those that saw him or heard him" (201). From a man who never did either, this is quite a testimonial. Bacon's assurance concerning the fluency of Perkin's English—about which earlier histories are less clear or confident, thinking of Perkin as foreign born—is equally strong, for "living much in English company" has made the "English tongue" of Bacon's Perkin "perfect" (203).[37] Measured by his sources, Bacon also exaggerates greatly the coaching Margaret of Burgundy gave Perkin's acting, explaining that she detailed for him everything about young Richard of York, his family, and his experiences needed to make the impersonation complete and convincing.[38]

To take a variant instance, Bacon is rightly praised for clearing away confusion regarding the role Perkin actually played on first going into Ireland, where he willingly took the part of Richard of York from the start, instead of being forced to take it, as he claimed in his confession.[39] But even this sound perception owes as much to plausibility and especially to Bacon's conception of Perkin, as to fact. It comes at the conclusion of Bacon's introductory portrait of Perkin. Bacon proclaims it "the truth" first, a statement we are likely to understand in the light of the preceding portrait, and only thereafter does he add that he is aware of letters from Perkin proving this fact (207). Presumably, too, it is in the clear, consistent light of Perkin's imagined character that Bacon uses one fact, the letters, to disprove another fact, the confession, upon which Bacon relies for other information about Perkin, such as the names of his parents. Plausibility—or probability, as Fussner would have it in this case—can be a Baconian strength, as well as a weakness, in writing history.

Every Baconian mistake is not significant, of course. Bacon does make simple errors; for example, he follows Speed in dating Henry's death April 1508, instead of a year later. The point is, however, that very many of Bacon's apparent errors reveal deliberate method and imposed pattern. Hitherto I have concentrated on those mistakes whose evolution sooner or later involves deliberate manipulation, purpose, and invention. Before proceeding, we might profitably consider an instance in which Bacon does not corrupt his sources by accident or design but tries to *make* sense of their confused or erroneous facts and chronology. In this instance Bacon treats Henry's efforts to discourage France from annexing Brittany.

Spedding offers a fascinating gloss on these efforts that can serve us as an introduction to them. After first remarking that it "seems early" for Henry to give "Brittaine for lost," worrying about Bacon's grounds for this conclusion, and making a halfhearted attempt to find Bacon some grounds, Spedding admits that Bacon's conclusion is more likely to have been "an *inference* from what went before and followed." Spedding's apology next takes a curiously twisted tack, urging us to overlook Bacon's inferential license because Bacon "was proceeding upon false grounds." Bacon, he continues, "was going upon the supposition that the French had had their own way in Brittany, without any effectual check, since the battle of St. Aubin. He knew nothing of the events of 1489, or of the treaty of Frankfort; of which not the slightest hint is to be found in any of our old historians. And believing . . . that the negotiation he was speaking of took place in the spring of 1491, he was endeavouring to *conceive* the case as it would have been then." As we observed in the previous chapter, Sidney put the matter more simply: "Many times" the historian "must tell events whereof he can yield no cause; or, if he do, it must be poetically."[40]

What is striking about Bacon's treatment of his defective sources this time is that you would never know just by reading Bacon there is anything wrong with them:

> The King could not well tell what to think of the marriage of Brittaine. He saw plainly the ambition of the French King was to impatronise himself of the duchy [of Brittany]; but he wondered he would bring into his house a litigious marriage [with the Duchess], especially considering who was his successor. But weighing one thing with another, he gave Brittaine for lost; but resolved to make his profit of this business of Brittaine, as a quarrel for war. . . . [165–66]

Here is stated no evidence of anyone's indecision and resolve except the King's—so long, of course, as we refrain from identifying the King wholly with Bacon. The King's resolve once taken, "keeping himself somewhat close," he calls Chancellor Morton "to him apart" and bids him speak to the French ambassadors "in such language as was fit for a treaty that was to end in a breach" (168). Henry's political nature and nose for profit thus give him a purpose, and his "closeness" gives him a method in proceeding with the French. Bacon's conception of Henry's character and more exactly of his "spirit of government" enables Bacon to infer Henry's conclusion in the absence of accurate facts—or, in Spedding's words, "to conceive the case as it would have been then."

Not until Bacon's sources were painstakingly examined in the nineteenth century did we begin to realize how much of his *Henry* is fiction, or what nineteenth-century historians more simply termed "imagination." Again, Bacon's manipulation and embellishment of "things," while metamorphic, are not conspicuous and are therefore best illuminated by references to his less artful sources or, as the case may be, to his lack of sources. With such reference, the subtler designs underlying the whole, as well as those more local and specific, become increasingly evident. The center of Bacon's initial representation of Henry, the latter's concern to ground his title to the throne on the securest possible base, is basic to these larger designs. Henry's concern and at times his anxiety are among the shaping conceptions of *The Historie* and may be its deepest root, even as textually its beginning and, earlier in the present discussion, the beginning of our examination of the work. This concern, for example, helps otherwise eccentric fictions concerning Henry's attitude toward his Queen and the execution of Sir William Stanley, which first seem unrelated, together fall into place.

In light of Bacon's sources, Henry's hostility to Queen Elizabeth is without any basis in fact. An "aversion toward the house of York" that "found place not only in his [Henry's] wars and counsels, but in his chamber and bed," it is unique to Bacon and opposed to what little information we do have concerning Henry's domestic arrangements.[41] The circumstances surrounding the execution of Stanley, Lord Chamberlain to King Henry, brother-in-law to Henry's mother, and the nobleman whose aid had proved crucial to the victory at Bosworth that made Henry king, are at least somewhat more soundly based on facts than is Henry's aversion to his wife. We are sure at least that Stanley's loyalty became tainted and that he suffered beheading as a result.[42] According to Bacon himself, however, "yet [is it] to this day left but in dark memory, both what the case of this noble person was, for which he suffered; and what likewise was the ground and cause of his defection and alienation of his heart from the King" (227). And so, according to the redoubtable Wilhelm Busch, "from his own invention" Bacon "fills in the scanty account of Stanley's end."[43] Obviously, in view of Bacon's own statement on the "darkness" of Stanley's case, he acted deliberately in doing so. To look in greater detail at the evolution of these two Baconian fictions—the Queen's marriage and Stanley's end—is to realize ever more fully the pervasive, formative influence of Bacon's opening analysis of Henry's resolve to settle his claim to the throne first and foremost on his own Lancastrian right.[44]

Although Henry had sworn prior to Bosworth to marry Elizabeth of York, thus uniting the Lancastrian and Yorkist heirs to the throne, he waited nearly five months after Bosworth and nearly three after his coronation to fulfill his oath. Bacon perceives this delay as Henry's deliberate policy to avoid any suggestion that he is relying on Elizabeth's claim to the title, insofar as he realized such reliance would make him "but a King at courtesy" and give him "rather a matrimonial than a regal power" (48). Further, Bacon informs us, Henry was aware of the persistent rumor that the two sons of Edward IV were yet living, which, if true, would have "prevented the title of the Lady Elizabeth" (49). Whether Elizabeth's title is valid or invalid, then, Bacon's Henry sees it as a potential threat, as well as a potential support, to his own right.

After Henry's own coronation and his first Parliament, which legally entailed the crown upon him and his heirs, Henry proceeds to marriage. Bacon stresses that for Henry marriage with Elizabeth is the last and least of his four chief claims to power (conquest, birthright, law, marriage) and alone of them all is reluctantly embraced: "which day of marriage was celebrated with greater triumph and demonstrations (especially on the people's part) of joy and gladness, than the days either of his entry or coronation; which the King rather noted than liked."[45] Here Bacon's gratuitous additions to his sources, even where, as in the present quotation, they are parenthetical or subordinate and, indeed, syntactically ex post facto, are persistent and, for once, almost intrusive. The fiction of Henry's hostility to his Queen is clearly an important one for Bacon. In a later passage, as an afterthought, Bacon perfunctorily mentions the birth of Prince Arthur less than eight months after the marriage. The opportunities it offered for the symbolism of restoration and renewal, union and continuity, opportunities exploited by other historians, were evidently of little interest or use in Bacon's characterization of Elizabeth's role.[46]

Bacon has another angle of vision, essentially external to Elizabeth, if often enough identified with Henry's view of things in *The Historie*. Referring to Simnell's imposture little over a year and a half after Henry's coronation, Bacon observes, "The root of all [this] was the discountenancing of the house of York, which the general body of the realm still affected. This did alienate the hearts of the subjects from him daily more and more, especially when they saw that after his marriage, and after a son born, the King did nevertheless not so much as proceed to the coronation of the Queen, not vouchsafing her the honour of a matrimonial crown; for the coronation of her was not till almost two years after, when danger had taught him what to do" (70). We have seen that Henry's failure to look "afar off" is one of Bacon's shaping conceptions of Henry's character and of the events in his reign. The chief cause of Henry's "shortness of foresight," according to Bacon, is his insensitivity to the strength of Yorkist sympathy. To the continuing dismay of modern historians, Elizabeth, Henry's Queen, becomes for Bacon the focus and symbol of a deep and repeatedly aggravated aversion Henry has to the house of York. Having reached this conclusion, it is only reasonable, if also highly "poetic," of Bacon to extend this aversion to the privacy of the King's chamber and bed.

We can almost see Bacon's conviction of the matrix of Lancastrian aversion and Yorkist aggravation unfolding:

> But for the extirpating of the roots and causes of the like commotions in time to come, the King began to find where his shoe did wring him; and that it was his depressing of

the house of York that did rankle and fester the affections of his people. And therefore being now too wise to disdain perils any longer, and willing to give some contentment in that kind (at least in ceremony), he resolved at last to proceed to the coronation of his Queen. [93–94]

What we really see, of course, is the growing realization by Bacon's reluctant husband Henry of the political consequences of hostility to the Queen. But again, Bacon's interpretation of this hostility has become increasingly fictional—internally rather than externally coherent, subjectively rather than objectively referential. His interpretative role has also become increasingly intrusive:

the Queen was with great solemnity crowned at Westminster, the twenty-fifth of November, in the third year of his reign, which was about two years after the marriage (like an old christening that had stayed long for godfathers); which strange and unusual distance of time made it subject to every man's note that it was an act against his stomach, and put upon him by necessity and reason of state. [94]

Stomach aching and, just above, shoe wringing, the wise historian variously implies a considerable grasp of, if not a sympathy with, the aversion of the wise King.

Bacon grounds the fiction of Henry's aversion to his Queen in the simple facts of his delaying the marriage and coronation and beyond that in the more fundamental question of Henry's right to the throne. With respect to the marriage, Chrimes wonders aloud how Henry "could possibly have proceeded in any other way." Chrimes's reasons range from political, to personal, to legal and theological ones: from agreeing with Bacon's (literally Henry's) view that Henry had to claim the title as his birthright, to which the marriage was irrelevant; to arguing that Henry had urgently to concentrate his time and energy on a new and unsettled regime and that "Even Henry could hardly have plunged into matrimony with a total stranger" upon whom he had most probably never laid eyes, to reminding us that Elizabeth (as Bacon well knew) was legally "stigmatized as a bastard" when Henry ascended the throne and that she and Henry could not be married without dispensation because they were "related in the fourth degree of kinship and perhaps in the fourth degree of affinity." Chrimes concludes that "To overcome these obstacles took time, and, on the whole, things moved fast to enable the marriage to take place on January 18, 1486."[47] It is surely significant that all these reasons, perhaps excepting the last, should have been available for Bacon's consideration, had he not already decided on another tack.

Indeed, Chrimes even notes that there is little if any basis in contemporary accounts of Henry's reign for the view that Henry's right to the throne was a controverted issue.[48] Thus even Bacon's extended analysis of Henry's resolving to claim the throne in his own right looks still more like an expression of Baconian wisdom than an historical account. That leaves only the delay in the coronation of Henry's Queen, without the supposition upon which Bacon grounds his explanation of it. Chrimes's understanding of this delay is not unlike that of Speed, Bacon's contemporary, who attributes the delay to Henry's not being assured and confident of his throne until after the suppression of the Yorkist revolt incident on Simnell's imposture. Bacon, having read Speed, could think his own interpretation the right one—even the true one—but surely he recognized, if only dimly, that it is, in fact, an interpretation.

Bacon's initial analysis of Henry's right to the throne influences his explanation of Stanley's betrayal more suddenly and conspicuously than it does Henry's domestic aversion. Moreover, because this analysis is still more incidental to Stanley's betrayal, Bacon's pronounced invocation of it further demonstrates the extent of its shaping influence. The ill-fated Stanley, once examined, confesses, hoping vainly thereby to get mercy. But Stanley's claims on the King, Bacon explains, were overweighed by other things "predominant in the King's nature and mind." He then elaborates: "First, an over-merit," not easily repaid to Stanley and therefore embarrassing to the King; next, "the sense of his [Stanley's] power;" thirdly, "the glimmering of a confiscation; for he was the richest subject . . . in the kingdom;" and "Lastly, the nature of the time; for if the King had been out of fear of his own estate, it was not unlike he would have spared his life; but the cloud of so great a rebellion hanging over his head made him work sure" (226–27).

At this point, after accounting so fully and systematically for the King's motives, Bacon plainly acknowledges how "dark" is the cause of Stanley's condemnation, defection, and alienation from the King. He next turns to the legalities of Stanley's case, namely, Stanley's reputedly having said, "That if he were sure that that young man [Perkin] were King Edward's son, he would never bear arms against him." Bacon worries the conditional clause and then considers the "positive words" in the main clause. His conclusion is quick, unerring, and, in the light of his opening analysis of Henry, predictable:

> though the words seem calm, yet it was a plain and direct over-ruling of the King's title, either by the line of Lancaster or by act of Parliament; which no doubt pierced the King more than if Stanley had charged his lance upon him in the field. For if Stanley would hold that opinion, That a son of King Edward had still the better right . . . it was to teach all England to say as much. And therefore, as those times were, that speech touched the quick. [228]

Stanley's end is referred essentially to Henry's perception rather than to the merits of the case itself. From here, Bacon proceeds to Stanley's motives for breaking with the King: "conceit of his [own] merit," ambition, and ingratitude. Although Bacon recounts these motives confidently, he does not analyze them with the same degree of comprehension, engagement, and intimacy that he reserves for the King. He does not participate in them so fully.

* * *

"*WHAT is Truth?* said [Bacon's] jesting Pilate" and thereby provided what is probably the best known opening of any essay by Bacon. This essay, "Of Truth," purports less to have an answer to Pilate's skeptical jest than to reject deliberate falsehood. Judicious, equivocal, and upright, it affords a suitable commentary on Bacon's practice in *Henry VII*.

Ending part I of this book, I suggested that Renaissance *Lives* violate modern standards of factual accuracy not because their authors simply fail to value fact but because they value (and at times overvalue) the truth of fiction. I expect this is also true in Bacon's case. For all Bacon's condescension to poetry (understood specifically as an ideal fiction), the truth he thoughtfully, skillfully, consciously espouses in *Henry VII* is so full of imaginative inventions insecurely or inadequately based on fact as often to qualify in our eyes purely as fiction. To the characteristics of this fiction as a narrative I should now turn more closely.

CAUGHT IN A COBWEB OF WORDS

Examining Bacon's narrative manner in *The Historie* without benefit of the X-ray illumination shed by his sources, we shall again find his role more latent and subdued. As we notice patterns of words and images, themes, and especially internalized perspectives, we recognize his artistic presence but we are unlikely to suspect its real extent. The margins of my own copy of the *Henry* are dotted with such queries as "Is there any basis for this in Bacon's sources" or "How much of this is Bacon," and until I went to the sources, I could not anticipate their answers, at least not to the extent that I could with Walton's more openly artful *Life of Donne*. The lines cited just above, which so reasonably and confidently describe the King's response to Stanley's treasonous opinion ("For if Stanley would hold that . . . it was to teach all England to say as much"), got one of the queries in point. The following lines, which I offer the reader without benefit of Bacon's sources, got another. They refer to the report to Henry by his ambassadors of new evidence of the French king's designs on Brittany: "After consultation with the ambassadors, who brought him no other news than he expected before (though he would not seem to know it till then), he presently summoned his Parliament" (114). On simply reading this statement, no one could reasonably be sure how much of it is in the sources and how much is plain fiction on Bacon's part.[49]

Similarly when, during the sitting of Henry's first Parliament, Bacon refers to the future prominence of the King's natural avarice, we are likely to note the reference without quite realizing how operative a conception it is to become in Bacon's interpretation of Henry's character: these laws "being points of profit to his coffers, whereof from the very beginning he was not forgetful; and had been more happy at the latter end, if his early providence, which kept him from all necessity of exacting upon his people, could likewise have attempered his nature therein. He added during parliament to his former creations the ennoblement or advancement in nobility of a few others" (63–64). The last sentence of the quotation shows the lack of emphasis this first reference to Henry's avarice receives.

Only in retrospect do we really see that Bacon has from the beginning a settled conception of Henry's nature to which he alludes early in *The Historie* and in the light of which he interprets or invents Henry's responses. What is significant, however, is that Bacon does not introduce Henry as a fully realized character. He does not give us an opening portrait, or characterization, of Henry equivalent to More's depiction of Richard III's nature, of "what maner of manne this was," as More expresses it. Instead, he presents Henry's engagement with a problem, the ground of his title to the throne; an objectified image, Henry's entrance into the City in a close chariot; a chronicle-style report of an outbreak of sweating-sickness, and an account of the King's decisive actions, his coronation and summoning of Parliament.

Internalized perspectives notwithstanding, then, Bacon's narrative *manner* is objective, issue oriented, and, above all, dispassionate. In numerous ways, he is at pains to give this impression of it. Among the most telling is his definite, sometimes abrupt, and seemingly unshaped alternation of an annalistic approach with one relatively more personal, psychological, or analytical: by "Poynings' Law," for example,

> all the statutes of England were made to be of force in Ireland. For before they were not; neither are any now in force in Ireland, which were made in England since that time; which was the tenth year of the King.
>
> About this time began to be discovered in the King that disposition, which afterwards nourished and whet on by bad counsellors and ministers proved the blot of his times: which was the course he took to crush treasure out of his subjects' purses, by forfeitures upon penal laws. At this men did startle the more (at this time), because it appeared plainly to be in the King's nature, and not out of his necessity; he being now in float for treasure. . . . [233–34]

In a second example, the fuller, more focal, and more searching attention to Henry again emerges suddenly, as if the result of history itself, rather than of art. To avoid distortion, an unbroken citation is needed: the Cornishmen

> encamped upon Blackheath, between Greenwich and Eltham; threatening either to bid battle to the King (for now the seas went higher than to Morton and Bray), or to take London within his view; imagining with themselves there to find no less fear than wealth.
>
> But to return to the King. When first he heard of this commotion of the Cornishmen occasioned by the subsidy, he was much troubled therewith; not for itself, but in regard of the concurrence of other dangers that did hang over him at that time. For he doubted lest a war from Scotland, a rebellion from Cornwall, and the practices and conspiracies of Perkin and his partakers, would come upon him at once: knowing well that it was a dangerous triplicity. . . . [267][50]

Especially as the *Henry* develops, the alternation of annalistic and analytical passages is Bacon's method of balancing and even resisting subjective patterning, of ensuring that we do not become too interested in Henry's character and unrealistically lose sight of events outside his initiation and control. Indeed, although Bacon applies Ockham's razor relentlessly to chronicle details marginally relevant to main issues, he keeps just enough of them to remind us that history is untidy, such as the burning of "the King's palace of Shyne" or the death of Sir James Parker, who "by accident of a faulty helmet . . . was stricken into the mouth at the first course [in a joust], so that his tongue was borne unto the hinder part of his head" (293, 192). Because such digressive elaboration is infrequent in the *Henry*, it is noticeable when it occurs and effective in intimating the "true" historicity of the work.

A relatively greater proportion of annalistic notations occurs in the final third of the *Henry*. In part this results from the fact that the material for Henry's later years is thinner in Bacon's sources; the ticking off of Henry's years simply quickens. At the same time, however, this kind of presentation is entirely appropriate to the unfolding of Henry's character, already achieved as his life draws to a close. It constitutes a further disengagement from the historical process of characterizing him.

The narrative manner of *Henry VII* enforces modified engagement with character. While factual and specific, it is curiously disembodied. Much as we observe of Henry's process of thought and response, he remains almost faceless until the end. We hear little of his person; his background prior to Bosworth or the closeness of his relation to his mother and to his much-trusted uncle Jasper Tudor does not exercise Bacon's imagination.[51] We do not even learn what Henry looks like until three paragraphs from the end of *The Historie*, near the end of the character that concludes it. Comparing passages from Bacon's *Henry* with their parallels in Polydore and Hall, Robert Adolph has specially noted Bacon's excision of the earlier writers' "dramatic and sensuous touches" and has remarked a consequently "abstract" quality in the prose style of the *Henry*.[52] But Bacon's method, at least, might better be described as analytical than as abstract, since it is abstracted neither from temporal and material actors and events nor from interior process or assessment of them.

Although Bacon has a preconception of Henry's character, he does not argue explicitly from character to cause and from characterization to action as More does with Richard III. As Bacon presents Henry's character, it is a process of evaluation and response to the problems of governing the realm. Henry's difficulties are engaging, but he himself is laid out a little flatly, impersonally, clinically. He is sentient but faceless, individual but exemplary, always thinking but thinking always about some matter of state. Of course this is partly the man Henry Tudor, as Bacon sees him, and partly the method of portraying him. As with the earlier life-writers, it is virtually impossible quite to distinguish life-lived and *Life*-written in *Henry VII*.

Bacon gives the impression of testing and refining what preconceptions he has about Henry and his reign against historical situations as *The Historie* progresses. Ironically this process may account for some of his invention: that is, if his conceptions proved true enough, grounded firmly enough in the realities of events, they ought to enable him to fill in a few gaps. The same process, though at one more remove than a chronological account from the events themselves, is nowhere more evident than in the concluding character of Henry, where we might least have expected to find it. Moving in this character from the King's mercy to the relatively small number of executions in his reign, to the correlatively large number of financial penalties and exactions, Bacon turns again to the subject of the King's greed: "Of nature assuredly he coveted to accumulate treasure; and was a little poor in admiring riches" (357). Fortunately for monarchies, Bacon next explains, the people prefer to impute their wrongs to the prince's counselors instead of to the prince and in this instance to Morton and Bray, who actually managed to temper Henry's greed, whereas their successors Empson and Dudley not only gave means to his greed but also actively encouraged it, even finding new outlets for it. Henry's excess, Bacon continues, "had at that time many glosses and interpretations" (358). Some thought Henry had grown "to hate his [restless and rebellious] people." Others thought it done to humble them and render them more governable. Others, "that he would leave his son a golden fleece" or that he had foreign designs and ambitions:

> But those perhaps shall come nearest the truth that fetch not their reasons so far off; but rather impute it to nature, age, peace, and a mind fixed upon no other ambition or pursuit. [358]

This excerpt from the concluding character, which I have partly summarized and partly quoted, encapsulates the method of the larger *Historie*. It begins with the assertion that we have come to recognize as one of Bacon's settled conceptions when he began the work: "*Of nature* assuredly he coveted to accumulate treasure" (my emphasis). This conception is next aligned with the actual facts and situations (Morton, Bray, Empson, Dudley) and refined by them. Through this process the truth—at least the near truth, "perhaps" —then emerges for Bacon. Here, in short, are preconception, reconsideration, and likely conclusion.[53]

But Bacon does not end his final consideration of Henry's avarice with even the likely truth about the cause of Henry's excess. Instead he appends an assessment of its practical consequences: "whereunto I should add . . . the necessities and shifts for money of other great Princes abroad . . . did the better by comparison set off to him the felicity of full coffers" (358). He then comments that Henry never hesitated to spend money when "his affairs required" and built magnificently but gave limited rewards: "So that his liberality was rather upon his own state and memory than upon the deserts of others." Consideration thus ends on a morally ambiguous note: first the political advantage of full coffers, next the astuteness to spend whatever was needed, and finally the stinginess and selfishness—the closeness—at the base alike of royal strength and weakness.

The portion of the long character ending *The Historie* just examined is not an isolated instance of the process of assessment in the whole. The following is another example that begins with one of Bacon's familiar preconceptions regarding Henry's "nature," speculates further as to its cause, and ascertains its practical and political effects. Bacon describes Henry's nature as "almost marred . . . by troubles" and then explains,

> His wisdom, by often evading from perils, was turned rather into a dexterity to deliver himself from dangers when they pressed him, than into a providence to prevent and remove them afar off. And even in nature, the sight of his mind was like some sights of eyes; rather strong at hand than to carry afar off. For his wit increased upon the occasion; and so much the more if the occasion were sharpened by danger. Again, whether it were the shortness of his foresight, or the strength of his will, or the dazzling of his suspicions, or what it was; *certain it is* that the perpetual troubles of his fortunes (*there being no more matter out of which they grew*) could not have been without some great defects and main errors in his nature, customs, and proceedings. [363–64: my emphasis]

The conclusion, the certainty that Henry's troubles were related to flaws in his nature, is stated conditionally and couched in terms of negative evidence ("could not . . . without"). The claim to certainty, though hardly mocked or canceled in this context, is thereby muted.[54] Most interesting is the parenthetical and therefore subsumed, positive claim that Henry's character, because other material causes were lacking, was in fact the source of all troubles in his reign. Not until the end of the *Henry* does Bacon so explicitly ground the troubled events of the reign in Henry's character, and even here, having done so, he pulls back: "But those [defects] do best appear in the story itself" (364). In *The Historie* of his reign, Henry is focal, and yet he is parenthetically and conditionally so, subject to our sorting out for ourselves the center of his story. As Bacon's *Henry* is and is not objective, is and is not true, it is and is not life-writing.

Having just sent us back to "the story itself" in the passage at hand, Bacon recalls our attention in the very next sentence—"Yet take him with all his defects . . ."—and proceeds to compare Henry favorably to the monarchs of France and Spain contemporary with him. Bacon finds Henry "more politic" than Louis XII and "more entire and sincere" than Ferdinand. Then he decides to substitute Louis XI for Louis XII and declares the former, plus Henry and Ferdinand, "the *tres magi* of kings of those ages" (364). He ends the paragraph and, this time, the substance of the character as well on an equivocal note: "if this King did no greater matters, it was long of himself; for what he minded he compassed." Paraphrase shows the circularity of this conclusion: if Henry did nothing greater, it was his own doing, for what he had a mind to do, he got done. More freely, the limits of Henry's measurable achievements were those of his vision. But the circularity of Bacon's insight is itself significant. Henry's external and internal actions are coextensive for Bacon. Henry's recorded behavior bodies forth his thought, and to analyze one is to analyze the other. Herein lies the warrant for Bacon's interiorized analyses of Henry's thinking.

In *The Historie* as a whole and even in its concluding character, Bacon's method of exposition insists on process; typically, instead of arguing from character to cause, he analyzes character causing. More's method, on the other hand, might be said to discover the same process somewhat reluctantly. More's view of Richard's own nature, his evil character, is fixed, yet as More's history unfolds, he tests an ideal conception of human nature against the phenomenon of Richard and the effects of his reign.

While Bacon's conception of Henry is subject to process in *The Historie*, however, his more general notion of human nature is not. Whether analyzing Henry's avarice or his shortsightedness, Bacon invariably finds—as he puts it elsewhere—"that everything human is subject to imperfection, and good is almost always associated with evil" or, for that matter, evil with good.[55] His view of human nature is at once morally mixed and philosophically settled. It underlies his investigative treatment of individual character and his apparent conviction that individuality, properly analyzed by the wise historian, is what exemplifies truly.

In the course of *The Historie*, Bacon's minor characters, his sketches of figures other than King Henry, also belong more to process and continuing narrative than do those in More's *Richard*. More at least tries to use characters—Hastings, Shore's Wife, Edward IV—as islands of principle, islands of resistance to instability and inhumanity. Such characterizations are powerful instances of subjective patterning in the *Richard*. Bacon's characters are less autonomous and more contextual. They merge with the overall development of the *Henry*. A case in point is the character of Cardinal Morton, which Bacon introduces in good annalistic style: "This year also died John Morton, Archbishop of Canterbury, Chancellor of England, and Cardinal" (310). This notice is followed by a quick, ambiguously balanced assessment: "He was a wise man and an eloquent, but in his nature harsh and haughty, much accepted by the King, but envied by the nobility and hated of the people." There immediately follows a rather surprising regression to Perkin's Proclamation, reported some sixty pages earlier, from which, Bacon only now informs us, Morton was excluded because of the inseparability of his image from the Pope: "Neither was his name left out . . . for any good will" (311). The abruptness of this gratuitous association ("hated of the people" / Perkin's Proclamation) indicates unfinished business, assessment in process, and, indeed, the interpreting presence of Bacon. The next consideration reaches even further back, to get at the origin of Morton's acceptance by the King, namely, his "secrecy and diligence," loyalty, and "inveterate malice against the house of York." Then, moving his consideration of the King's high regard for Morton toward the present, Bacon soon aligns the "envy" or ill will directed at Morton with the envy directed at Henry himself: Morton

> was willing also to take envy from the King more than the King was willing to put upon him. For the King cared not for subterfuges, but would stand envy, and appear in any thing that was to his mind; which made envy still grow upon him more universal, but less daring. [311]

So much is this character in process that Bacon actually becomes distracted here by the topic of envy from his ostensible concern, Morton, to Henry, his larger and more abiding one.[56] In effect, he reconsiders his opening assessment of Morton ("envied . . . hated") in relation to a fuller historical context involving the stoutness of the King's will, another characteristic Bacon associates with both Henry's achievements and their limitations.

Bacon turns easily from the topic of envy to Morton's part in Henry's exactions and then again back in time to Morton's influence on another Henry, "the Duke of Buckingham, whom he did secretly incite to revolt from King Richard" and after abandon. He concludes the character first with a noncommittal gesture—"But whatsoever else was in the man"—next with recognition of Morton's real achievement—"he was the principal means of joining the two Roses"—and finally with the annalistic observation of Morton's great age but "strong health and powers." He then turns quickly and uneventfully to "The next year, which was the sixteenth year of the King and . . . the year of jubilee at Rome," an occasion for the Pope to levy huge sums of money within England as well as within the other countries of Christendom.

Cardinal Morton is the leading example of the numerous churchmen employed by Henry in positions of wealth and power, a practice that Bacon criticizes sharply as "one of the causes of his troublesome reign."[57] Yet, if the progression from the Cardinal's character right to the papal levies is designed by Bacon for ironic effect, its potential goes largely unexploited. Still, it does not quite pass unremarked: three sentences after characterizing Morton, Bacon comments slyly that the levies were more tactfully handled in England than those which fomented the Reformation in Germany less than two decades after.[58] While present as a fact in the text, Bacon's associative selection and arrangement of material—Cardinal-Chancellor-Archbishop Morton followed directly by Papal impositions—are subsumed and understated. They are typical of the artful but unintrusive manner in which Bacon works.

Taken by itself, the character of Morton has more point than an arbitrary obituary notice and has also a specific relation to the themes, as well as to the historical events, of *The Historie*. It is thoughtful and, although brief, avoids merely simplifying Morton's complexity. At the same time, the potential in it for reflection on "what maner of manne this was," as More put it, is barely touched. Bacon is far more interested in this character's relation to the central impulses of *The Historie of the Raigne* as a whole. With Morton, it is clear that Bacon's vision of history and causation encompasses individual characters and is fundamentally broader than any but perhaps the one character most focal among them. And even in Henry's case, virtue and fortune, inner will and outer forces and circumstances, count nearly alike: "in him as in all men (and most of all in Kings) his fortune wrought upon his nature, and his nature upon his fortune" (363).

As before, Bacon's handling of formal characterizations in the *Henry* can be set in perspective by comparison with that of Lord Herbert of Cherbury in his history of Henry VIII. Lord Herbert's *Henry* is similar enough in method and close enough in time to Bacon's to offer a fair comparison and different enough to illuminate more sharply Bacon's art—an art whose unintrusiveness belies its presence and makes its nature elusive. Lord Herbert's *Henry* is characterized by an overwhelming accumulation of fact, a general directness and openness of interpretation, careful and judicious (if also prolix and loosely focused) examination of evidence, and on the whole a greater objectivity and plainer historicity than Bacon's *Henry.* Despite evidence that Lord Herbert, too, invented speeches to fit what he knew of the speaker and occasion, his history still has authority as a source, largely for the original documents he prints and translates in the text.[59]

Lord Herbert's concluding character of Henry VIII, while relatively simpler and more straightforward in its assessment than Bacon's, is morally complex and even ambiguous enough to pass as a reflection of Bacon's concluding character of Henry VII.[60] Taking issue with those who criticize Henry VIII for covetousness, for example, Lord Herbert considers this King's prodigality more pernicious. He contrasts it unfavorably with Henry VII's accumulation of treasure, which was well known by foreign powers always to be sufficient to "pay an Army Royall." In contrast, Henry VIII not only exhausted his treasury and had "to have recourse to unusuall and grievous" measures to relieve his wants but also "exposed his Kingdom to the Invasion of his Neighbours" through his obvious lack of financial readiness. Lord Herbert concludes that the apparent covetousness of Henry VII "was a royall Vertue: whereas the excessive and needlesse expences of *Henry* VIII drew after them those miserable consequences . . . so much reproached" (573–74). Lord Herbert then turns round on his own reasoned view of political virtue and vice, wondering whether the elder Henry's excessive "Vertue"—covetousness in this case—might not have led in a vicious circle to the opposite vice of his son: "whether . . . the young Prince his Son, finding such a mass of money, did [not] first carelessly spend, and after strive to supply as he could." Although Lord Herbert's concluding character is a process of moral and intellectual assessment, it is less broadly and persistently one than is Bacon's. Despite Lord Herbert's relative openness of mind, he remains more concerned with an objective and impartial truth than with a thought-provoking method and more concerned with the interpretation of fact than with the wisdom of insight.

The contrast between Lord Herbert's manner in introducing the concluding character and Bacon's manner is striking. Bacon introduces his lengthy character in a single short sentence and acknowledges his own presence only parenthetically: "This King (to speak of him in terms equal to his deserving) was one of the best sort of wonders; a wonder for wise men" (354–55). Lord Herbert contemplates the prospect of a character considerably less confidently and apparently sees it as a necessary but artificial formality:

> And now if the Reader (according to my manner in other great Personages) do expect some Character of this Prince, I must affirm, (as in the beginning) that the course of his life being commonly held various and diverse from it self, he will hardly suffer any, and that his History will be his best Character and description. Howbeit, since others have so much defamed him, as will appear by the following Objections, I shall strive to rectifie their understandings who are impartiall lovers of truth; without either presuming audaciously to condemn a Prince, heretofore Soveraign of our Kingdom, or omitting the just freedom of an Historian.[570]

If there is a touch of defensiveness in Lord Herbert's tone, it is presumably directed against his own forthcoming effort to characterize Henry VIII. Otherwise his apology suggests an ingenuousness that would be hard to imagine in Bacon's *Historie*. Nothing so outspoken is characteristic of Bacon's *Henry*. Lord Herbert's claim to truth is essentially objective rather than interpretative, and it is based on impartiality rather than on wisdom.

The ends of both works, which extend or comment on the preceding characters, sharpen the contrast between them. Once again, and this time without offering any alternative, Lord Herbert sends the judicious, or perhaps the wise, reader back to the body of the history: "But what this Prince was, and whether, and how far forth excusable in point of State, Conscience or Honour, a diligent observation of his Actions, together with a conjuncture of the times, will (I conceive) better declare to the judicious Reader, then any factious relation on what side whatsoever" (575). Despite the greater openness of Lord Herbert's presence in his history—indeed, perhaps, because of it—he tends to distinguish his interpretations and opinions more fully and carefully from the actual record of events than does Bacon. The end of Bacon's *Henry*, we have noted previously, refers to his own work as a monument and expresses his hope that Henry might endure in Bacon's art. In comparison, Lord Herbert's final sentence seems deliberately to negate this traditional claim. Whereas Bacon wishes Henry might dwell "in this monument of his fame," Lord Herbert writes simply, "To conclude; I wish I could leave him in his grave." Lord Herbert's outspoken acknowledgment of his own presence earlier in *Henry VIII* and then his final negation of art illuminate by contrast Bacon's elusive presence throughout *Henry VII* and his final affirmation of art. This Baconian presence has been with us for a long time: in Bacon's manipulation of facts and images from his sources, in his interiorized analyses of Henry, and more recently in his parenthetical observations and associative sequences and in the continuous process of his assessment of character. I should now turn to this presence more directly.

As processes, interiorized analyses and even formal characters might be said to belong to their subjects. Henry VII's thinking is to an extent a mimetic, dramatic technique of portraying him: the complexity and moral ambiguity of Bacon's method of characterizing Henry at the end of *The Historie* is not separable from the very mixed character of Bacon's Henry himself. We have observed such a correspondence between choice of method and subject in life-writing before this. Apart from interiorized analyses and formal characters, however, Bacon's narrative has a process of its own:

> As for Empson and Dudley's mills, they did grind more than ever. So that it was a strange thing to see what golden showers poured down upon the King's treasury at once. The last payments of the marriage-money from Spain. The subsidy. The benevolence. The recoinage. The redemption of the city's liberties. The casualties. And this is the more to be marvelled at, because the King had then no occasions at all of war or troubles. He had now but one son; and one daughter unbestowed. He was wise. He was of a high mind. He needed not to make riches his glory, he did so excel in so many things else; save that certainly avarice doth ever find in itself matter of ambition. Belike he thought to leave his son such a kingdom and such a mass of treasure, as he might choose his greatness where he would. [335–36]

This is the prose of the engaged observer, the storyteller, not the annalistic reporter of facts. Hearing it read aloud we might almost expect also to hear in the background the arranging of the set upon which it comments. Of course Bacon, presumably aware and indeed in control of its dramatic potential himself, defuses it in the subsequent paragraph of one sentence: "This year was also kept the Serjeant's feast, which was the second call in this King's days."

The passage in question is simultaneously an observation of and on Henry's avarice. Examined more closely, it has two counterbalanced sections, each with a series of short sentences or fragments that are nominally sentences and its second stage beginning with a relatively longer sentence, whose comparative construction ("the more . . . marvelled at") is literally a step up, the intensification of wonder from "a strange thing" to a marvel. This second stage leads through further reflection to a conclusion, which is for the Baconian reader predictably subordinate to the main clause of the sentence in which it occurs ("*save* that *certainly* avarice doth *ever* find in itself matter of ambition"), even while it is distinguished by the certainty of a morality ever true. As predictably, this conclusion leads promptly to another thought, the possibility that Henry's avarice has behind it a motive larger than itself or even than a merely personal ambition, namely, the "greatness" of his dynasty in the person of his son. This possibility is more rational, more charitable, more likely ("Belike"), but for all that, not necessarily true. It supersedes but does not cancel the self-enclosure of the avaricious man.

The movement we have been examining is not even analysis so much as observation, reflection, and insight; further, it is Bacon's alone, not Henry's. Its syntax is especially distinctive: informal ("As for," "So that," "And this"), fragmentary, progressive, and at moments rhythmically self-perpetuating ("The subsidy. The benevolence. The recoinage. The redemption of the city's liberties . . . He was wise. He was of a high mind. He need not . . ."). Although far less frantic and far more orderly, such rhythms and lists are curiously suggestive of Robert Burton's observer of the madding crowd: "Today we heare of new Lords and officers created, tomorrow of some great men deposed, and then again of fresh honors conferred; one is let loose, another imprisoned; one purchaseth, another breaketh: he thrives, his neighbor turns bankrupt; now plenty, then again dearth and famine; one runs, another rides, wrangles, laughs, weeps. . . ."[61] Repunctuation of Bacon's passage to remove nearly all the full stops and as far as possible to make it a single sentence increases the resemblance. But even as Bacon's short, fragmentary sentences stand, they reflect the irrational round of collection, accumulation, and exaction.

There is every sign of deliberation and control in Bacon's passage, including pacing (and punctuation) and details of diction and structure that the ear hears as unified effect but analysis discovers by dissection. In the first line, for example, the verbal form "did grind" rather than simply "ground" prolongs and in this way mirrors the unrelenting, endless working of Empson's and Dudley's mills. The use of "did grind" in this way is unusual in English, since its force but not its form is imperfect or past descriptive; in fact, "did," as used here, looks even more like a descendant of Middle English "gan" ("did"), which introduces an action that is logically incomplete. Another sign of Bacon's attention to detail is his use of the passive infinitive "to be marvelled at" (about halfway through the passage). Although it can be argued that the infinitive's passivity impersonalizes it, the use of the verbal form, instead of the corresponding adjective, is an invitation to marvel, to engage in an action, rather than an assertion or an action completed (e.g., "This is marvelous.").

Still another, more extensive indication of Bacon's care can be seen in the difference between the sentence fragments of the first section of the passage and the short sentences of the second section. Aside from the obvious contrast in length and syntax, the fragments consist of material or objective things, while the sentences refer to less tangible considerations—family responsibility, wisdom, high-mindedness, excellence. The sentences refer to Henry's "virtue," the fragments to his "fortune" or actually to a parody of his fortune, an effort to reduce it to a quantifiable and controllable mass of treasure.

The imagery and even the mythology allusively present, though not explicitly developed, in the passage also attest to the fineness of Bacon's work.

Jove's "golden showers" now pour down "upon the King's treasury" instead of upon a fertile lap and thereby suggest the unnaturalness of the King's avarice.[62] The image of Empson's and Dudley's mills, good in its own biblically resonant simplicity, finds fulfillment in the repetitive rhythm of the short and fragmentary sentences that follow and in the circularity of King Henry's avarice, which "doth ever find in itself matter of ambition." The "ever" of this clause completes the "ever" of the grinding of those mills in the first sentence quoted; and after the insistent recurrence of the subject "He" in the immediately preceding lines, "avarice," the depersonalized subject of the same clause, comments tacitly on the dehumanizing process of greed.

The fact that Bacon's exteriorized narrative can become a process of reflection and insight makes it less surprising that his narrative should move so easily into and out of an interiorized analysis of his characters—Henry in particular, although to a lesser extent other figures as well, for example, the ambitious and devious French king or the rebellious Earl of Lincoln.[63] Since further examination of this technique will require the citation of about three pages of text, I shall adopt the expedient of quoting the phrases that indicate the interiorizing of Bacon's analysis of Henry's thought without quoting their full context but shall quote Bacon's subsequent commentary on this thinking more fully. The instance I have selected is one of several in which Bacon analyzes Henry's thinking from within but also explains why Henry is mistaken. As a result, there is no question of the fact of distance in judgment between Bacon and Henry, as there can be when Bacon is focusing on Henry's responses to the exclusion of all else. Strikingly in the following passage, Bacon's explanation of what Henry *fails* to think begins, for all the world, to sound as if his own character Henry were thinking it:

> For (as was partly touched before) the King had cast the business thus with himself. He took it for granted in his own judgment . . . he conceived . . . and besides . . . He conceived likewise . . . So then judging it would be a work of time, he laid his plot . . . Wherein first he thought . . . knowing . . . And because he knew . . . he chose . . . considering . . . he saw no other expedient . . . Besides he had in consideration . . . He thought likewise . . . So that in substance he promised himself money, honour, friends, and peace in the end. But those things were too fine to be fortunate and succeed in all parts; for that great affairs are commonly too rough and stubborn to be wrought upon by the finer edges or points of wit. The King was *likewise deceived* in his two main grounds. For although *he had reason to conceive* . . . yet *he did not consider* that Charles was not guided by any of the principal of the blood or nobility, but by mean men, who make it their master-piece of credit and favour to give venturous counsels which no great or wise man durst or would. *And for Maximilian, he was thought* then a greater matter than he was; his unstable and necessitous courses *being not then known*. [112–14: my emphasis]

Only the negatives really remind us that these are no longer Henry's views. "And for Maximilian," the opening of the final sentence, belongs to the storyteller for whom the issues are once more coming alive. The passive "was thought" again impersonalizes the act of thinking, since, after all, we lack an historical thinker, but it also opens this process of thinking to any who would join it. "Being not then known" is the passive, impersonal substitute for Henry's knowing, but it is also a state of *being*, a curiously present and active condition. This use of the present passive participle (being known), actually the present participle in combination with the past one, effectively moves the missing knowledge to the forefront of consideration and experience.

"History and experience," wrote Bacon, "I consider . . . to be the same thing," and as earlier noted, he thereby implied a continuum between experience past and present, between that of the historical actor and that of his true interpreter.[64] Surely one reason Bacon enters so naturally into Henry's analyses is that they merge with or grow out of his own. Experience, the experience that feeds wisdom and upon which wisdom feeds, is the common denominator between Bacon and Bacon's Henry, with the qualification, of course, that Bacon's present vision is privileged by the perspective of history—of memory, as he himself put it—and thus privileged by the greater wisdom of hindsight and emotional distance.

There is one point in the *Henry* where Bacon refers conspicuously to himself, making the continuum between past actor and present interpreter explicit. He apologizes for recounting yearly in detail and at length the laws in King Henry's reign:

> whereof I have these reasons; both because it was the preeminent virtue and merit of this King, to whose memory I do honour; *and because it hath some correspondence to my person;* but chiefly because in my judgment it is some defect even in the best writers of history, that they do not often enough . . . set down the most memorable laws that passed in the times whereof they write, being indeed the principal acts of peace. [147–48: my emphasis]

Bacon's awareness as a rhetorician and as an historian, as a manipulator of words and facts, can hardly be longer in question. His awareness of his own presence in the *Henry* is, however.

It would be supersubtle, I suppose, to see Bacon aware of the *Henry* as a reflection as much of his own mind as of Henry's and therefore aware of the relativity of his own interpretation—to see him aware that its real subject is the political mind playing over recorded material or aware that the work as a whole might turn autobiographically inward, much as his images of the rough seas and storms of Henry's external fortunes turn inward to the currents of his avarice. On the other hand, to imagine the writer of the *Henry* as simply unaware, self-deceived, and confident of his own objectivity is, on the basis of the evidence we have examined, unwarranted—indeed, plainly wrong. "Those perhaps shall come nearest the truth"—to borrow Bacon's own phrasing—who see some irreducible ambiguity in Bacon's awareness.

Lord Chancellor Bacon's impeachment for taking bribes occurred in the same year in which the *Henry* was written. The *Henry* was, in fact, the first work to which Bacon turned after his disgrace. While it might be true, as is usually assumed, that Bacon hoped to regain favor by writing a fair sample of the history of England in which James I had once expressed interest, it is naive to assume that he would not choose to write the history of a man with special relevance to himself—to his interests, to his expertise, to his insight, and perhaps even to his failings; to his political and legal experience, to his psychological and moral wisdom, and perhaps to his greed or, at least in one serious case, his shortsightedness. In the context of seventeenth-century politics, it would also be incredible to think that the *Henry* courts favor or forgiveness without offering some sign of apology and acknowledgment.[65] Certainly as seen from the outside, the former storms of Bacon's own external fortunes do turn inside when he is foolish and shortsighted enough to tolerate and indeed to accept the practice of bribery; and yet in his view of Henry, at least, wisdom and service ultimately outweigh vice.

And as for the courting of favor through the exhibition of one's own talents and use, the reference of Speed, Bacon's fellow historian, to that man who would write a history of Henry VII could not have failed to catch Bacon's eye. Such "an argument," Speed had written, "for the worthy doing thereof, requires as wise a man as *Henry* himselfe."[66] Speed's comment is the more likely to have been noted by Bacon since it falls on the same page on which Speed reports that "a learned, eloquent Knight, and principal Lawyer of our time," namely Bacon, has already made "very regardable" observations on "the *Character* of this famous wise Prince," Henry VII.

In a book that has often invoked analogies with portraiture and has examined pictorial metaphors, it is difficult for me at this juncture not to think of Rembrandt's paintings of persons other than himself, out of nearly every face of which look the eyes of Rembrandt's self-portraits. At the same time it is difficult not to suspect as well that Bacon's awareness of his own presence in the *Henry* is in some degree my own invention. Perhaps the effect on an author of a book on life-writing is like the effect on an author of writing a *Life*, and this one is becoming my own fiction. The final chapter of a book on the truth of Renaissance life-writing could have no more appropriate and no truer ending.

Throughout this study I have intended to demonstrate how an awareness of truth in fiction, or of fiction in truth, exists with increasing complexity in Renaissance depictions of historical figures. With the near exception of Shakespeare's *Henry VIII*, such awareness in the works I have treated never becomes so tensely and skeptically an oxymoron as it has tended to be in modern times. The nature of such awareness (or its lack, as in Bede) is inseparable from a conception of truth, and the Renaissance conception cannot be equated with one in our own century. We have always known these things, but as the more polemical moments in these pages suggest, we have not fully explored or acknowledged their implications.

With the ending of this book, Woolf's truth of fiction and truth of fact, Frye's constructive and descriptive elements of thought, and White's truth of coherence and truth of correspondence come again to mind. While the Renaissance practice of life-writing can offer no model for our own time, it can sharpen our questions about the ways in which and the extent to which such truths are finally opposed, and it can, perhaps, cause us to wonder whether the earlier period did not possess, more than half-consciously, an insight into their relationship that we have only begun to reinvent or rediscover. The biographical fictions of the Renaissance period are not ours, but they alert us to the fact—not to say the still factual character—of our own. They caution us against the reduction that simply or subtly collapses one kind of biographical truth into another, whether present in a medieval monk's confusion of fact with fiction or in a neopositivist's subversion of fiction by fact. These Renaissance fictions at least suggest the elusive possibility of a balanced reality and a balanced interpretation.

NOTES

GENERAL INTRODUCTION

1 Donald A. Stauffer, *English Biography before 1700* (Cambridge, Mass.: Harvard Univ. Press, 1930).

2 In order, places of publication and dates are Cambridge, Mass.: Harvard Univ. Press, 1973; Baltimore: Johns Hopkins Univ. Press, 1978; Chicago: Univ. of Chicago Press, 1980.

3 "The Boundaries of Fiction in the Renaissance: A Treaty Between Truth and Falsehood," *ELH*, 36 (1969), 31.

4 Pp. 1–2.

5 "Boundaries of Fiction," p. 31.

6 *Fact or Fiction*, p. 1.

7 Woolf, *Collected Essays* (New York: Harcourt, Brace & World, 1967), IV, 234; for the context of this quotation, see p. 70 of my discussion; Frye, *Fables of Identity: Studies in Poetic Mythology* (New York: Harcourt, Brace & World, 1963), p. 56; and White, p. 122.

8 White, p. 122, uses the phrase "something beyond itself" to define the "correspondence" of fiction.

9 White, p. 125; R. G. Collingwood, *The Idea of History* (1946; rpt. Oxford: Oxford Univ. Press, 1980), p. 246; Frye, pp. 54–58.

10 *A Defence of Poetry*, in *Miscellaneous Prose of Sir Philip Sidney*, ed. Katherine Duncan-Jones and Jan Van Dorsten (Oxford: Clarendon, 1973), p. 89. See my discussions of Sidney and Bacon, pp. 124–25, 164–66. On the Renaissance identification of poetry with fiction, cf. also Nelson, *Fact or Fiction*, pp. 8, 50.

11 White, pp. 97–98, 123.

12 For more detailed discussion, see Collingwood, pp. 245–46 ff., 9–10, and White, p. 121.

13 Quotations are from Greenblatt, pp. 3, 254, 1 (my emphasis). Because often missed, Greenblatt's specific disclaimer that he intends his book as a comprehensive explanation of Renaissance self-fashioning should be noted (p. 8); yet it should also be noted that he sees the book as analyzing the culture's "larger" and "dominant" patterns (pp. 6–7).

14 Among Greenblatt's governing conditions are the following: (1) "None of the figures [examined] inherits a title, an ancient family tradition or hierarchical status"; (2) "Self-fashioning . . . involves submission to an absolute power or authority"; (3) "Self-fashioning is achieved in relation to something perceived as alien, strange, or hostile . . . [a] threatening Other" (pp. 8–9). (If the date of *Othello* is 1604 [alternatively 1603], it is not technically a Tudor work and is therefore a nominal exception to my description of Greenblatt's examples.)

15 *Sir Walter Ralegh: The Renaissance Man and His Roles* (New Haven, Conn.: Yale Univ. Press, 1973); the quotation just below citation in text is from p. ix. Mazzeo's essay is in *Renaissance & Revolution: Backgrounds to Seventeenth-Century English Literature* (New York: Random House, 1967), pp. 131–60.

16 *Self-Fashioning*, pp. 2–3, offers a helpful list of quotations including the verb *to fashion*.

17 John Dryden, "The Life of Plutarch," in *Works*, ed. H. T. Swedenberg, Jr., et al.; vol. XVII, ed. Samuel Holt Monk et al. (Berkeley: Univ. of California Press, 1971); the actual words of Dryden's definition read "the History of Particular Mens Lives" or "the Histories of particular Lives" (pp. 273, 275).

18 Collingwood, p. 304. White, p. 111, remarks a relationship between history and biography

as forms of discourse when he observes, "No one and nothing *lives* a story."

19 E.g., Stauffer, pp. 219–21, but see also my discussion of Bede on pp. 12–13 and my chapters on More and on Bacon.

20 *The Nature of Biography* (New York: Knopf, 1957), p. 28. The association of Garraty's definition with the work of Frye and Collingwood is mine.

21 Collingwood, pp. 240–43. Collingwood (after Kant) also refers to the historical imagination as the a priori imagination.

1. BIOGRAPHICAL TRUTH

1 See David Novarr, *The Making of Walton's "Lives"* (Ithaca, N.Y.: Cornell Univ. Press, 1958), pp. 24–25; I. A. Shapiro, "Walton and the Occasion of Donne's *Devotions*," *RES*, n.s. 9 (1958), 22; John Butt, *Biography in the Hands of Walton, Johnson, and Boswell* (Los Angeles: Univ. of California, 1966), pp. 4–5; and R. C. Bald, *John Donne: A Life*, ed. Wesley Milgate (Oxford: Oxford Univ. Press, 1970), pp. 11–13, 489, 503, 525.

2 "Vita Sancti Cuthberti Auctore Beda," in *Two Lives of Saint Cuthbert: A Life by an Anonymous Monk of Lindisfarne and Bede's Prose Life*, ed. and trans. Bertram Colgrave (1940; rpt. New York: Greenwood Press, 1969), pp. 142–44: "nec sine certissima exquisitione rerum gestarum aliquid de tanto uiro scribere, nec tandem ea / quae scripseram sine subtili examinatione testium indubiorum passim transcribenda quibusdam dare praesumpsi . . . ablatis omnibus scrupulorum ambagibus ad purum, certam ueritatis indaginem simplicibus explicitam sermonibus commendare menbranulis . . . curaui." Bede's Latin, as Colgrave prints and I quote it, often contains eccentricities and medieval spellings, but it is impossible to reproduce Colgrave's variants and notes here. Although I have repeatedly consulted Colgrave's translation, I have altered it to the extent that I should have to call translated passages from Bede's *Life of Cuthbert* my own. I have also consulted the freer translation of this *Life* by J. F. Webb in his *Lives of the Saints* (Baltimore: Penguin, 1965). Both translations have been of great help. My translations of Bede's *Life* are based throughout on Colgrave's Latin text, hereafter cited as *Vita Cuthberti.* On the conventionality of Bede's protestations of truthfulness, see Charles W. Jones, *Saints' Lives and Chronicles in Early England* (Ithaca, N.Y.: Cornell Univ. Press, 1947), pp. 54–55, but also Thomas W. Mackay, "Bede's Hagiographical Method: His Knowledge and Use of Paulinus of Nola," in *Famulus Christi*, ed. Gerald Bonner (London: SPCK, 1976), pp. 84–85.

3 *Vita Cuthberti*, p. 144: "alia multa nec minora his quae scripsimus praesentibus nobis ad inuicem conferentes, de uita et uirtutibus beati uiri superintulistis, quae prorsus memoria digna uidebantur, si non deliberato ac perfecto operi noua interserere, uel supradicere minus congruum atque indecorum esse constaret."

4 *Bede's Ecclesiastical History of the English People*, ed. and trans. Bertram Colgrave and R. A. B. Mynors (Oxford: Clarendon, 1969), p. 444: "e quibus aliqua in libro uitae illius olim memoriae mandauimus. Sed et in hac historia quaedam, quae nos nuper audisse contigit, superadicere commodum duximus." The translation given is mine.

5 Donald A. Stauffer, *English Biography before 1700*, p. 11; cf. p. 233: "Biography to the Venerable Bede was only history viewed more closely."

6 Cf. Paul Murray Kendall, *The Art of Biography* (New York: Norton, 1965), p. 4: "The historian frames a cosmos of happenings, in which men are included only as event-producers or event-sufferers. The biographer explores the cosmos of a single being."

7 See Robert W. Hanning, *The Vision of History in Early Britain* (New York: Columbia Univ. Press, 1966), p. 67 and chap. 3, passim; and for a related but variant view, Jones, p. 82.

8 Stauffer, p. 14, considers Eadmer's *Anselm* modern in spirit, and, certainly, Eadmer's close association with Anselm afforded him a kind and quantity of material lacking in Bede's *Cuthbert*—an atypical, "unexpected combination of circumstances and talents," as R. W. Southern characterizes Eadmer's *Vita: Saint Anselm and His Biographer: A Study of Monastic Life*

and Thought 1059–c.1130 (Cambridge: Cambridge Univ. Press, 1963), p. 336. But the essential distinction Eadmer himself makes between his *Historia Novorum in Anglia* and his *Vita Sancti Anselmi* is, like Bede's, between a public and private or an historical and individual perspective. Thus the *Historia*, Eadmer explains, records events "which took place between the kings of England and Anselm archbishop of Canterbury . . . [and] were open to the inspection of any contemporary who wished to know the truth about them, but it left out anything which seemed to belong merely to Anselm's private life, or to his character, or to the setting forth of his miracles"; these the *Vita* treats (*The Life of St Anselm*, ed. and trans. R. W. Southern [1962; rpt. Oxford: Clarendon, 1972], p. 1).

9 George Cavendish, *The Life and Death of Cardinal Wolsey*, ed. Richard S. Sylvester, EETS, No. 243 (London: Oxford Univ. Press, 1959), p. 3. All references are to this edition, hereafter cited as Cavendish. I have silently expanded the contractions in Sylvester's text and in other Renaissance texts quoted. Following the initial citation, references to primary texts will generally be parenthetical.

10 William Roper, *The Lyfe of Sir Thomas Moore, knighte*, ed. Elsie Vaughan Hitchcock, EETS, No. 197 (London: Oxford Univ. Press, 1935), p. 3. All references are to this edition, hereafter cited as Roper. Bracketed inserts in quotations from Roper are italicized if they are mine; if not italicized, they indicate Hitchcock's editorial emendations in accordance with her practice in the printed text.

11 Nicholas Harpsfield, *The life and death of Sr Thomas Moore, knight, sometymes Lord high Chancellor of England*, ed. Elsie Vaughan Hitchcock, intro. R. W. Chambers, EETS, No. 186 (London: Oxford Univ. Press, 1932), p. 4. All references are to this edition, hereafter cited as Harpsfield. Bracketed inserts in quotations from Harpsfield are italicized if they are mine; otherwise they are Hitchcock's.

12 Novarr, e.g., pp. 25, 82, and Part I, passim.

13 Izaak Walton, "The Life of Dr. *John Donne*, Late Dean of St. *Paul's* Church, London," 4th rev. ed., in *The Lives of Dr. "John Donne," Sir "Henry Wotton," Mr. "Richard Hooker," Mr. "George Herbert"* (London: Tho. Roycroft for Richard Marriot, 1675), rpt. in *"The Lives" of John Donne, Sir Henry Wotton, Richard Hooker, George Herbert, and Robert Sanderson* (London: Oxford Univ. Press, 1927). Unless otherwise specified, all references are to this modern edition, hereafter cited as Walton. Citations from this edition, whose accessibility recommends it, have been verified against the 1675 edition, and such insignificant discrepancies in punctuation and capitalization as exist have silently been emended.

2. BEDE: CONVENTIONS OF PORTRAYAL

1 *Vita Cuthberti*, p. 154: "usque ad octauum aetatis annum." On Cuthbert's age, see Charles W. Jones, *Saints' Lives and Chronicles in Early England*, p. 74.

2 *Vita Cuthberti*, p. 156: "sanctissime antistes et presbiter."

3 *Vita Cuthberti*, p. 154: "ita ut illud beati Samuelis tunc de ipso posset testimonium dici. *Porro* Cuthbertus *necdum sciebat Dominum, neque reuelatus fuerat ei sermo Domini*"; p. 156: "*Cum* enim *esset paruulus, ut paruulus sapiebat, ut paruulus cogitabat*, qui postmodum *factus uir*, plenissime ea *quae paruuli erant deposuit*."

4 *Vita Cuthberti*, pp. 202, 222: "In aqua uidelicet elicita de rupe, factum beati patris Benedicti qui idem pene et eodem modo legitur fecisse miraculum, sed iccirco uberius quia plures erant qui aquae inopia laborarent. Porro in arces/sitis a messe uolatilibus reuerentissimi et sanctissimi patris Antonii sequebatur exemplum, qui a lesione hortuli quem ipse plantauerat uno onagros sermone compescuit."

5 Cf. Jones, pp. 60–64, 118–19.

6 *Vita Cuthberti*, p. 266: "et uisa est ei aqua quasi in saporem uini conuersa, tantique sibi testem uolens adhibere miraculi fratrem qui / proxime astabat, porrexit ei poculum. Qui cum et ipse biberet, eius quoque palato pro aqua uinum sapiebat." While the transformation of water to

wine is not unprecedented in hagiographical writings, its origin—unlike that of such wonders as the extinguishing of house-fires or the kindly ministrations of sea otters (chaps. 14, 10)—is specifically Christological. Moreover, in recounting it, rather than interjecting intermediary precedents, Bede allows our imagination to go directly to the memorable transformation at Cana.

7 *Vita Cuthberti*, p. 178: "ad exemplum uiuendi praesentibus"; p. 178: "Et aliquando quidem palam, aliquando autem uelate, quasi sub persona / alterius id facere curabat. Quod tamen qui audiere, quia de se ipso dixerit intelligebant, iuxta exemplum magistri gentium, qui modo aperte suas uirtutes replicat, modo sub praetextu alterius personae loquitur dicens, *Scio hominem in Christo ante annos quattuordecim raptum usque ad tertium coelum.*" Karl Joachim Weintraub, *The Value of the Individual: Self and Circumstance in Autobiography* (Chicago: Univ. of Chicago Press, 1978), chap. 3, "Individuality in the Middle Ages," affords support to my argument in this chapter.

8 Cf. Bertram Colgrave, "Bede's Miracle Stories," in *Bede: His Life, Times, and Writings*, ed. A. Hamilton Thompson (Oxford: Clarendon, 1935), pp. 201–02, 229: there may well be "something more in these strange stories than the earlier editors of Bede believed."

9 Although there are several comparisons between Cuthbert's life and the New Testament early in Bede's work, comparisons of the young saint's life with the Old Testament are proportionately conspicuous.

10 *Vita Cuthberti*, p. 160: "mittente illo qui quondam Raphaelem archangelum ad sanandos Tobiae uisus destinare dignatus est"; p. 160: "si cui uidetur incredibile angelum in equo apparuisse, legat historiam Machabeorum, in qua angeli in equis, et ad Iudae Machabei, et ad ipsius templi defensionem aduenisse memorantur."

11 *Vita Cuthberti*, p. 180: "sicut Herefridus familiaris eius presbiter et abbas quondam monasterii Lindisfarnensis ipsum referre solitum testatur"; p. 266: "postea in nostro monasterio quod est ad hostium Wiri fluminis non paruo tempore demoratus . . . sua mihi relatione testatus est"; p. 170: "Haec mihi religiosus nostri monasterii quod est ad hostium Wiri fluminis presbiter nomine Inguuald . . . ab ipso Cuthberto iam tunc episcopo se audisse perhibuit"; p. 240: "nunc usque superest, et in aecclesia Lindisfarnensi presbiterii gradum officio tenens . . . qui et mihi hoc ipsum quod refero miraculum narrauit"; pp. 270–72: "Cuius obitum libet uerbis illius cuius relatione didici describere, Herefridi uidelicet." Jones, pp. 75–76, affirms the ethical and moral—as against the factual—character of such testimony. Cf. Colgrave, "Bede's Miracle Stories," pp. 224–26; but also Wilhelm Levison, "Bede as Historian," in *Bede: His Life, Times, and Writings*, pp. 128–29: "Given, as he [Bede] is, to the belief in miracles, he nevertheless endeavours to ascertain the truth of the related facts"; and Paul Meyvaert, "Bede the Scholar," in *Famulus Christi*, pp. 51–55.

12 *Vita Cuthberti*, p. 294: "Adiecitque mirando quae quondam uersibus dixi, et ait. . . ."

13 *Vita Cuthberti*, p. 202: "At ego et mei similes propriae fragilitatis et inertiae conscii, certi quidem sumus quia contra ignem materialem nil tale audemus, incerti autem an ignem illum inextinguibilem futurae castigationis immunes euadere queamus"; p. 202: "indignis nobis et nunc ad extinguenda uiciorum incendia, et ad euadendas in futuro poenarum flammas."

14 Cf. Jones, p. 74.

15 *Vita Cuthberti*, p. 300: "Unde *meminisse iuuat*, quia *haec* est *inmutatio dexterae excelsi*, cuius memoranda ab initio mirabilia mundo fulgere non cessant."

16 See "Vita Sancti Cuthberti Auctore Anonymo," in *Two Lives of Saint Cuthbert*, pp. 59–139, and introduction, p. 14: "Of the forty miracles recorded in the Prose Life, only eight are peculiar to Bede . . . and of these eight, two . . . are mentioned by the earlier writer but passed over."

17 *Vita Cuthberti*, p. 252: "Quadam autem die dum parrochiam suam circuiens . . ."; p. 222: "Libet etiam quoddam beati Cuthberti in exemplum praefati patris Benedicti factum narrare miraculum"; p. 254: "Neque huic dissimile sanitatis miraculum . . . multi qui praesentes

fuere testati sunt . . . Dum enim more suo pertransiret uniuersos docendo, deuenit in uicum quendam"; pp. 254–56: "Nec silentio praetereundum arbitramur miraculum, quod . . . cognouimus"; p. 248: "Non multo post tempore idem famulus Domini Cuthbertus ad eandem Lugubaliam ciuitatem rogatus aduenit"; p. 194: "Quadam quoque die cum predicaturus iuxta consuetudinem suam populis, de monasterio exiret . . ."; p. 256: "Quodam quoque tempore dum sanctissimus gregis dominici pastor, sua lustrando circuiret ouilia. . . ." On time in Bede's works, see Jones, pp. 31, 74, 82, and William J. Brandt, *The Shape of Medieval History: Studies in Modes of Perception* (New Haven, Conn.: Yale Univ. Press, 1966), pp. 66–69.

18 *Vita Cuthberti*, p. 214: "postquam in eodem monasterio multa annorum curricula expleuit, tandem diu concupita, quaesita, ac petita solitudinis secreta . . . laetabundus adiit"; p. 242: "Igitur dum Egfridus rex ausu temerario exercitum in Pictos duceret, eorumque regna atroci / ac feroci seuicia deuastaret, sciens uir Domini Cuthbertus adesse tempus de quo anno praeterito interroganti eius sorori praedixerat, non eum amplius quam uno anno esse uicturum, uenit ad Lugubaliam ciuitatem."

19 E.g., *Vita Cuthberti*, pp. 156, 198, 200, 204, 252, 256, 268, 290.

20. *Vita Cuthberti*, p. 210: "acerrimis . . . iniuriis"; p. 276: "minus quam dimidia parte corrosa"; pp. 162–64 (jeering peasants); p. 218: "calciatus tibracis quas pellicias habere solebat."

21 *Vita Cuthberti*, p. 186: "Solebat autem ea maxime loca peragrare, illis predicare in uiculis, qui in arduis asperisque montibus procul positi aliis hor/rori erant ad uisendum, et paupertate pariter ac rusticitate sua doctorum prohibebant accessum. Quos tamen ille pio libenter mancipatus labori, tanta doctrinae excolebat industria, ut de monasterio egrediens, sepe ebdomada integra . . . nonnunquam etiam mense pleno domum non rediret, sed demoratus in montanis plebem rusticam uerbo predicationis simul et exemplo uirtutis ad coelestia uocaret."

22 *Vita Cuthberti*, p. 234: "mater uirginum Christi Elfled."

3. CAVENDISH: PATTERNS WITHOUT MEANING

1 F. J. Levy speculates that "in Cavendish's mind the pagan goddess and the Hebrew God probably merged more and more into one another": *Tudor Historical Thought* (San Marino, Calif.: Huntington Library, 1967), p. 28. This view, while provocative, derives from the highly questionable belief that "it was the Reformation itself," rather than Wolsey, that Cavendish "had to explain" (p. 27).

2 On dating *The Life of Wolsey*, see Richard S. Sylvester's discussion in Cavendish, p. xxvii.

3 The Byble in Englyshe (London: Edwarde Whitchurch, 1541 [1540]), i.e., The Great Bible. I Chron. 29: 11–12 in the Vulgate, which could be the source for Cavendish and is the likely source for Wolsey, reads as follows: "Tua est Domine magnificentia, et potentia, et tibi laus: cuncta enim quae in coelo sunt, et in terra, tua sunt: tuum, Domine, regnum, et tu es super omnes principes. Tuae divitiae, et tua est gloria: tu dominaris omnium, in manu tua virtus et potentia: in manu tua magnitudo, et imperium omnium." See also I Sam. 2:7: "The Lord maketh pore and maketh ryche: bringeth lowe, and heueth vp on hye" (Great Bible, 1541); "Dominus pauperem facit et ditat, humiliat, et sublevat." All subsequent biblical quotations in Latin are from the Vulgate.

4 Ps. 22 (23):4: "Virga tua, et baculus tuus, ipsa me consolata sunt"; "thy rod and thy staf confort me." Cf. Isa. 36:6: "Ecce confidis super baculum arundineum confractum istum, super Aegyptum; cui si innixus fuerit homo, intrabit in manum eius, et perforabit eam; sic Pharao rex Aegypti, omnibus qui confidunt in eo"; "loo, thoū puttest thy trust in a broken staffe of rede (I meane Egypte) whyche he that leaneth vpon, it goeth into hys hande and shutteth hym thorowe. Euen so is Pharao the kynge of Egipte, vnto all them that trust in hym" (Great Bible, 1541).

5 Cf. Warren W. Wooden, "The Art of Partisan Biography: George Cavendish's *Life of*

Wolsey," *Ren&R*, n.s. 1 (1977), 33. Wooden's comments are perceptive, but I disagree, as here, with his reading of specific passages (p. 33), as well as with his interpretation of Cavendish's purpose as merely partisan and of Cavendish's method as essentially schematic, rather than experiential and lifelike.

6 Matt. 27:35 "diviserunt vestimenta eius . . . Diviserunt sibi vestimenta mea"; The Byble ([Antwerp?]: sold by Rich. Grafton and Edward Whitchurch, London, 1537), i.e., The Matthew Bible, reads: "they parted his garmentes . . . They deuyded my garments amonge them." (Great Bible, 1541, reads "departed" for "deuyded.") John 13:1: "sciens Iesus quia venit hora eius ut transeat ex hoc mundo ad Patrem"; "when Jesus knewe that his houre was come that he shulde depart out of this world vnto the father" (Great Bible, 1541). Cf. Matt. 26:18: "Tempus meum prope est"; "my time is at hande" (Great Bible, 1541). Also cf. Luke 9:51.

7 A. F. Pollard, *Wolsey: Church and State in Sixteenth-Century England* (1929; rpt. New York: Harper & Row, 1966), p. 273. Cf. F. George Steiner, "A Note on Cavendish's 'Life of Cardinal Wolsey,' " *English*, 9 (1952), 54.

8 Pollard, *Wolsey*, p. 301. Richard S. Sylvester, "Cavendish's *Life of Wolsey:* The Artistry of a Tudor Biographer," *SP*, 57 (1960), 68–71, reaffirms Pollard's observation. Sylvester's editorial and critical work on Cavendish is seminal to my discussion.

9 Cavendish, pp. 81, 83–84, 89: in order, Queen Catherine, King Henry (6), the Bishop of Rochester, Cardinal Campeggio (2).

10 E.g., Cavendish, p. 79: "yf eyes be not blynd men may se/ if eares be not stopped they may here/ And if pitie be not exiled they may lament/ the sequell of this pernycious and inordynat/ Carnall love/ the plage wherof is not seased." Cavendish refers here to Henry's love for Anne Boleyn. Lacey Baldwin Smith's defense of the authenticity of Henry's preoccupation with conscience illuminates the complexity of assessing the King's "Great Matter": "A Matter of Conscience," in *Action and Conviction in Early Modern Europe*, ed. Theodore K. Rabb and Jerrold E. Seigel (Princeton: Princeton Univ. Press, 1969), pp. 32–51.

11 Cavendish, pp. xxx–xxxii and Appendix C. More recently, Steven May has argued (in part persuasively) for a heavier dependence by Cavendish on Hall in the first half of *The Life:* "Cavendish's Use of Hall's *Chronicle*," *Neophil*, 59 (1975), 293–300. While Cavendish most probably did use Hall to refresh his memory or to fill in some details, however, May greatly exaggerates the amount and nature of Cavendish's dependence on Hall and, as a curious consequence, minimizes Cavendish's art.

12 Cavendish, p. xxxviii.

13 Edward Hall, *The Vnion of the Two Noble and Illustre Famelies of Lancastre & Yorke* (1548; rpt. London: for J. Johnson et al., 1809), pp. 754–55, 757, hereafter cited as Hall's *Chronicle*. In one verifiable detail of the trial, Sylvester points out, Cavendish is more accurate than Hall: see Cavendish, p. 268, n. 1.

14 On dating, see *Metrical Visions*, ed. A. S. G. Edwards (Columbia: Univ. of South Carolina Press, 1980), p. 9, and Cavendish, pp. x–xi. The passage quoted from *Visions* is from p. 32 (vs. 155–61). Sylvester (Cavendish, p. xxxvii) cites two other lines from *Visions* about which we hear just a hint in *The Life of Wolsey:* "to fforrayn potentates [I] wrott my letters playn / Desireng ther ayd / to restore me to fauor agayn" (Edwards, ed., p. 34, vs. 209–10). See also Cavendish, pp. 150–51, 249, n. 151/13–14; Pollard, *Wolsey*, pp. 294–97; and on Wolsey's judicial conduct, John A. Guy, "Thomas More as Successor to Wolsey," *Thought*, 52 (1977), 280–81.

4. ROPER: DELIBERATED DESIGN AND DESIGNER

1 Richard S. Sylvester and Davis P. Harding, eds., *Two Early Tudor Lives: "The Life and Death of Cardinal Wolsey," by George Cavendish; "The Life of Sir Thomas More," by William Roper* (New Haven, Conn.: Yale Univ. Press, 1962), pp. xv–xvi.

2 Cf. Jean Starobinski's definition of autobiography as "A biography of a person written by

himself": "The style of Autobiography," trans. Seymour Chatman, in *Autobiography: Essays Theoretical and Critical*, ed. James Olney (Princeton: Princeton Univ. Press, 1980), p. 73. Cf. also pp. 70–71 of my discussion.

3 Roper, p. xlv: More dies in 1535; Roper's *Life* is written over twenty years later, "not long before 1557."

4 Roper, pp. xlvi–xlvii: Hitchcock notes 11 minor historical inaccuracies in Roper. Given the lapse of time since More's death, this is hardly a great number. See Harpsfield, pp. ccii–cciv, for Chambers' high assessment of Harpsfield's accuracy.

5 E.g., Roper, p. 76; Harpsfield, pp. 17–18.

6 The only recorded variant of interest is in Roper: goe] goe off. See also Harpsfield, p. 73, and Roper, pp. 23–24.

7 The liberties of classical historians, especially in constructing formal speeches, clearly bear on the practices of Renaissance historians and biographers. But they cannot be invoked automatically or exclusively as the explanation—rather than as the source or analogue—of Renaissance practice without obscuring the complexity and variety of Renaissance attitudes toward biographical truth.

8 Roper, pp. 99–100; *The Correspondence of Sir Thomas More*, ed. Elizabeth Frances Rogers (Princeton: Princeton Univ. Press, 1947), p. 564. Hitchcock, Roper's editor (p. xlv, n. 4), draws attention to Roper's use of More's letters.

9 *The Correspondence of Sir Thomas More*, p. 489 (my emphasis). Roper's use of this letter was first noted by John Maguire, "William Roper's *Life of More:* The Working Methods of a Tudor Biographer," *Moreana*, 23 (1969), 61. Maguire does not analyze the difference between letter and *Life*. While other provocative instances of resemblance between More's letters and Roper's narrative exist, they are either susceptible of alternative explanations or close enough only to be suggestive: but see Maguire, pp. 59–65, and n. 12 below. If Roper had available to him *as he wrote* all the suggestive letters, the really surprising fact is that he did not make more use of them.

10 Roper, p. 52. Although Hitchcock's emendations in this passage (bracket and asterisks) appear silently to have been guided by More's letter, they do not significantly alter the near identity of this passage in letter and *Life*.

11 Roper, pp. 12–16, 92–95; by the second speech (or speeches) I mean the entirety of More's final answer to his judges prior to their condemnation of him; it is interrupted briefly by the reply of the Lord Chancellor.

12 The ambiguity of Henry's words, as Roper gives them, is further illustrated by contrast with a passage in one of More's letters to Cromwell that otherwise resembles the present speech: "his Highnes graciousely takyng in gre my good mynd in that byhalfe vsed of his blessed disposition in the prosecuting of his great mater onely those (of whom his Grace had good nombre) whose conscience his Grace perceived well and fully persuaded vppon that parte . . ." (*The Correspondence of Sir Thomas More*, p. 496). Cf. G. R. Elton, "Sir Thomas More and the Opposition to Henry VIII," in *Essential Articles for the Study of Thomas More*, ed. R. S. Sylvester and G. P. Marc'hadour (Hamden, Conn.: Archon, 1977), p. 80: Henry "had a high opinion of his powers of persuasion and a low one of people's consciences." Cf. also J. J. Scarisbrick, *Henry VIII* (1968; rpt. Berkeley: Univ. of California Press, 1970), p. 477.

13 For another example, see Roper, p. 102 (St. Cyprian).

14 Matt. 22:21 is also pertinent, though less pointedly so; its first concern, unless read ironically, is Caesar. On use of this text by the propagandists of Henry VIII, see Scarisbrick, p. 388.

15 Morton became a Cardinal in 1493. He was Archbishop of Canterbury and Lord Chancellor of England from 1486 to 1500. More was in Morton's household from 1490 to 1492. (On the date of Morton's appointment as Chancellor, see S. B. Chrimes, *Henry VIII* [1972; rpt. London: Eyre Methuen, 1977], p. 57.)

16 *DNB*, s.v. Amias Paulet (d. 1538).

17 John Donne, *The Elegies and The Songs and Sonnets*, ed. Helen Gardner (1965; rpt. Oxford: Clarendon, 1970), pp. 62–64. All references to this kind of poetry by Donne are to Gardner's edition, hereafter cited as *Songs and Sonnets.* Gardner, pp. 188 and xxix, rejects Walton's belief, but cf. Novarr, *Making of Walton's Lives*, pp. 110–18, and Bald, *John Donne*, p. 242.

18 Harpsfield, pp. 17–18; Roper, pp. 29, 76.

19 Harpsfield, pp. xlvii, xlix. Cf., however, Chambers' description of Roper's *More* as "probably the most perfect *little* biography" in English: *Thomas More* (New York: Harcourt Brace, 1935), p. 24 (my emphasis); on Harpsfield, see p. 32.

20 Cf. Chambers, *Thomas More*, p. 400. "More placed the right of the State to silence the individual very much higher, and the right of the individual to claim liberty of conscience from the State very much lower" than we would: "Yet he died for the right of the individual conscience, as against the State." Likewise, Lacey Baldwin Smith, *This Realm of England: 1399–1688* (Boston: D. C. Heath, 1966), p. 126: Smith considers More's "unwillingness to acknowledge the state as the be-all and end-all of human existence" the real issue at stake. To More, Henry "was violating the unity ["the common conscience"] of Christendom, the common heritage of Western Europe." For a much less idealistic view of More, see Greenblatt, *Renaissance Self-Fashioning*, chap. 1: e.g., More's "was a truth . . . capable of *canceling*, but not *clarifying*, human politics" (pp. 14–15). For an account of "The Tradition of Early More Biography" by Michael A. Anderegg, see *Essential Articles for the Study of Thomas More*, pp. 3–25, and in the same volume, R. S. Sylvester on "Roper's *Life of More*," esp. pp. 190–91. Sylvester's introduction to another volume he has edited, *St. Thomas More: Action and Contemplation* (New Haven Conn.: Yale Univ. Press, 1972), pp. 1–14, affords a sampling of other recent views of More: Richard J. Schoeck's "Common Law and Canon Law in Their Relation to Thomas More," pp. 17–55, in this volume is especially pertinent (e.g., p. 48), but see also Donald R. Kelley, "The Conscience of the King's Good Servant," *Thought*, 52 (1977), 293–99.

21 See Germain Marc'hadour, "Thomas More's Spirituality," in *St. Thomas More: Action and Contemplation*, p. 156, n. 48.

22 As Chambers notes, "Most of . . . [Harpsfield's] material is still extant elsewhere": *Thomas More*, pp. 32–33.

5. WALTON: LIKENESS AND TRUTH

1 The marginal glosses are most likely Walton's rather than a printer's since they recur in the revised editions (sometimes in variant form); in any case, Walton obviously sanctioned them. Unless otherwise noted, references to the text of Walton's *Life of Donne* in this section are to the 1675 version: see chap. 1, n. 13, above. Francisque Costa, *L'Oeuvre D'Izaak Walton* (Paris: Didier, 1973), pp. 127–28 ff. offers a useful discussion of Walton's sources.

2 Novarr, *Making of Walton's "Lives,"* p. 491. Although I often disagree with the angle of Novarr's judgment of Walton, I have found his work on *The Lives* immensely helpful. For a brief but provocative discussion of Walton's achievement that takes issue with several of Novarr's conclusions, see John Butt, *Biography in the Hands of Walton, Johnson, and Boswell*, pp. 1–18; also his review, with Peter Ure, of Novarr's book (*MLR*, 54 [1959], 588–91). For additional commentary on Walton's inaccuracy, see Bald, *John Donne*, pp. 220, 242, and idem, "Historical Doubts Respecting Walton's *Life of Donne*," in *Essays in English Literature from the Renaissance to the Victorian Age Presented to A. S. P. Woodhouse*, ed. Millar MacLure and F. W. Watt (Toronto: Univ. of Toronto Press, 1964), pp. 69–84.

3 *The Likeness of Thomas More: An Iconographical Survey of Three Centuries*, ed. and supplemented by Nicolas Barker (New York: Fordham Univ. Press, 1963), pp. 68, 55–58; figs. 27, 28; p. 62; fig. 32.

4 See John Pope-Hennessy, *The Portrait in the Renaissance* (New York: Pantheon, 1966): "The conquest of physical appearance [in Renaissance portraiture] is in turn bound up with a change in the function of the artist." He becomes "an interpreter whose habit is to probe into the mind and for whom inspection connotes analysis" (pp. 3–4). See also Roy Strong, *The English Icon: Elizabethan & Jacobean Portraiture* (London: Routledge & Kegan Paul, 1969), esp. pp. 13–42; also n. 8 below.

5 According to Jakob Rosenberg, we know "about sixty painted self-portraits" by Rembrandt, plus "more than twenty etchings and about ten drawings": *Rembrandt: Life & Work*, rev. ed. (London: Phaidon, 1964), p. 37. On Dürer's self-portraits, see Pope-Hennessy, pp. 124–30.

6 *Songs and Sonnets*, p. 29.

7 *The Satires, Epigrams and Verse Letters*, ed. W. Milgate (Oxford: Clarendon, 1967), p. 90.

8 The Ditchley portrait of Elizabeth is the familiar illustration on the cover of *The Norton Anthology of English Literature*, I. See Strong, fig. frontispiece and pp. 289, 23; also Frances A. Yates, *Astraea: The Imperial Theme in the Sixteenth Century* (London: Routledge & Kegan Paul, 1975), Part II, esp. pp. 29–87, and pp. 215–19 (allegorical portraits of Elizabeth I). In *The Cult of Elizabeth: Elizabethan Portraiture and Pageantry* (London: Thames & Hudson, 1977), Roy Strong describes Elizabethan portraiture as really "a branch of the study of emblematics" (pp. 111–12). He also posits a sharp distinction between the visual premises of the Elizabethan and Jacobean ages that seems to me to be considerably softened by his own recognition of the self-consciousness and deliberation of artifice under Elizabeth. The visual premises of the Elizabethan court, unlike those of the medieval period they otherwise resemble, were at least as much a matter of conscious construction as of presumed fact—as much deliberate imagination as objective record. See also Strong's earlier *Portraits of Queen Elizabeth I* (Oxford: Clarendon, 1963), pp. 36, 39–40: "the Elizabethan state portrait is a magnificent—one is almost tempted to say a deliberate—archaism." Strong's views on the deliberation of Elizabethan archaism are never entirely clear.

9 See Pope-Hennessy, "Donor and Participant," chap. 6; also pp. 249–51 and chap. 1.

10 *Catalogue of Portraits in the possession of the University, Colleges, City, and County of Oxford*, compiled by Mrs. Reginald Lane Poole (Oxford: Clarendon, 1912), I, 16: cited in Harpsfield, p. cxciii.

11 Cf. Pope-Hennessy, p. 226.

12 Perhaps the qualification "most modern viewers" would be prudent: recently it has been fashionable for young couples to don the garb of the mid-nineteenth century for formal family photographs. The degree and extent of such modern self-consciousness in costume, I might add, are no more identical to those of the Elizabethans than theirs are to those of Bede.

13 For the 1670, 1658, and 1640 versions of Walton's *Donne*, in order see: *The Lives of Dr. "John Donne," "Sir Henry Wotton," "Mr. Richard Hooker," "Mr. George Herbert"* (London: Tho. Newcomb for Richard Marriott, 1670); *The Life of "John Donne," Dr. in Divinity, and Late Dean of Saint "Pauls" Church London* (London: J. G. for R. Marriot, 1658); "The Life and Death of Dr *Donne*, Late Deane of St Pauls London," in *LXXX Sermons Preached By That Learned And Reverend Divine, John Donne, Dr In Divinity, Late Deane of the Cathedrall Church of S. Pauls "London"* (London: for Richard Royston and Richard Marriot, 1640).

14 See *Songs and Sonnets*, Appendix E; also Bald, p. 54.

15 Novarr, p. 484.

16 The first quotation is from George Herbert Palmer, ed., *The English Works of George Herbert* (Boston: Houghton Mifflin, 1905), I, 46: Palmer refers to Walton's *Life of Herbert* but considers this *Life* generally typical of Walton's biographical procedures. The second quotation is from Novarr, p. 485. Cf. Margaret Bottrall, *Izaak Walton* (London: Longmans, Green, 1955), p. 28: "Having made up his mind which are the most striking lineaments in each man, and from what angle they appear to the best advantage, Walton sets up his easel."

17 Bald, pp. 535–36, suspects that "the role" Donne was trying to enact was the resurrection of the body; thus "the shrouded figure is rising from the funeral urn, and what seems at first glance to be a crouching attitude suggests rather that he is still emerging."

18 *OED*, s.v. *Biography: "biographist* was used by Fuller 1662, *biography* by Dryden 1683, *biographer* by Addison 1715, *biographical* by Oldys 1738: all the others are later." But Donald A. Stauffer, *English Biography before 1700*, pp. 218–19, documents the use of *biography* twice and *biographer* once between 1661 and 1663.

19 *Psevdo-Martyr* (London: W. Stansby for Walter Burre, 1610): subsequent reference is to this edition.

20 See Novarr, pp. 60–61, for further examples and discussion.

21 See Holy Sonnets 4, 6, in *The Divine Poems*, ed. Helen Gardner, 2nd ed. (Oxford: Clarendon, 1978), and *Devotions Vpon Emergent Occasions* (London: A. M. for Thomas Jones, 1624), "17. Meditation," pp. 415–16: "No Man is an *Iland*, intire of its selfe; euery man is a peece of the *Continent*, a part of the *maine;* if a *Clod* bee washed away by the *Sea*, *Europe* is the lesse . . . Any Mans *death* diminishes *me*, because I am inuolued in *Mankinde*."

22 From Walton, p. ix.

23 "Walton's Use of Donne's Letters," *PQ*, 16 (1937), 30–34; cf. also Novarr, pp. 98–99, and Costa, pp. 139–40.

24 Costa's description of the use of letters as an innovation of seventeenth-century biographers (p. 421) is not entirely accurate: e.g., Roper (see my discussion pp. 42–43); likewise Harpsfield. Stauffer, pp. 257–58, also notes Stapleton's use of letters in the *Lives* of Becket and More (1588: in Latin).

25 Compare Walton, p. 73, "in *January* 1630" and, p. 74, "after *Candlemas*" with *Letters to Severall Persons of Honour* (London: J. Flesher for Richard Marriot, 1651), p. 243: "as I do not much hope before Christmas." Also see Novarr, pp. 44 ff. On p. 491, Novarr enumerates this "misuse" of fact and two others as Walton's chief biographical faults. The other two are less persuasive instances since they are based on the telescoping of chronology (account book) or on omission (will) rather than on commission.

26 Quotation from Novarr, p. 51. For a relevant analysis of Walton's patterned structure in the biography of Herbert, see Clayton D. Lein, "Art and Structure in Walton's *Life of Mr. George Herbert*," *UTQ*, 46 (1977), 165 ff.

27 Costa, pp. 171–72, attributes Walton's awareness of his own extravagance in praising Donne's preaching to Walton's awareness of contemporary criticisms of Donne's style. Such an attribution seems needlessly limited, if not forced, to me. See also Evelyn M. Simpson, "The Biographical Value of Donne's Sermons," *RES*, n.s. 2 (1951), 342 (the preacher in a cloud).

28 Cf. Novarr, p. 56: Walton's "apparent objectivity is an extremely real subjectivity." But see also p. 55; by subjectivity Novarr means "selection of details" and "correlative omissions" rather than psychological interest and novelistic technique, as I do in this instance.

29 Walton, pp. 47–48; my emphasis on "now" and "new."

30 On Walton's digressions, cf. Costa, pp. 424–26.

31 Cf. pp. 15–17.

32 Novarr's remarks on Walton's use of detail are provocative, although I should again interpret the evidence he cites differently: pp. 54–55 but also pp. 126, 489.

33 Walton's associating Donne particularly with David and Paul imitates two of Donne's own preferences, as stated and practiced in his sermons. See Bald, p. 322, and *The Sermons of John Donne*, ed. George R. Potter and Evelyn M. Simpson, 10 vols. (Berkeley: Univ. of California Press, 1953–62), II, 49 (No. 1); subsequent reference is to this edition, unless otherwise noted.

34 Biblical references in discussion of Walton are to the King James version.

35 Costa suggests that Walton's references to Stephen allude to Donne's sermons but specifies no further (p. 155). See *Sermons* VIII, 175 (No. 7): "Christs earliest witness, his Proto-Martyr . . . [was] St. *Stephen,* and in him that which especially made him his witness, and our example, [is] his death, and our preparation to death, what he suffered, what he did, what he said, so far as is knit up in those words, *When he had said this, he fell a sleep*"; cf. also p. 181: "the Libertines . . . were not able to resist the wisedome and the Spirit by which hee spake"; p. 183: "propose to thine imitation *Stephen,* who though enriched with great parts, and formerly accustomed to the conversation of others of a different perswasion, applied himself early to Christ as a Disciple, and . . . in a particular function and office as a Deacon." This sermon was preached at Whitehall in 1628 and, although unpublished until 1660, is likely to have been available to Walton at some point (see Novarr, pp. 26–28). Curiously, Walton fails to employ Donne's text for the sermon, Acts 7:60 (italicized passage cited above). To Donald Ramsay Roberts, Stephen—specifically in death—becomes Donne's "self-imposed pattern and example in later life": "The Death Wish of John Donne," *PMLA,* 62 (1947), 962, 972. Like Simpson ("The Biographical Value of Donne's Sermons," pp. 351, 355–56), however, I find Roberts' claim an overstatement in an otherwise fine essay.

36 "Sermon No. 11: Deaths Duell," in *Sermons,* X, 240–41, 247. Donne's text for the sermon is "And Unto God the Lord Belong the Issues of Death. i.e. From Death": Psalm 68:20. (St. Stephen is not mentioned in this sermon.)

37 Cf. the words of Donne to Bishop Morton in Walton, p. 34: "some irregularities of my life have been so visible to some men" as perhaps to dishonor "that sacred calling."

38 Novarr, p. 73, suggests that Walton's scriptural quotations are the result of carelessness or inadequate acquaintance with the Bible. Literary analysis of Walton's practice makes this possibility unlikely.

39 For another example in a more secular context, see the "*Pelican in the wilderness*" (Walton, p. 51) and Psalm 102:6.

40 Costa, p. 164, takes a similar position: Walton offers us "le témoignage d'un homme qui était le contemporain de ses modèles et partageait ainsi mieux que nous leur mentalité, leurs goûts, leur culture, et offre, de plus . . . une interprétation qui est celle des sujets eux-mêmes."

41 John A. Garraty describes the financial incentives of biographical "fictionizers" in the first half of the twentieth century: *Nature of Biography,* pp. 124–30.

42 Sir John Hayward, *The Life* . . . (London: for John Partridge, 1630); Michael Drayton, *Works,* ed. J. William Hebel (Oxford: Basil Blackwell, 1932), II, 451–75. Stauffer classifies both these works as biographies (pp. 324, 376).

43 Cf. Alan Shelston, *Biography* (London: Methuen, 1977), pp. 16, 73.

44 See p. 5.

45 *Collected Essays,* IV, 234.

46 The passage quoted from Woolf continues, "Yet if he [the biographer] carries the use of fiction too far, so that he disregards the truth, or can only introduce it with incongruity, he loses both worlds; he has neither the freedom of fiction nor the substance of fact" (p. 234).

47 *Art of Biography,* pp. 89, 125. Barbara W. Tuchman employs the term "primary" biography for such works: "Biography as a Prism of History," in *Telling Lives: The Biographer's Art,* ed. Marc Pachter (Washington, D.C.: New Republic Books/National Portrait Gallery, 1979), pp. 141–43.

48. E.g., Kendall, p. 110; Georges Gusdorf, "Conditions and Limits of Autobiography," ed. and trans. James Olney, in *Autobiography: Essays Theoretical and Critical,* pp. 31, 43–44; Roy Pascal, *Design and Truth in Autobiography* (Cambridge, Mass.: Harvard Univ. Press, 1960), pp. 83, 195.

6. MORE'S *RICHARD III*

1 St. Thomas More, *The History of King Richard III*, ed. Richard S. Sylvester, in *Works* (New Haven, Conn.: Yale Univ. Press, 1963), II. All references are to this edition, hereafter cited as More, *Richard III*. I have again silently expanded the contractions in Sylvester's text and in citations to other Tudor texts.

2 Quotations, in order: "Literary Problems in More's *Richard III*," *PMLA*, 58 (1943), 28; "Sir Thomas More's 'Richard III,' " *History*, 17 (1933), 320; "The Making of Sir Thomas More's *Richard III*," in *Historical Essays in Honour of James Tait*, ed. J. G. Edwards, V. H. Galbraith, and E. F. Jacob (Manchester: for the Subscribers, 1933), pp. 231, 235; More, *Richard III*, p. lxxx; "The Dramatic Structure of Sir Thomas More's *History of King Richard III*," *SEL*, 12 (1972), 223–24; *Richard III and His Early Historians 1483–1535* (Oxford: Clarendon, 1975), p. 155. Cf. Elizabeth Story Donno's learned, witty essay "Thomas More and *Richard III*," which appeared when this book was at press: *RenQ*, 35 (1982), 401–47. Since, as Donno notes, epideictic converges with history (and biography) in Roman writers, her observations on More's rhetoric are consonant with mine but her conception of his overall purpose is not. She considers the *Richard* essentially ahistorical and implies that the use of certain rhetorical techniques cancels other meanings. Classifying the *Richard* as a paradoxical encomium, she very nearly asserts that the work is a Lucianic exposure of rhetoric. Although I, too, reject "moralistic" readings of the *Richard*, I find it much more than an exercise or a joke.

3 *SEL* actually published Kincaid's article on the *Richard* in the annual issue on Elizabethan and Jacobean drama rather than in that on the nondramatic Renaissance. Hanham takes the *Richard* to be a five-act satiric drama, which is essentially comic but has an unfinished satiric tragedy appended to it. She calls the portion of the work that follows Richard's accession a "continuation' (pp. 184, 188, and chap. 7 passim).

4 See, e.g., "More and his School: Use of Dialogue: The Chelsea Academy of Dramatic Art," in Chambers' introduction to Harpsfield's *Moore*, pp. clvii–clxvii.

5 Letter to John Astley, in *Works*, ed. J. A. Giles (London: J. R. Smith, 1864–65), III, 5–6. Interestingly, Stauffer, *English Biography before 1700*, p. 374, includes Chaucer's St. Cecilia (Second Nun's Tale) and Monk's Tale in his list of biographies. Ascham's list of histories would doubtless have included Chaucer's *Troilus and Criseyde*. For additional discussion, see Walter F. Staton, Jr., "Roger Ascham's Theory of History Writing," *SP*, 56 (1959), 125–37.

6 More, *Richard III*, p. 2: "The history of king Richard the thirde (vnfinished) writen by Master Thomas More than one of the vndersheriffis of London . . . VVich worke hath bene before this tyme printed, in hardynges Cronicle, and in Hallys Cronicle. . . ."

7 Pollard, "The Making of Sir Thomas More's *Richard III*," p. 230. On the development of the term *history* in Greek, Latin, and Renaissance English, see Tom F. Driver, *The Sense of History in Greek and Shakespearean Drama* (1960; rpt. New York: Columbia Univ. Press, 1961), pp. 6–8.

8 *Utopia*, ed. Edward Surtz, S.J., and J. H. Hexter, in *Works* (New Haven, Conn.: Yale Univ. Press, 1965), IV, 42: "florem illi gratiamque nouitatis historiae suae praeripere" (23–24).

9 Hanham, pp. 155, 160, 190.

10 See Levy, *Tudor Historical Thought*, pp. 7, 13–14; F. Smith Fussner, *Tudor History and the Historians* (New York: Basic Books, 1970), p. 235; Myron P. Gilmore, "The Renaissance Conception of the Lessons of History," rev., in *Facets of the Renaissance*, ed. William H. Werkmeister (1959; rpt. New York: Harper & Row, 1963), pp. 73–101; and Felix Gilbert, *Machiavelli and Guicciardini: Politics and History in Sixteenth-Century Florence* (Princeton: Princeton Univ. Press, 1965), pp. 215–18. Even in the 1570s Thomas Blundeville describes the principal purposes for which histories are written as follows: "First that we may learne thereby to acknowledge the prouidence of God . . . Secondly, that by the examples of the wise, we maye learne wisedome wysely to behaue our selues in all our actions . . . Thirdly, that we maye be stirred by example of the good to followe the good, and by the example of

the euill to flee the euill": *The true order and Methode of wryting and reading Hystories, according to the precepts of Francisco Patricio and Accontio Tridentino* (London: Willyam Seres, 1574), F2v–F3r.

11 Cf. Albert H. Buford, "History and Biography: The Renaissance Distinction," in *A Tribute to George Coffin Taylor*, ed. Arnold Williams (Chapel Hill: Univ. of North Carolina Press, 1952), pp. 100–12. Buford's examples (1579–1618) are considerably later than More. Although Buford seeks the theoretical distinction between history and biography, his essay addresses and illustrates their overlapping concerns: e.g., Hayward, "like Bacon and Bolton, looks on history as being more comprehensive than biography but definitely embracing it" (p. 111). Irving Ribner, *The English History Play in the Age of Shakespeare* (Princeton: Princeton Univ. Press, 1957), pp. 193–223, relies on Buford's article in distinguishing "the biographical play" from "the history play." More's *Richard III* does not readily accommodate a sharp distinction; nor without substantial qualification does Shakespeare's (chaps. 7, 9 of my discussion).

12 Citations for the preceding paragraph, in order: *Richard the Third up to Shakespeare* (1900; rpt. Totowa, N.J.: Rowman & Littlefield, 1976), pp. 121, 201; *English Biography before 1700*, pp. 37–40; A. R. Myers, "The Character of Richard III," *History Today*, 4 (1954), 515. Cf. Levy, *Tudor Historical Thought*, p. 68.

13 Dean, "Literary Problems in More's *Richard III*," p. 38. Cf. Walter M. Gordon, "Exemplum Narrative and Thomas More's *History of King Richard III*," *ClioI*, 9 (1979), 75–88.

14 Cf. More, *Richard III*, pp. xci–xcii; but also pp. lxxx–civ.

15 Chambers, in Harpsfield's *Moore*, p. xlviii.

16 Robert E. Reiter sees the *Richard* as an inverted version of a saint's *Life*—to my mind pushing a very general resemblance (or analogy) to a specific one: "On the Genre of Thomas More's *Richard III*," *Moreana*, 25 (1970), 12, 14.

17 Charles Ross, *Edward IV* (Berkeley: Univ. of California Press, 1974), p. 416: Edward was three weeks shy of age 41 at death. More himself was born in February 1477 or 1478; the earlier date is the likelier one: G[ermain] M[arc'hadour], "Thomas More's Birth: 1477 or 1478?" *Moreana*, 53 (1977), pp. 6–10.

18 More's "precise computation" suggests to Sylvester that More was "following a now lost written source": More, *Richard III*, p. 157, n. 3/1.

19 On More's knowledge of Fabyan, see More, *Richard III*, pp. lxxiii–lxxv. Quotation is from Fabyan's *New Chronicles of England and France* of 1516, ed. Henry Ellis (London: F. C. and J. Rivington et al., 1811), p. 667.

20 Fabyan, p. 577. Cf. examples in *The Great Chronicle of London*, ed. A. H. Thomas and I. D. Thornley (London: G. W. Jones, 1938), p. 229, and "Historiae Croylandensis Continuatio," ed. William Fulman, in *Rerum Anglicarum Scriptorum Veterum* (Oxford: E Theatro Sheldoniano, 1684), I, 564. Cf. also Polydore Vergil on the death of Edward IV, in *Polydori Vergilii Vrbinatis Anglicae Historiae, libri XXVI* (Basel: J. Bebelium, 1534), p. 532: Polydore reckons Edward about 50 at death ("annum agens aetatis circiter quinquagesimum"); his catalogue of Edward's children includes a bastard son ("tertium ex concubina, nomine Arthurum") whose name More's list omits. Citing Polydore, I should note that I am unpersuaded by Hanham's view that his work is "the basis" of More's *History* and "in a broader way . . . the begetter" of it (pp. 159, 163–64, 146–47). This is an exaggerated and unsubstantiated view of the relationship between the two works.

21 More, *Richard III*, pp. 4–5, 161–62, nn. 4/20, 5/1.

22 *Great Chronicle*, pp. 229–30.

23 "Vomitum provocare solitum accepi, ut voluptate edendi iterum stomachum referciret": Dominic Mancini, *The Usurpation of Richard the Third*, ed. and trans. C. A. J. Armstrong (London: Oxford Univ. Press, 1936), pp. 80–83; see also More, *Richard III*, pp. 160–61.

24 Cf. Mancini's "intemperantissimus," p. 80; also "tam corpulento" in "Historiae Croylandensis Continuatio," p. 564.

25 As Ross observes, p. 423, Edward's "own contemporaries, and the early Tudor commentators . . . admired and respected him." Modern historians are likewise inclined to assess his reign in a generally favorable light (Ross, pp. 419–22).

26 Polydore thinks Edward about 50; *The Great Chronicle*, presumably compiled by Fabyan, declares Edward 46 (n. 22 above). Neither of these works was in print while More was composing the *Richard*, but it is likely that he knew both their authors and entirely possible that he had access to their work (More, *Richard III*, pp. lxxiii–lxxvi). See also Pollard, "The Making of Sir Thomas More's *Richard III*," p. 231, n. 4, and Cora L. Scofield, *The Life and Reign of Edward the Fourth*, 2 vols. (London: Longmans, Green, 1923), I, 1–2; the *Annales* (in progress in 1491) and other manuscript sources give Edward's year of birth correctly. (On the *Annales*, formerly attributed to William of Worcester, see Ross, p. 432.)

27 "Making of Sir Thomas More's *Richard III*," p. 231; also More, *Richard III*, p. 157, n. 3/1. The error in age would have Edward born in 1429 rather than in 1442. *DNB*, s.v. Richard, Duke of York (1411–60); Edward's birth is misdated in this article but given correctly s.v. Edward IV.

28 For the date of marriage, see George Edward Cokayne, *The Complete Peerage*, rev. ed. Geoffrey H. White and R. S. Lea (London, St. Catherine Press, 1959), XII, pt. 2, 908, s.v. York (1415). For Cecily's date of birth: "Wilhelmi Wyrcester Annales Rerum Anglicarum," in *Letters and Papers Illustrative of the Wars of the English in France*, ed. Joseph Stevenson, Rolls Series (1864; rpt. Kraus-Thomson, Nendeln/Liechtenstein, 1968), II, pt. 2, 759 (1415).

29 "Wilhelmi Wyrcester Annales Rerum Anglicarum," p. 762 (1439: b. Anne), p. 763 (1441, 1442). On the several steps toward marriage, of which until 1439 the church wedding was not the sacrament, see Lawrence Stone, *The Family, Sex and Marriage in England 1500–1800* (New York: Harper & Row, 1977), p. 31.

30 More, *Richard III*, pp. lxiii–lxv; More, *Utopia*, xv–xxiii. Hanham suggests that More wrote the *Richard* between 1518–19 and 1520–21 but adds that he might have been working on it as late as 1524 and perhaps even after 1527 (pp. 218–19). Any date between 1514 and 1524 is possible since there is no hard evidence against it (and very little evidence of any sort to inform a choice). Hanham's inclination to see the work continued beyond 1521 (execution of Edward, Duke of Buckingham) derives from her literary interpretation of the *Richard* and correlatively from her view that the version(s) of the *Richard* printed in the chronicles of Grafton and Hall were composed by More after the version Rastell printed. That I do not agree with her position will be evident in succeeding pages.

31 *The Acts and Monuments*, ed. Josiah Pratt, 4th ed. (London: Religious Tract Society, 1877), IV, 688.

32 More, *Richard III*, pp. 168–69, n. 8/13–14; but cf. also Churchill, p. 120.

33 More, *Richard III*, p. 169, nn. 8/23, 27; pp. 165–66, nn. 7/1–2, 5, 9–10; cf. Churchill, pp. 44, 51, 65, 156, esp. 120–21. Richard's complicity in Clarence's death appears original with More's account.

34 See Pollard, "Making of Sir Thomas More's *Richard III*," p. 235; More, *Richard III*, p. 170, nn. 9/8, 9.

35 See More, *Richard III*, p. 9 (Latin), ll. 18–20.

36 More, *Richard III*, p. lxix.

37 More, *Richard III*, pp. 28–32, 37–40, but see also pp. 33, 34–37, and p. 195, n. 28/19: I. D. Thornley, "The Destruction of Sanctuary," in *Tudor Studies Presented to Albert Frederick Pollard*, ed. R. W. Seton-Watson (1924; rpt. New York: Russell & Russell, 1970), pp. 182–207, esp. 200–03.

38 *The Likeness of Thomas More*, pp. 18, 21, 3, 5–6; Morison cites David Piper, "Holbein the Younger in England," *Journal of the Royal Society of Arts*, 111 (1963), 736–55. Piper, p. 742, describes the picture as "A not quite fully resolved adaptation of a religious formula for secular, indeed domestic, purposes"; he adds, "If a naked Holy Child were placed in the

rather void foreground, the group would at once cohere in an Adoration." Cf. Pope-Hennessy, *Portrait in the Renaissance*, pp. 99–100.

39 See Roper, p. 43, on More's reverence for his father.

40 Roper, p. 25.

41 More, *Richard III*, p. 212, n. 44/22–23; but also Churchill, pp. 126–27. For the passage in *Thyestes*, see *Seneca's Tragedies*, ed. and trans. Frank Justus Miller, Loeb series, rev. ed. (Cambridge, Mass.: Harvard Univ. Press, 1929), II, vs. 957–60.

42 Cf. Chaucer's handling of dreams as omens in The Nun's Priest's Tale: *Works*, ed. F. N. Robinson, 2nd ed. (Boston: Houghton Mifflin, 1957), vs. 3338–54. Hastings' fate, like Chauntecleer's, even falls on a Friday. Like Ascham in the Letter to Astley, More thinks of Chaucer repeatedly when writing history. In this instance, More's debt to Chaucer is undeniable.

43 More, *Richard III*, pp. 51; 224, n. 51/15: Sylvester finds no historical record of "one Hastinges a purseuant." Hanham, p. 173, n. 1, finds reference to one in 1480 and perhaps in 1485. Scofield, II, 319 and n. 2, records a reference to "Hastings Pursuivant," sent to Louis XI in 1481 with a couple of horses, gifts from Edward IV. Because Scofield's note, which is not listed in her index, has eluded others, I reproduce it here: Account Book of John Cheyne, master of the horse, 21–22 Edw. IV, Exchequer Accounts, Equitium Regis, bundle 107, no. 15.

44 More, *Richard III*, pp. 49–52, 52–55.

45 Roper, pp. 35, 69. Morison, p. 18; an eleventh figure, who is unidentified, appears in the right background of the Holbein sketch.

46 More, *Richard III*, pp. lxxxvii, xcv: Sylvester suggests Tacitus' apology as the source of More's recognition and notes similarities between Shore's wife and Sallust's Sempronia. Although Tacitus' apology is verbally relevant to the *Richard*, its emphasis and context in *Annals* IV, 32, are substantially different. Tacitus considers the trifles he introduces distasteful ("ita minimum oblectationis adferunt") and continues, "Descriptions of countries, the vicissitudes of battles, commanders dying on the field of honour, such are the episodes that arrest and renew the interest of the reader" (IV, 33): *Annals*, ed. and trans. John Jackson, Loeb series (Cambridge, Mass.: Harvard Univ. Press, 1937), III. Despite a few verbal similarities, Sallust's Sempronia has little in common with Shore's wife: *The War with Catiline*, ed. and trans. J. C. Rolfe, rev. ed., Loeb series (Cambridge, Mass.: Harvard Univ. Press, 1931), xxv; e.g., "Even before the time of the conspiracy she had often broken her word, repudiated her debts, been privy to murder . . . Nevertheless, . . . she possessed a high degree of wit and of charm." For further discussion, see Esther Yaël Beith-Halahmi, "Angell Fayre or Strumpet Lewd: Jane Shore as an Example of Erring Beauty in 16th Century Literature," *ElizS*, 26–27 (1974), pp. 47–48; also Lee Cullen Khanna's acute comments on Mistress Shore in "No Less Real than Ideal: Images of Woman in More's Work," *Moreana*, 53–56 (1977), pp. 45–47 ff.

47 *Bede's Ecclesiastical History of the English People*, pp. 338–43 (Owine), pp. 414–20 (Caedmon). Roger D. Ray, "Bede, the Exegete, as Historian," in *Famulus Christi*, p. 133, notes that while "Bede frequently calls his full work *historia*" and so titles it, he twice refers to it "as his 'histories' " and once speaks of inserting "into his *historia* a certain brief *historia*" (*Eccles. Hist.*, pp. 512, 128, 404). He adds that Bede's practice reflects "biblical norms," e.g., the Gospel of Luke, which was for Bede a larger *historia* containing many small *historiae*.

48 Mancini, pp. 74–75: "fama est, pugione ab Eduardo eius iugulo admoto, ut in libidinem consentiret, imperterritam constitisse; morique potius statuisse, quam cum rege impudice vivere." See also More, *Richard III*, p. 239, n. 61/7.

49 Readers have remarked an alteration of tone in More's work after Richard's accession: e.g., A. W. Reed, "Philological Notes," in *The English Works of Sir Thomas More* (London: Eyre and Spottiswoode, 1931), I, 189–90, but cf. 192–93; Hanham, pp. 185 ff. This alteration corresponds to a shift in More's point of view and in his assessment of history's meaning. As

we have seen, there are signs of it well before the accession.

50 Hanham, p. 187, divorces "style" from content in commenting on the passage that ends with this description and that includes a great deal of alliterative reference to the princes, "these innocent tender chil[e]dren, borne of moste royall bloode, brought vp in great wealth, likely long to liue to reigne and rule in the realme. . . ." Hanham writes that "The passage is basically entirely serious, but at the same time More is indulging himself by reproducing the heavy alliterative style considered appropriate to such subjects by less sophisticated writers." It is hard to see how such a passage can be basically serious and parodic at the same time.

51 Churchill, pp. 40–41, 124, 159; More, *Richard III*, p. 267, nn. 87/14–15, 18.

52 Hanham's speculations about More's failure to finish the *Richard* depend heavily on her views that the work is satiric-parodic throughout and that it has a five-act structure, plus an anomalous appendage. Her theory (pp. 188–89) about the ending is itself an appendix to her theory of the whole—or rather the five-act whole—and not by itself debatable or now relevant.

53 Pollard, "Making of Sir Thomas More's *Richard III*," p. 237. Hanham (p. 218) refers non-committally to this explanation but in doing so moves the date on which More might have recognized the danger to Buckingham forward to 1521, the date of his execution.

54 Richard S. Sylvester, ed., *The History of King Richard III and Selections from the English and Latin Poems*, by St. Thomas More (New Haven, Conn.: Yale Univ. Press, 1976), pp. xv–xvi, appears to favor this suggestion.

55 Kincaid, pp. 230–31.

56 Dean, "Literary Problems in More's *Richard III*," p. 41.

57 According to More's biographers, as a member of Parliament he incurred Henry VII's indignation with the result that More's father was imprisoned and fined, and More himself was spared flight from England only by Henry's death (1509): see Roper, pp. 7–8; Harpsfield, pp. 15–17; and 308–09, nn. 15/15–16, 21.

58 More, *Richard III*, p. xxx, and p. 87: "King Richarde himselfe as ye shal herafter here, slain in the fielde. . . ."

59 Harpsfield, pp. 10, 12; 306, n. 12/13.

60 Morton died in 1500; Wolsey became Chancellor in 1515, and More in 1529.

61 For More's punning on his own name, see Germain Marc'hadour's engaging essay, "A Name for All Seasons," in *Essential Articles for the Study of Thomas More*, pp. 539–62; also More, *Richard III*, p. xxi, n. 1.

7. SHAKESPEARE'S *RICHARD III*

1 Cf. Waldo F. McNeir, "The Masks of Richard the Third," *SEL*, 11 (1971), 168: "the naturalistic man, the stylized monster, and the synthetic man-monster . . . are all implicit in Shakespeare's source."

2 *Narrative and Dramatic Sources of Shakespeare*, ed. Geoffrey Bullough (London: Routledge & Kegan Paul, 1960), III, 222–28. All references to Shakespeare's *Richard III*, unless otherwise noted, are to Herschel Baker's edition in *The Riverside Shakespeare*, ed. G. Blakemore Evans et al. (Boston: Houghton Mifflin, 1974).

3 *Historical Drama: The Relation of Literature and Reality* (Chicago: Univ. of Chicago Press, 1975), p. x.

4 Cf. Jan Kott, *Shakespeare Our Contemporary*, trans. Boleslaw Taborski, rev. ed. (London: Methuen, 1967), p. 9.

5 *Angel with Horns*, ed. Graham Storey (London: Longmans, 1961), p. 2. F. W. Brownlow's view that Richard is thoroughly unhistorical is still more extreme: *Two Shakespearean Sequences: "Henry VI" to "Richard II" and "Pericles" to "Timon of Athens"* (Pittsburgh: Univ. of Pittsburgh Press, 1977), pp. 63–69.

6 Roland Mushat Frye notes an especially suggestive example of the influence of Shakespeare's

"stage villain" on actual portraits of Richard III: "The 'Shakespearean' Portrait of Richard III in Edward Alleyn's Picture Collection," *SQ*, 32 (1981), 352–54. But see also the alteration of a 1518–23 portrait of Richard in Pamela Tudor-Craig, *Richard III*, 2nd ed. (Totowa, N.J.: Rowman and Littlefield, 1977), p. 93 (P44); Shakespeare's play intensifies the distortion of Richard's figure but hardly initiates it.

7 Quotation from Rossiter, p. 2.

8 Theodore Weiss notes a similar tension: *The Breath of Clowns and Kings: Shakespeare's Early Comedies and Histories* (London: Chatto & Windus, 1971), p. 177. Perceptive as Nicholas Brooke's analysis of *Richard III* is, it seems to me, though more subtly than Rossiter's, to slight the basic historicity of the play and thereby to lessen its real impact: *Shakespeare's Early Tragedies* (London: Methuen, 1968), pp. 48–79. For Brooke, "events" get lost in "a generalized momentum" (p. 52), and the figure of Richard, already implicit in Shakespeare's historical sources, becomes, in *opposition* to history, "an emblem of the tragic enfeeblement of man" (p. 79). The meaning of "history/historical" is at issue in his analysis. (In it, history, by Coleridge's distinction, might be said to subserve plot: see n. 10 below.)

9 Since my purpose is not to define the history play or the biographical play as a genre but to relate specific historical/biographical plays to Renaissance life-writing, I have relied on the common denominator of nearly all attempts at definition, namely, the dependence of Shakespeare's English history plays on the facts and political issues (i.e., the matter) of the chronicles. See Irving Ribner, *The English History Play in the Age of Shakespeare*, pp. 5–12, 24–25; if a play fulfills what "the Elizabethans considered to be the legitimate purposes of history" and is "drawn from a chronicle source . . . that at least a large part of the contemporary audience accepted as factual, we may call it a history play." See also Hardin Craig, "Shakespeare and the History Play," in *Joseph Quincy Adams Memorial Studies*, ed. James G. McManaway, Giles E. Dawson, and Edwin E. Willoughby (Washington, D.C.: Folger Library, 1948), p. 56: "there is no available criterion [for the history play] until plays began to deal actually and faithfully with history." Andrew S. Cairncross, "Shakespeare and the History Play," *EIRC*, 1 (1974), 68–69, similarly connects "the factual-episodic view of history" with the history play. For other relevant efforts, cf., in addition to n. 10 below, Lily B. Campbell, *Shakespeare's "Histories": Mirrors of Elizabethan Policy* (San Marino, Calif.: Huntingon Library, 1947), pp. 8–17, 306; F. P. Wilson, "The English History Play," in *Shakespearian and Other Studies*, ed. Helen Gardner (Oxford: Clarendon, 1969), esp. pp. 2–4; Josephine A. Pearce, "Constituent Elements in Shakespeare's English History Plays," in *Studies in Shakespeare*, ed. Arthur D. Matthews and Clark M. Emery (Coral Gables, Fla.: Univ. of Miami Press, 1953), p. 148; M. M. Reese, *The Cease of Majesty: A Study of Shakespeare's History Plays* (London: Edward Arnold, 1961), pp. 66, 74; Robert Ornstein, *A Kingdom for a Stage: The Achievement of Shakespeare's History Plays* (Cambridge, Mass.: Harvard Univ. Press, 1972), pp. 1–7; and David Riggs, *Shakespeare's Heroical Histories: "Henry VI" and Its Literary Tradition* (Cambridge, Mass.: Harvard Univ. Press, 1971), pp. 23–24; relating Shakespeare's conception of history primarily to heroical literature rather than to the chronicles, Riggs nonetheless acknowledges "the more restrictively 'historical' " nature of plays drawn from the English chronicles, i.e., from "more closely specified historical environments."

10 The title in the Quartos suggests a similar mixture; the first Quarto is representative: "The Tragedy / of King Richard the third. / Containing, / His treacherous Plots against his brother Clarence: / the pittiefull murther of his innocent nephewes: / his tyrannical vsurpation: with the whole course / of his detested life, and most deserued death": *The Tragedy of Richard the Third: with the Landing of Earle Richmond, and the Battell at Bosworth Field*, Variorum ed. by Horace Howard Furness, Jr. (Philadelphia: J. B. Lippincott, 1908), XVI, 431–32. S. T. Coleridge's distinction is useful: "In the purely historical plays [e.g., *Henry VI*], the history *informs* the plot; in the mixt [e.g., *Henry IV*], it *directs* it; in the rest, as *Macbeth*, *Hamlet*,

Cymbeline, *Lear*, it subserves it": *Coleridge's Shakespearean Criticism*, ed. Thomas Middleton Raysor (London: Constable, 1930), I, 143. "Classifying a play as a History," James Winny sensibly observes, Shakespeare's first editors "did no more than indicate its subject-matter very broadly"; he adds, "The Histories are works of an indeterminate literary kind, capable of extension towards either the comic or the tragic": *The Player King: A Theme of Shakespeare's Histories* (London: Chatto & Windus, 1968), p. 10; cf. Wolfgang Clemen, *A Commentary on Shakespeare's "Richard III,"* trans. Jean Bonheim (London: Methuen, 1968), pp. 223–24, and David Scott Kastan, "The Shape of Time: Form and Value in the Shakespearean History Play," *CompD*, 7 (1973–74), esp. pp. 259–63. Cf. also Madeleine Doran, *Endeavors of Art: A Study of Form in Elizabethan Drama* (Madison: Univ. of Wisconsin Press, 1954), pp. 112–15; A. C. Hamilton, *The Early Shakespeare* (San Marino, Calif.: Huntington Library, 1967), pp. 186–87; and Brooke, pp. 48–50. While the three preceding authors, like many others, see *Richard III* as essentially tragic or as tragedy, D. A. Traversi refers to the play as "comedy" (in nervous quotation marks): e.g., *An Approach to Shakespeare*, 3rd ed. (New York: Doubleday, 1969), I, 32. Thomas F. Van Laan assigns the "genre" of melodrama to *Richard III*: *Role-playing in Shakespeare* (Toronto: Univ. of Toronto Press, 1978), pp. 146–47. See also chap. 6, n. 11, above, regarding Ribner's classification.

11 For More's ending, see John Stow, *The Chronicles of England* (London: Ralphe Newberie, for Henrie Bynneman, 1580), p. 835; Raphael Holinshed et al., *Chronicles* (London: for John Harison et al., 1587), III, 737: subsequent reference is to this edition of Holinshed.

12 Recent editors have either rejected or silently dismissed the possibility that the wooing scenes were influenced by Thomas Legge's *Ricardus Tertius:* e.g., John Dover Wilson, ed., *Richard III*, corrected ed. (1961; rpt. Cambridge: Cambridge Univ. Press, 1971), p. xxix; E. A. J. Honigmann, ed., *King Richard III* (Harmondsworth, Middlesex: Penguin, 1968); and Antony Hammond, ed., *King Richard III* (London: Methuen, 1981), p. 82. Hammond also notes that Bullough, who printed excerpts from Legge's play as an analogue to Shakespeare's, overestimated its relevance. Richard P. Wheeler, "History, Character and Conscience in *Richard III*," *CompD*, 5 (1971–72), is one of the few critics sensitive to the reality of the psychological violence and the perversity of the wooing scenes: e.g., p. 314, but cf. the note of Hammond, ed., on IV.iv.423 (p. 295).

13 On Shakespeare's use of More, cf. Wilson, ed., *Richard III*, p. xv; Moody E. Prior, *The Drama of Power: Studies in Shakespeare's History Plays* (Evanston, Ill.: Northwestern Univ. Press, 1973), p. 296; Riggs, pp. 143–44; Edward I. Berry, *Patterns of Decay: Shakespeare's Early Histories* (Charlottesville: Univ. Press of Virginia, 1975), pp. 84–86, 88–90; and Emrys Jones, *The Origins of Shakespeare* (Oxford: Clarendon, 1977), pp. 211–16.

14 Richard actually married Anne in 1472, according to Paul Murray Kendall, *Richard the Third* (London: Allen & Unwin, 1955), pp. 106–10; she was promised to Richard by Edward IV in 1471, however.

15 *King Lear*, ed. Frank Kermode, in *The Riverside Shakespeare:* V. iii.240, 244–45 (my emphasis).

16 E.g., the parenthetical remark cited on p. 97. A similar interiorization of More's editorial remarks occurs in Hastings' reiterated and penitent realization of "the blindnes of our mortall nature":

> I now repent I told the pursuivant,
> As too triumphing, how mine enemies
> To-day at Pomfret bloodily were butcher'd,
> And I myself secure, in grace and favor.
>
> [III.iv.88–91]

And five lines later: "O momentary grace of mortal men, / Which we more hunt for than the grace of God!" In More's *Richard*, Hastings' blindness is recognized only by More (p. 52).

17 Clemen, p. 220, similarly reads the last three lines of Richard's speech. Cf. Robert G. Hunter, *Shakespeare and the Mystery of God's Judgments* (Athens: Univ. of Georgia Press, 1976), pp. 97–99, and Wilbur Sanders, *The Dramatist and the Received Idea: Studies in the Plays of Marlowe & Shakespeare* (Cambridge: Cambridge Univ. Press, 1968), pp. 107–08.

18 Sigmund Freud, *Complete Psychological Works*, trans. and ed. James Strachey et al. (1957; rpt. London: Hogarth Press and The Institute of Psycho-Analysis, 1973), XIV, 314–15. Robert B. Heilman treats Richard's psychology provocatively in "Satiety and Conscience: Aspects of Richard III," *AR*, 24 (1964), 57–73.

19 Prior, pp. 309–10.

20 From a different but relevant perspective, Bridget Gellert Lyons discusses Richard's "emblem," the boar, in " 'Kings Games': Stage Imagery and Political Symbolism in 'Richard III,' " *Criticism*, 20 (1978), 25–27. On Richard as Vice, see Bernard Spivack, *Shakespeare and the Allegory of Evil: The History of a Metaphor in Relation to His Major Villains* (New York: Columbia Univ. Press, 1958), pp. 386–407.

21 E.g., Sidney Thomas, *The Antic Hamlet and Richard III* (New York: King's Crown Press, 1943), p. 17.

22 *The Tempest*, ed. Hallett Smith, in *The Riverside Shakespeare:* I.ii.397–403; subsequent reference is to this edition.

23 Garden of Adonis, originally the name for a forcing bed or place of heightened fertility, became in the Renaissance a "ioyous Paradize" and the seminary of created things (cf. n. 26 below, on "seminal reasons"). The center of Spenser's paradisal Garden is a mons veneris. See Edmund Spenser, *The Faerie Queene*, ed. A. C. Hamilton (London: Longman, 1977), Bk. III.vi.29–30 (and notes, p. 360); the deadly boar is imprisoned "In a strong rocky Caue . . . Hewen vnderneath that Mount" in the mythic Garden (III.vi.48, and notes, p. 364). The babes returning from the world through a gate of death "in that Gardin *planted* be againe; / And grow afresh, as they had neuer seene / Fleshly corruption, nor mortall paine" (III.vi.33: my emphasis). On the Mount, Venus "takes her fill" of Adonis' "sweetnesse," and

> There yet, some say, in secret he does ly,
> Lapped in flowres and pretious *spycery* [my emphasis],
> By her hid from the world, and from the skill
> Of *Stygian* Gods. . . .
>
> [III.vi.46]

Similarity of situation and explicit echoes leave little question that Shakespeare had Spenser's Garden in mind. (Harold F. Brooks's proof that Shakespeare drew on other parts of Spenser's Books II and III—Cave of Mammon, Bower of Bliss, Rich Strand—earlier in the play makes the present allusion virtually certain: " 'Richard III': Antecedents of Clarence's Dream," *ShS*, 32 [1979], 148–50.) For still another plausible echo of Book III in the present scene, see *Richard III*, IV.iv.218, and *Faerie Queene*, III.iv.27, vs. 1; i.37, vs. 9. All references to *The Faerie Queene* will be to Hamilton's edition.

24 *Richard III*, IV.iv.388–90, 395–96. Contrast the renewing circularity of mythic time in the Garden of Adonis.

25 Mikhail Bakhtin's discussion of this association is classic: *Rabelais and His World*, trans. Hélène Iswolsky (Cambridge, Mass.: MIT Press, 1968), esp. chap. 5.

26 Frederick Copleston, *A History of Philosophy* (1950; rpt. New York: Newman Press, 1971), II, 76–77. Cf. *Faerie Queene*, p. 360, note on stanza 30. The present association of Elizabeth's "reasons" further suggests that the context of Spenser's Garden of Adonis is recurrently in Shakespeare's mind in this scene. For numerous additional examples of the seminal reasons in Renaissance thought, see James Nohrnberg, *The Analogy of "The Faerie Queene"* (Princeton:

Princeton Univ. Press, 1976), pp. 537–54, and John Erskine Hankins, *Source and Meaning in Spenser's Allegory: A Study of "The Faerie Queene"* (Oxford: Clarendon, 1971), pp. 234–86.

27 *Richard III*, I.iii.130–32; see also vs. 134–36: while Richard is yet unaware of Margaret's presence, her words join his to give voice in the court to the guilt Clarence will confront in his dream (I.iv. 48–62). Margaret has an intimate, symbolic relation both to Richard and to the deathly realm of Clarence's dream, his psychic hell.

28 Cf. A. L. French, "The World of *Richard III*," *ShakS*, 4 (1968), 35: Clarence's dream "works potently to create eschatological terrors which show up the hollowness of the religious feelings presented elsewhere." Wilbur Sanders' notion of "a natural providence," incipient in *Richard III* (p. 95), and Richard P. Wheeler's notion of a " 'villainizing' of the idea of individuality in the person of Richard" (p. 320) could by extension be integrated profitably with my own point of view, though they are unconnected with its origin. The same is, perhaps, even true of Michael Neill's position—more extreme and less ambiguous than mine—that the Deity of this play is "a Cosmic Ironist," or in some sense "a greater and more competent Richard . . . a malign demiurge delighting in the monstrous shadow of his own ugliness": "Shakespeare's Halle of Mirrors: Play, Politics, and Psychology in *Richard III*," *ShakS*, 8 (1975), 126.

29 I do not argue that Shakespeare meant us to respond to Richmond in the manner which I describe, only that this is in fact the way we do respond. For similar views of Richmond, see, for example, Robert B. Pierce, *Shakespeare's History Plays: The Family and the State* (Columbus: Ohio State Univ. Press, 1971), p. 119: "a dramatic nonentity"; Riggs, p. 148: Richmond's "flatness"; Hunter, p. 73: "a dramatic nonentity, a vacuum in shining armor"; Sanders, p. 93: Richmond's "wooden rectitude"; Brooke, p. 61: an "angelic figure" the play makes us distrust; Wheeler, pp. 306–07: "a redemptive figure" that works thematically but not emotionally; French, p. 31: "a cipher"; Ornstein, pp. 79–80; Clemen, pp. 197, 202–16. Prior, p. 310, suggests, "The [suitable] nemesis of the perfect Machiavellian virtuoso of power is a highly idealized figure," i.e., Richmond. Prior's observation has merit but accounts for only half the story; the half it omits is clearer in Reese's more (or possibly less) logical formulation of the same point: "In its context the lifelessness of the character [of Richmond] shows how seriously Shakespeare took him" (p. 212). For still another, subtler version of this position, see Robert Y. Turner, *Shakespeare's Apprenticeship* (Chicago: Univ. of Chicago Press, 1974), pp. 142, 73–74.

30 *Works*, ed. James Spedding, Robert Leslie Ellis, and Douglas Denon Heath, 15 vols. (Boston: Brown and Taggard [imprint varies; vols. 6–10: Taggard and Thompson], 1860–64), XI, 45: all future reference to Bacon's works, unless specified otherwise, is to this edition. Another contemporary writer, John Milton—admittedly not a neutral observer of kings—also found in More and the chronicles a true picture of Richard III, so true, in fact, that Milton thinks Shakespeare "us'd not much licence in departing from the truth of History": *Eikonoklastes*, ed. Merritt Y. Hughes, in *Complete Prose Works*, ed. Don M. Wolfe et al. (New Haven: Yale Univ. Press, 1962), III, 362. Neither Bacon's nor Milton's notion of what truth is appears to differ much in this instance from Izaak Walton's.

8. SHAKESPEARE'S *HENRY VIII*

1 "Of the Proficience and Advancement of Learning Divine and Humane," in *Works*, VI, 203; hereafter cited as *Advancement*.

2 F. J. Levy, ed., *The History of the Reign of King Henry VII*, by Francis Bacon (Indianapolis: Bobbs-Merrill, 1972), p. 28; similarly, Anne Righter, "Francis Bacon," p. 310, and John L. Harrison, "Bacon's View of Rhetoric, Poetry and the Imagination," pp. 253–68, both in *Essential Articles for the Study of Francis Bacon*, ed. Brian Vickers (Hamden, Conn.: Archon, 1968); also, Brian Vickers, "Bacon's Use of Theatrical Imagery," p. 212, and Benjamin Farrington, "Francis Bacon after His Fall," pp. 153–54, both in *SLitI*, 4 (1971). For opposing

views of this relation, see Murray W. Bundy, "Bacon's True Opinion of Poetry," *SP*, 27 (1930), 244–64, esp. 253–54; Leonard F. Dean, "Sir Francis Bacon's Theory of Civil History-Writing," *ELH*, 8 (1941), 183; and Eugene P. McCreary, "Bacon's Theory of Imagination Reconsidered," *HLQ*, 36 (1973), 317–26: while McCreary rightly distinguishes Bacon's poetics from Sidney's, his characterization of Bacon's poetics as "idealist" and Sidney's as "realist" (pp. 322–24) seems to me radically to invert the basic features of each, e.g., Sidney's Neoplatonism and Bacon's materialism. Elizabeth Sewell, *The Orphic Voice: Poetry and Natural History* (New Haven, Conn.: Yale Univ. Press, 1960), pp. 77, 106–09, 125, acknowledges indirection, ambiguity, weakness, and self-betrayal in Bacon's opinion of poetry, but she also argues for an essential unity in his thought that denies significance—or indeed reality—to these deficiencies. For further discussion, see my chap. 9.

3 *Miscellaneous Prose of Sir Philip Sidney*, ed. Katherine Duncan-Jones and Jan Van Dorsten, pp. 89–90: unless otherwise specified, all references are to this edition of the *Defence*.

4 Introduction to his edition, *King Henry VIII*, corrected ed. (1964; rpt. London: Methuen, 1968), pp. xxviii–xxix: all references, unless otherwise specified, are to this edition; I have altered the spelling of Bullen, Katherine, and Campeius in Foakes's edition to conform to my earlier discussions of Cavendish. William M. Baillie, "*Henry VIII:* A Jacobean History," *ShakS*, 12 (1979), 247, argues that the *original* title of the play must have been "All is True." His suggestion, if valid, disputes the claim that the play is centered on Henry VIII because it bears his name.

5 Most interpretations of *Henry VIII* uphold the dominance either of an idealized, masque-like, mythic, romantic movement in the play or of a realistically dramatized, historical, and pessimistic movement; that is, they tend to see the play either as a Romance or as a Problem. I find myself in the second camp and often in agreement with Lee Bliss's fine essay "The Wheel of Fortune and the Maiden Phoenix of Shakespeare's *King Henry the Eighth*," *ELH*, 42 (1975), 1–25. Bliss is, however, somewhat harder on Henry (e.g., pp. 8–9) and generally on Wolsey than I; for me, consequently, the play's truths are still more essentially ambiguous than for Bliss, and they are also more historical in both nature and origin. Cf. also Frank V. Cespedes, " 'We are one in fortunes': The Sense of History in *Henry VIII*," *ELH*, 10 (1980), 413–38: "in the pattern of the play itself" is a "conflict between historical ends and means" (p. 415). Frederick O. Waage, Jr., writes of "Shakespeare's *inability* to mythologize history in *Henry VIII*" and characterizes this problem (reductively, I think) simply as "a function" of the dramatist's "reaction to the death of Prince Henry in 1612": "*Henry VIII* and the Crisis of the English History Play," *ShakS*, 8 (1975), 297. Whereas Waage combines contemporary allusion with a sense of pessimism in the play, Eckhard Auberlen, "King Henry VIII—Shakespeare's Break with the 'Bluff-King-Harry Tradition,' " *Anglia*, 98 (1980), 318–47, finds in the play regenerative purpose politically relevant to the Stuart monarchy. For strongly romantic views of the play, see Howard Felperin, *Shakespearean Romance* (Princeton: Princeton Univ. Press, 1972), pp. 196–210; G. Wilson Knight, *The Crown of Life: Essays in Interpretation of Shakespeare's Final Plays* (London: Oxford Univ. Press, 1947), pp. 256–336; Ronald Berman, "*King Henry the Eighth:* History and Romance," *ES*, 48 (1967), 112–21; and with qualification, e.g., p. 404, John D. Cox, "*Henry VIII* and the Masque," *ELH*, 45 (1978), 390–409. Edward I. Berry, "*Henry VIII* and the Dynamics of Spectacle," *ShakS*, 12 (1979), 229–46, holds a mixed view of the play's movement, seeing it as "one of poetic and visual redefinitions" but also as fundamentally a redemptive rather than a problematic movement, one "like the masque's" (p. 237). Berry further regards these redefinitions as a questioning of the "naive moralizing" of the *Mirror* tradition (p. 234). While I agree that the play questions the nature and meaning of truth, I do not agree that it responds directly and primarily to the *Mirror* itself or even to the *de casibus* tradition, rather than to what Shakespeare found in his more immediate, more historical sources; less directly, of course, the *Mirror* and any other simplistic response/vision are implicated. See n. 35 below.

6 Cf. Cespedes, p. 424.

7 John P. Cutts notes the additionally relevant "divorce" (separation) of Eurydice from Orpheus: "Shakespeare's Song and Masque Hand in *Henry VIII*," *SJ*, 99 (1963), 187–88.

8 *Faerie Queene*, IV.i.19.

9 *King Henry the Eighth*, ed. J. C. Maxwell (1962; rpt. Cambridge: Cambridge Univ. Press, 1969), p. xxxv. Maxwell follows Knight, pp. 309–10: "One is to respond [to the lines in question] with an amused tolerance. . . . we, being human, condone it [Henry's desire], rather as we condone Antony's love for Cleopatra." So much for conscience.

10 P. 229. The fact that reference is made in the play to Catherine's advancing years makes the word "able" further suspect (III.i.119–22). Catherine was 5½ years Henry's senior and in her forties when rumors of a divorce were first bruited.

11 The exquisite subtlety of associations in these (and related) lines at issue is easily misinterpreted as the King's innocent simplicity or, at the other extreme, as his lascivious wordplay. For widely differing readings, cf., for example, Paul Bertram, *Shakespeare and "The Two Noble Kinsmen"* (New Brunswick, N.J.: Rutgers Univ. Press, 1965), pp. 164–66; Bliss, p. 9; and Brownlow, *Two Shakespearean Sequences*, pp. 193–95.

12 On Henry's conscience, cf. Scarisbrick, *Henry VIII*, pp. 217, 477; but also chap. 3, n. 10, above.

13 Robert Ornstein, *A Kingdom for A Stage*, pp. 203–20, describes *Henry VIII* as "deliberately ambiguous" (pp. 214–15) but believes the play flawed by the essentially superficial quality of its ambivalence (e.g., pp. 204–05). He does not connect the play's ambiguity with the writing of *Lives* or of history.

14 On the authorship of *Henry VIII*, see R. A. Foakes, ed., *King Henry VIII*, pp. xv–xxviii; also his *Shakespeare: the dark comedies to the last plays: from satire to celebration* (London: Routledge & Kegan Paul, 1971), p. 173. See also Maxwell, ed., *King Henry the Eighth*, pp. ix–xxviii; Bertram, pp. 124–59.

15 *Narrative and Dramatic Sources of Shakespeare*, ed. Geoffrey Bullough, IV, 435–51, esp. 446; Foakes, ed., xxxv–xxxix; Maxwell, ed., xxviii–xxxi. As these editors note, Foxe's *Acts and Monuments* is the source for the story of Cranmer in Act V.

16 Confusion exists about the date of the conservatives' attempt to overthrow Cranmer: Bullough, p. 443, suggests 1540; Herschel Baker, ed., *Henry VIII*, in *The Riverside Shakespeare*, p. 977, suggests 1544. I use the date given by Jasper Ridley, *Thomas Cranmer* (Oxford: Clarendon, 1962), pp. 238–39; also by Scarisbrick, pp. 421–22, 481. The date of Henry's marriage to Anne is January 25, 1533: Scarisbrick, p. 309.

17 See my chapter on Book V in *The Growth of a Personal Voice: "Piers Plowman" and "The Faerie Queene"* (New Haven, Conn.: Yale Univ. Press, 1976).

18 Cf. Larry S. Champion, *Perspective in Shakespeare's English Histories* (Athens: Univ. of Georgia Press, 1980), pp. 169, 180.

19 Cf. Bliss, p. 14.

20 Review of Foakes's edition, *JEGP*, 59 (1960), 291; the quotation in the next sentence also comes from this review.

21 Scarisbrick suggests, on the basis of Hall, a source available to Shakespeare, that Henry was not even present at Elizabeth's christening and queries, "Was he too disappointed to attend?" (pp. 323–24).

22 In order, quotations in this paragraph are from Richard S. Sylvester, ed., in Cavendish's *Life of Wolsey*, p. 271, and Wiley's "Renaissance Exploitation of Cavendish's *Life of Wolsey*," *SP*, 43 (1946), 129. Holinshed (III, 917), Stow, and John Speed each set off their portrait of Wolsey with an introductory statement that interrupts the ongoing narrative conspicuously. These introductions or "pointings" emphasize the importance and special quality of the sketch of Wolsey still more: for Stow, *The Annales of England* (London: by Ralfe Newbery, 1592), p. 831; for Speed, *The Theatre of the Empire of Great Britaine* (London: sold by John Sudbury &

Georg Humble, 1611), II, 756; subsequent reference is to these editions. As Larry S. Champion observes, Henry speaks 16.5%, and Wolsey 15.8%, of the lines in *Henry VIII:* "Shakespeare's *Henry VIII:* A Celebration of History," *SAB*, 44 (1979), 2.

23 E.g., see Stow, pp. 841, 920, 924, 927, 933, 941.

24 On p. 834, however, Stow designates Cavendish (instead of "me") as the person to whom Wolsey tells his story.

25 P. 929; this quotation, remarkable for its cutting edge, is not found in Holinshed (e.g., III, 923, 928).

26 *King Henry VIII*, p. 121 *n*.

27 *King Henry VIII*, pp. 123 *n*–124 *n*; Cavendish, p. 113.

28 Stow, p. 931; cf. Cavendish, pp. 125–26; also pp. 112, 123–27, 129–32.

29 See Cavendish, pp. 107, 105–06, 110.

30 See Stow, p. 927, and Cavendish, p. 113.

31 See Stow, pp. 930–31, and Cavendish, pp. 125–26.

32 Cavendish, pp. 127–28.

33 Stow, p. 941; cf. Cavendish, pp. 178–79.

34 Stow, p. 927: my emphasis; cf. Cavendish, p. 114.

35 Frederick Kiefer, "Churchyard's 'Cardinal Wolsey' and Its Influence on Shakespeare's *Henry VIII*," *ELWIU*, 6 (1979), 3–10, suggests Shakespeare's portrayal of Wolsey is indebted to that in the *Mirror for Magistrates.* While right in observing distinctions between the portrayal of Wolsey in the play and in Holinshed, Kiefer has located a somewhat distant analogue to, rather than the source for, them. The similarities he finds between the *Mirror* and the play are much more fully, precisely, and pertinently present in Stow's version of Cavendish or else are too general or commonplace to be persuasive in the presence of more exact echoes from Stow. Striking in the former category is a relatively more sympathetic attitude toward the Cardinal in adversity, and in the latter, references to Fortune and change.

36 *DNB*, s.v. Thomas Howard I (1443–1524), p. 64.

37 Bliss, p. 4.

38 Scarisbrick, buttressing his view with Cavendish's *Wolsey*, supports Henry's claim: pp. 153–54.

39 Knight, pp. 280–81, advances a similar view.

40 Scarisbrick, pp. 214–17, is helpful in clarifying the historical circumstances behind the Cardinals' visit and perhaps indirectly in casting some light on the possible origin of its ambiguity in the play.

41 Cf. Holinshed, III, 922: Wolsey was "double both in speach and meaning." Both Foakes (p. 136 *n*) and Maxwell (p. 204 *n*) in their editions of *Henry VIII* gloss the word "double" as "ambiguous." Again one thinks of the "meaning" of Spenser's Ate. An essentialist streak of meaning is never so foreign to Renaissance writers, no matter how realistically dramatic their work, as it tends to be to us.

42 As Foakes notes in *Shakespeare: the dark comedies to the last plays*, p. 179, "the deliberate design of the dramatist" is also evident in his "rearranging history"—more exactly, in his bringing together two pictures of Wolsey widely separated in his historical source, in this case, Holinshed (III, 917, and III, 922).

43 *King Henry VIII*, V.iv.33–36, and p. 175 *n*.

44 As Foakes, ed., p. 176 *n*, suggests, the darkness may have biblical echoes but these do not eliminate its unfortunate resonance in the speech. Responses to Cranmer's prophetic vision vary tremendously: for generally positive responses, see, for example, Champion, *Perspective*, pp. 182–84; Bertram, pp. 175–76; Knight, pp. 131–36; and additional interpretations cited as being "romantic" in n. 5 above. For severely qualified, highly skeptical, or downright negative responses, see, for example, Rossiter, *Angel with Horns*, pp. 40–41; Clifford Leech, "The Structure of the Last Plays," *ShS*, 11 (1958), 29; idem, *Shakespeare: The Chronicles*

(London: Longmans, 1962), pp. 38–39; Bliss, pp. 16–17, 20–23; Waage, p. 299; and Cespedes, p. 416.

45 Frances A. Yates's conclusion to her celebrated essay, "Queen Elizabeth I as Astraea," affords a fitting final comment on Cranmer's symbolism: "in place of the facile optimism of official propaganda," Shakespeare's dramatizations of monarchy gain their "poignancy from the imagery, which so often suggests universal possibilities forever betrayed" (*Astraea: The Imperial Theme in the Sixteenth Century*, p. 87).

46 *Songs and Sonnets*, vs. 31–34.

9. BACON'S THEORY OF LIFE-WRITING

1 Levy, *Tudor Historical Thought*, p. 245.

2 George H. Nadel, "History as Psychology in Francis Bacon's Theory of History," *History and Theory*, 5 (1966), 280–81.

3 Edward I. Berry, "History and Rhetoric in Bacon's *Henry VII*," in *Seventeenth-Century Prose: Modern Essays in Criticism*, ed. Stanley E. Fish (New York: Oxford Univ. Press, 1971), pp. 290, 294, 305 (quotation in next paragraph). I owe a great deal to this fine essay, although I disagree with it in many specifics.

4 "Advancement," *Works*, VI, 189–90.

5 *OED*, s.v. *Native* a., I.i., I.i.c. For *true* and *lively*, cf. Spenser, *Faerie Queene*, III.Pro.4, vs. 1–3: "But if in *liuing* colours, and *right* hew, / Your selfe you couet to see pictured, / Who can it doe more *liuely*, or more *trew* . . ." (my emphasis); also my discussion of these lines in *Poetic Traditions of the English Renaissance*, ed. George deForest Lord and Maynard Mack (New Haven, Conn.: Yale Univ. Press, 1982), pp. 50–51.

6 Quotation from "Advancement," *Works*, VI, 133.

7 "Of the Dignity and Advancement of Learning," *Works*, VIII, 424–26 (Bk. II.vii); cf. "De Dignitate et Augmentis Scientiarum," *Works*, II, 205: "Vitae autem fructu et exemplis." This work is cited hereafter as *De Augmentis;* all parenthetical references to it in the text are to *Works*, VIII.

8 See Robert Adolph, *The Rise of Modern Prose Style* (Cambridge, Mass.: MIT Press, 1968), pp. 55–56.

9 *Works*, XI, 35

10 "Sir Francis Bacon's Theory of Civil-History Writing," *ELH*, 8 (1941), 170–71: hereafter cited as "Bacon's Theory." Felix Gilbert's description of earlier humanist historians' assumptions sounds remarkably like Bacon's practice, as Dean characterizes it: "This humanistic distinction [found "regularly"] between two forms of historical writings—one containing chiefly facts and thereby providing the material from which the other, the true history, could be constructed—placed the true historian far above those who just collected and described facts" (*Machiavelli and Guicciardini: Politics and History in Sixteenth-Century Florence*, pp. 224–25; cf. p. 223).

11 *OED*, s.v. *Counsel sb.*, I.1, 2, 3, 4, 5. While I.2 and 3 neither can nor should exclude the other possible meanings, they are of particular interest: "Opinion as to what ought to be done given as the result of consultation; aid or instruction for directing the judgement; advice, direction"; "The faculty of counselling or advising; judgement; prudence; sagacity in the devising of plans." Cf. Bacon's essay "Of Counsel," *Works*, XII, 146–47.

12 *OED*, s.v. *Negotiation*, 2: "A process or course of treaty with another (or others) to obtain or bring about some result, esp. in affairs of state. Freq. in *pl.*"; 3: "The action or business of negotiating or making terms with others." By "negotiation," Bacon usually means "business" or "conduct": cf. "De Augmentis," *Works*, IX, 236–97 (Bk. VIII.ii), and Lisa Jardine, *Francis Bacon: Discovery and the Art of Discourse* (Cambridge: Cambridge Univ. Press, 1974), pp. 165–66; also Bacon's "Of Negociating," *Works*, XII, 246: "All practice [*negotiatio*] is to discover, or to work"—i.e., roughly, to unmask, ascertain, or to manipulate (lead, persuade,

awe, govern). See also "De Augmentis," *Works,* VIII, 438 (Bk. II.xii): "for instruction in civil prudence, still greater help is derived from letters written by great men on weighty subjects. . . . And when there is a continued series of them in order of time (as we find in the letters of ambassadors, governors of provinces, and other ministers of state, to kings, senates, and other superior officers; or, again, in the letters of rulers to their agents), they are of all others the most valuable materials for history." While it could be argued that such letters are to provide the "counsels" with which the Baconian historian enriches history, both this passage and the one at issue in the text imply that such letters are among the "originals" and "materials"—the "negotiations of state"—upon which the historian works.

13 Bacon gets much of Perkin's Proclamation and most of Perkin's speech to James from Speed's chronicle-history: see Spedding et al., eds., *Works,* XI, 245, n. 1; 250–51, n. 2; I treat Bacon's use of sources in *Henry VII* in chap. 10.

14 Cf. Jardine, pp. 157–59; Thomas Wheeler, "The Purpose of Bacon's *History of Henry the Seventh,*" *SP,* 54 (1957), 11–13; and idem, "Sir Francis Bacon's Concept of the Historian's Task," *RenP* (1955), 40–46. My position shares considerable ground with Jonathan Marwil's study *The Trials of Counsel: Francis Bacon in 1621* (Detroit: Wayne State Univ. Press, 1976), pp. 156–57 ff., but it also differs in specific and in fundamental respects. Marwil's book is at once so useful and so wrongheaded as to require further comment. In effect, I argue that, while Bacon might have had a conception of truth different from Marwil's, he knew what he was doing in *Henry VII* (see my introduction and end of chap. 5). Marwil, repeatedly and pervasively patronizing Bacon and his work, denies to Bacon any significant awareness of what he was about. On pp. 160–62, for example, Marwil first denies to Bacon any inkling that he was in fact shaping Henry's character and then—in a seemingly inconsistent afterthought—wonders whether Bacon might not have tampered with historical truth, as Bacon himself saw it, in order to affect his audience. Again, on p. 187, when Marwil catches Bacon "misrepresenting the statutes" and then asserts that "Bacon was not consciously misrepresenting" them, he fails to address what Bacon was consciously doing; he does not consider that Bacon might not only have been consciously shaping their significance but also, by his own lights, doing so prudently, wisely, and therefore conscientiously. When Marwil sees as a "distortion" Bacon's statement that Henry's policy was to encourage a merchant marine, we might ask, "a distortion of what kind of truth, on what grounds and by whom considered a distortion, and, if ascertainable, distorted for what conscious purpose?" Despite frequent avowals to the contrary, Marwil refuses to see the work for what it is rather than for what it is not, i.e., a "modern" history. Like critics of Walton earlier discussed, he keeps giving lip service to the work's being an *X* but insists on assessing it as a *Y*; i.e., this is an apple but it's really a lemon. As a result some distortion of evidence is inevitable in his assessment.

15 Phrase quoted is Levy's (*Tudor Historical Thought,* p. 269).

16 *The Letters and the Life of Francis Bacon,* ed. James Spedding, Robert Leslie Ellis, and Douglas Denon Heath (London: Longmans, Green, Reader, and Dyer, 1868), III, 249–50. Cf. "Advancement," *Works,* VI, 188; "De Augmentis," *Works,* VIII, 422 (Bk. II.vi): "Civil History is of three kinds, not unfitly to be compared with the three kinds of pictures or images. For of pictures and images we see some are unfinished, and wanting the last touch; some are perfect; and some are mutilated and defaced by age. So Civil History (which is a kind of image of events and times) may be divided into three kinds, corresponding to these,—*Memorials, Perfect History,* and *Antiquities.*"

17 E.g., see virtue and fortune in Machiavelli's *Prince,* trans. Edward Dacres, in *Three Renaissance Classics* (New York: Scribner's, 1953), pp. 93–96, 98. Gilbert, p. 179, describes *virtù* as "the strength and vigour from which all human action arose" and *fortuna* as "external circumstance or chance"; for extensive refinements, see pp. 180, 194–97. In *Renaissance & Revolution: Backgrounds to Seventeenth-Century English Literature,* Joseph Anthony Mazzeo defines

Machiavelli's concept of *virtù* as "the human power to effect change and control events" and his concept of *fortuna* as "a host of related concepts"—e.g., "all the impersonal agencies active in the lives . . . of men . . . the logic of history . . . blind chance or, at times, an equally blind fate" (p. 91). With others, he sees in the two the "polar concepts" or indeed the polar "symbols" of Machiavelli's thought (pp. 91–94).

18 The phrase occurs conspicuously in Sidney's *Defence* and in Jonson's *Timber* (after Plutarch, who uses the phrase repeatedly in reference to poetry). For these and many other examples, see *Elizabethan Critical Essays*, ed. G. Gregory Smith (1904; rpt. London: Oxford Univ. Press, 1959), I, 386, n. 158/8, and Sir Philip Sidney, *An Apology for Poetry*, ed. Geoffrey Shepherd (1965, rpt. Manchester, Eng.: Manchester Univ. Press, 1973), pp. 159–60, nn. 33 ff.

19 Dedication added to the 1609 edition: *The Civil Wars*, ed. Laurence Michel (New Haven, Conn.: Yale Univ. Press, 1958), p. 68; cf. Levy, *Tudor Historical Thought*, p. 275.

20 "On the Fortunate Memory of Elizabeth Queen of England," *Works*, XI, 443; see p. 425 for the original Latin.

21 "De Augmentis," *Works*, II, 214–15 (Bk. II.x), reads: "Licet enim Historia quaeque prudentior politicis praeceptis et monitis veluti impregnata sit, tamen scriptor ipse sibi obstetricari non debet." Cf. "Advancement," *Works*, VI, 197.

22 On Bacon's use of imagery, see Brian Vickers, *Francis Bacon and Renaissance Prose* (Cambridge: Cambridge Univ. Press, 1968), esp. chap. 5. Vickers finds "no evidence in his [Bacon's] style which either contradicts his thought or attitudes, or points to aspects of which he was himself unaware" (p. 18). Paolo Rossi's chapters on "The Classical Fable" and "Language and Communication" are more generally relevant: *Francis Bacon: From Magic to Science*, trans. Sacha Rabinovitch (1968; rpt. Chicago: Chicago Univ. Press, 1978). Also, Karl R. Wallace, "Francis Bacon on Understanding, Reason, and Rhetoric," *Speech Monographs*, 38 (1971), 79–91.

23 *Works*, XI, 33.

24 "The New Organon," *Works*, VIII, 86: Aphorism LIX (my emphasis); hereafter cited as *Organon*.

25 See pp. 124–25.

26 "Advancement," *Works*, VI, 202–03 (my emphasis); virtually the same statement carries an equally, if not more, negative thrust in "Descriptio Globi Intellectualis," *Works*, X, 403–04. Cf. also the reference by John Speed, Bacon's contemporary historian, to unjustly fabricated charges against the Earl of Warwick as "their bloody Poetry": II, 746.

27 "De Augmentis," *Works*, VIII, 440 (Bk. II.xiii) is commonly cited as evidence of Bacon's high regard for poetry, which shows "there is agreeable to the spirit of man a more ample greatness, a more perfect order" than is found in nature since the Fall. Equally often, the immediate context of the statement is ignored, for it depicts poetry as a distraction from useful endeavors, as an anodyne, and as a departure from truth ("*seems* to bestow," "to *satisfy* . . . with the *shadows* of things," not "the substance": my emphasis). Likewise ignored is the larger context: time spent on poetry not in the service of Baconian truth is wasted (p. 444); poetry is outside the palace of wisdom (p. 469). In another passage of *De Augmentis* commonly cited to show Bacon's esteem for poetry, he acknowledges that poets and historians best portray the operations of the affections (*Works*, IX, 220: Bk. VII.iii). While Bacon's thinking lacks the logical consistency of a professional philosopher's, his giving poetry its due again cannot randomly be detached from related statements, whether a few pages earlier (pp. 216–17: "so among the poets . . . are everywhere interspersed representations of characters, though generally exaggerated and surpassing the truth. . . . But far the best provision and material" for this knowledge "is to be gained from the wiser sort of historians"), or whether in the next book, where fables are said formerly to have been "substitutes and supplements" of actual (true) examples, "but now that the times abound with history, the aim is more true and active when the mark is alive" (p. 266: Bk. VIII.ii). Occasional qualifications and inconsis-

tencies aside, the dominant tenor of Bacon's opinion of poetry is negative. See also chap. 8, n. 2, above.

28 I refer there to Sidney as the best known and most pertinent representative of a well-established association of poetry with the idealizing imagination: see Murray W. Bundy, "Bacon's True Opinion of Poetry," pp. 252–54, 263; and in particular, George Puttenham, *The Arte of English Poesie*, ed. Gladys Doidge Willcock and Alice Walker (Cambridge: Cambridge Univ. Press, 1936), pp. 3–5, 18–20. The quotation from Sidney that follows in this paragraph is from *A Defence of Poetry*, p. 89.

29 Dean, "Bacon's Theory," p. 183.

30 "Organon," *Works*, VIII, 87: Aphorism LIX.

31 "Advancement," *Works*, VI, 122. The limit to which Bacon refers is analogous to the limit nature places on the mechanical or experimental arts: see "De Augmentis," *Works*, VIII, 410–11 (Bk. II.ii: "where the case does not admit this . . ."), and my discussion of these arts later in this chapter. Cf. also "Organon," *Works*, VIII, 131–32: "Those who have handled sciences have been either men of experiment or men of dogmas. The men of experiment are like the ant; they only collect and use: the reasoners resemble spiders, who make cobwebs out of their own substance. But the bee takes a middle course; it gathers its material from the flowers of the garden and of the field, but transforms and digests it by a power of its own. Not unlike this is the true business of philosophy; for it neither relies solely or chiefly on the powers of the mind, nor does it take the matter which it gathers from natural history and mechanical experiments and lay it up in the memory whole, as it finds it; but lays it up in the understanding altered and digested. Therefore from a closer and purer league between these two faculties, the experimental and the rational . . . much may be hoped" (Aphorism XCV).

32 "Advancement," *Works*, VI, 132: my emphasis.

33 "De Augmentis," *Works*, VIII, 441 (Bk. II.xiii). "Reason," but not "history," occurs in the earlier version of this sentence in "Advancement," *Works*, VI, 203.

34 "Advancement," *Works*, VI, 184; the remaining quotations from Bacon in this paragraph come from "De Augmentis," *Works*, VIII, 409–11 (Bk. II.ii). Cf. Rossi, chap. 1 (e.g., p. 26), on mechanical arts; and James C. Morrison's provocative article "Philosophy and History in Bacon," *JHI*, 38 (1977), 585–606: "the 'coincidence' of knowledge (*scientia*) and power (*potentia*) ultimately consists" in the "transformation of knowing into making—of *theoria* into *praxis* and *poēsis*" (p. 592); but see also n. 38 below.

35 "De Augmentis," *Works*, II, 189–90 (Bk. II.ii), reads: "Sed et illabitur etiam animis hominum aliud subtilius malum; nempe, ut ars censeatur solummodo tanquam additamentum quoddam naturae, cujus scilicet ea sit vis ut naturam (sane) vel inchoatam perficere, vel in deterius vergentem emendare, vel impeditam liberare; minime vero penitus vertere, transmutare, aut in imis concutere possit." This is a much neglected passage in discussions of Bacon's work. Quoting its surrounding context, Jardine (p. 138) excises it; F. H. Anderson, *The Philosophy of Francis Bacon* (Chicago: Univ. of Chicago Press, 1948), p. 151, is evidently so disturbed by it that he rejects Spedding's accurate translation and substitutes for it a total and flatly impossible reversal of meaning. Morrison, p. 594, renders the passage accurately, as does Gilbert Watts, the distinguished seventeenth-century linguist who translated *De Augmentis*. Watts reads: "But there is a yet more subtile deceit which secretly steales into the mindes of Men, namely, that *Art* should be reputed a kind of *Additament* only to *Nature*, whose virtue is this, that it can indeed either perfect *Nature inchoate, or repaire it when it is decaied, or set it at liberty from impediments; but not quite alter, transmute, or shake it in the foundations*"; *Of the Advancement and Proficience of Learning or the Partitions of Sciences* (Oxford: by Leon Lichfield for Rob: Young & Ed: Forrest, 1640), p. 80. Neglect and misreading of this passage are the more significant in view of the recurrence of the same idea in Bacon's works: e.g., in nearly identical terms, "Descriptio Globi Intellectualis," *Works*, X, 407–08 (cf. the Latin in *Works*, VII, 289); also "Parasceve," *Works*, VIII, 357: "For in things artificial

nature takes orders from man, and works under his authority: without man, such things would never have been made. But by the help and ministry of man a new face of bodies, [*veluti:* even as] another universe or theatre of things, comes into view" (cf. the Latin in *Works*, II, 47). Sewell, *Orphic Voice*, pp. 124–26, also observes the importance of such passages in Bacon's thought but interprets their meaning more freely than I.

36 *Defence of Poetry*, p. 78.

37 *Defence of Poetry*, p. 79: "Neither let it be deemed too saucy a comparison to balance the highest point of man's wit with the efficacy of nature; but rather give right honour to the heavenly Maker of that maker, who having made man to His own likeness, set him beyond and over all the works of that second nature: which in nothing he showeth so much as in poetry, when with the force of a divine breath he bringeth things forth surpassing her doings."

38 "De Augmentis," *Works*, VIII, 415 (Bk. II.ii). Morrison, p. 587, remarks the significance of Bacon's classification: "Philosophy or rational knowledge does not ground itself but is grounded in the non-philosophical science of history. The importance of this radical inversion of the tradition should not be underestimated." Although Morrison himself may underestimate the significance of Bacon's distinction between poetry and history and of his transference of true (real) making (manufacture, invention, fabrication) from poetry to natural and civil history (pp. 586, 588), his argument that "The grounding function of natural history implies that it—and not method—is the real heart of Bacon's thought" (p. 590) is persuasive and seems in good measure right.

39 *Works*, XI, 34.

40 See Nadel, p. 286: "In Bacon's theory . . . history functions as behavioral science."

41 "Advancement," *Works*, VI, 187.

42 Quotation from "De Augmentis," *Works*, VIII, 407 (Bk. II.i). On *Inventor*, see esp. Bacon's "Of the Interpretation of Nature," in *The Letters and the Life*, III, 84–85: "the work of the Inventor . . . is felt everywhere and lasts for ever"; he is "the benefactor indeed of the human race,—the propagator of man's empire over the universe, the champion of liberty, the conqueror and subduer of necessities." See also "De Augmentis," *Works*, IX, 64 (Bk. V.ii), 83–84 (Bk. V.iii), and Murray W. Bundy, " 'Invention' and 'Imagination' in the Renaissance," *JEGP*, 29 (1930), 535–45. In her study of Bacon, Jardine distinguishes two meanings of the word "invention," as Bacon uses it, from one another, i.e., "discovery" from "art of discourse" (p. 2). She acknowledges Bacon's use of the word for both meanings (pp. 69, 170–71) but also seems to attribute to Bacon her own distinction in terminology: "Throughout his work Bacon stresses the, to his mind basic, distinction between 'discovery', that is, the investigation of the unknown . . . and 'invention', that is, the selection of received assumptions about the natural world as premises for argument or for display" (p. 6). While admiring the considerable clarity Jardine brings to Bacon's thought, I cannot help wondering whether the ambiguity present in his terminology (here as elsewhere) is not inseparable from his philosophical position—from its richness and suggestiveness, as well as from its looseness and equivocation. The rationalization of terminology is inherently interpretative and can be editorial.

10. BACON'S *HENRY VII*

1 *Works*, XI, 43: cited hereafter as *Henry VII*.

2 See pp. 15–16.

3 *England Under the Tudors: King Henry VII*, trans. Alice M. Todd (London: A. D. Innes, 1895), p. 417. On these and Bacon's other sources, see Busch, pp. 416–23; Marwil, *Trials of Counsel*, pp. 154–56, 223–25, nn. 16–25; Spedding et al., eds., *Works*, XI, 13–15; and notes to *Henry VII*, passim: Spedding's notes indicate Bacon's use of Speed more fully and fairly than does his Preface.

4 For the influence of Continental historians on the presentation of persons and events in Bacon's *Henry*, see Vincent Luciani, "Bacon and Guicciardini," *PMLA*, 62 (1947), 96–113, esp. 98, 103–04; also Marwil, p. 224, n. 21.

5 *Henry VII*, pp. 293–96. Busch, p. 418, claims but does not document Hakluyt as Bacon's source. Marwil, p. 156, rejects Busch's claim in favor of Stow (1592), p. 802. For the following reasons, I believe Busch to have been right. Stow describes Cabot as "a Genoas sonne, borne in Bristow"; whereas Bacon describes him more accurately as a Venetian by birth, who was "dwelling in Bristow." While *Vitellius Ms A XVI* might have given Bacon Cabot's nationality, it would not have told him of Cabot's dwelling in Bristow: *Chronicles of London*, ed. Charles Lethbridge Kingsford (Oxford: Clarendon, 1905), p. 224. Hakluyt, *Principall Navigations*, Hakluyt Society, extra series No. 39 (1589; rpt. Cambridge: Cambridge Univ. Press, 1965), pp. 509–15, 602, provides the first piece of information and grounds for the second. Moreover, in close proximity to the data on Cabot, Hakluyt, like Bacon, provides both the story of Henry VII's near sponsorship of Columbus and the suggestion that Cabot might have desired to emulate Columbus: *Henry VII*, pp. 296, 293; Hakluyt, pp. 507–09, 512. The proximity of this material in both texts is unlikely to have been coincidental. Bacon's use of Hakluyt is still more likely in view of Speed's marginal note, II, 744, directing the reader to Hakluyt for information on Cabot's discoveries. On the confused dating of the Cabots' voyages in the Tudor period, see J. A. Williamson, *The Voyages of John and Sebastian Cabot*, Historical Association Pamphlet, No. 106 (London: G. Bell, 1937), pp. 3–4, 7–8; see also *Great Chronicle of London*, ed. Thomas and Thornley, p. 287 (marginal note) and pp. 445–46 *n*; and Kingsford, ed., *Chronicles of London*, pp. 327–30 *n*. Hakluyt, *Divers Voyages touching the discovery of America and the Islands Adjacent* (1582; rpt. London: for the Hakluyt Society, ed. John Winter Jones, 1850), p. 23, dates the voyage 1498: *anno regis* 13; Stow, p. 802, dates it 1498: *anno regis* 14. As Spedding notes, *Works*, XI, 296, n. 2, Bacon's dating may be based on Stow's. With the sole exception of *The Great Chronicle* (Stow's probable source), Stow alone of the sources I have cited gives the combination 1498/ *an. reg.* 14. But again see Spedding's note 2, p. 296, and *Henry VII*, p. 293 ("Somewhat before this time"), and *Principall Navigations*, p. 512, where a date as early as 1496 is to be found: the inconsistent dating of the Cabots' voyages in Bacon and elsewhere is highly volatile evidence. In sum, Hakluyt is a definite source for Bacon's treatment of Cabot, and Stow is at most a likely additional one.

6 The two occasions are the French ambassador Gaguin's libel of Henry VII and Henry VI's prophecy of Henry Tudor's accession to the throne: see Marwil, pp. 156, 224, n. 22; Busch, pp, 417–19; but also n. 7, below.

7 *Henry VII*, pp. 364–65; John Fisher, *Here after foloweth a mornynge remembraunce had at the moneth mynde of the noble prynces Margarete countesse of Rychemonde* (London: Wynkyn de Worde, 1509), A3v. Marwil, p. 156, attributes "two prophecies about Henry that are to be found at the end of . . . [Bacon's] *History*" to André, but he offers no further documentation, either of the *Henry* or of André. One of the prophecies, as noted by Busch, is Henry VI's, found in Bacon's *Henry*, p. 365, and in André's "Historia," in *Memorials of King Henry the Seventh* (London: Longman, Brown, Green, Longmans, and Roberts, 1858), p. 14. The second "prophecy" I take in the absence of other candidates at the end of the *Henry* to be Margaret's vision, which counsels her to marry Edmund Tudor. A source for Margaret's vision in André eludes me. On Cotton's library and, indirectly, on the possibility that it might have contained Fisher's book, see Kevin Sharpe, *Sir Robert Cotton 1586–1631: History and Politics in Early Modern England* (Oxford: Oxford Univ. Press, 1979), pp. 48–83.

8 Busch, p. 418; *Letters of the Kings of England*, ed. James Orchard Halliwell (London: Henry Colburn, 1846), pp. 194–96. See also *Henry VII*, p. 207 and n. 2, on Perkin's letters.

9 *Henry VII*, pp. 251–57, 374–79. Unlike Bacon's, Speed's rendition of the Proclamation, II, 741–42, omits Empson's name and Perkin's assurances of the absence of self-serving designs on the part of the Scotch King.

10 *Henry VII*, pp. 328–29; cf. Chrimes, *Henry VII*, p. 332, regarding Henry VII's surviving books of payments, initialed by Henry himself.

11 Busch, p. 418; Marwil, p. 179.

12 *The Life and Raigne of King Henry the Eighth* (London: by E. G. for Thomas Whitaker, 1649), p. 1; see also "Epistle Dedicatory," A_2v: subsequent reference is to this edition. Lord Herbert (1583–1648) began work on *The Life* around 1632: *DNB*, s.v. Herbert, Edward, first Lord Herbert of Cherbury.

13 Cf. Karl R. Wallace, *Francis Bacon on the Nature of Man* (Urbana: Univ. of Illinois Press, 1967), p. 77: Bacon "might well have preferred, with Aristotle, a probable impossibility to an improbable possibility."

14 For a divergent discussion of the same passage, see Edward I. Berry, "History and Rhetoric in Bacon's *Henry VII*," pp. 282–84: cited hereafter as "History and Rhetoric." Berry reads the brief character of Richard as a parody of history-writing in the humanist tradition, including More's *Richard.* Instead of being directed at a particular style of writing history, however, this character is aimed at a particular way of running a realm, tyranny. Bacon's essential concern is a style of ruling. Years before the *Henry*, incidentally, in the prospectus to "The History of the reign of K. Henry the Eighth . . . ," *Works*, XI, 37–40, Bacon had similarly offered a brief character of the person and reign of Henry VII, the only example of history-writing in the work and presumably intended as the beginning—again the political context—of the proposed work on the other Tudor monarchs.

15 "History and Rhetoric," p. 284. For More, see my discussion, pp. 90–91.

16 "Advancement," *Works*, VI, 327; for additional examples, see *Works*, X, 556–57, s.v. Machiavelli; and for discussion, Vincent Luciani, "Bacon and Machiavelli," *Italica*, 24 (1947), 26–40; Thomas Wheeler, "Bacon's Henry VII as a Machiavellian Prince," *RenP* (1957), 111–17; Jardine, *Francis Bacon*, pp. 163–68; F. Smith Fussner, *The Historical Revolution: English Historical Writing and Thought 1580–1640* (London: Routledge & Kegan Paul, 1962), pp. 269, 271; and Howard B. White, *Peace Among the Willows: The Political Philosophy of Francis Bacon* (The Hague: Martinus Nijhoff, 1968), pp. 48–56. See also chap. 9, n. 17, above.

17 Cf. Sidney, *Defence of Poetry*, p. 79, and my discussion of Sidney, chap. 9.

18 *Works*, XI, 37–38.

19 "History and Rhetoric," pp. 292–93.

20 Levy, ed. *King Henry the Seventh*, p. 52; Chrimes, p. 268.

21 E.g., *Henry VII*, p. 58.

22 André, pp. 34–35: all citations are to James Gairdner's edition of André.

23 Speed, II, 729: excepting proper names, my emphasis. Gairdner, ed., *Memorials of King Henry the Seventh*, p. xxvi, n. 2, suggests that both Speed and Bacon might have been following an inaccurate transcript, but in light of Bacon's clear debt to Speed elsewhere, he greatly doubts this to be the case. Cf. Marwil, pp. 224–25, nn. 22, 31. The Cottonian Ms *Domitian XVIII* edited by Gairdner is the one presumably used by Speed; in it, *laetanter*, spelled *letanter* (f. 165r), is very legible. Speed, it should be noted, also misconstrues André's version of Perkin's parentage: see my discussion, pp. 181–82.

24 *Henry VII*, pp. 70–71, 92, 293, 359, 104, 361–62, 328–29, 357, 364. On nearness of sight, see also p. 92.

25 Adolph, *Rise of Modern Prose Style*, p. 34, makes a similar observation.

26 *Henry VII*, pp. 134, 69, 229; on poetry, see p. 220, for example.

27 *Henry VII*, p. 324; "History and Rhetoric," p. 297.

28 Speed, II, 730, 733, 743; but cf. Hall's *Chronicle*, pp. 429, 432, 459, 462, 463, 464, 465, 472, 475, 482 ("a vayne shadowe and vntrue fyccyon," "ydoll," "Mawmet," "fayned fable," "ficcion," "peinted image," and so on). Brian Vickers treats *Henry VII* in "Bacon's Use of Theatrical Imagery," *SLitI*, 4 (1971), 219–24.

29 Speed, II, 738; *Henry VII*, pp. 209, 199.

30 Busch, p. 419; *Letters of the Kings of England*, p. 196: "this our realm is now environed, and, in manner, closed in every side with such mighty princes, our good sons, friends, confederates, and allies, that, by the help of our Lord, the same is and shall be perpetually established in rest and peace,and wealthy condition. . . ."

31 The title of Robert Greene's *Friar Bacon and Friar Bungay* would, one might imagine, have attracted Francis Bacon's attention: for the wall of brass, see scene ii.33, 154, 184, in *English Drama 1580–1642*, ed. C. F. Tucker Brooke and Nathaniel Burton Paradise (Boston: D. C. Heath, 1933). The references to brazen walls in both Spenser and Drayton belong to episodes treating British history. For Spenser, see *Faerie Queene*, Bk. III.iii.10; for Drayton, see *Poly-Olbion*, Song IV.331–32, in *Works*, ed. J. William Hebel (Oxford: Basil Blackwell, 1933), IV. If Bacon indeed recalls Merlin's brazen wall, his reference might be seen as the final laying of Margaret-le-Fay's ghost, since Merlin is in myth her opposite, more benign number and the support of Arthur's kingdom, which, Bacon notes (p. 69), had at least nominally been renewed in the line of Tudors.

32 Speed, II, 738. In Hall's *Chronicle*, pp. 463–64, Perkin's identity and performance are variously a "poeticall and feyned inuencion," "a pernicious . . . ficcion," a "golden tale."

33 *Henry VII*, p. 211, n. 1; see *The Tempest* (Riverside), I.ii.99–103:

> —like one
> Who having into truth, by telling of it,
> Made such a sinner of his memory
> To credit his own lie—he did believe
> He was indeed the Duke. . . .

34 *Henry VII*, pp. 245, 117, 178, 159. Marwil, p. 163, endeavors to locate the meaning of *Henry VII* primarily in Bacon's experiences and personality. Thus, pp. 164–68, Bacon's persecution of conspirators in his political/judicial life accounts for his exaggeration of Margaret of Burgundy's plots and presumably for his interest in Perkin. Such reasoning strikes me as reductive; while there may be a correlation between Bacon's life and events in the *Henry*, there is not so simple a cause-effect relation. Similarly reductive is Marwil's insistence on a one-to-one relationship between events in the *Henry* and specific lessons for the English monarch (e.g., pp. 169, 171). The *process* of kingly (political) thinking is for Bacon more important than any given test case or any precise parallel between Henry VII and James I.

35 Speed, II, 737; André, pp. 65–66, 72. Cf. Polydore Vergil, *The Anglica Historia of Polydore Vergil*, ed. and trans. Denys Hay, Camden Series, vol. 74 (London: Royal Historical Society, 1950), pp. 62–63. See *Henry VII*, p. 201, n. 4; Gairdner, ed., *Memorials of King Henry the Seventh*, p. xxxiv; Busch, p. 420; and for a recent, factual account, Chrimes, p. 81, n. 2.

36 Speed, II, 745; Hall's *Chronicle*, p. 488.

37 See Busch, p. 419; Speed, II, 737, 745; Hall's *Chronicle*, pp. 462, 488–89; and Polydore Vergil, ed. Hay, pp. 62–63.

38 Gairdner, ed., *Memorials of King Henry the Seventh*, pp. xxx–xxxiii; *Henry VII*, p. 204.

39 See Fussner, *Revolution*, p. 268; Speed, II, 745; and Hall's *Chronicle*, p. 488.

40 *Henry VII*, pp. 165–66, n. 2 (my emphasis on "conceive"); and my discussion, p. 165. Fussner, *Revolution*, pp. 267–68, helpfully summarizes Bacon's chronology of the events connected with Henry's efforts. Marwil, pp. 172–77, conceives Bacon's practice differently here, as a somewhat guileful expression of Bacon's ulterior motives.

41 *Henry VII*, pp. 66–67; see Chrimes, pp. 302–04.

42 Chrimes, p. 85; and W. A. J. Archbold, "Sir William Stanley and Perkin Warbeck," *EHR*, 14 (1899), 529–34: Stanley sent Clifford abroad in the first instance to communicate with Perkin and this "constituted his special act of treason."

43 Busch, p. 420; cf. Speed, II, 739; Hall's *Chronicle*, pp. 469–70; Polydore Vergil, ed. Hay, pp. 74–77. There are suggestions of Bacon's view of Henry's motivation in Bacon's sources;

nonetheless, Bacon's explanation of Stanley's end answers primarily to his own theories regarding Henry VII's motivating obsessions.

44 These views differ substantially from Marwil's, p. 194: "Quite unintentional is our feeling that Bacon's portrait of Henry bears a remarkable likeness to himself. This, however, was inevitable. . . . Bacon necessarily had to substitute his own thoughts and values for the historical Henry's." While I do not know what an "unintentional feeling" is or whose it is in the first sentence or what the referent of "This" is in the second sentence, I consider the word "substitute" in the third sentence entirely inappropriate to what Bacon set out to do or, indeed, to what he did. In a Renaissance setting, participation is not synonymous with substitution, or invention, whether rhetorical or interpretative, synonymous with distortion.

45 *Henry VII*, p. 65. Cf. Hall's *Chronicle*, pp. 424–25, and Speed, II, 729–30. Nearly six months after Henry's marriage on January 18, 1486, a fifth "claim" to the throne, recognition by Papal authority, is added to the already existing four: *Tudor Royal Proclamations*, ed. Paul L. Hughes and James F. Larkin (New Haven, Conn.: Yale Univ. Press, 1964), I, 6–7 (No. 5); cf. *Henry VII*, p. 59.

46 *Henry VII*, p. 69: parenthetically, Bacon does mention that Henry names Arthur "(in honour of the British race, of which himself was)," but he develops the significance of the event no further. On the symbolism of Arthur's birth, see Sydney Anglo, "The *British History* in Early Tudor Propaganda," *BJRL*, 44 (1961–62), 24, 28–31, and idem, *Spectacle, Pageantry, and Early Tudor Policy* (Oxford: Clarendon, 1969), pp. 19–20, 36, 46, 55–56.

47 Chrimes, pp. 65–67.

48 Chrimes, p. 50 and n. 5.

49 Although there are some suggestions for Bacon's statement in his sources, his statement is highly interpretative—indeed, downright inventive: e.g., see Hall's *Chronicle*, p. 440; Speed, II, 734; and Polydore Vergil, ed. Hay, pp. 34–35.

50 Cf. other examples, *Henry VII*, pp. 237–38, 314–15.

51 On Henry's mother and uncle, see Chrimes, pp. 301–02, 13–15, 54, 250.

52 Adolph, pp. 69–72. This quality, as I refer to it, is generally rather than exclusively characteristic of Bacon's depiction of character and specifically of Henry's. It tends to subsume rather than to exclude the patterns of imagery, rhythmic effects, and the like observed in this chapter.

53 Marwil's interpretation of the *Henry* seems to miss the considerable extent to which the work is *experiment*, discovery, process, invention: e.g., "The *History* is a book about kingship . . . and the reader is obliged to spend his attention on the model for imitation" (p. 193).

54 Stanley Fish's chapter on Bacon's prose in *Self-Consuming Artifacts: The Experience of Seventeenth-Century Literature* (Berkeley: Univ. of California Press, 1972), pp. 78–155, has general relevance to this discussion.

55 "De Augmentis," *Works*, VIII, 426 (Bk. II.viii).

56 *Envy* is a recurrent thematic word in *Henry VII:* e.g., pp. 74, 82, 103–04, 113, 127, 131, 183, 197, 265, 290, 303, 305, 324.

57 *Henry VII*, p. 361: Bacon interprets Henry's employment of churchmen as his choice to have servants who were "more obsequious to him, but had less interest in the people" than the members of his nobility, a choice "which made for his absoluteness, but not for his safety."

58 On the German levies, see Roland H. Bainton, *The Reformation of the Sixteenth Century* (1952; rpt. Boston: Beacon Press, 1960), pp. 37–38.

59 On the value of Lord Herbert's historical scholarship, see Fussner, *Revolution*, pp. 158–59, and H. A. L. Fisher, "The Speeches in Lord Herbert of Cherbury's 'Life and Reign of Henry VIII,' " *EHR*, 20 (1905), 498.

60 Bacon's work could have influenced Lord Herbert's: e.g., for conceptual and verbal similarities, see *Henry VII*, pp. 358–59, 335–36, and *Life and Raigne of King Henry the Eighth*, pp. 573–75.

61 *The Anatomy of Melancholy* (Oxford: for Henry Cripps, 1651), p. 4.
62 The fertile lap is Danae's: e.g., Ovid, *Metamorphoses,* trans. Frank Justus Miller, Loeb series, 2nd ed. (Cambridge, Mass.: Harvard Univ. Press, 1921), I: Bk. IV.610–11.
63 *Henry VII,* pp. 98–99, 88–89.
64 See p. 162; cf. Marwil, p. 157; also n. 44 above.
65 Analogy with Bacon's experiences during his trial in 1621 is pertinent here; whereas Bacon first tried to avoid an abject admission of wrongdoing, Parliament insisted on one: see Joel J. Epstein, *Francis Bacon: A Political Biography* (Athens: Ohio Univ. Press, 1977), chap. 9, esp. pp. 148–55; also Marwil, pp. 56–61. But the latter's view of Henry VII as virtually "a mirror image of Bacon's talents, ideas, and personality" is totally unbalanced by any properly historical sense of Bacon's objectivity; and it is curiously inconsistent with his subsequent view that "Bacon at least half-consciously *did* identify himself with Bishop Foxe, 'a wise man, and one that could see through the present to the future' " (p. 195).
66 Speed, II, 728.

INDEX OF NAMES

If scholarly works are merely cited or discussed briefly in the notes, they are not included in the index, except in a few instances to facilitate bibliographical reference. The index does not record occurrences of such terms as *truth, fiction, history,* and *biography,* which are everywhere present. Names of persons/characters are usually cited as they appear in my texts, for example, Stanley rather than Derby, but Buckingham rather than Stafford.